A Dictionary of Maqiao

WEATHERHEAD BOOKS ON ASIA

Weatherhead Books on Asia
Columbia University

LITERATURE
David Der-wei Wang, Editor

Ye Zhaoyan, *Nanjing 1937: A Love Story*, translated by Michael Berry
Makoto Oda, *The Breaking Jewel*, translated by Donald Keene

HISTORY, SOCIETY, AND CULTURE
Carol Gluck, Editor

A Dictionary of Maqiao

Han Shaogong

TRANSLATED BY JULIA LOVELL

Columbia University Press NEW YORK

This publication has been supported by the

Richard W. Weatherhead Publication Fund of

the East Asian Institute, Columbia University

Columbia University Press

Publishers Since 1893

New York   Chichester, West Sussex

Library of Congress Cataloging-in-Publication Data

Han, Shaogong.

[Maqiao ci dian, English]

A dictionary of Maqiao / Han Shaogong ;

translated by Julia Lovell.

p. cm.

ISBN 0–231–12744–8 (cloth : alk. paper)

1. Maqiao (Huanan Sheng, China)—Fiction.

I. Lovell, Julia. II. Title.

PL 2861.A662M3613   2003

895.1'35—dc21   2002041712

∞

Columbia University Press books are printed on
permanent and durable acid-free paper.

Printed in the United States of America

Designed by Linda Secondari

c 10 9 8 7 6 5 4 3 2 1

Contents

Translator's Preface

In 1968 the Chinese Communist regime under Mao Zedong instigated one of the twentieth century's most sweeping movements of human upheaval. The Great Proletarian Cultural Revolution (1966–76) resulted in a cataclysmic disruption of Chinese society and the relocation of millions of intellectuals, predominantly high-school and university students (*zhiqing*, "Educated Youth"), from the cities and towns to the countryside, where they were expected to settle for the rest of their lives, laboring alongside the peasants. Often dispatched thousands of miles to remote, impoverished areas on the borders or in the rural hinterland of China, they were confronted with languages and ways of life that were entirely alien. Han Shaogong, age sixteen in 1970, was sent to villages in northern Hunan (south China), to spend his life planting rice and tea.

That life plan came to an end in 1976, along with the Cultural Revolution and Mao Zedong himself. Han returned to the Hunan provincial capital Changsha, where he attended college and began a career as a writer in the post-Mao political and cultural thaw. By the mid-1980s, he was at the forefront of one of the key liberating developments in post-Mao literature: the Root-Searching Movement (*xungen pai*). The Root-Searchers set about reopening fiction to influences from Chinese traditional culture, aesthetics, and language, rebelling against decades of stifling Communist controls. From Mao's proscriptive 1942 *Talks at Yan'an on Art and Literature* up until his death, the Chinese Communist Party had defined the function of literature as serving China's hundreds of millions of workers, peasants, and soldiers (whose own thoughts and desires were also defined by the Party). In the interest of increasing its control over literary production, the Maoist regime made ever more strenuous efforts to regulate language through manuals dictating correct forms of grammar, rhetoric, and characterization. After Mao's death, Han and his peers emerged, blinking, from a world in which the limits of literary expression had been so closely prescribed that fictional output had dwindled alarmingly: an average of eight novels had been published every year between 1949 and 1966; this figure fell even lower during the Cultural Revolution.* Not surprisingly, the

---

* Figures from Perry Link, ed., Roses and Thorns: *The Second Blooming of the Hundred Flowers in Chinese Fiction, 1979–1980* (Berkeley: University of California Press, 1984), p. 7.

question of how to break out of the strangulating "Mao Style" in language and form dominated literary discussion of the 1980s and beyond.

A *Dictionary of Maqiao* (completed in 1995) is, among many other things, Han Shaogong's answer to this question. It is a rebuttal both to the insanity of Maoist thought control and to the linguistic dogmatism that persists within contemporary Communist China in the form of continuing censorship of public expression. As its title suggests, the novel is structured as a dictionary. Its headings are words from the dialect of Maqiao, a tiny village in southern China, noted down by Han during his time in the countryside and confined for years in exercise books, until they became his focus for this philosophical meditation on the impossibilities of creating a universal, normalized language, and on the absurdities and tragedies that ensue when such an attempt is made.

The book is also a fictional account narrated by Han Shaogong as an Educated Youth, recording the history, language, and customs of the area to which he was sent down—from before, during, and after the Cultural Revolution. A Contents page appears at the start of the novel, in theory permitting the reader to treat it as a reference book or lexicon, to dip into entries at will. As the novel progresses, however, entries start to assume knowledge of dialect words and of characters already introduced—the Party Branch Secretary Benyi, the old village leader Uncle Luo, the local opera aficionado Wanyu, the special Maqiao understanding of words such as "awakened" and "precious"—thus requiring a linear reading. Han Shaogong's compilation of dictionary entries, it soon becomes apparent, is neither alphabetical nor random, and the book is very far from a dry catalog of anthropological and linguistic detail. A *Dictionary* is the biography of a community, told through its history, people, plants, and animals.

Through entry headings that range from people and places to dogs and mosquitoes, from brief vignettes to lengthy sequences, Han combines the variety of a short-story collection with the satisfactions of a sustained narrative. (By breaking up the narrative into shorter episodes and observations, he is also harking back to well-established genres in the Chinese literary heritage, in particular the "jottings" (*biji*) essay form much beloved of premodern literati.) Chinese history, in particular the traumatic recent past, has a large part to play, as Han presents his and the village's own unique interpretation and experience of events: the pre-1949 struggles between the Communist and Nationalist parties, Land Reform and the Great Leap Forward in the 1950s, the Cultural Revolution and the post-Mao economic reforms. But Han's story telling always has a larger, philosophical point to make. Even against the Orwellian backdrop of Maoist China, Han shows us, language and history do not become fixed, controllable entities; words and meanings are mutated, misrepresented, and invented by everyone, including Benyi, the local Party mouthpiece.

One of the most intriguing aspects of the novel is Han's own position as an Educated Youth—as an educated outsider living within the village. Many of the Educated Youth enthusiastically embraced the idea of banishment to the countryside as a way of assuaging the long-standing Chinese intellectual guilt complex toward the People. The legitimacy of the Chinese literary elite is traditionally rooted in the Mencian theory of government—namely, that the mandate to rule was deserved only if the People's welfare were properly attended to—and modern literati have continually agonized over how to portray the lives of the Masses, rather than the preoccupations of the group they belonged to and most understood, the urban bourgeoisie. This sense of guilt opened the way to intellectual support for Communism and, later, for the radical plan of sending millions of students to the countryside to reform their filthy intellectual thoughts by practicing the clean laboring habits of peasants.

Many of the episodes Han relates, however, testify to the difficulties these "sent-down kids" had in adjusting to the local dialect and customs, and to the tragicomic clashes between peasants and students that resulted. Han Shaogong's Maqiao is very far from being a rural paradise: life is often violent, arbitrary, and oppressive (especially for women); food is in short supply, privacy nonexistent, the work backbreaking, and the cultural and recreational possibilities limited and generally monotonous. But Han achieves a balanced portrayal of the country-dwellers he worked alongside, one that neither romanticizes nor betrays contempt for its subjects. Throughout the book, Han never behaves like a moralizing spectator, but as a guilty participant, even leader, in some of the more ridiculous and insensitive episodes. As an earnest youth with a Maoist schooling, Han is at one point instructed to write a revolutionary opera glorifying the lives of the laboring peasants. Wanyu, one of the stars of the show, reacts badly to Han's script: "Sing this? Hoes and rakes and carrying poles filling manure pits watering rice seedlings? Comrade, I have to put up with all this stuff every day in the fields, and now you want me to get on stage and sing about it?'" Han and the local "cultural officials" arrogantly tell him to get on with it—this is art.

Han's musings on the impossibility of universalizing or normalizing language and truth reveal a deeply Chinese, unmistakably Daoist strain of thought. "The Way that can be spoken is not the constant Way," pronounced Laozi, the great Daoist philosopher, and Han constantly draws attention to the confusion, comedy, and calamity that result from the uses and abuses of language, from the failure to accept the insufficiency of language. Yet neither, as A.C. Graham tells us, do Daoists reject language as useless.

> Taoists are trying to communicate a knack, an aptitude, a way of living. . . . [They] do not think in terms of discovering Truth or Reality. They merely have the good sense to remind us of the limitations of the language which they use to guide us towards that altered perspective on the world and that knack of living. To point the direction they use stories, verses, aphorisms, any verbal means which come to hand. Far from having no need for words, they require all available resources of literary art.

Equally, how could Han, in undertaking the daunting task of compiling a dictionary, deny his esteem for language? Instead, his range of writing styles, subjects, and discussion reveal a truly Daoist openness to using all linguistic means available. Any component of Maqiao—its "purple-teeth soil," its demonic maple trees, its stubborn oxen—has a story to tell and a part to play of no less importance than the characters that people his pages. Several of Maqiao's inhabitants are also strongly Daoist in outlook—for example, the dropout Ma Ming, whose withdrawal from the corruption and hypocrisy of Communist/Confucian life encapsulates the archetypal life choice of the Daoist hermit through Chinese history.

In tune with this Daoist receptiveness to ideas and influences, the book is as international and universal as it is local and particular. Han places himself within a broad channel of influences, from Confucius to Freud, and he is not afraid to leap between different countries and periods in his exploration of language. His frame of reference contains both Chinese and Western history and culture—the Crusades, American anti-Communism, modernist art and literature—resulting in a novel that is both fascinatingly Chinese and accessibly Western in approach. He is equally comfortable with conventional and magical realism, with philological musings and story telling. And although his characters live in Maqiao, "a little village, impossible to find, almost dropped off the map," we would do well to remember the conviction of the modern Irish poet Patrick Kavanagh that "Parochialism is universal; it deals with the fundamentals." The inhabitants of Han Shaogong's Maqiao are as universal and three-dimensional as a reader could hope for: Benyi, the loud-mouthed local Mr. Big; Tiexiang, his femme fatale wife; Zhihuang, the brutish *idiot savant*; Zhaoqing, the eccentric miser; Zhongqi, the village busybody; Yanwu, the "strange talent" who's just a bit too clever for his own good. As explored in Han Shaogong's *Dictionary*, the dialect, life, and inhabitants of Maqiao are fully deserving of their place in world literature.

A Note About the Translation

When I first wrote to Han Shaogong asking for his permission to translate *A Dictionary of Maqiao*, I received a friendly but slightly bemused response. "I am very happy that you wish to translate the book, but I'm afraid it will be terribly difficult." He probably thought I was mad even to have suggested translating a book written in Chinese, about the language of one tiny corner of southern China, into English.

I plunged on regardless and, for the most part, I have translated the novel in its entirety, from the 1997 Shanghai wenyi chubanshe edition. There are, however, five entries from the novel that I deemed to be so heavily dependent in the Chinese original on puns between dialect and Mandarin Chinese as to make extensive and distracting linguistic explanations necessary in English. I therefore decided, with the author's permission, to omit from my translation the following entries: "Bayuan"; "Lian xiang"; "Liu shi"; "Po nao"; "Xian"; and the final paragraph of the entry "Reincarnation."

On the theme of dictionaries, the reader will find an alphabetically arranged glossary at the end of the book to explain any possibly unfamiliar terms that occur in the text. I have included also a list of principal characters and a guide to pronunciation of Chinese words.

—*Julia Lovell*

Guide to Pronunciation of Transliterated Chinese

According to the pinyin system, transliterated Chinese is pronounced as in English, except for the following:

VOWELS :

a (as the only letter following a consonant): *a* as in after
ai: *I* (or *eye*)
ao: *ow* as in how
e: *uh*
ei: *ay* as in say
en: *on* as in lemon
eng: *ung* as in sung
i (as the only letter following most consonants): *e* as in me
i (when following c, ch, s, sh, zh, z): *er* as in driver
ia: *yah*
ian: *yen*
ie: *yeah*
iu: *yo* as in yo-yo

o: *o* as in fork
ong: *oong*
ou: *o* as in no
u (when following most consonants): *oo* as in food
u (when following j, q, x, y): *ü* as the German ü
ua: *wah*
uai: *why*
uan: *wu-an*
uang: *wu-ang*
ui: *way*
uo: *u-woh*
yan: *yen*
yi: *ee* as in feed

CONSONANTS:

c: *ts* as in its
g: *g* as in good
q: *ch* as in chat
x: *sh* as in she
z: *ds* as in folds
zh: *j* as in job

Editorial Note*

Producing the dictionary of a village has been a somewhat experimental undertaking for us.

We received this offering from the dictionary's compiler, Han Shaogong, a renowned gentleman of letters whose oeuvre includes "Homecoming," "Dadada," "Womanwomanwoman," and a host of other hugely influential works, and whose mighty skills in penmanship extend to both fiction and essays; not, however, to dictionaries. But having considered the specialized content of this dictionary, as well as the opportunity that a lexicon affords for exploration and discussion, we encouraged his brave experiment and permitted him to retain his own distinctive literary style within the work.

To clarify for the reader:

1. The compiler originally arranged the entries in alphabetical order. In order to make it easier for readers to grasp the narrative thread and to increase the readability of the novel, the entries were rearranged into their present order. The original index of headings (presented in the "List of Entries" which follows this section), however, was retained to make the book easier to consult.

2. Each word has a certain geographical range. If the symbol ☆ appears before an entry, it means use of the word is not limited to Maqiao. Conversely, if the symbol * appears before an entry, it means that use of the word is limited to Maqiao, or even that it is used only by one individual in Maqiao.

3. For ease of reading, the author has used as little dialect as possible in the definitions. However, this should not prevent interested readers from using the knowledge of dialect this book provides by mentally replacing corresponding words in definitions with dialect as they read. In so doing, a reader can get even closer to the original feel of life in Maqiao.

* This Editorial Note was included in the original Chinese edition.

List of Entries*

* This list is explained above in the Editorial Note.

A Dictionary of Maqiao

✫**River** [江]: The word for river (*jiang* in Mandarin) is pronounced *gang* by Maqiao people (in southern China)and refers not just to vast bodies of water, but to all waterways, including small ditches and streams. In northern China, on the other hand, the word "sea" is used to cover everything from lakes to ponds, which must seem equally strange to southerners. Size, it appears, is something left for people to worry about later.

In English, difference in size can be expressed by "stream" or "river." Yet in French, *fleuve* refers to rivers entering the sea and *rivière* indicates an inland river or tributary entering another river, while size remains unspecified. It seems that the world contains many systems of naming, which do not necessarily relate to each other.

Although Maqiao people later on became more specific about size, they still didn't seem to attach much importance to it, only differentiating it slightly by tone. *Gang* pronounced in a high, level tone refers to a large river, and in a rising tone to a rivulet or stream; it takes some time for outsiders to attune their ears to avoid misunderstandings. As a newcomer to Maqiao, I ran into such difficulties myself when I went off in excited search of a river, following directions from locals. My destination turned out to be a gurgling brook so narrow I could reach the other side in one flying leap. Some dark waterweed lay within and watersnakes would flash by unannounced, but for washing or swimming it was of no use.

Rising-tone *gang* is very different from high-tone *gang*. Following this rising-tone *gang* for a stretch, I wandered alternately between torrents and calm, and then back to torrents. I felt myself scattering in pieces then coming together again, as if repeatedly lost, then found. When I came across an old herdsman, he said not to dismiss the river for its size—in the past, its water had been so oily it could be used to light lamps.

✫**Luo River** [羅江]: Maqiao's water flowed into the Luo River, a good half-day's walk from the village. There was a little rowboat for crossing, and if the boatman wasn't there then people wanting to cross simply rowed themselves over. If the boatman was there, it cost five cents per person. He moored the rowboat on the opposite side, stuck the boat pole well into the ground, and stood on the bank taking each person's money, one by one, licking a finger to count each note.

Once he'd collected a good handful of notes, he tucked them in a tattered wool hat and pulled it firmly onto his head.

The cost of crossing the river remained the same whether in summer or winter. In fact, the river in summer was much wider, and the water much more turbulent. If it happened to be the flood season, the bottomless brown soup overflowed unstoppably, obscuring all reflections, expelling layer upon layer of mire onto the banks, along with sour-smelling piles of foam which the slow lapping of the water marooned on the shallow bends. But the worse the conditions became, the more people gathered on the riverbanks, patiently waiting for dead ducks, dead pigs, broken tables or old wooden pots, along with bamboo canes split off from bundles, to come bobbing along: fishing them out and taking them off home was called "making a flood fortune."

Of course, sometimes perhaps a woman or a child, swollen up into an enormous white flesh ball, would suddenly roll up out of the waves, their glazed stare scattering people, provoking cries of terror.

Some strong-stomached children would search out a long bamboo pole and amuse themselves by prodding at the flesh ball.

People at the riverbank also fished, by casting nets or with line and hook. Once, as I headed toward the bank, some women in front of me suddenly screeched in panic, turned, and ran–something, it would seem, had happened. When I took a more careful look at where they'd run from, I saw that all the men, old and young, carriers and herders, had stopped what they were doing, ripped off their pants, and run, stumbling, toward the river in a line of ten or more pairs of glistening buttocks, shouting at the tops of their voices. Only then did it occur to me that the muffled noise I had just heard was the sound of firecrackers. That is to say, firecrackers had been set off in the river to blast the fish. After the explosion, the men had pulled off their pants to go and hook the fish. Not wanting to get their pants wet, they hadn't foreseen that their spontaneously coordinated initiative would frighten anyone.

During my six years in Maqiao, I never had much to do with the Luo River, only crossing it when I happened to be walking to the county seat. Speaking of river crossing, five cents often seemed like a lot of money. None of the Educated Youth had much money and once the male students got together, a kind of resistance-hero-versus-Jap-devil-oppressors mentality set in: whenever we crossed the river, we always considered fare dodging. One Educated Youth, nicknamed Master Black, was particularly heroic when it came to this kind of stunt, and once, after getting onto the bank, he took on the role of Underground Worker Sacrificing Himself for the People—giving us a meaningful look, he told us to walk right on and that he'd pay for us all himself. He patted his right pocket, groped in his left pocket, and generally dragged his feet until he saw that we'd walked on a long way, when he snarled at the boatman that he didn't have any money, and even if he did he wouldn't hand it over, so what was he going to do about it? He then picked up his heels and ran. He fancied himself as something of a basketball player, and thought there was no way the old ferryman could catch him up. It turned out, though, that the issue of speed was irrelevant to the old man: shouldering an oar, he ran slowly and trailed further and further behind us, but he never stopped. He followed us for one *li*, two *li*, three *li*, four *li*. . . . When finally we were staggering along, dripping with sweat, the tiny black dot far back in the distance still held on fast. Everyone truly believed that he would pursue us to the edge of heaven, brandishing the oar as he went, for as long as we hadn't paid him those thirty cents; short of us killing him, nothing else would persuade him to turn back. He wasn't half as clever as us and hadn't thought things through properly; not once did regret at abandoning his boat or the large crowd of customers waiting at the side of the river cross his mind.

There was nothing to be done but meekly gather together the money and send Master Black back to avoid trouble in the future. In the distance, I glimpsed the old man actually giving Master Black his change, his mouth making big open and shut movements, probably to swear at him, but as he was standing against the wind, not a single word reached us.

I never saw the old man again. When the movement to purge counterrevolutionaries began, a pistol in our possession became the target of investigation. We'd got hold of the pistol while waging Cultural Revolution in the city. After the bullets had all been used up, we were loath to give it up, and secretly brought it down to the countryside. When things got tense later on, we were afraid we'd be hauled up on a charge of hoarding weapons, so Master Black dropped it in the river as he crossed and we agreed amongst ourselves to keep our mouths shut. Even now I'm still not sure how the whole business came out into the open. I'm just sorry that we were too clever for our own good, that we reckoned losing it in the river would be the tidiest solution. We hadn't realized that until the authorities found the gun, the case simply couldn't be closed; in fact, they even suspected we were still secretly harboring this gun with intentions of our own. We endured endless grillings and interrogations until winter came and the water of the Luo River crept back, exposing a large stretch of sandy bank. Clutching rakes, we dug deep and sifted meticulously over the place where we'd dropped the gun, determined to excavate our innocence. We dug in the riverbank for a full five days, covering an ever-widening area. Lashed by winds that bit into our bones, we dug over almost the entire Good Earth of the People's Commune, but never heard the clunk of rake on metal.

There was no way such a heavy gun could have been swept away by the current. Neither was there any way anyone could have taken it away, sunk beneath the water as it was. Strange—where could it have gone?

I could only suspect that this strange river harbored ill feeling toward us for some unknown reason, and was determined to have us locked up.

Only then did we sense its mystery, only then, for the first time, did we size it up properly. It was strewn with the winter's first snow, reflecting a piercing white glow, like a sudden bolt of lightning that had illuminated the world, then petrified for eternity. On the riverbank was a track of light footprints, which had alarmed a few waterbirds into flight. Sometimes they merged into the icy background so that people had no way of differentiating the two, sometimes emerged from nowhere, a few white threads breaking up the dark green surface of the narrow waterway. As I stood in the path of this eternal streak of lightning, tears sprang uncontrollably to my eyes.

There was hardly anyone crossing the river. The boatman was no longer the old guy from before, it was now someone middle-aged, quite a bit younger, who squatted for a while on the riverbank with his hands in his sleeves, then headed home.

I suddenly spun around, but the bank was still empty.

☆**Savages (and Savages of the Luo Clan)** [蠻子(以及羅家蠻)]: In Mandarin Chinese, sturdy young men are also known as *hanzi* (lads). In Maqiao, men are more often called savages, or "savages of the three clans." I haven't been able to ascertain the origins of this "three clans." The ancients had a saying: "although there are only three clans in Chu, the Chu must extinguish the Qin"; it seems the "three clans" of this saying don't just refer to men.

This term "savage of the three clans" clearly referred to a single person, but it brought with it the mark of the "three clans," as if the individual had to carry out the mission of the "three clans"; I've never managed to discover whether this was a tradition from Chu ancestry. I once had a thought: if a person's bloodline comes from his two parents, but the parents' bloodline comes from their set of four grandparents, the grandparents' bloodline also comes from their set of eight great-grandparents. By this sequencing system, within a few dozen counts all mankind in its vast totality would be traced back to a single forebear, a universal common ancestor. Through this simple operation of arithmetic, the hope expressed in the Chinese saying that "over ocean and sea, all are brothers" ceases to be a beautiful but empty platitude; it is borne out by biological proof. In theory, everyone is descended from all mankind, all people carry within them the accumulated, concentrated inheritance of all mankind, passed down along a few dozens of generations. If so, is an individual still only an individual? As I've commented in an article elsewhere, the concept of the "individual" is incomplete in itself; everyone is at the same time a "group person." I hope that the "three" in Maqiao's "savages of the three clans" is a traditional synonym for "many." So if "savages of the three clans" is another name for "group person," thus emphasizing the group background of the individual, it corroborates my strange hypothesis.

The word "savage" is popular in the south, and for a long time it served as a general term for southerners. Historical records state that in the Spring and Autumn Period (c. 700 b.c.) there existed a Luo Kingdom, also known as the "Savages of the Luo Clan." *The Chronicles of Zuo* tell us that "in the twelfth year of Lu Huangong's reign, the Chu army divided and reached the Peng. The Luo people wanted to attack them." This is the earliest mention of them. The Luo people settled in southwest Yinan county (modern Hubei), adjacent to the southwestern Ba kingdom. They subsequently named it Luochuan City, which gets a mention in the 28th chapter of *The Waterway Records*. The Savages of the Luo Clan were also known as the Kingdom of Luozi, and they made use of the Peng River as a natural frontier against fearsome northern invaders. After the Chu army had been seen fording down south, they were forced to put up a fight and won an unexpected victory. But their kingdom was far smaller than the Kingdom of Chu, and in the end peace was made. We know from *The Chronicles of Zuo* that the Luo people twice fled for their lives. The first time, they fled to Zhijiang County, none other than the historical birthplace of the "Ba people"; the second time was about twenty years later, in the time of King Wen of Chu, when they once again fled to Xiangbei, the area composed of present-day Yueyang, Pingjiang, and Xiangyin county.

The river took on the name of the people—that was how the Luo River got its name.

It's hard to imagine the scene as children and old people were helped along that long trek across the river. From the records available, it appears that after arriving, the Luo people rebuilt the city of Luo, but there is no trace left of it today. I suspect the town of Changle on the bank of the River Luo is the Luo City of old (the two are linked by the similarity in sound between *le* and *luo*). It's a small town, positioned between mountains and a river, which I had to cross on my way carrying bamboo from the mountains. A cobblestone street, over whose stones floated the scent of sweet rice wine and the clop of wooden clogs, traversed the entire town, linking it to a damp, bustling wharf. The town's windows and doors were jammed so tightly shut it seemed a human face would never poke out. The local people said that there were iron pillars below the wharf, visible only at low tide, on top of which were written many blurred ancient inscriptions. I had no great interest in archaeology then, and so never went to look. Every time I passed through, I was dazed with exhaustion, and after drinking down a bowl of sweet wine, I'd topple over at the side of the street and fall asleep with my clothes on, before preparing to continue my journey. Plenty of times I was woken in deep winter by a glacial blast of wind. As I opened my eyes, only the distant stars hung above me, swaying as if about to fall.

If Changle isn't Luo City, other researchable possibilities are Luopu, Luoshan, Baoluo, Tongluodong, all of which include a syllable homophonic with "luo" (although the character is written differently), and all of which I have a passing acquaintance with. Even now, glimpses of ancient walls and stone steps, and of the furtive watchfulness that flashed momentarily in the eyes of their men and women, float up out of my recollections of these places.

The Luo people have close ties with the Ba people (an ancient people who inhabited the area now known as Sichuan). "Songs of the Ba people" is a phrase often used to refer to ancient folk songs. The terminus of the Luo River, appropriately, is "Baling," in what is present day Yueyang. The 493rd chapter of the *Song History* speaks of the third year of Zhezong Yuanyou (1088 A.D.), when the "Savages of the Luo Clan" went in for a period of rebellion. Amnesty was not declared until the ancestral chieftain of the Tujia (a nationality found in Hunan and Hubei provinces) took steps to control the revolt. It appears thus that there was some degree of cooperation between the Luo and the Tujia peoples; the Tujia have moreover been widely acknowledged by historians to be descended from the Ba people. Another piece of evidence worthy of note is that Tujia legends contain many stories relating to "Luo brothers and sisters," proving that "Luo" forms an immutable link within Tujia ancestry.

The strange thing is that on neither bank of the Luo River have I ever found a village or town that contains this very same character *luo*, or heard of someone with this character in their surname, apart from an old village leader from my village, originally a hired farm laborer, an outsider through-and-through. I could only suppose that following a cruel wave of persecution, a reign of terror that eludes both our knowledge and imagination, this word *luo* became taboo here, and the Luo people simply had to change their surname, obliterate their own history, or flee to distant parts, as is related by certain historians: gathered in groups, eating and sleeping in the wilds, they departed for Xiangxi, Guizhou, Guangxi, Yunnan, and the towering mountain ranges and lofty ridges of Southeast Asia, never to return. From this time on, the Luo River was so-called in name only. All that remained was an empty name, a mouth that would never again utter forth sounds, from which sprang only boundless silence. Even if we unearth this mouth from its open grave, we have no way of knowing what it once said.

In fact, their country is already lost forever, beyond all hope of recovery. All that remains is a few green bronze vessels, already corroded to powder, ready to disintegrate at the slightest touch. When digging wasteland in the area, I would often dig up vast numbers of arrowheads and spearheads, but they were very small, much smaller than the ones you see in books; this shows what a premium there was then on metal, that it had to be used so sparingly. The local people were so used to these relics that they weren't in the least surprised by them, in fact ignored them totally, simply threw them onto the ground by the side of the road; kids would heap baskets with them and take them away to fight or play with—nothing more. Later on, whenever I saw closely guarded bronze vessels displayed in a museum, I always felt nonplussed. What did these things count for? In Maqiao, anywhere I stepped took me into pre-Han history as I trampled into smithereens who knows how many precious cultural relics.

*Third of the Third [三月三]: Every year, on the third day of the third month of the lunar calendar, Maqiao people all ate rice dyed black with the juice from a type of wild grass, until every mouth was tar black. On this same day everyone sharpened knives. The earth trembled as every single family and household roared in unison and the leaves on the trees that lined the mountains shuddered and quivered uncontrollably. As well as axes, sickles, and hay cutters, each family also had to have a dagger which they polished until it shone snowy white, the icy gleam of the knife edge rippling, pulsating, scintillating, arousing a certain savagery in people. These knives, once sunk in deep, rusty sleep, now returned to glinting consciousness and exploded into life in the hands of the savages, the Savages of the Luo Clan, sowing subliminal tensions. If they weren't gripped tightly by the handle, it seemed they'd take on a life of their own, whizzing through doors, each making for their own targets, scaring the life out of people—sooner or later this was bound to happen.

This custom could be seen as a new-year ritual linked to farming preparations, empty of all aggressive implications. But while sharpened hoes and ploughs were obviously needed for farming, it was never quite made clear why they sharpened daggers.

Once the knives gleamed, then spring would come.
On the third of the third, the air quivered on knife-edge.

*Maqiao Bow [馬橋弓]: The full name for Maqiao is "Maqiao Bow." Bow means village, including the land covered by a village: it's obviously a traditional unit of area, one "bow" representing the stretch of land covered by the trajectory of an arrow. Maqiao Bow had forty-odd households, about ten head of cattle, and pigs, dogs, chickens and ducks, with two long narrow paddy fields hugging its perimeters. The eastern boundary lay where the village met the fields of Shuanglong Bow with a view of the Luo River in the distance; the northern edge was marked by the ridge that carried water from the top of Tianzi Peak to Chazi Valley, which you could see if you looked up toward the undulating skylines of the Tianzi mountain range. To the west, the village was bordered by Zhangjia District, and its southern reaches extended right up to Longjia Sands, where a narrow road linked up with the Chang Qin highway, built in the 1960s; anyone taking the bus to the county seat would have to travel by this road. It took a good hour to walk from the top to the bottom of the bow. The strength of the ancients is a source of perpetual wonder: what mighty warriors they must have been, to be able to shoot an arrow over such an expanse of land.

Could it be that people are shrinking, generation by generation?

It's said that Maqiao (literally "Horsebridge") Bow was originally spelled differently, with the characters meaning "Motherbridge" Bow, but the only evidence is an old title deed. Maybe this is just a spelling mistake left over from the past. Thanks to the establishment of a fairly clear system of record-taking in the modern era, the changes to its name can be roughly summarized as follows:

— before 1956, called Maqiao Village, part of Tianzi Township;
— from 1956 to 1958, called Maqiao Group, part of Dongfeng Cooperative;
— in 1958, called 22nd production team, part of Changle People's Commune (Large Commune);
— from 1959 to 1979, called Maqiao Production Team, part of Tianzi People's Commune (Small Commune);
— since 1979, when the People's Communes were disbanded, up to the present day, Maqiao Village, along with a section of Tianzi Township, has become part of Shuanglong Township.

Most people in Maqiao were surnamed Ma, and it was roughly divided into an upper and a lower village, or an upper and a lower Bow. Previously, wealthy people, and those surnamed Ma, were concentrated in the upper part of the village. The prevalence of this surname in the village was far from normal for the area. The inhabitants of Zhangjia

District (literally Zhang Family District) were in fact surnamed Li, and the inhabitants of Longjia Sands (literally Long Family Sands) were surnamed Peng. Though it struck me as rather strange that the name of the village and the clan surname were different, I'd estimate that this was the case in more than half the county.

According to the *Annals of the Ministry for the Suppression of Rebellion*, at the start of the reign of the Qing emperor Qianlong (1736–96), Maqiao Bow enjoyed a period of prosperity. At that time it was called Maqiao Prefecture, a settlement encircled by walls, with a population of more than a thousand. There were four blockhouses, and its defences were strongly fortified; there was no way vagrant bandits could break in. In the 58th year of Qianlong's reign, a certain Ma Sanbao, a resident of Maqiao Prefecture, suddenly went insane at a banquet in a relative's house and started proclaiming himself the offspring of a union between his mother and a spirit dog, saying he was the reincarnation of an ordained son of heaven, the Great Lord of the Lotus Flower, destined to found the Lotus Flower Kingdom. Three members of his clan, Ma Youli, Ma Laoyan, and Ma Laogua, also promptly accompanied him into insanity: hair standing on end, shouting to whomever might listen, they thronged around Ma Sanbao and acclaimed him as king. They produced an imperial edict conferring the title of empress on his wife, who was of the Wu clan, and conferred the title of concubine on a niece of Ma Sanbao and on another girl surnamed Li. They spread notices everywhere, drumming up soldiers and rebellion, and managed to assemble unruly elements from areas up to eighteen bows away, seizing the goods of traveling salesmen, raiding government grain barges, and killing uncounted numbers of people. On the eighteenth day of the first month of the 59th year, the leader of the Zhen'gan forces, Ming Antu (a Mongol), with his deputy general Yi Sana (a Manchu), led a force of eight hundred men, divided into two columns, to suppress the rebellion. The left-hand column attacked Qingyu Embankment, charging directly at the stockade, taking guns and cannon along with them. They fired cannon at the robbers' stockade, which caught fire, forcing the robbers to flee to the river, where countless of them died. After the assault, the right-hand column crossed the river by laying down trees at Hengzipu and made a nighttime raid on the bandits' lair, Maqiao Prefecture. At dawn, more than two hundred robbers broke out of the stockade and fled chaotically to the east, where they were headed off by the left-hand column of government soldiers, who surrounded them and killed every one, down to the last man; the heads of Ma Youli and his five phoney ministers were soon cut off and hung up as an example to all. Every single bandit stockade

surrounding Maqiao that had joined the rebellion and helped the robbers was razed to the ground. Only those with a spotless record in helping quell the disorder could avoid persecution by government troops.
They stuck in their threshold a red government-issued flag, on which
were written the words "good people."

The *Annals of the Ministry for the Suppression of Rebellion* left me
rather melancholy. The Ma Sanbao that the *New County Annals*
included in its roll of "Peasant Rebellion Leaders"—the Ma Sanbao who
in Maqiao legend was a Son of Heaven of bona fide dragon origin—
made an extremely poor showing in this version edited by the Qing
authorities. In his brief three months of rebellion, he never contemplated any bold vision for establishing government, founding a dynasty,
resisting his enemies, and saving the world—all he did was appoint five
imperial concubines. From the historical materials available, it appears
he lacked a talent for rebellion: apparently, when the government troops
arrived, his only strategy for warding off the metal guns and cannon of
the government troops was to ask shamans to consecrate an altar and
plead with the spirits, make paper cuts, and sprinkle beans (the idea
being that generous use of paper and beans would produce generals and
soldiers in similar quantities). He lacked also the morals of rebellion:
once captured, he didn't have the integrity to lay down his own life, but
wrote out a fulsome confession more than forty pages long, filling the
sheets with groveling self-deprecations, "humble this," "humble that,"
obtaining only pity from his vanquishers. The lack of any coherence to
his confession clearly demonstrated his insanity. In the rise and fall of
the "Lotus Flower Kingdom" (according to official statistics), the death
toll of peasants in Maqiao and its environs exceeded seven hundred, and
even women who had left up to ten years earlier to be married in faraway
places determinedly returned from all directions in order to join their
kinsmen and fellow villagers in a life and death struggle. Drenched in
blood, they battled through fire and through water, only to put their own
destinies in the hands of such a madman.

Was it a false confession? I truly hope so—that these confessions are
part of a history fabricated by the Qing dynasty. I also hope that Ma Sanbao met his end soaked in paraffin, tied to a large tree and lit up like a
magic lantern, not as he was described in the *Annals of the Ministry for
the Suppression of Rebellion*, and that the fates of the seven-hundred-odd
dead souls who followed him were not demeaned by such a madman.

Is there perhaps more than one version of history?

The disorder wrought by the "Lotus Bandits" is the most significant
event in the history of Maqiao, as well as the main cause of Maqiao's

decline. Henceforth, Maqiao people gradually began migrating in greater numbers to other areas, leaving fewer and fewer people behind. By the start of the century, the whole village had fallen into a state of dereliction. When the authorities were making arrangements for resettling Educated Youth, they normally looked for fairly poor villages, whose fields were sparsely populated; Maqiao was one of the villages that the authorities selected.

***Old Chum** [老表]: The end of the Ming Dynasty [1368–1644] witnessed even greater upheaval than the disorder caused by the "Lotus Bandits": when the rebel Zhang Xianzhong took up arms in Shaanxi, he clashed repeatedly with the Hunanese hatchets, the "Rake troops" in the government army. The heavy casualties Zhang suffered generated in him a deep hatred of all Hunanese, and on several later occasions he led an army into Hunan, leaving countless dead. He was dubbed "No Questions Zhang," meaning that he killed without asking name or reason. There were always human heads hanging from his soldiers' saddles, with strings of ears at their waists, to back up their demands for rewards.

Hunan was overrun with Jiangxi people as a result of this bloodbath. It's said that because of this historical episode, Hunanese started calling all Jiangxi people "old chum" and grew to be on very close terms with them.

There are no major geographical barriers between Hunan and Jiangxi, so the population can move back and forth with little difficulty. There was at least one surge in migration from Hunan into Jiangxi, occurring at the start of the 1960s. When I had just arrived in Maqiao to start working the land, the favorite topic of conversation among the men, apart from women, was eating. When they uttered the word "eat" (*chi*), they pronounced it with the greatest intensity, using the ancient pronunciation *qia*, rather than the medieval *qi*, or modern *chi*. *Qia* was pronounced in a falling tone: the bold "a" sound of the syllable in combination with a light, crisply percussive falling tone displayed to the maximum the speaker's intensity of feeling. *Qia* chicken duck beef mutton fish dog, and meat—this last was the abbreviation for pork. *Qia* stuffed buns steamed buns fried dough cakes fried crispy cakes noodles rice-noodles glutinous rice cakes and, of course, rice (that would be boiled rice). We talked with great gusto, never bored with the topic, never bored with its minutiae, never bored with its repetitiousness. It was a source of constant talk, constant novelty, constant delight, and we talked compellingly, unstoppably, our hearts dancing, faces glowing, every word drenched in a deluge of saliva, then catapulted violently out of the mouth off the tongue, the reverberation of the explosion lingering in the sunlight.

Most of this talk was based on memories, for example recollections of some birthday banquet or funeral feast engraved on a deeply appreciative memory. All this talk, talk, talk would then turn into speculation and boasting. As soon as someone announced that they could eat three pounds of rice in one go, then someone else would announce that they could eat twenty stuffed buns. That was nothing, some superman would interrupt with a snort, he could eat ten pounds of pork fat with two pounds of noodles thrown on top, and so on. Arguments, and assiduous research, would inevitably ensue. Some refused to be convinced, some wanted to take bets, some proclaimed themselves referees, some suggested competition rules, some volunteered to watch over the combatants to prevent them from cheating, for example stopping them from burning the pork fat into crackling, and so on and so forth. This excitement reproduced itself endlessly and identically, and always when mealtimes were still a long way off.

At moments like these, the local people would often speak of the year they "opened canteens"—this was the way they generally referred to the Great Leap Forward. They always recalled the past through their stomachs, giving past events a real texture and taste. "Eat grain" meant military service, "eat state grain" meant people going to the city to labor or do cadre work, "the last time they ate dog meat" meant some cadre meeting in the village, "eat new rice" meant early autumn, "make *baba* cakes" or "kill the new year pig" meant the new year, "there are three or four tables of people here" meant the numbers present at some group activity.

No one had enough to eat during what they called the "canteen" years. Although everyone's eyes were green from hunger, they still had to tramp through ice and snow to repair the irrigation works, and even women were forced to bare their upper bodies, breasts hanging pendulously down as they heaved earth on their backs, wielding red flags, drums, gongs, and slogan boards as they went, to demonstrate their undaunted revolutionary zeal. Unable to manage another breath, third father Ji (I never met him myself) toppled over and died on the construction site. Many young people, in the prime of life, couldn't bear the hardship and fled to Jiangxi. They didn't return for many years.

I later came across a man who had returned to Maqiao from Jiangxi to visit relatives; his name was Benren, and he was about forty years old. He offered me cigarettes, and called me "old chum." In response to my curious inquiries, he said that the reason he fled to Jiangxi that year was because of a pot of maize gruel (see the entry "Gruel"). He'd taken a pot of maize gruel home from the commune canteen, the evening meal for the whole family, but as he waited for his wife to get back from the fields, waited for his two children to come back from school, he felt just too hungry and couldn't help eating his own portion first. Hearing the voices of his children at the mouth of the village, he hurried to divide the gruel into bowls, but when he lifted the lid, he discovered that the pot was already empty. Anxiety turned everything black before his eyes. The gruel had been there a minute ago—where had it gone? Could he have wolfed down the lot without realizing it?

He searched all over the room, disbelieving and panic-stricken: there was no gruel anywhere, all the bowls, dishes, pots were empty, everything was empty. That year there were no dogs or cats who would come and steal food—even all the earthworms and locusts in the ground had long since been devoured.

No sound had ever been as terrifying as the footsteps of his children, growing nearer, and nearer.

He felt that he could not face a soul, let alone tell his wife, and ran panic-stricken to the slope behind the house where he hid in the clumps of grass.

He heard the faint sound of his family's cries, heard his wife calling out his name everywhere. He didn't dare reply, didn't dare release the sound of his own sobs. He never stepped into his home again. He said that he now worked in a valley in southern Jiangxi, chopping wood, burning coal, you know the kind of thing. . . . Ten years had already passed, and he had a new nest of children there.

His original wife had also remarried, and bore no grudge against him, even had him over to her house, cooked him a meal with meat. The only thing was, her two children were shy with strangers; they'd gone to play in the hills and hadn't come back even after it got dark.

I asked him if he still planned to move back.

As soon as the words were out of my mouth, I realized this was a very clumsy thing to ask.

He gave a brief, slight smile, and shook his head.

He said it was all the same, life over there was just the same. He said he might get to be a permanent laborer at the forestry center. He also said that he'd set up home with some other people who had left Maqiao, and their village was also called "Maqiao." The people over there also called Hunanese people "old chum."

A couple of days later, he returned to Jiangxi. A light rain was falling on the day he left, and he walked in front, his former wife following about ten paces behind, probably seeing him off for part of the way. They only had one umbrella, which the woman held but hadn't opened. When they crossed a ditch, once he had pulled the woman over, they quickly resumed their ten paces separation, one in front, one behind, battling forward through the thick misty drizzle.

I never saw him again.

*Sweet [甜]: Maqiao people have a very simple way of expressing flavors. Normally, one umbrella term suffices for anything that tastes good: "sweet." Sugar is "sweet," fish and meat are also "sweet," boiled rice, chilli pepper, bitter gourds are all "sweet."

Outsiders have found this hard to understand: was it because their sense of taste was crude, and therefore they lacked vocabulary to describe flavors? Or was it the other way around: had a lack of vocabulary to describe flavors caused their palate to lose the ability to differentiate? Their predicament is virtually unheard of in a country as gastronomically developed as China.

Similarly, there is only one name for all sweet foods: "candy." Candied fruits are "candy," biscuits are "candy," sponge cake, shortcake, bread, cream, absolutely everything is "candy." The first time they saw popsickles in Changle, they called them "candy" too. There are, of course, exceptions: the specialities of the region each have their own name, for example "glutinous rice cake" and "rice cake." Use of the umbrella term "candy" is restricted to all foodstuffs that are Western, modern, or just from distant regions. Most Educated Youth bought biscuits from street stalls to take back home: these were called "candy." This always sounded strange to us, and we never quite got used to it.

Perhaps in the past, Maqiao people had had only just enough food to avoid starvation, and had never achieved a thorough understanding and analysis of food flavors. Years later, I met some English-speaking foreigners and discovered that they suffered from a similar poverty of vocabulary for taste sensations. For example, any piquant flavor—pepper, chilli, mustard, garlic, anything that made your head sweat—was described as "hot." I secretly wondered to myself, did they too, like Maqiao people, have a history of famine that prevented them from selecting their food and differentiating flavors? I can't joke about this, because I know what starvation tastes like. There was one time when, having groped my way back to the village in the darkness, I didn't bother to wash my hands or face (I was covered in mud from head to toe), didn't bother slapping at the mosquitoes (which were swarming densely around me), I just gulped five bowls of rice (each one holding half a pound of rice). After gulping it all down, I still couldn't say what I'd just eaten, what it tasted of. At that moment, I could see nothing, hear nothing, my only sensation was a violent wriggling in the stomach. All those words used by the upper classes to describe taste, all that precise, detailed, flatulent chatter, meant nothing to me.

The word "sweet" exposes a Maqiao blind spot with respect to food and drink, demarcating the boundaries of their knowledge in this area. But once you take a careful look at anything, you'll discover that everyone has all kinds of blind spots. The boundaries of human awareness do not snugly nestle back-to-back, and the weak flame of human perception is a long way from illuminating the whole world. Even today, the majority of Chinese people still have great difficulty in distinguishing the facial types of western, northern, and eastern Europeans, and in making out cultural differences between the British, the French, the Spanish, the Norwegians, the Poles, etc. The names of each European people are no more than empty symbols in school textbooks, and many Chinese, when put on the spot, are still unable to make any link between them and corresponding characteristics in facial type, clothing, language, and customs. This baffles Europeans, just as it baffles the Chinese that Europeans cannot differentiate clearly between people from Shanghai, Canton, and the Northeast. Thus, the Chinese prefer to use the general term "Westerner" or even "old foreigner," just as Maqiao people prefer the word "sweet." This type of generalization will naturally seem ridiculous to a British person who objects to being lumped together with Germans, or to a French person who objects to being lumped together with Americans. Similarly, even today, the vast majority of Chinese, even the majority of economists, still can't make out any apparent differences between capitalism in America, capitalism in western Europe, capitalism in Sweden and other northern European countries, and capitalism in Japan. Neither is any significant distinction made between 18th-century capitalism, 19th-century capitalism, 20th-century prewar capitalism, 1960s capitalism, and 1990s capitalism. For many Chinese, the term "capitalist" is quite sufficient to convey their intended sense of admiration or of loathing.

When I was in America, I came across an anticommunist political journal in which I was perplexed to discover that the editors' sense of political taste was stuck at the same level as Maqiao people's "sweet." For example, sometimes they lambasted such-and-such a Communist Party for its false Marxism, for betraying Marxism, and at other times just lambasted Marxism (in which case, isn't falsification or betrayal of it a good thing?). On the one hand they exposed the extramarital affairs and illegitimate children of Communist Party members, on the other hand derided the asceticism of Communist Party members for their excessive oppression of human nature (in which case, aren't extramarital affairs and illegitimate children completely in harmony with human nature?). They perceived no confusion or contradictions in their logic; they only perceived that anything anticommunist was worth cheering on, was very good, was sweet. It was in this journal that I happened across a certain news item: a woman named Chen, who had just fled from Hainan Island to Hong Kong, was proclaiming herself an anticommunist dissident and, thanks to the kindness of a Western government, had been given asylum as a political refugee. A few months later, on meeting an official from this country's embassy, I was seized with deep indignation on behalf of his government. At the dinner table, I told him that I knew this Miss Chen. She'd never participated in any political activities on Hainan Island. All she'd done was organize an "Island Heat Literary Contest," in which she'd swindled young writers from all over the country out of nearly 200,000 yuan in entry fees, dumped a huge pile of competition entries in a hotel, then picked up her heels, along with the money, and fled to Hong Kong. She hadn't managed to persuade me to act as a judge for the contest, but this hadn't proved an obstacle: in the call for contributions that she placed in a newspaper, she had cited the names of ten world-famous writers, Marquéz, Kundera, Borges, and so on, who had all, amazingly, become her judges. She had envisaged a Super Nobel Literature Prize, to be adjudicated on Hainan Island.

My revelations seemed to puzzle the embassy official somewhat. He said, wrinkling his brow, maybe she had committed fraud, maybe she had acted badly, but couldn't her behavior be seen as a particular form of political opposition?

He gesticulated strenuously.

I dropped the subject. I didn't want to sway this diplomat's political standpoint over the dinner table. You can endorse or you can oppose any type of serious, scrupulous and peaceful political position, but you can't not respect it. I simply felt that I was in a difficult situation. Just as in the past I had no way of making Maqiao people distinguish linguistically between all the different kinds of "candy," neither did I at that moment have any way of making this diplomat distinguish between all the different kinds of "opposition" in China. In what he saw as a mysterious, alien country, fraud counted as no more than another piece of delicious "candy."

*Tincture of Iodine [碘酊]: The Chinese use a lot of popular names for industrial products. I was born in the city and reckoned myself really quite advanced, until I went down to the countryside. I knew about iodine solution, but I didn't know about tincture of iodine. In the same way, I'd got into the habit of calling mercury "red medicine," gentian violet "purple medicine," a storage battery "electric medicine," an ammeter "firemeter," a ceramic cup "foreign mug," an air-raid siren "nee-naa," whistling "tooting."

After I arrived in Maqiao, I often corrected the even more rustic terms used by the villagers. For example, a public square in a city should be public square, not "field," and certainly not "drying field."

So I was flabbergasted to discover that everyone here, men and women, young and old, all used a formal scientific term: tincture of iodine. They, on the contrary, didn't know what iodine solution was, and found it very strange that I used such an odd phrase. Even old grannies with clouded vision and foggy hearing talked in a more scholarly tone than I did. When they pronounced "tincture of iodine" in their Maqiao accent, it was as if they'd unconsciously uttered a secret code, a code that normally remained buried out of sight, only spoken in times of dire necessity, to make contact with the remoteness of modern science.

I inquired about the history of this word, since I got nowhere with my own conjectures. Maqiao had been visited neither by foreign missionaries (Westerners might have opened hospitals and used the scientific names of medical products) nor by large new-style armies (the soldiers might have been wounded and used the new names for medical products); most teachers would have studied in the county seat, and some would have gone even farther, to Yueyang or Changsha, but they wouldn't have brought back phraseology more modern than anything in use there. I finally discovered that this term was linked to one mysterious person.

Uncle Luo, the old village leader of the lower village, told me as he sucked on his bamboo pipe that a person called Long Stick Xi was the first person to use the phrase "tincture of iodine" here.

☆**Rough** [鄉氣]: I know very little about Long Stick Xi. No one knew where he came from, what class status he had, or why he moved here. No one even knew his real name—"Xi" was a pretty odd-sounding surname. Some remarked on how his receding chin and his eyelids were different from other people's. It was only much later that I came to understand the significance of these features.

From all the various legends I heard, I concluded that he most probably came to the village in the 1930s, and lived there for ten or so years, or twenty or so years, or even longer. He brought an old man with him, who helped him cook food and look after a few caged birds. He talked "rough," which meant he spoke with an accent from outside Maqiao that people found difficult to understand. Take, for example, "tincture of iodine." Another example: he would replace "see" with "regard"; "play" with "mess about"; "soda," meaning soap, also became very common here and afterwards spread to neighboring areas for miles around.

One might guess that he was someone who had some knowledge of

"New Studies," or at the very least knew something about chemistry. Since he apparently liked to eat snake, it isn't entirely fanciful to imagine him as a snake-eating Cantonese.

He left a rather complex impression on Maqiao people. Some were well-disposed toward him: when he arrived in the village, he'd brought with him foreign medicine, cloth, and fire, which he'd exchanged for grain at a fair price. If he came across someone with a snake to exchange, he would beam and happily negotiate a discount. He could also cure disease, and even deliver babies. The local quacks used to rail against him en masse, saying it was no more than black magic and mumbo-jumbo, even the *yin*, *yang*, and eight hexagrams were blocked—he couldn't cure his way out of a cloth bag! How could anyone who ate poisonous stuff like chessboard snake not have a poisoned mind? This kind of talk, however, later petered out. A woman from Zhangjia District was having a difficult labor, rolling around on the ground in agony, mooing like a cow, neighing like a horse, yelling so much the quack had run out of ideas and the villagers were at their wits' ends. Her uncle finally volunteered to take action: picking up a kitchen knife, he sharpened it on the stone steps and prepared to split open her stomach.

But just as the kitchen knife was put in position, Long Stick Xi luckily rushed over and yelled out, scaring the knife wielder into staying his hand. Slowly and calmly, he had a drink of his tea, washed his hands, and shouted at idle onlookers to get out of the room. After an hour or so, the sound of crying was heard from inside the room and again, slowly and calmly, he strolled out to have a drink of tea. When the crowd went in to have a look, the child had been born, and the woman, amazingly enough, was safe and peaceful.

When he was asked how he'd done it, he talked too rough and no one could understand him.

Afterwards, the child grew up healthy, and when he could talk and run everywhere, his parents forced him to visit Long Stick Xi and make a few kow-tows to him. Long Stick Xi seemed to rather like the child and would often chat with him, as well as to other children who came with him to play. Gradually, the children also began to talk a bit rough, even said how delicious snake meat was and nagged their parents to catch snakes for them.

Maqiao people had never eaten snake. They believed that snakes were the most poisonous creatures in the whole world and that snake meat surely poisoned a person's mind. They regarded Long Stick Xi's ability to drink raw snake's blood and swallow raw snake's innards as supremely horrifying, and would cluster around to whisper about how this boded ill for the village. One by one, they forbade their children ever to go back to Long Stick Xi's house to play, terrified that Long Stick Xi would turn them bad with snake meat. They spoke to the children in menacing tones: you seen that Xi? He sells children—next thing you know, he'll have you tied up in a hemp sack and slung over his back to sell on the street—haven't you seen all the hemp sacks he has in his house?

The children stopped to think: they didn't have any strong recollection of hemp sacks in the house, but when they saw the serious expressions on the adults' faces, they didn't dare visit Xi. They would at most band together and sneak a look from far-off. When they saw Xi's friendly wave, none of them dared go closer.

Because Xi was good at delivering babies, the village people in the end refrained from torching his house and driving the young and old in his household out of the village. But they never harbored any good will towards the Xi family. Everyone resented his laziness (the thick hair on his legs was proof of laziness). Neither could they bear his extravagance: he actually fed caged birds on eggs and slices of meat. Even more objectionable was his sinister greenish-pale complexion, frigidly indifferent and arrogant. He also lacked all respect for the aged and never understood that he should give up his seat, much less offer cigarettes or tea. He would always grumble at whoever had come, and if the target of these remarks didn't understand, he would give an icy laugh and mumble to himself as he went about his own business. With that hideous expression on his face, he had to be muttering rough talk. Did he think that if other people didn't understand him then he could use filthy language? He was the precise embodiment of the word "rough": it wasn't just a question of speech—there was definitely a certain air about him, a blast of cold, frigid air, spiteful air that sowed fear and discord. He transformed "rough," a word that already jarred the ear, into a term yet more derogative, a term spat out between snarled teeth. There can be little doubt that this brought calamity to the door of subsequent newcomers, that it had an unstated influence on Maqiao attitudes to all outsiders.

When the land reform work team arrived in the village, they inquired whether there were any landlords or local bullies there. At first, the ordinary people were still rather fearful, they muttered and mumbled, even slammed their doors as soon as they saw the work team people. Finally, though, the work team killed the biggest tyrant from Longjia Sands, paraded around with his head lifted up high, bang-bang-banging drums and gongs to get people to come and look; once the masses saw blood, they threw open their doors and rubbed their hands together, itching to be a part of it all. A lot of men went looking for the work team, and the first name they brought up was Long Stick Xi.

"What crimes is he guilty of?"

"Exploitation, greed, laziness, never grows his own vegetables."

"Anything else?"

"He wears a foreign chain, goes ticktock ticktock."

"A pocket watch? A pocket watch is movable property. Anything else?"

"He eats poisonous snakes—disgusting, bleurgh!"

"Eating snakes doesn't prove a specific problem. The most important thing is whether he has mountains, whether he has land. We need to control the limits of policy."

"He's got land all right, oh yes, I should say so."

"Where?"

The men became vague, said they should go and have a look, it was around here somewhere.

"Whereabouts?"

Some pointed to the east, some to the west.

The work team went to check, but discovered that Long Stick Xi actually had neither land nor mountains and that apart from a few caged birds, his house was empty and bare. He had no pocket watch, either; it was said that he'd sent it to a lover in Longjia Plain. Someone like him could be labeled neither a landlord nor evil tyrant, nor could he be regarded as an enemy. The work team's conclusion annoyed all the local men, who grumbled they couldn't count on anything anymore. On and on they muttered about their grievances: if Peng Shi'en (a super-bully from Longjia Bay) could be killed, then why not him? He was far worse than Peng Shi'en; he swindled people like there was no tomorrow! What was Peng Shi'en compared to him? He treated his own old man like his grandson!

When they first started talking about the business of treating his old man like his grandson, the work team didn't understand. A few days' investigation, however, produced a rough outline of the affair. At one point, a startling piece of news had secretly spread around Maqiao: apparently, Xi was in fact more than a hundred years old. He'd taken a Western elixir of life and lived to a ripe old age in the pink of health, his face glowing with youth. The old man who followed him around wasn't his dad at all, but his grandson, who, stubborn by nature, hadn't obeyed the family rules and had refused to drink the precious Western potion, thereby turning into a desiccated old prune. Some were flabbergasted by this piece of news. Eyeing Xi with new respect, they timidly approached his door to make inquiries. The old chap in the Xi household was as rough as they came, and couldn't utter a single intelligible word. Long Stick Xi wouldn't say too much either, but once, when he came up against someone who wouldn't be put off, when enough bowing and scraping had been done, after Xi had hedged a while, then, finally, with great reluctance, he said he didn't really remember how long he'd actually lived, but the emperor had changed a few times, he'd seen everything, nothing surprised him. As he said this, he told the old man to go to bed. His listeners heard very clearly that he didn't call the old man Dad, but said "laddie" instead, his tone definitely that used for dismissing those of a younger generation.

Maqiao people were naturally very interested in an elixir of life. Some offered money, meat, and wine to beg for the treasure from Xi. Some even offered up their wives, because Xi said people's physiques were not the same, sometimes the male element was too weak, and he needed to add a woman's "three peaks"—that is, saliva, breast milk, and vaginal fluid—into the elixir, because only this would gather up the *yin* to balance the *yang*, making the elixir effective. Of course, this was very complicated and needed a lot of careful research, something he was most unwilling to do. Sometimes the seeker of elixir got it wrong time and again, and the "three peaks" sent over were useless, but after the man begged abjectly, he'd finally relent and agree to help him out, calling on him to sort out a replacement. He'd shut himself up with the man's wife and pull down the mosquito net, making the bed wheeze and creak in a highly disconcerting way. Since this greatly sapped his energy, normally he'd be forced to charge even more for it.

When this kind of thing started happening more and more often, talk began to spread among the people involved. First, angry suspicions gradually formed in the minds of the women; subsequently, the men also started to pale with fury, but they didn't know quite what to say. Shortly before the work team went into the mountains, a little girl was dispatched by her mother to get to the bottom of the Xi mystery. When she came back, the little girl reported that as soon as outsiders weren't around, Xi called the old man "Dad"!

This meant that Xi had all along made his dad pretend to be his grandson in front of other people, he was not one hundred years old at all, and he had no elixir of life!

"The swindler." The head of the work team understood, and nodded his head.

Another cadre said, "whatever he's swindled you of, money, grain, women, just let us know—we'll settle accounts with him."

Though they were spitting with anger, the men would talk only in vague terms, wouldn't spell things out in detail. The work team saw their difficulty, thought things over and over again, and at last came up with a solution: they got someone highly learned to mull it all over until he finally concluded that Long Stick Xi was guilty of moral bankruptcy plotting with landlords and tyrants colluding with bandits forcibly resisting land reform illegal commerce, and so on, producing a list of crimes ten items long which, in conclusion, made him a counterrevolutionary carbuncle who should be tied up double-quick.

"So, d'you actually have an elixir of long life?"

"No, no, I haven't." Long Stick Xi trembled all over before the work team. His arrogance had completely evaporated and snot was streaming from his nose.

"What did you sell them?"

"A . . . aspirin."

"Why'd you lie like that?"

"I . . . I . . . a counterrevolutionary stance, moral bankruptcy, plotting with landlords and tyrants. . . ." He'd memorized the list of crimes item by item. Not one word was incorrect.

"Got that?"

"I've got a good memory, I don't like to blow my own horn, but—"

"Cut it out! This is your criminal record. You have to confess honestly."

"I confess, I confess."

The work team sent him to the county seat under escort. A member of the People's Militia was responsible for the escort, but he must have eaten something funny on the way, because he started vomiting yellow, then green and black bile; he vomited till you could see the whites of his eyes—quite extraordinary, it was. Long Stick Xi knelt down and gave him mouth-to-mouth resuscitation, then found a bucket of water to sluice out his guts. When his condition had stabilized a little, he carried him on his back all the way to the county seat and handed him over, together with his gun holster. Of course, he also handed himself over. Apparently, people later on asked him, why didn't he take this opportunity to flee? He said, I couldn't run away, I just couldn't, I wanted to remold myself, escape the dung heap, serve the people.

His law-abiding behavior while under escort was taken into account when the government judged his case, and his sentence was reduced by two years, after which he was sent to some farm for labor reform. Some people also said that the above version of events was incorrect, and that he didn't serve any part of his sentence; a senior officer took a fancy to him, bailed him out, and sent him to some mountainous mining area where he could make use of Xi's medical skill. Other people had seen him in teahouses in the county seat drinking tea. He had by then cut off his long hair and shaved his head. Oddly enough, his speech was not in the slightest bit rough any more. When he'd talked himself into a state of self-satisfaction, he wouldn't be able to resist some private boasting: in order to get off lightly, he'd first poisoned that soldier escort, then saved his life, thereby reducing his sentence by two years, and so on.

I don't know how near the truth this version is.

His old dad soon died. The signs of their roughness also soon disappeared from Maqiao, leaving only those few random words, like "tincture of iodine" and "soda," which so surprised me all those years later. Of course, he also left behind in Maqiao at least three sons, all three with that receding chin particular to him, who will appear in some of my subsequent entries, and who will be the focus of later stories about Maqiao.

☆**Same Pot** [同鍋]: Maqiao people don't talk in terms of same ancestry, or same clan, or same parents. They call sons of the same parents "same-pot brothers." When men remarry, they call their former wife "former-pot wife" and call the wife married after the death of the first "later-pot wife." This shows the importance they attach to blood ties doesn't equal the importance they attach to pots, that is to say the importance they attach to eating.

After the Educated Youth arrived in Maqiao, seven people lived together in a household, all eating from the same pot. The fact that they had seven different surnames, were from seven different families, had seven different sets of blood ties was of no importance to locals; the fact that there was only one pot formed the basis for making a lot of important decisions. For example, there was the question of going to the market in Changle on the fifth day of every month. When it was the busy season for farming, the team leader decreed that each pot could at most spare one person to send to the market; everyone else had to stay in the village and work. The Educated Youth, who all wanted to go to town, argued themselves hoarse, protesting that they were not one family, that all had their own individual right to go to the market—to no avail. The household's communal pot stood behind them as cast-iron proof of the final verdict they were futilely disputing.

At one time, the fires of love blazed between two Educated Youth who, as they settled down to begin their blissfully happy life together, separated their pot off from those footloose and fancy-free Educated Youth. This brought an unexpected bonus when the team leader was distributing oil. Because there was very little, it wasn't distributed according to labor capacity, or by person; in the end, each pot was allotted one catty, so that everyone could have a little oil to grease the pot and enjoy the "righteous glow of shared good fortune." When the storeman came to have a look at the Educated Youth's stove, he certified that they had two pots and allotted two catties of oil to them, fully double the amount they'd been expecting.

They fried up a feast of profligate oiliness, wiping their greasy mouths in blissful happiness.

***Placing the Pot** [放鍋]: When women leave home to get married, the most important of the wedding rites is when the bride places a new pot on the stove of her husband's family, draws water to wash the rice, chops wood to light the fire, and boils a pot of rice, showing she has become a member of her husband's family. This is called "placing the pot," synonymous with getting married. Placing the pot is normally scheduled for the winter, not only to avoid the busy season for farming, and not only because people can only afford the expense after the autumn harvest—there is a yet more important reason. I was told that only in winter could the bride wear the several layers of padded clothing needed to protect herself from the boisterous japes, punches, and kicks that young men go in for giving at weddings.

Once Fucha dragged me along to one. Under the dusky light of oil lamps and candles, in which elegant shadows flickered and the smell of alcohol stung the nose, I sat squeezed into a seam of people in a corner cracking sunflower seeds when suddenly I heard a cry of alarm; a black shadow speedily loomed towards me and hurled me violently against the wall, pressing so hard I could barely breathe. Struggling to poke my head out from behind this black shadow, I discovered that it was a person; that it was in fact none other than the bride dressed in her flowery jacket, her face obscured by a tangled bird's nest of hair, and on the verge of tears. I was terrified, but before I had time to break free from the suffocating force that seemed to emanate from her legs and back, hands closed in from all sides to grab at her; amongst roars and cheers, she made her limping escape, sheltered against the chest of another male guest. Her shrill cries were drowned out by thunderous laughter all around.

The next day, I heard that although the bride had wrapped herself in four layers of padded clothes, tightly tied up with six belts, she had still been mauled black and blue on several parts of her body, testament to the boisterous excess of the young men.

There was no way the husband's family could register any objection.

Quite the contrary; if people didn't get carried away, it meant a loss of face for the husband's family, made them the object of general contempt. When a villager called Zhaoqing held the reception for his eldest son, he did everything in a miserly way, watering down the wedding wine, cutting the pieces of meat too small. Highly disgruntled, the guests conspired to take revenge. And so it came about that nobody lifted a finger in the direction of the bride throughout the entire wedding night. If they saw her, they either hardly stirred and pretended not to have seen her, or scuttled away. The next day, the bride threw a huge tantrum: how could everyone have snubbed her like that, she wept, how could she ever show her face again? The two uncles who had come with her to place the pot also flew into a rage and, oblivious to the bride's feelings, heaved up the pot from the stove top and walked out of the door, carrying it back home on their backs. The bride hadn't originally intended her tantrum to extend to revoking her vows, but seeing the pot gone, there was nothing she could do but tearfully follow it back to the family home.

A village marriage was thus annulled.

☆**Little Big Brother (etc.)** [小哥(以及其他)]: "Little big brother" means big sister. Clearly, by the same token, "little little brother" means little sister, "little paternal uncle" means an aunt on the father's side, "little maternal uncle" means an aunt on the mother's side, and so on.

I noticed very early on that because Maqiao and places nearby didn't appear to have an independent system for female nomenclature, most female names were formed simply by preceding the male name with the word "little," thus tying women forever to the diminutive. This meant, in effect, that women were people of little consequence, petty people. I can't be certain whether there's any link between this kind of ruling and ancient sayings such as Confucius's dictum that "women and petty people are hard to handle."

Language, it seems, is never absolutely objective or neutral. A linguistic space will always be distorted under the influence of a particular set of beliefs. Bearing in mind the namelessness of females, it's easy to draw further conclusions about their social status around here; it's easy to understand why they always bound their chests flat, crossed their legs tightly, and lowered their eyes timidly onto steps or short grass, harboring a deep-felt fear and shame that sprang from their status as females.

To be given a name is a right of life, the product of love and respect. People always give names to pampered pets, like "Kitty," or "Lulu." It's only the names of criminals that are usually ignored and replaced by numbers, as in stock-taking. We only refuse to acknowledge the names of people we most hate, "that so-and-so," "you scoundrel," and so on, depriving them of their linguistic position. Those we deem nameless vermin are those whose names have no function in public life or are used with such infrequency that they become erased. Thus, in the Cultural Revolution, names like "professor," "engineer," "Ph.D.," "artist" were expunged. The aim was not to abolish these professions and jobs, neither was it to physically annihilate these people. Instead, it expressed a yearning for every form of employment to develop exclusively in the name of revolution. Intense psychological pressure was exercised in order to weaken, even totally undermine, these individuals' rights to a professional label—because any form of title can provide the breeding ground for a body of thought or entire system of beliefs.

In ancient China, the study of names and principles infiltrated all philosophy. Naming is the fulcrum, the point of departure, the focal point and result of all theoretical debate.

In Maqiao, female unnamedness is in fact male namedness, which, of course, is not such a very unusual phenomenon. Even though the English language passed through the tumultuous baptism of humanistic enlightenment several hundred years ago, feminists still now continue to attack the masculinization of a range of prestige terms (for example, using "man" to mean "human," and words such as "chairman" and "minister"). But even though gender-neutral or unisex terms have carved out an enclave only under the shadow of male hegemony, English has never been masculinized to the same degree as Maqiao dialect, where female terms were completely deleted. I've had great difficulty in working out whether this linguistic misrepresentation had any influence on the sexual psychology or even sexual biology of Maqiao women—whether it had to any degree altered reality. From the looks of things, the women all seemed to use coarse, vulgar language, had even learned how to fight and curse. Once they gained the upper hand in relation to a man, they often became complacent. Their hands and faces were hardly ever clean, hardly ever fresh and bright, and their bodies were always hidden in masculine clothing that covered their female figures with loose, straight pants or stiff, rough-padded jackets. They were also embarrassed to talk about menstruation, and referred to it as "that thing." "That thing," again, is no kind of name. When I was laboring in the paddy fields, I hardly ever saw a woman ask to rest because of her period. They could ask for leave to go to the market, to deliver pigs, to help with farm work, and so on, but the period of leave would not be given over to their own health. I figured that in order to affirm their position in male roles such as "little big brother" they had to obliterate even their own periods.

*__House of Immortals (and Lazybones)__ [神仙府(以及爛桿子)]:** In Maqiao Upper Bow there was a stretch of cobbled road, along both sides of which stood a few cottages. The buildings on one side of the road were fronted by a perfectly ordinary wall of wooden planks, leaning this way and that. They were, however, still crowned by a high, square terrace built out of bricks. Once you looked carefully, you realized that these platforms were trading counters from many years before, that these old houses retained the faint appearance of storefronts. Such trading counters represented the fossils of commerce. The *Annals of the Ministry for the Suppression of Rebellion* record that this area experienced a period of prosperity in the reign of the Qing emperor Qianlong, of which these damaged, peeling counters, besmirched with chicken and duck droppings, were probably material evidence.

Another mysterious relic from the past was a big iron pot, now full of holes, long cracks, and splits; abandoned in the woods behind the state granary and minded by no one, the bottom of the pot had filled with rotten leaves and rainwater. The pot amazed people by its size, which was big enough to steam two baskets of rice, and the spoon used to stir it would have had to be at least as big as a rake. Nobody could say to whom this pot had belonged in the past, why they'd needed such a big pot, why the pot's owner had subsequently discarded it. If this pot had been used to cook food for regular hired labor, its owner must have been a great village landlord. If this pot had been used to cook food for ordinary soldiers, then its owner must have been a general of no little standing. These conjectures were enough to unsettle me.

Of the prosperity that the *Annals of the Ministry for the Suppression of Rebellion* described, there still remained one last corner in an old house in Maqiao Upper Bow. It was a house made of blue bricks and large tiles, whose main gate had disappeared; it was said a stone lion behind the main gate had been smashed during the revolution, but stone portals which came more-or-less up to people's knees gave an indication of how impressive it had looked in earlier days. Inside the house, a window casement that hadn't been ripped out still remained, on which flying dragons and dancing phoenixes were intricately and exquisitely carved, and which brought with it a faintly oppressive air of extravagant wealth. The local people jokingly referred to this ownerless construction as the "House of Immortals." It was only later that I found out the word "immortals" referred to its lazybones residents who didn't do honest work in the fields. These people were also known as Maqiao's "Four Daoist Immortals" and had lived here for a very long time.

I went to the House of Immortals once: dispatched by a cadre with orders to paint quotations by Chairman Mao everywhere in red and yellow paint, I couldn't leave out this corner of the village. When I went, I knew that all the other Daoist Immortals in the House of Immortals had either passed away or departed, leaving only one Ma Ming. He wasn't at home, and having received no response after coughing several times at the gate, I had no choice but to advance timidly up a few dilapidated stone steps into this dust-smothered darkness, into a state of hopeless and overpowering fear and trepidation. Fortunately, after proceeding sideways into the right wing of the house, I found a few tiles were missing from a corner of the house and a shaft of light had sneaked in, finally helping me out of the desperate obscurity. Only slowly did I begin to make out an expanse of brick wall, for some unknown reason bulging outwards, shaped like a Buddha's belly. The wooden plank wall was riddled with woodworm, and everywhere I went there were grass rushes and the crunching sound of broken tile residue. Next to the wall was a large coffin, also covered with rushes and a piece of torn polyethylene. I spotted the owner's bed, a piece of worn matting in amongst a grass nest in one corner. On top there was a mound of wadding as black as ashes—probably the end that kept his feet warm, bound tightly together with a length of grass rope, demonstrating the owner's ingenuity in keeping out the cold. To the side of the grass nest were two old batteries, a wine bottle, and a few multicolored paper cigarette packets— these must have been the few trophies in the House of Immortals seized from the world outside its door.

My nostrils encountered an aggressively pungent stench which, if I leaned a little over to one side, disappeared. If I leaned back, there it was again. I couldn't help but feel that the bad smell here was not caused by a gas, but was a formless solid, built up over a long period of time, already coagulated into a concrete form, a heavy mass. The owner of the house would surely have had to watch where he stepped to avoid stirring up such a deeply accumulated stench.

I also took care to avoid this solidified stench, and found a place where my nose could be more at ease to paint a board of quotations. They went like this: "When busy, eat dry food, when leisured eat liquid, at normal times eat half dry, half liquid." I hoped it would have some illuminative value for the owner of the house.

I heard someone behind me exclaim with a sigh: "When time is confused, it must be a time of confusion."

As I hadn't heard footsteps approach, I didn't know when he'd appeared. He was so thin his temples were deeply sunken, and he was wearing a cotton hat and unlined cotton jacket unusually early in the day. As he upbraided me with a slight smile, his hands in his sleeves, it occurred to me this must be the owner of the house. The brim of his hat was just like that of other men round here, always worn twisted at a great angle.

When asked, he nodded his head, and confirmed that he was Ma Ming.

I asked him what he had just said.

He gave another slight smile and said that these simplified characters had no logic at all. Full-form Chinese characters fall into six categories, the picto-phonetic type (in which one element represents meaning and the other sound) being easiest for communication. Take the full-form character for "time" [時]: its meaning derives from the left-hand element, the character for "day" [日]; its sound *shi* derives from the right-hand element, the character [寺], which is pronounced *si*. If it means [日] and sounds like [寺], why change something that works perfectly well? In simplified form [时], its side component became [寸], pronounced *cun*. The reader now had nothing to orient himself by and the character didn't lend itself to quick memorization. What was introduced as a measure to reduce confusion in fact completely confused the texture of Chinese characters. Time being thus confused, confused times could not be far-off.

Such an educated remark gave me a fright, and also fell outside my range of knowledge. I quickly changed the subject and asked him where he had just been.

He said he'd been fishing.

"What, no fish then?" I saw that both his hands were empty.

"Do you also fish? You must know that the fisherman's intent lies not in obtaining fish, but in the Dao. Big fish, small fish, fish or no fish at all, in fishing all has its own Dao, its own pleasure, of incalculable worth. Only the fierce and cunning will be blinded with greed, poisoning the water, setting off dynamite, casting nets, beating the water, ruining the atmosphere, vile evil practices, vile, vile, vile!" At this point, his face flushed with unexpected animation, and he burst into a fit of coughing.

"Have you eaten?"

He pursed his lips and shook his head.

I was terribly afraid that next thing he would ask me to lend him some rice, so before he had finished coughing, I burst in with "fishing—good idea. Nice steamed fish."

"What's so great about fish?" he grunted contemptuously. "Like eating dung, bleurgh!"

"So, do you . . . eat meat?"

"Ai, pigs are the most stupid of animals. Pork only wakes up after you've stabbed it. Oxen are the most idiotic, beef damages the intelli-

gence. Goats are the most cowardly, eating goat will make you lily-liv-
ered. All no good."

I'd really never heard anything like this before.

Seeing that I was puzzled, he smiled dryly. "With heaven and earth
this big, you're worried there's nothing to eat? Take a look, butterflies
have beautiful colors, cicadas sing a clear song, mantises can fly over
walls, leeches can divide up a body. The hundred insects are thus, they
gather the essence of heaven and earth, collect the ingenuity of the old and
the new. They are the most elusive delicacies. Delicacies. Tsk tsk tsk. . . ."
With insatiable gusto he smacked his lips and tongue, then suddenly
thought of something, turning back to the side of his nest, where he took
out a ceramic bowl and held out to me a long thin black something.
"Here, have a taste, this is leftover pickled golden dragon. It's a pity
there's only a bit left, it's really fresh."

At one glance I took in that the golden dragon had started off life as
an earthworm, and my entire digestive system did a back-flip.

"Taste it, taste it." His mouth opened wide in enthusiasm, a gold tooth
glinting out. A yellow cloud of vapor reeking of fermented urine hit my
face.

I stumbled out and fled.

After that, it was a long time before I saw him again—I hardly ever
had reason to cross paths with him. He never came out to work. The
Four Daoist Immortals hadn't touched a pickaxe or carrying pole for the
last ten years or more. Apparently it made no difference what rank of
cadre went to argue with them or curse them, even tie them up with
rope, it was all to no avail. If the authorities threatened to lock them up
in jail, they seemed delighted, since being in jail saved them the trouble
of cooking for themselves. Actually by this time they hardly ever cooked
anyway, and their relish of jail was just part of a scheme to take laziness
to an absolute, pure extreme.

They didn't bunch together in a group at all, and never had a fixed
time for eating; whenever one of them got hungry, he would disappear
for a while, then return wiping his mouth, perhaps after having eaten
some wild berries or bugs, or stolen a radish or some maize off someone's
floor and just swallowed it down raw. For any of them, lighting a fire to
cook food counted as the most incredibly laborious, unbearably tire-
some thing for which they would be ridiculed by the other Daoist
Immortals. None of them had any possessions, and the issue of ownership of the House of Immortals was of course extremely hazy. But neither was it the case that they owned nothing whatsoever: in Ma Ming's
words, "the mountains and rivers have no owner, the idler is the master

of all." They wandered around happily the whole day long, playing chess, humming operas, surveying the scenery, climbing up high to admire the view, taking in all that lay around, swallowing up the new and the old; it was as if they were borne aloft on the wind, freed from this world, had taken wing and become immortal. Those working on the land down below couldn't suppress their smiles when they first saw them standing on the mountains. The Daoist Immortals saw things differently, and instead laughed at the plodding work of the villagers, day in, day out, eating to work, working to eat, the old working for their sons, sons working for their grandsons, one generation after another suffering like beasts of burden—was this not pitiful? Even if they accumulated ten thousand strings of cash, a person could never wear more than five feet of cloth, or eat more than three meals a day, and how could this possibly compare with courting the friendship of the sun and moon, with taking the heavens and earth as their abode, enjoying beautiful scenery and experiences in luxurious leisure!

Later on, people were no longer surprised to see them in broad daylight just standing still, looking around, and took no notice of them.

The Daoist priest among the Four Daoist Immortals sometimes went to distant parts to perform a few rites. One Hu Erce once went to the county seat to beg and didn't return to the village for a month or more. There began to be talk in the county that it looked very bad if Maqiao people were going into town to beg for food. The village should impose strict controls and give assistance to those with real economic problems—people couldn't starve to death under socialism. The old village leader Uncle Luo had no alternative but to send the accountant Ma Fucha over to the House of Immortals with a basket of grain from the granary.

Ma Ming was an extremely unyielding kind of person, and just glared and said: "Nay. This is the blood and sweat of the common people—how can it be right for you to give it away out of pity?"

There was in fact something in what he said.

Fucha had no choice but to carry the basket of grain back.

Ma Ming didn't eat food that had been cadged, he didn't even use other people's water. He hadn't dug stones or hauled mud for the village well, so there was no way he would draw water from it. Off he'd go, wooden bucket in hand, to a stream two or three *li* down the road, often so exhausted the blue veins on his forehead bulged out, taking huge panting breaths, all the bones in his body twisted into one chaotic mass under the weight of the water bucket. Every few steps he'd have to rest, moaning and wailing, nose and mouth distorted into unrecognizable shapes. When they witnessed this, people did manage a little sympathy: the well was for all the villagers, how could we grudge you a mouthful of water? He would grind his teeth ferociously and say "as ye sow, so shall ye reap."

Or he would put on a show of bravado in self-justification: "The stream water tastes sweeter."

Once, someone treated him to a bowl of ginger-salted sesame vegetables and insisted that he swallow it down. After he'd swallowed it and before he'd walked ten steps, he threw up violently—so violently that long strings of saliva hung down from his mouth and you could see the whites of his eyes. He said it wasn't that he wasn't grateful, it was just that his guts couldn't cope with coarse food like that, and the well water stank of duck shit—how in heaven's name could he let it pass his lips? Of course, it wasn't quite the case that he received no charity at all: for example, the padded unlined jacket that he wore all year round, in summer and winter, was given to him by the village. At first he categorically refused it, until the old village leader took a different tack and said this wasn't charity, it was more a case of him helping out the village; if he went out of the village dressed too shabbily, it would be bad for Maqiao's face. Only then, as a special favor, just to keep people happy, did he accept, with enormous reluctance, the new jacket. Furthermore, whenever this matter was raised in the future, he acted as if a great misfortune had come over him, and said he hadn't cared how old and venerable the village head was, he'd absolutely refused to bow down—the jacket burned his bones, made him feel ill when he was perfectly healthy.

He wasn't in fact afraid of the cold, and would often sleep out in the open. If, while walking somewhere, he didn't feel like walking anymore, he would yawn, lie down in his clothes, and curl up into a ball, sometimes under the eaves of a house, sometimes at the side of a well—and he'd never ended up ill from all his curling up. As he put it, when sleeping in the open your upper surface could be at one with the spirit of the heavens, and your lower surface could make contact with the spirit of the earth, from 11 P.M. to 1 A.M. you could absorb the *yang* in the *yin*, from 11 A.M. to 1 P.M. you could pick out the *yin* in the *yang*; this was the best way of making up deficiencies in the body. He also said that human life was a dream and that dreams were the most crucial part of life. If you slept next to an ants' nest, you could dream the dreams of emperors; if you slept among clumps of flowers, you could dream romantic dreams; if you slept in front of a pit of quicksand, you could dream golden dreams; if you slept on a grave, you could dream ghostly dreams.

He would forego anything for the rest of his life, apart from dreams. During his whole life he was particular about nothing, except for where he slept. For him, the most pitiful of beings were those for whom life meant only the awakened state and who didn't experience the life of sleep. Sleeping—awakening—sleeping—awakening: it was always sleeping that had to come first. A life with no dreams was a life half lived, was, in fact, a gross outrage of the Way of heaven and earth.

Other people regarded these remarks of his as the talk of a madman, or as a joke. This made his feelings of rancor towards the villagers grow ever deeper, made him even more stonily silent in public.

He was, in point of fact, someone who lacked all public connections, someone who had no connections with Maqiao's laws, morality or any of its political changes. Land reform, the campaign against bandits and landlords, the mutual aid teams, the cooperatives, the People's Communes, the Socialist Education Movement, the Four Clean-ups, the Cultural Revolution, none of these had any effect on him, they weren't part of his history, they were no more than a play that he enjoyed from a great distance, but which was incapable of having any influence on him. The year they opened canteens, a cadre from outside the village—who wasn't in the know—tied him up with a rope and dragged him down to the construction site for labor reform. No matter how much they beat him with sticks or whipped him, he remained coldly contemptuous, preferring to die rather than labor, to die rather than stand up. He just lay there, stubbornly prostrate, rolling around in the soupy mud, refusing to get up. What's more, once they'd gotten him there, it wasn't so easy to get him home again: he repeated over and over that he wanted to die in front of the cadre, and wherever the cadre went, he would crawl after him; in the end, everyone had to lend a hand lifting him back to the House of Immortals. Since he didn't want to be counted as a person, he overpowered any authority. Having easily foiled society's last attempt to harass him, he henceforth became in Maqiao even more of a nothing, a blank space, a drifting shadow. As a result, when it later came round to checking class status, grain allocation, family planning, even carrying out the census—I helped the village do this—nobody thought about whether there was still a Ma Ming, and nobody felt he should be included in the calculations.

He was definitely not included in the full national census.

He was definitely not included in the worldwide census.

Obviously, he didn't qualify as a person.

If he wasn't a person, then what was he? Society means People, writ large. He rejected society, and society canceled his qualifications as a person. My guess is that he finally brought the situation to a head because he'd always wanted to become an immortal.

The slightly surprising thing is that in the stretch of land near Maqiao, there were quite a number of creatures like Ma Ming who were perfectly happy to withdraw from the normal run of human society. Fellows like Maqiao's Four Daoist Immortals, it was said, were still to be found in most villages from far around; it was just that outsiders tended not to know of them. If an outsider didn't discover them by chance or curious inquiry, the locals wouldn't talk about these creatures, would even forget they existed. They were a world inside this world that has already caved in and disappeared.

Fucha once said that they weren't at all awakened (see the entry "Awakened"). Most of their parents weren't hard-up, and there was an insolent cleverness about them. As an early indication of what they'd become, though, they'd been a bit mischievous as children, not very diligent as students. Ma Ming, for example, never did his homework, but when it came to writing couplets, they'd spring from his mouth fully formed. One example: "See the national flag, everyone goes spare, do the rice sprout dance, we're got nowhere." Agreed, it was counterrevolutionary, but the sound and sense of the lines (in Chinese, at least) are flawless. Even while they were struggling him for it, everyone praised the kid's phenomenal literary aptitude. Once someone like him lost his parents, he started to turn bad, turned scientific (see the entry "Science"). Who knew what possessed him.

*Science [科學]: When Maqiao people chopped firewood on the mountainside, they'd carry it home on their backs, then lay it out on the ground to dry in the sun before burning it. Wet firewood is very heavy, and carrying it on the back really bit into the shoulders. We Educated Youth later on came up with the idea of leaving the firewood, after it had been cut, to dry in the sun on the mountainside. Once it had dried, we would come back to carry it down the next time we came to cut firewood. We still carried a whole load of firewood every time, but as it was dry firewood, it was quite a lot lighter. Uncle Luo had heard that this technique was quite effective, and swapped loads with me to give it a try; eyes wide in astonishment, he agreed that it was a lot lighter.

I said that at least half the water had evaporated out.

He put my load down, then took up once more the wet firewood he had just cut and set off down the mountain. A little perplexed, I went after him to ask why he didn't give our method a try.

"People who chop wood but won't carry it have missed the whole point."

"It's not that we won't carry it, we just want to carry it a bit more scientifically."

"What d'you mean scientific? You mean lazy! Those city automobiles, railroads, flying machines of yours—name me one that hasn't been thought up by a lazybones! Who else but lazybones would've thought up such a devilish set of names?"

This outburst quite took my breath away.

He went on: "With all these scientific comings and goings, we'll all be like Ma Ming before you know it."

He was referring to the owner of the House of Immortals. Ma Ming, its resident-in-chief, had never come out to work, didn't even want to see to his own needs. Sometimes he would bring back a bit of gourd, but he was too lazy to light a fire, so he would eat it raw. He'd got used to eating things raw like this, and so when he'd scavenged out some uncooked rice, he'd put it straight into his mouth and crunch away on the grains until the corners of his mouth were a mass of powdery rice starch. People would laugh at him, but still he came up with justification after justification, saying that cooked things lacked nutritional value; that tigers and panthers in the mountains had always eaten their food raw, and see how much stronger they were than humans, how much less prone to illness—so what could be wrong with it? He never used a urine bucket either, but instead poked a hole in the wall at crotch height, and fixed a length of hollow bamboo stem leading out of the house; any urine was discharged into the stem. He considered that this method was more scientific than hauling a urine bucket: the water flow was carried along, and it was better to let things run out than have them pile up.

Once winter came, he never washed his face. A crust formed around his face, which fell off in pieces once he gave it a rub or pinched and picked at it. He wouldn't say he was afraid of cold water, but would argue that frequent washing of the face wasn't scientific—washing your face clean of its natural organic oils damaged the skin.

The absurdest thing of all was the way it took him an hour to carry a load of water back home from the stream. Particularly when going uphill, he would walk in a Z-shape, taking ages twisting and turning back and forth, then still find he was only halfway there. Onlookers idling around the hillside would watch in bemusement: wouldn't it be better if you just put down your water buckets and sang us a song? Ma Ming said: "What do you know? This is the only way to preserve your strength when walking. Zhan Tianyu built the railroad at Badaling in a Z-shape."

His listeners had no idea who on earth Zhan Tianyu was.

"How on earth would you know?" His face set into a mask of arrogant aloofness as if he disdained to waste his breath on the masses, he picked up his two buckets of water and continued on his way, twisting and turning as before, saving his precious energy all the way to the House of Immortals.

From this time on, people said that as the lazybones in the House of Immortals were each more scientific than the other, it should really become an academy of science. It's easily to imagine, then, that for Maqiao people the implications of the word "scientific," once projected onto Ma Ming, were far from positive. I suspect that henceforth they barely glanced at the pamphlets on crop-sowing distributed from above, simply ripped them up into cigarette papers, that they remained entirely indifferent to the endless broadcasts on scientific pig-feeding, that they even cut the metal wire serving as a lead to use as a hoop for the piss bucket; all this was a form of psychological inertia. To put it another way, science became an extension of the general mockery of the Daoist Immortals. There was the time a group of Maqiao lads set off to carry lime into Changle; on the highway they passed a big bus that was being repaired, which struck them as a great novelty. They gathered round, unable to help themselves from knocking at the body of the vehicle with their carrying poles until it rattled and shook, until, before they knew it, they'd bashed two dents in the body, which had been hitherto in perfectly good condition. The driver, who had been lying under the car making repairs, sprang out furiously and started cursing them, jumping up and down, spoiling for a fight, until they finally scattered. But still the Maqiao lads were unable to suppress a kind of nameless impulse, turning to shout and yell, picking up stones to hurl at the big bus after they'd fled some distance away.

They harbored no ill will toward the driver. Neither had they ever displayed any wantonly destructive tendencies: when walking past any household, for example, they'd never dream of knocking against the walls or door with their carrying poles. Why, then, could they not restrain themselves on encountering a motor vehicle? I can only suspect that underneath their joking and laughter there lay concealed a kind of unconscious loathing, a loathing of all new-fangled gadgets, of all the fruits of science, of all the mechanized oddities that came out of modern cities. In their opinion, the so-called modern city was nothing other than a great big bunch of scientific—or lazy—people.

To blame this assault on a bus on Ma Ming is, or course, rather far-fetched, and not entirely fair. But the process behind understanding a word is not just an intellectual process, it's also a process of perception, inseparable from the surroundings in which the word is used and the actual events, environment, facts relating to it. Such factors often largely determine the direction in which understanding of this word proceeds. "Model Operas" (the eight revolutionary operas deemed "politically correct" during the Cultural Revolution) are an appalling concept, but someone whose memories of love or youth are interlinked with the strains of a model opera tune will perhaps feel an unstoppable surge of heightened emotion on hearing these words. "Criticism," "position," "case for investigation" are not made up of inherently evil words, but someone whose memories have been colored by the red terror of the Cultural Revolution may well start to tremble with deep, uncontrollable revulsion on hearing them. Actual understanding of these words in their final form will perhaps have a far-reaching influence on the subsequent psychological state and existential choices of a person or race, but the literal meaning of these words can't be held responsible for this understanding. Thus, the word "science" can't be held responsible for the vicious attacks on "science" expressed in the views of Uncle Luo and other Maqiao people; neither can it be held responsible for the chance encounter on the highway in which Maqiao lads picked up their carrying poles to launch a unified assault on the fruits of science.

Who was responsible? Who made "science" so hateful that it became something that Maqiao people must shun at all costs?

All I can say is that perhaps it was not Ma Ming alone who was responsible.

*Awakened (*Xing*) [醒]: Out of the many Chinese dictionaries that exist, not one gives a pejorative sense for the word *xing* (awaken). For example, the *Origins of Words* (Commercial Press, 1989) defines it as "recover from drunkenness," "rouse from dream," "become conscious" and so on. Awakening is thus the opposite of befuddlement and confusion, and implies only rationality, clarity, and intelligence.

There is a famous line in Qu Yuan's poem *The Old Fisherman*, "Throughout the world all is muddy, I alone am clear; everyone is drunk, I alone am awakened (*xing*)"—a line which did much to boost the prestige of "awakened."

Maqiao people don't see things this way. Quite the opposite: Maqiao people have long used this word, spat out with a disdainful wrinkling of the nose and thinning of the lips, to refer to all kinds of idiotic behavior. "Awakened" means stupid. Someone awakened is a stupid fool. Could it be this custom dates from when their ancestors encountered Qu Yuan?

In c.278 b.c., Qu Yuan the Awakened, Qu Yuan the self-proclaimed member of the Awakened, unable to tolerate the drunken disorder prevailing throughout the world, resolved to make a martyr of himself, and to oppose evil through death. He threw himself into the Miluo River (the lower reaches of the Luo River) and drowned—in the area nowadays called Chutang township, where he went after having been condemned to exile. At that time in the state of Chu, which he had loyally served, "crowds of ministers vied jealously for success and toadied to gain advancement, while good ministers were dismissed and banished far from the hearts of the common people" (taken from *The Record of the Warring States*). He was thus no longer wanted in Chu. He looked back over the city of Ying, Chu's capital, composing aloud poems to vent his grief. His lofty aspirations thwarted, he released cries of deep melancholy to the heavens. If he was not to be the savior of this world, he could at least reject it. If he could not tolerate the betrayal and falseness that surrounded him on all sides, he could at least shut his eyes to it. Thus he finally chose to settle his suffering heart in the dark quiet of the riverbed. It is worth noting that his route to exile took him through Chenyang, Shupu, and so on, leading him finally to the edge of the River Xiang, which winds up to the land of Luo. In fact, this was one of the last places on earth that a dismissed Chu minister should go. This was the first place to which the Luo people had fled for refuge after being brutally routed by the mighty state of Chu. When the people of Chu had themselves been brutally routed by the even mightier state of Qin, Qu Yuan himself drifted there soon afterwards, following almost exactly the same route. History was repeating itself, simply with the roles switched around. Why revive old grievances between those who wander together in desperation through foreign lands?

Qu Yuan had been a top official in the state of Chu, in charge of official court documents, and so would naturally be very familiar with the history of Chu, and thus also be well aware of the rout of Luo by Chu. When he climbed mournfully up onto the bank of the Luo River, saw faces, heard words, or experienced local customs that seemed familiar, when he encountered all this that had by some lucky chance escaped all the executioners' knives of Chu, what thoughts and feelings were in the mind of this exile? I don't know. I find it even harder to guess whether, when the humiliated and impoverished Luo people faced the former minister of the invading state, when they silently approached, mutely grasping the handles of their swords, when finally they held out bowl and spoon, did the hands of the great minister tremble?

History has recorded none of this.

Suddenly, I feel that there are complex reasons for Qu Yuan's choice of final resting place, reasons that remain beyond our comprehension.

The land of Luo was a mirror which permitted him to see clearly the absurdity of concepts of rise and fall, of division and unity. The land of Luo was a dose of bitter medicine, sweeping away all self-control in the innermost being of this court official. The chill billow of the waves on the river made him question all his memories, not only his grievance against the state of Chu, but also his loyalty to Chu, his lifelong self-love, and his lifetime's devotion to these causes. This was not the first time he had had to endure rejection, and he ought to have had sufficient experience and psychological resources to cope with exile. He had already spent many days journeying through wild lands, and he should have been used to the hunger, cold, and hardship of exile. His eventual death at the side of the Miluo river, leaving behind a vast, empty riverbank, meant that he must have received some fundamental shock which induced in him a feeling of terror towards the yet vaster life that existed beyond life, a feeling of unassailable confusion at the yet vaster history that existed beyond history. The only thing he could do was to take a step into the unknown.

Where else could he have experienced such a dazzlingly rude—*awakening*?

Where else could he have come to understand better his long-prized sense of—*awakening*?

All this is conjecture.

Qu Yuan wandered barefoot far and wide through the land of Luo, wrapped only in flowers and grasses, drinking dew and eating chrysanthemums, greeting the wind and rain, conversing with the sun and the moon, sleeping alongside the insects and birds. By then, I think he can't have been quite right in the head. He had *awakened* (as he, as well as the later *Origins of Words* and the like understood it), and truly was *awakened* (as Maqiao people understand it).

His leap into the river generated a dual meaning for the word "awakening": wisdom and ignorance, heaven and hell, the physical present and metaphysical eternity.

The Luo people couldn't really understand the staunch loyalty of the Chu minister, but they empathized with a fallen enemy, and expressed their sorrow for Qu Yuan in the annual tradition of dragon-boat racing on May Fifth that later developed. They throw rice dumplings into the river, hoping this will persuade the fish and shrimps to leave Qu Yuan's corpse in peace. They bang deafeningly on drums and gongs, hoping to waken the poet from his deep sleep on the riverbed. Time and again they shout themselves hoarse trying to summon his soul: men and women, young and old all shout till their veins almost burst, their eyeballs bulge, their throats hurt, the sweat pours off them. Their shouts fill the heavens, obliterating their age-old enmity toward the Chu army, as they apply themselves only to saving the life of a man, of a foreign poet.

The earliest mention of this custom is in *The Record of the Four Seasons in Jingchu*, written at the time of the Southern Dynasties (440–589 A.D.) by Zong Bing, a man of Liang. Before this, no one spoke of commemorating Qu Yuan on the fifth day of the fifth month. In fact, dragon-boat racing had long been a common sight in the south, a part of their ritual sacrifice to the spirits that lacked any verifiable connection to Qu Yuan. The link between the two was most probably fabricated by the historical fantasy of literati. It was done for Qu Yuan, but also for themselves. Therein lies the rationale of the ever more elaborate celebration of ritual sacrifices: aren't those who martyr themselves to civilization reassured by the promise of eternal glory as final compensation?

Qu Yuan never saw this glory, and in any case, not just any aspiring Qu Yuan could win this glory. Looking at things from the opposite angle, the way in which Maqiao people understood and used the word "awakened" concealed another viewpoint, concealed the dislike of their forefathers for the politics and foreign culture of a powerful state, concealed the necessary ambiguity between different historical positions. This use of the word "awakened" to mean "ignorant" or "stupid" is a fossil seam running through the unique history and beliefs of the Luo people.

*Asleep (*Qo*)* [覺]: The character pronounced *jue* in Mandarin is pronounced *qo* in the Maqiao accent, with a rising tone, and means "clever," the opposite of the Maqiao meaning of "awakened."

In fact, when pronounced *jiao* in Mandarin, this character happens also to mean not clever at all, but muddle-headed, confused, dazed, as in the phrase *shui jiao*, meaning "asleep."

"Awakened" and "asleep" are antonyms. Directly opposed to normal understanding in standardized Chinese thinking, this pair of antonyms exchanged places when their meanings were extended in Maqiao: as Maqiao people see it, regaining consciousness is stupid, while sleeping is in fact clever. This inversion always sounded rather odd to outsiders who were new to the village.

We have to allow that different people will judge cleverness and stupidity from different angles and using different yardsticks. We must, it seems, also permit that Maqiao people are perfectly entitled to draw from their own experience original metaphors from "awakened" and "asleep." Take Ma Ming: people can sigh about what a down-and-out he was, and laugh at how he was smelly and stubborn and crazy and stupid and how he lived, quite frankly, like a dog. But if we look at things from a different angle? From Ma Ming's angle? Far from lacking happiness or unfettered freedom, his existence could often be compared even with that of the immortals. And if we consider how act upon act of bitter farce have played themselves out: the Great Leap Forward, the Anti-Rightist Movement, the Cultural Revolution . . . far too much human brilliance dissipated into absurdity, far too much diligence turned into mistakes, far too much enthusiasm diverted into wrongdoing; at least Ma Ming, this distant onlooker, remained pure and unblemished, with no trace of blood on his hands. Even with all the natural hardships he endured, he lived to be healthier than most.

Now, does that make him stupid or clever?

Was he "awakened" or "asleep"?

Every pair of antonyms is in fact the fusing of different understandings, the intersection of different lives and paths of practice, leading in turn to two paradoxical extremes. This type of intersection is concealed in a secret language which often gives those traveling abroad pause for thought.

*Delivering Songs [發歌]: If you happen to spot Maqiao men getting together in twos and threes, squatting down by walls, or crouching by the fireplace, cupping their chins or covering their mouths in a way born of long habit, then you know they are singing. They have a secret way of singing: not only do they keep their voices low, they also avoid the eyes and ears of outsiders and do it in out-of-the-way places. For them, the activity of singing is closer in spirit to a game of chess within a small circle of friends than to a kind of public performance. Originally, I thought this resulted from fear of official censorship and political criticism; later, however, I found out that this secretive style of singing existed many years before the Cultural Revolution. I don't know why this was so.

In Maqiao, "singing" (*chang ge*) is also called delivering songs, or dealing songs (*fa ge*), similar in sense to "delivering a speech" at a meeting, or "dealing cards" at a card table. In Chinese, this word *fa* can also mean "incite" or "exhort," and in the Han (202 b.c.–220 a.d.), Mei Sheng wrote the famous "Seven Exhortations," a type of *fu* rhapsody poem, mostly made up out of a question-and-answer structure. "Delivery of songs" in Maqiao is also structured around a question-and-answer opposition, one singer inciting, exhorting the other, but I have no way of knowing whether this is the same as the "exhortation" of the Han dynasty.

Young people like listening to people deliver songs, and react promptly to each phrase in the song with comments or cheers. If there's someone fairly generous in their midst, he may fish out some money to buy a bowl of wine or use "face" to buy a bowl on credit, as a reward for the singer. After the singer has finished singing a round, he'll take a sip of wine, after which, fueled with alcohol, he can of course make up lines that are even more vigorous, cutting, and impossible to answer, forcing his opponent into a corner, so heavily under siege that all around is blocked out, yet still the hand cupping the chin or covering the mouth won't be released.

Their songs have always derived from great affairs of state. One might ask an opponent, for example, who is the country's Premier? Who is the country's Chairman? Who is the country's Chairman of the Military Commission? Who is the elder brother of the country's Vice-chairman of the Military Commission? What illness has the elder brother of the country's Vice-chairman of the Military Commission had recently, and what medicine did he take? and so on. I was amazed by the difficulty of these questions. I read the newspapers every day, but I'm afraid I couldn't recite details about these remote great personages as if they were members of my own family, or recall with such exactitude their lung cancer or diabetes. I can only guess that the amazing memory of these men, who stank from head to foot of ox dung, must have developed out of a particular type of training. Just as vagabond barbarians did not forget their sovereigns, their ancestors must have had a tradition of paying attention to court affairs.

They later move on to delivering filial songs. The singers often find fault with each other, blaming their opponent for failing to fluff cotton wadding for their beloved parents, or for not having bought a coffin for their godfather when he died, or for not having sent cured meat over to their uncles on the fifteenth day of the first month, or saying that the fat on the meat wasn't even two inches thick, or even that the meat was swarming with maggots, and so on. They always sing with the force of justice behind them, calling their opponent to account: isn't this stingy miserliness? Isn't this rank ingratitude? Isn't this someone who, eating animals every day, has grown the heart of an animal? Of course, their opponent has to keep his wits about him under this barrage, use the weather or a lame foot as a pretext to exonerate himself from his own wrongdoing, then quickly launch a counterattack, seeking out his opponent's recent unfilial behavior—neither adversary balks in the slightest before exaggeration of the facts. They have to face up to sung interrogation; this kind of folk morality is strictly enforced.

The above forms the necessary opening struggle, setting up the standpoint of the adversaries.

After this has been delivered, they can relax and deliver a few *qoqo* songs. *Qo* can also mean "joke," for example "*qoqo* talk" can mean "funny talk." It can be further extended to mean indecent, and "*qoqo* songs," for example, often mean flirting songs. *Qoqo* songs excite the physical senses, and these are the numbers that animate young men the most. They can still be delivered in adversarial mode, as long as one side plays the male role and the other plays the female; one side has to love, and the other has to refuse this love.

Here's one I wrote down:

Think of her and I lose my wits,
When I walk on rocks, I don't feel a thing,
When I'm eating, I can't hold my chopsticks,
When I squat, I don't know how to get up.

Another verse was even sillier:

Think of her and I get in a rage
I eat every day but never put on weight,
If you don't believe me, then look under my clothes,
I'm nothing but skin and bones.

Some were quite terrifying, such as this one about a foolish woman's secret plot to kill her husband:

My husband's ever so handsome and smart,
My husband's like a stick of firewood,
Three chops, two chops, he drops dead,
All my friends come to have a barbecue.

Some were melancholy:

When I'm with you I hate to leave,
I paint a picture and stick it on the wall,
We haven't seen each other for weeks on end,
Hugging your shadow, I cry awhile.

Some expressed desperation in love:

What a waste for us to love each other,
Makes more sense to grind rice for other people's chickens,
Her children have already grown up,
But they don't call me father, just hey you!

All these were love songs. After reaching a certain point with love songs, the singers moved on to "low songs":

I see you, a girl twenty years old
You don't bolt the door too tightly
I see your face, peach-blossom pink
My crotch is already soaked through

Nonstop shouting from your house
The water flowing out is thick and white
A thousand pounds are thumping down on your bed
Stamping out a hole in the ground . . .

Every time these songs started, any women in the audience would hastily depart, cursing as they went, their faces burning scarlet; the young men would follow the more eye-catching back views with their eyes, like a line of restless fighting cocks, necks stretched out, eyes red, spoiling for a fight, springing up, then squatting down, their faces contorting into bursts of scorching laughter. They would deliberately make their laughter resound exaggeratedly so that the women would hear far away.

There were also songs about female suffering; for example, one sung by Wanyu from the lower village, describing the scene as a woman watched her illegitimate child float off downstream in a wooden basin along the Luo River:

Go slow and steady, steady and slow,
Don't crack your head on the rocks you pass,
It's not that your ma doesn't want you here,
You have no pa, she can't take the shame,
Go slow and steady, steady and slow,
Don't get wet in the wind and waves,
It's not that your ma wants to let you go,
Three times each night, she cries out loud . . .

In Wanyu's version, the wooden basin drifted into a whirlpool, made a circle and floated back, as if reluctant to leave, wanting to return wailing to its mother's bosom. When he'd sung up to this point, there wasn't one among the women listening whose eyes weren't red-rimmed, who hadn't begun to wipe her eyes on the edges of her clothes, each woman's snivels rising up one above another. Benren's wife's mouth fell at the corners, the basket of pig's fodder dropped from her hand, and she bent over another woman's shoulder and bawled.

*Striking Red [撞紅]: I heard that taking a virgin bride used to be taboo in Maqiao, and that "striking red," as it was called, on the nuptial night was seen as something highly inauspicious. Contrarily, the husband's family would be very content with a female pregnant before marriage, whose stomach stuck out a long way. Li Minggao, a scholar of Dong minority customs from the provincial Cultural Association in Hunan, told me there was nothing odd about this: in areas and periods of low production rate, people were the most important productive force and giving birth was the most important task for women, much more important than maintaining moral chastity. It was pretty common in many parts of the South for men to favor a big stomach when choosing a spouse.

Since it seemed to be an explanation that made sense, I made a note of it for reference.

In connection with this custom, Maqiao men harbored animosity toward their first-born, viewing it as wild spawn of unascertainable origin, not of their flesh and blood, and they either stuffed it into the piss bucket or smothered it in the mattress; they were always glad to be rid of it. This type of custom was called "favoring younger brothers"—in other words, murdering the eldest—and was for a long time practiced tacitly by people in Maqiao. Those mothers unable to bear it would swaddle the baby in a padded jacket and place it on the main road before their husband had struck, or place it in a wooden basin to float downstream, entrusting the fate of their own child to heaven—a common occurrence, this was.

After the Communist Party arrived, they prohibited such brutality and very little more was heard about it. There's no way of telling whether or not some people continued the practice in secret. Of course, when Wanyu sang ballads such as "Farewell from the Riverbank," it's easy to understand how, as the sound of weeping rose up on all sides, the song evoked for its female listeners the misery of earlier days.

☆**The *Qoqo* Man** [覺覺老]: The best singer in Maqiao was Wanyu, but I only got to know him a long time after I arrived in Maqiao. Orders had been issued for the village to organize an arts propaganda team to propagate Mao Zedong thought, which meant performing documents or editorials sent down from above to the sound of clappers. Performers were sent off to other villages banging drums and beating gongs, and other villages did the same thing. When the performance was finished, they would always have to yell a few slogans. Since everyone would be yelling at once, it was very difficult to yell them in a neat, coordinated fashion. Therefore, they would often divide up the long slogans into several sentences for the purpose of yelling, which created some unavoidable problems. There was one quotation from Chairman Mao which divided into three sentences: (1) Strike at poor peasants! (2) Means! (3) Strike at revolution! The first and last sentences thus became reactionary slogans. But everyone, as ever, raised their arms together and shouted, not hearing anything odd about it.

Orders were also issued to perform model revolutionary operas. As resources in the countryside were limited, people had to make do with what was available—you couldn't be too particular about props and costumes. When the White-haired Girl got on stage, a length of flax hung from her head, transfixing the faces of small children with terror. The hero Yang Zirong didn't have a proper cape, and had to make do with a rush cape to go up the mountain and fight the tiger. Once in late autumn, a very strong wind blew over the wooden scenery, along with a door plank covered in cotton, and poor Comrade Yang Zirong, who had just finished fighting the tiger with his lofty ideals, was knocked sideways by the snowy mountain. His eyes glazed over, as he swayed left and right, before toppling over onstage. Luckily, the oil lamps on stage were quite dim, and the audience couldn't see very well, or even thought that the hero falling to the ground was planned as part of the fight, and gave him a round of applause.

The peasants said that although the old plays were still the best, the new ones were also fun in their own way.

Although Yang Zirong was injured, he still gave a pretty good performance. As his brain was a bit fuzzy, he forgot his lines, but he came up with an emergency solution. When he saw gongs and drums, he would sing "gong," "drum"; if he saw chairs and tables, he would sing "chair," "table." When he finally sang in one breath "Land Reform Cooperative and People's Commune repairing irrigation sowing rape plants," the whole theater burst into spontaneous cheers. Not having heard properly, the commune cadre said again and again how good it was. He decided to choose the Maqiao propaganda team to represent the whole commune at the theater festival in the county seat.

Going to the county seat was a very rare treat. Rehearsals, moreover, were bound to be a lot more relaxing than hauling pond sludge. The men and women could also make use of this rare opportunity to mix freely, make each other up, fiddle with each other's costumes, and so on. Everybody was overjoyed. The Party Branch Secretary in the village, Ma Benyi, felt it gave him face and explained to me in great excitement that he wanted a play with four girls. He didn't care what it was about, as long as it had four girls in it.

I asked why.

"Didn't you have four red mandarin jackets made up last year? Those jackets cost the production brigade more than two carrying poles of grain, it's a shame to leave them locked in a case."

Back then, he hadn't wanted to sink two carrying poles of grain into the jackets.

Everyone thought this suggestion was spot on.

In order to improve the play, two people came from the Cultural Center in the county seat and suggested we add a mountain song to represent the folk characteristics of Maqiao. Benyi took a moment to think, then said, no problem: Wanyu had a fine pair of lungs, could do just about anything, funeral songs, comic songs, you name it. Let him sing!

All the villagers laughed—especially the women, who simply collapsed. Somewhat perplexed, I inquired who this person was, and they gave a brief description of someone who sounded vaguely familiar: beardless, eyebrows twisted but extremely thin, head always shaved smooth, rather like a shiny oiled radish. I remembered that he always left the village bearing a carrying pole, but I didn't know what he went off to do. I also remembered that when he stood looking on while others were singing, and people asked him to join in, he'd whine old-fashioned classical Chinese in shrill girlish tones: "Nay, nay, I'll sing not, thou must not jest with little me, comrades." He even blushed as he spoke.

He lived in two thatched huts in the lower part of the village, divorced, with a small child. It was said he was a bit of a lowlife: his high-pitched voice always appeared in places where there were a lot of women, and he always provoked guffaws or was chased away by them with stones. He'd started off as a miller, one of those people who came to the door to mill rice, and so had a lot of dealings with housewives. As time went by, the word "mill" started to take on connotations of low behavior because of its association with him. People would often ask him, so how many women have you actually milled? He would give an embarrassed laugh, "Tease me not, don't you know that in the new society we should be civilized?"

Fucha told me that once, when Wanyu went to Longjia Sands to mill rice, a child asked him what his name was. He said he was called old officer Ye. The child asked him what he'd come to do. Mill your mommy's *baba* cakes, he said. The little child rushed back into the house in excitement and reported what he'd been told. There was a group of women gathered at home drinking ginger tea, and they burst into raucous laughter on hearing the news. The child's elder sister was furious, and set the dog onto Wanyu, who scurried away like a terrified rat before losing his footing and falling into the manure pit.

Covered in manure, he climbed up onto a ridge between fields, leaving a great big hole in the pit, as if an ox had been asleep there. On the way back, people asked him in surprise, "Miller Wan, why did you leap into the manure pit today?"

"I wanted to see . . . how deep the manure pit really is."

"Did you come to check on production then?"

He hurried off, muttering away to himself.

A few children followed behind him, clapping their hands and laughing, and he picked up a stone as a threat and twisted round a few times in preparation for throwing it, but even straining every muscle he lacked the strength to toss it a bamboo-pole length away. The children laughed even more uproariously.

From then on, "checking on production" became a Maqiao allusion, referring to a Wanyu-type of sticky situation and to covering up difficulties. For example, if someone fell over, Maqiao people would laugh and ask "Have you been checking on production too?"

Wanyu was Benyi's same-pot cousin. At one time, when there was a pretty female guest at Benyi's place, he would turn up at Benyi's almost every day to sit around, hands in sleeves, his girly voice shrilling out deep into the night. One evening, he casually barged his way with a chair into the circle of people by the fireside. "What are you doing here?" Benyi asked ungraciously.

"The young lady's ginger tea smells good, really good," he answered virtuously.

"We're having a meeting in here."

"A meeting? Oh good, I'll have one too."

"This is a meeting for Party members. D'you understand?"

"That may be, but I haven't had a meeting for months. I really feel like one today, I'm getting desperate."

Uncle Luo asked "Eh, eh, eh, when did you become a Party member?"

Wanyu looked at the people around him, then looked back at Uncle Luo. "I'm not a Party member then?"

"Have you got a member?" said Uncle Luo, at which everyone guffawed.

Wanyu finally started to look embarrassed. "Bah, your humble slave stumbled into the royal sanctum, I take my leave, I take my leave."

Once he'd stepped outside the threshold, he exploded in anger, and said menacingly to a Party member on his way in, "When I feel like having a meeting, they don't let me come. Next time there's a meeting, don't ye come bothering me!"

As threatened, he subsequently attended no meetings, each time justifying his refusal with "Why did you stop me having a meeting when I felt like one? Fine, you have all the good meetings, then drag me along to the rotten leftover meetings—let me tell you, you can forget it!" As a result of his resentment at having been driven out of the Party meeting, he gradually started whining more and more. Once, for example, when helping a few women dye clothes, working up a happy sweat, he was talking away, getting more and more pleased with himself, until his mouth ran away with him. He said that Chairman Mao didn't have a beard—d'you reckon he looks anything like old Mother Wang San from Zhangjia District? He had two cherished portraits of the leader, he continued, one stuck on the front of his rice bucket, one stuck on the front of his piss bucket. If there was no rice in the bucket to scoop, then he'd give the portrait a clip round the ears. If there was no piss in the bucket to carry, he'd whack that portrait too.

Seeing the women grinning from ear to ear, he felt even more pleased with himself and said that next year he wanted to go to Beijing for a bit, to talk things over with Chairman Mao, ask him why the cold-water paddies have to be planted two seasons in a year.

Once his remarks reached the ears of a cadre, the cadre immediately got the People's Militia to grab their rifles, tie Wanyu up, and send him under guard to the commune. He returned a few days later, muttering away, somewhat paler than before.

"Well, what happened? Did the commune invite you to check on production?" people asked.

He rubbed his face and smiled bitterly: "Luckily the cadre who came with me had respect, the punishment wasn't too heavy, not too heavy."

He meant that the commune had seen he was a poor peasant and only fined him one hundred catties of grain.

From then on, "have respect" or "the cadre had respect" also became a Maqiao allusion, meaning to explain away personal ridicule, or a grain fine.

When he first appeared in the propaganda team, he seemed really down on his luck: his thin, tattered jacket was held together with a straw cord, he wore a crooked woollen hat and his stockingless feet stuck out from pants that were too short for him, revealing a length of leg that was raw from the cold. He still had an ox whip in his hand, as he'd just come back from the fields. What on earth were we playing at! he said. One minute we wouldn't allow him to sing, the next we'd want him to sing, then we wanted him to go to the county seat to sing—he felt like a chamber pot at the foot of the bed, dragged out when needed, shoved back when he wasn't needed. Nothing good could ever come out of Commune Head He!

None of this, in fact, had anything to do with Commune Head He.

He asked mysteriously "Can I sing *qoqo* songs now? The Communist Party . . . ?" He made a toppling over gesture.

"What are you blathering on about?!" I thrust a piece of paper at him, some lines about spring ploughing. "Memorize them today, tomorrow we rehearse, the day after the commune are going to come and check it."

Having studied it a while, he suddenly seized me by the arm. "Sing this? Hoes and rakes and carrying poles filling manure pits watering rice seedlings?"

I wasn't sure what he meant.

"Comrade, I have to put up with all this stuff every day in the fields, and now you want me to get on stage and sing about it? Just thinking about hoes and carrying poles makes me sweat, gives me palpitations. What d'you really want me to sing?"

"What do you think we asked you here to sing? You'll sing what we want you to sing, if you don't sing then go and do some work!"

"Ooooh, comrade, temper, temper!"

He didn't give the lines back.

I didn't find his voice as beautiful as people said it was; though it was clear and sharp, it was too abrupt, too stark, too direct, sung throughout in a monotone, a real girly screech it was, as piercing as a knife edge scraping on tiles. I felt that the sinuses of listeners must be contorting horribly, that everyone must be listening not with their ears, but with their nasal cavities, their foreheads, the backs of their heads, in order to cope with these repeated knife cuts.

This kind of scraping noise must have been known in Maqiao. Yet except for the Educated Youth, the locals all had a high opinion of his singing voice.

The Educated Youth were even less impressed with how smug he was about his choice of costume, and wouldn't let him wear his old leather shoes. He also wanted to wear his candle-wick silk pants, even put on a pair of glasses. As the people from the County Cultural Center pointed out, how on earth could there be a toffee-nosed intellectual right in the middle of the spring ploughing? No way. They paused to think, and decided that he should be barefoot, roll up his trouser legs, wear a bamboo hat on his head, and carry a hoe on his shoulder.

He protested violently. "Carry a hoe? I'll look like an old water watchman! Horrible! Too horrible!"

The people from the Cultural Center said, "What do you know? This is art."

"Well, why don't I make it even more artistic by hauling a bucket of shit around?"

If Benyi hadn't been there supervising the rehearsal, the argument would never have ended. In fact Benyi wasn't that keen on the hoe himself, but since the county seat comrades said the hoe was good, the hoe stayed. "If they want you to carry it, you carry it." He scolded Wanyu: "You've got the wits of a pig, you have! You're going to look like an idiot on stage with nothing to do! What are you going to do when you start to sing?"

Wanyu blinked a couple of times, but remained blank.

Starting to get agitated, Benyi got up on to the stage to do a few sample actions to make Wanyu understand, holding the hoe upright, or carrying it on his shoulder, on his left shoulder for a bit, then on the right shoulder for a bit.

In the subsequent days of rehearsal, Wanyu's heart wasn't really in it as he stood on one side, a solitary figure holding a hoe. He was a good bit older than the other actors, and didn't seem able to join in with the chatter. Whenever any women came by to watch the fun, Wanyu's face always took on a shamed expression, his features screwed into a bitter smile. "Pray look not, ladies, it's too horrible."

In the end he didn't go with us to the county seat. The day we boarded the tractor in the commune, we waited and waited but there was no trace of him. When we finally saw him arrive, we discovered he hadn't brought his hoe. When asked where his hoe had got to, he mumbled no problem, no problem, I'll be able to borrow another in the county seat. The team leader said that the town wasn't like the country, where every household had a hoe—what if we couldn't borrow a suitable one, what would we do then? Quick, go back and fetch it! Wanyu just stood there hemming and hawing, with his hands in his sleeves. It was plain to see: he and that hoe just didn't mesh, and he didn't want to get on stage with it.

The team leader had no alternative but to go and borrow one from nearby. As we waited for him to borrow one, we discovered that Wanyu had disappeared, slipped away.

In fact, although he never made it to the county seat, he always very much wanted to go. From very early on, he was always washing his shoes and clothes, making preparations to go into town. He'd also secretly begged me that, when the time came, I should lead him across the roads in the city—he was terrified of cars. If a hooligan picked a fight with him, he would surely get the worst of it. The city women were good-looking, and he'd be so busy looking in all directions that he might lose his way. He hoped that I would rescue him as the need arose. But in the event he didn't go with us to the county seat, pitting himself against that hoe to the bitter end. He later explained that no matter how he tried, he simply couldn't remember the words to that song about manure pits, about digging the soil, scattering ox dung, watering the rice shoots. He just got confused and frustrated, and all that singing made him want to scream. If he'd really gone to the county seat to sing, there would have definitely been a major incident. It wasn't that he hadn't put in the effort, but even after he'd eaten pig brain, dog brain, ox brain, he still couldn't remember some of his lines, and then he was off on a spirit journey thinking about low doings between men and women. He had no choice but to slope off half-heartedly at the last minute.

Because he didn't say goodbye, Benyi later fined him fifty catties of grain.

This was how I saw it: Wanyu wasn't conscientious about a lot of things, but when it came to singing he was pretty conscientious. Many times he wouldn't stand firm, yet in his attachment to _qoqo_ songs, none stood firmer. Quite simply, he was intent on martyring himself to art, prepared to give up this cushy number in town, to give up work points and put up with punishment and abuse from cadres, rather than put up with hoe art, with this pathetic womanless excuse for art.

☆**_Ligelang_** [哩咯啷]:One day, Wanyu saw the stonemason Zhihuang beating his wife so violently that she cried out for help; Wanyu went to mediate, saying that he'd seen what was going on and that Zhihuang shouldn't be so brutal. One look at his bald head and smooth, beardless face sent the stonemason into a blind rage: "What business is it of yours if I beat my cheating wife to death, you piece of shit?" Wanyu replied that the New Society said we should all be civilized, and women were female comrades, not punching bags, don't you know?

After arguing a while, the stonemason finally smiled coldly and said, okay then, as your heart bleeds so much for female comrades, I'll strike a bargain with you. If you can take three punches from me, I'll respect what you say.

Wanyu normally acted like a weedy scholar, terrified of pain; a leech bite in the fields would make him bellow and bawl, and his face turned ashen at Zhihuang's challenge. Despite his terror, he probably didn't want to lose face in front of onlookers and decided to see the thing through; he squeezed his eyes shut, and shouted yes, while he braced his outer cranium for the blow.

He'd overreached himself, and shutting his eyes any tighter wasn't going to help. After just the first punch from Zhihuang, he hurled himself howling and yelling into the ditch and failed to re-emerge.

With an icy snigger, the stonemason left him there and walked off.

With great difficulty, Wanyu got himself back onto his feet and shouted at a black shadow in front of him, "Keep 'em coming! On the chin!" The black shadow remained motionless, but he sensed the people standing around were laughing. He rubbed his eyes to steady his vision; he then saw that the black shadow wasn't the stonemason but a grain winnower.

He roared furiously at the front door of the Zhihuang household: "What are you running from? Come out and fight, if you've got any guts! You vicious dog's bladder, you can't even keep your word, you owe me two punches, you, you chicken you!" Despite his heroism, he'd staggered dizzily to the wrong place: the stonemason wasn't there but had gone off to the mountains.

He stumbled back home. People he met on his way back laughed when they saw him covered in mud. "Hey, miller, you been checking on production again?"

He merely laughed bitterly. "I'm going to report him! Report! When the People's Government deal with it, they're not going to worry about our precious Master Huang knocking them around!"

He added: "I'd sooner be torn limb from limb than worry about Commune Head He's favoritism!"

In all matters his thoughts turned to Commune Head He, believing they were the result of Commune Head He's conspiracies. Listeners couldn't make heads or tails of this unreasoned hatred; when asked, he always failed to account for it.

Wanyu was very used to taking blows for women. Time after time, he rolled involuntarily into the midst of marital disputes, leaping inevitably to the defense of the woman, which he paid for successively in terms of physical pain, even in hair and teeth. Some of the women whom he sheltered thought him too meddlesome, and turned on him with their husbands, showering his head with enraged blows, which left him feeling rather aggrieved. Generally, he wouldn't argue with these women. People used to say that he was the *ligelang* for these women, and hearing this made him very happy. *Ligelang* (pronounced *lee-guh-lang*) is an onomatopoeic word, often used in describing tunes played in the traditional Chinese five-note scale; in Maqiao vocabulary, it's also used to refer to lovers and to lovers' talk. To be more precise, it's used for less formal, sincere, whole-hearted love; it has a more playful feel, the flavor of a burst of a tune on the fiddle, and stands for an ambiguous state somewhere in between love and friendship. For this very reason, the rather vague term *ligelang* has an unfixed meaning which can be elaborated into marginal, vague imaginings. Illicit fornication amongst clumps of grass is *ligelang*. Informal boistering and ribbing between men and women can also be called *ligelang*. It could be reasonably concluded that if Maqiao people saw ballroom dancing or men and women walking together in the city, they would place it firmly in the category of *ligelang*—a broad extramarital category lacking clear-cut analysis and explanation.

Maqiao people have many sketchy and muddled areas of consciousness, of which *ligelang* is one.

***Dragon** [龍]: Dragon is a swear word, referring to the male organ. It often comes up in Maqiao insults:

You, dead dragon, you!

Look at that stupid dragon!

Watch where you put your great big dragon feet!

Although Wanyu was no saint when it came to bad language, he couldn't bear other people calling him "dragon." Once thus insulted, he would grab the nearest likely weapon (stone, rake, whatever) and challenge his adversary to duel it out—I don't know why this was.

The last time I saw Wanyu was when I returned to Maqiao from the county seat and brought him the soap and women's socks he had asked me to buy for him. I spotted his son in front of his hut: he spat at me, guarding the door vigilantly. I said I'd come to see his dad.

Wanyu, lying on the bed inside, must have heard this. But he waited until I had reached the bed before suddenly pulling up the tattered, soya-black mosquito net. A face popped out. "What are you looking at, eh, eh? Here I am, like it or lump it!"

There was nothing comic about this. His face was waxy yellow, thin, and angular as a bunch of dead twigs—I had to hide my shock.

"I really missed you, I've been pining for days."

There was, once again, nothing comic about this.

After having asked about his illness, I said it was a pity he hadn't come to the city to sing. He waved his hands feelingly.

"Oh yes, very nice, very nice. Farming songs? That hoe and piss bucket, swing it here, swing it there stuff, you really call that singing?"

He sighed, and said the best times were past, from the first month to the eighth day of the third, when no one did any work, when all they did was enjoy themselves singing songs. This village would go perform in that village, this mountain in that mountain, now that was fun. The kids would sing "hallway songs," seated opposite each other to sing; once they'd completed a verse, they would shift their stool forward an inch, until the two stools were level with each other and the two singers snuggled up to each other, cheeks grazing, singing into each other's ear, their voices as quiet as the buzz of a mosquito, so that only their singing partner could hear clearly. This was called "earside singing." Wanyu's eyes shone with animation. "Tsk, tsk, tsk, those girls, they were like beancurd, squeeze 'em and the water'd come out!"

Since I happened to be feeling aimless myself that day, I felt a stirring of curiosity about Low Songs and begged him to sing me a bit of one. He came over all bashful for a time, and put up a show of refusing before he agreed. "You want me to get into trouble, then?"

"I bought you soap and socks, don't I deserve any thanks?"

His energy dramatically returned, and he jumped out of bed, pacing round the room once, then twice before he considered his throat properly moistened and his concentration properly focused. Suddenly, he burned with strength, vigor, power, his sickly color swept away, two beams of electric light shining from his eyes.

After he'd sung a few lines, but before I'd managed to understand them, he started waving his hands and coughing violently; unable to get any words out, he slowly groped his way back to the edge of the bed.

"I'm afraid my singing days are over." He grasped my hand tightly between his icy palms.

"Not at all, you sing really well."

"Really?"

"Of course, of course."

"Stop putting me on."

"I'm not putting you on."

"D'you reckon I can still sing?

"Of course, of course."

"What d'you know about it?"

I took a drink of my water.

His eyes dulled and he heaved a long sigh, leaning his head back onto the bed. "My singing days are over, all over. It's all Commune Head He's fault."

He began muttering darkly once more about Commune Head He. I didn't quite know what to say, but just drank my bowl of water good and slowly.

One day, a few months later, an ominous explosion of firecrackers was heard far off in the distance. When I went out to inquire, I discovered that Wanyu had scattered, or died (see the entry "Scattered"). I heard that when he died there was no one at his bedside, and his corpse lay there for a day or more before it was discovered by his neighbor Zhaoqing. I also heard that when he passed away, he had no more than three broad beans to his name, certainly not enough to eat for the next day. He left a child of about ten, whom some time ago he'd sent off to an uncle who lived far away. I'd seen the bare interior of his house, covered in spiders' webs and duck droppings; there wasn't even a cupboard inside this empty shell—clothes were always heaped on a tattered hanging basket over which his neighbors' chickens would jump back and forth. People said that he'd suffered all his life at the hands of women—otherwise, surely, his wife wouldn't have divorced him and would have made certain he had hot meals to eat.

He didn't even have a coffin for the funeral, and in the end Benyi donated a basket of grain which, supplemented by another basket from the team leader, could be exchanged for two lengths of fir wood to make a coffin.

In accordance with local custom, people placed a small bag of rice in his coffin as a pillow and put a copper coin in his mouth. While they were changing his clothes, Zhaoqing suddenly discovered, "Hey, he's got no dragon!"

Everyone was dumbfounded.

"Really!"

"Really, really, he's got no dragon!"

One after another they went up to the corpse to have a look, one after another discovered this male really had no dragon, no male organ, and one after another came away dumbfounded.

By evening, the news had spread through the whole village, and left the women whispering among themselves in shock and disbelief. Only Uncle Luo was a little disdainful of all the gossip, pronouncing in highly considered tones that there was no need for conjecture, his appearance made everything clear: if he wasn't a eunuch, how come he didn't have a beard or eyebrows? He also said that a long time back he'd heard people say ten or so years ago Wanyu had been arrested immediately upon assaulting the wife of a local grandee. This landlord controlled Changle, and headed up the defence grouping of the puppet regime; no matter how much Wanyu begged for mercy, they still cut off his dragon with one stroke of the knife.

When people heard this, there were sighs all around. They thought back to the way that Wanyu endlessly curried favor with women, helping them with their work, taking their punches for them—why had he bothered? He'd suffered decades of thunder, with never a drop of rain; fed decades of pigs, without getting a single meatball—was he mad? It turned out even his only child wasn't his own flesh and blood—when people came to think about it, the child didn't look anything like Wanyu.

With Wanyu gone, the village was much quieter, with far fewer songs. Sometimes you seemed to hear a faint screeching, but when you listened carefully it turned out to be the wind, not Wanyu.

Wanyu was buried under Tianzi Peak. When subsequently I went into the mountains to cut wood, several times I walked over his body. At the grave-sweeping festival, I took a look at his grave: it was the most colorful grave, all the straggling grasses had been pulled off the mound and there were masses of paper ashes, burnt candles, and incense sticks. There was also bowl after bowl of rice, laid there as a sacrifice. I also saw women there, both familiar and unfamiliar faces, some from the village and some from far away, all come to weep and wail, eyes red from grief.

There was nothing furtive about their weeping, nothing timid; a fat woman from Zhangjia District even plonked herself on the ground, slapping her enormous legs, howling that Wanyu was her liver, her lungs, wailing that her liver and lungs had lived a life of poverty with only three broad beans left when he died. It was no less than a spontaneous convention of the feminine world. I was surprised their husbands didn't have anything to say about this outpouring of tears.

Fucha said that they wouldn't say anything because they all owed Miller Wan money for work done. I think there was perhaps another reason: they felt that Wanyu wasn't a real man, and couldn't have had any untoward relations with their women; it wasn't worth putting up a fight, there was no need to settle scores.

☆**Dragon (continued)** [龍(續)]: Maqiao people always paint dragons in black, with horns, claws, snake bodies, ox heads, shrimp whiskers, tiger teeth, horse faces, fish scales, and so on—every single feature is necessary. These dragons are painted on walls, on mirrors, or carved onto beds, with billowing waves and clouds added on—sea, land, sky, everything present and correct. From this it seems that dragons belong to no animal species and bear no relation to the dinosaurs of prehistoric times. Dragons are a kind of Chinese-style synthesis of all animals, an abstracted summary of all life on the planet.

Dragons are a kind of concept. An exhaustive, all-inclusive, omnipotent concept.

Dragon Boats evolved out of the building of ships in the shape of dragons. When I was an Educated Youth in Maqiao, the Dragon Boat Festival had been criticized and prohibited as an old custom, because of the Cultural Revolution. I only heard from the villagers that the Dragon Boat race used to be very exciting, with both sides of the Luo River competing for supremacy; when the losing side got onto the bank each rower had to put his pants over his head and submit to endless mockery and humiliation. I also heard that the Dragon Boats were all painted hundreds of times over with tung oil, and that before starting to build the boats they burned incense and supplicated the spirits—endless fuss and ceremony—after which the boat couldn't get wet in the rain, or dry in the sun, or have water dropped on it, until the day of the race, when, thronged by drums and music, it would be lifted by the young men to the starting line. Even though the route was right along the side of the river, the men couldn't ride in the boat, instead the boat rode the men.

I asked why things were reversed this way.

They said that they'd wanted to let the dragon boat rest—it shouldn't be allowed to get tired.

At this time of year, the dragon became a real kind of animal, even a creature with limited stocks of energy.

***Maple Demon** [楓鬼]:Before I started writing this book, I hoped to write the biography of every single thing in Maqiao. I'd been writing fiction for ten or so years, but I liked reading and writing fiction less and less—I am, of course, referring to the traditional kind of fiction, which has a very strong sense of plot. Main character, main plot, main mood block out all else, dominating the field of vision of both reader and writer, preventing any sidelong glances. Any occasional casual digression is no more than a fragmentary embellishment of the main line, the temporary amnesty of a tyrant. Admittedly, there's nothing to say this kind of fiction can't approach one angle on the truth. But all you have to do is think a little, and you realize that most of the time real life isn't like that, it doesn't fit into one guiding, controlling line of cause and effect. A person often exists in two, three, four, or even more interlocking strands, outside each of which a great many other elements exist, each constituting an indispensable part of our lives. In this multifarious, scattered network of cause and effect, how valid is the domination of one main thread of protagonists, plot and mood?

Anything left out of traditional fiction is normally something of "no significance." But when religious authority is all-important, science has no significance; when the human race is all-important, nature has no significance. When politics is all-important, love has no significance; when money is all-important, art has no significance. I suspect the myriad things in this world are in fact all of equal importance; the only reason why sometimes one set of things seems to have "no significance" is because they've been filtered out by the writer's view of what has significance, and dismissed by the reader's view of what has significance. They are thus debarred from all zones of potential interest. Obviously, judgement of significance is not an instinct we are born with—quite the contrary, it is no more than a function of the fashion, customs, and culture of one particular time, often revealing itself in the form into which fiction shapes us. In other words, an ideology lurks within the tradition of fiction, an ideology which reproduces itself only on passing through us.

My memory and imagination aren't totally in line with tradition.

I therefore often hope to break away from a main line of cause and effect, and look around at things that seem to have no significance whatsoever, for example contemplate a stone, focus on a cluster of stars, research a miserable rainy day, describe the random back view of someone it seems I've never met and never will meet. At the very least I should write about a tree. In my imagination, Maqiao couldn't do without a big tree. I should cultivate a tree—no, make that two trees, two maple trees—on my paper, and plant them on the slope behind Uncle Luo's house in lower Maqiao. I imagine the larger tree to be at least twenty-five meters tall, the smaller around twenty. Anyone visiting Maqiao would see from faraway the crown of the trees, the tips of whose branches would spread out to encompass a panoramic view.

This is excellent: writing the biography of two trees.

A village without big trees is like a home without parents, or a head without eyes—it just doesn't look right, as if it lacks a center. These two trees were just that, the center of Maqiao. There wasn't a child in Maqiao who hadn't breathed in their cool shade, who hadn't drunk in the chirps of the cicadas, or in whom the bark's gnarled tumors hadn't induced bizarre and terrified imaginings. They didn't need any particular looking after: when people had things to do, they could just be left to themselves and forgotten about. But they were perfectly willing at any moment to welcome and provide company for the lonely, who would find their melancholy gently soothed away by the rustling of the leaves, and who under the leafy screen, on a patch of silver that was stippled and studded, dispersing and overlapping, sometimes tranquil, sometimes stormy, could set sail for a cloudless dream land.

There was no way of knowing who had planted these trees, and the old-timers in the village production team wouldn't shed any further light on the matter. As regards the name "Maple Demons," apparently there'd been a mountain fire many years ago in which all the trees on the slope were burned to death, except for these two, which escaped safe and sound; even their leaves and branches weren't damaged in the slightest. Henceforth, people eyed the trees with increasing awe and respect, and legends concerning them multiplied. Some said the gnarled patterns in the bark were in fact human shapes; in violent storms they secretly grew several feet, and only shrank back to normal when they saw people coming. Ma Ming told an even spookier story. Once, unthinkingly, he'd fallen asleep under the trees, hanging his bamboo hat on a broken forked branch. In the middle of the night, he was startled awake by the sound of thunder and made out, by a flash of lightning, that his bamboo hat was now hanging on the top of the tree. Very peculiar.

Ma Ming boasted that he used to be quite an artist when he was younger. He said that after painting these two trees, for three days afterwards his right hand swelled up dramatically and he ran a fever; he didn't dare try again.

You couldn't even paint them, much less cut them down. The two trees therefore grew taller and taller, and became a landmark for miles around. When someone had sawed off a branch, they hung a piece of red cloth from their door to ward off evil, or carved a wooden fish out of the wood, to beg the spirits to ward off misfortune; all of which was, apparently, very effective. Once, while taking part in an irrigation project, I went to the commune to draw up some plans. I went together with Teacher Fan from the Middle School (who had also been allocated to the project) to the county irrigation office and copied the map of the commune. I found out, as we choked on the archive room dust, that even after 1949 the government had still not drawn up a comprehensive map of the area, and that all plans were still based on the military maps left by the Japanese army at the time of their invasion of China. These looked to be the contour maps of great and resourceful strategists, drawn in black and white on a scale of 1:5000; the commune took up one large sheet. Instead of sea level, the map used the foundation stone of the Changsha city wall at Xiaowumen as its starting point for elevation. Apparently, before the Japanese invaded, they bribed Chinese traitors to draw up plans in secret. The ingenuity and thoroughness of their preparations are nothing short of astonishing.

I saw that on this map too, Maqiao's two maple trees were so awesomely imposing that they'd been ringed in red pen by the Japanese. Teacher Fan said knowledgeably that they'd been a landmark for navigating Japanese planes.

This set me to thinking that Maqiao people had actually seen Japanese planes. Benyi said that the first time they caught sight of this freak apparition, Benyi's elder uncle thought it was a big bird and yelled at some lads to spread grain on the ground to entice it down, and got everyone else to run and fetch ropes to catch it.

The plane didn't descend, and his uncle hurled abuse up at the sky:

I know you're up there! I know you're up there!

Only Long Stick Xi guessed then that it was a Japanese plane, come to drop bombs. Unfortunately, this outsider's rough speech was barely intelligible, and no one understood him. Benyi's uncle wondered how a Japanese bird could grow that big, since Japanese people were so very small.

For a day, the villagers watched and waited in vain for the plane to come and peck at the grain. The second time the planes came, they relieved themselves of bombs, setting off earth-shattering explosions. Benyi's uncle died right there, mouth blown off to the tree top, as if it wanted to nibble on the birds' nests. Benyi even today is still a bit hard of hearing, but I don't know if it's from the explosion or from the shock of seeing that mouth fly up the tree.

Three villagers were killed in the bombing. If you add Xiongshi (see the entry "Dear Life"), who died in a delayed explosion twenty years later, then the death toll rises to four.

When you think about it, if it hadn't been for those trees, would the Japanese planes have found their way there? Would they have dropped bombs? After all, there was no particular reason for the Japanese to take any great interest in a small mountain village. If they hadn't used those trees as a navigation mark, they wouldn't necessarily have flown through, probably wouldn't have seen the crowd of people down below shouting and yelling, and probably would have dropped their bombs somewhere they considered more important.

Everything, including the deaths of four people and all that subsequently occurred, happened because of those two trees.

From that point on, there was always a flock of crows perched on these two trees, a fractured blackness erupting as they flapped their wings. Sometimes people would try to chase them away by burning or smashing their nests, but these creatures of ill omen waited until people's backs were turned, then flew back, stubbornly defending the tops of the trees.

The crows cawed year in, year out. I heard it said that three woman hanged themselves under this tree, one after another. I don't know their backgrounds; I only know that one had had a big argument with her husband, and she hanged herself after poisoning him. All this happened a very long time ago.

When I passed by these two trees, it was like passing any tree, any blade of grass, any stone—I wouldn't take too much notice of them. I wouldn't think, aha, there they are, lurking in the depths of the day, concealing unfathomable possibilities, harboring menace under their canopies, rumbling and erupting at portentous moments, sealing such-and-such a person's fate.

Sometimes I think that one tree is very unlike another, just as people are very unlike one another. Hitler, say, was also a human being. Suppose aliens happened to read of him: on the basis of his possession of five senses, four limbs, upright posture and frequent emission of regulated sounds to others of his kind, the aliens, on leafing through the dictionary that they might possess, would define him as human. This would not be incorrect. *The Songs of Chu* is the title of a book excavated in the Han dynasty. If a copy was given to a Hebrew man who understood no Chinese, on the basis of the shape of its characters, writing implements, and its state on being unearthed, the Hebrew man might, through sufficient ingenuity and erudition, conclude that the writing was Chinese. This, similarly, would not be incorrect. But how meaningful is this "not incorrect"?

Just as we call the Maple Demon a tree, a maple tree, how meaningful is this degree of correctness?

A tree lacks human will and freedom, but in life's complex network of cause and effect it can often occupy a position of quiet importance. In this sense, the difference between one tree and another can sometimes be comparable to the difference between Hitler and Gandhi, to the distinction between the *Songs of Chu* and the instruction manual for an electric razor—it can be much greater than we imagine. Even if we've read cartloads of botanical books, when confronted with an unfamiliar tree our knowledge seems rudimentary indeed.

The two maple trees finally disappeared in early summer of 1972, when I was away from the village. On the journey back, I couldn't see the crowns of the trees from far off and immediately felt there was something not quite right about the panorama before me; I almost thought I'd taken a wrong turn. After I entered the village, I found that the houses seemed much more spaced out, much lighter, and that there was a rather striking patch of bare, empty ground. It turned out the shade from the trees was no longer there. Everywhere I saw wood chippings and sawdust reeking of sap, and mounds of branches and leaves sandwiched with birds' nests and spiders' webs, yet no one was taking them home for firewood; the soil lay overturned in waves, testifying to the violent struggle that had taken place not long before. I smelled something rather peppery, but couldn't say where it came from.

The crunching sound of feet trampling leaves and branches was the sound of advancing old age.

The trees were cut down under commune orders, to make, it was said, rows of seats for the newly built commune assembly hall and also to dispel the superstitions surrounding the Maple Demons. When the time came, absolutely no one was prepared to put hand to axe or saw, and in the end, the commune cadres had no choice but to order a landlord under official surveillance to get on with it. They also added workers from two hard-up families, to whom they had to promise to cancel a ten-yuan debt before they could finally make them hesitantly start work. Later I saw in the commune row upon row of those spanking new maplewood chairs, used for Party meetings, family planning meetings, irrigation and pig-feeding meetings, and so on. I also saw filthy footprints left behind, as well as oily banquet remains. It was probably from this time on that a kind of skin irritation started to rage through dozens of nearby villages: when sufferers, male or female, happened to meet, they would scratch wildly, pulling up their clothes all over the place, not knowing whether to laugh or cry. Some, unable to stand it, would place their backs to a wall and move up and down, or from side to side, or discuss instructions from the county with a hand down their pants all the while. Herbal remedies were tried, with no result. Apparently the county medical team were completely flummoxed, found it all very puzzling.

It was rumored that everyone had caught "maple pox," instigated by the Maqiao Maple Demons—they wanted to make people suffer for their arrogance, taking revenge on the murderers who'd chopped them down.

*Will/Willing (*Ken*)** [肯]: *Ken* (will/willing) is a word used to express wishes or preferences, to demonstrate desire and permission. For example, "*ken* with the head" (nod agreement), "*ken* do" (will do), "*ken* get my head around it" (will think about it) all describe a person's psychological inclinations.

Maqiao people use *ken* in a much broader sense—not only for people and animals, but for anything in the whole world.

Some examples:

· This plot of land *ken* grow crops.
· It's strange, but the firewood at home *ken* not burn.
· This boat *ken* go quite a ways.
· This sky *ken* not produce a drop of rain in a month.
· Benyi's hoe *ken* not dig very deep.

And so on.

On hearing these remarks, I couldn't stop a thought forming in my mind: everything has a will, a life of its own. Fields, firewood, boats, sky, hoes, and so on, they're all the same as men, should even have first names and last names of their own, stories of their own. Maqiao people in fact spoke to their objects as a matter of course, cajoling or cursing, praising or promising. For example, if they gave a plough a really savage talking-to, it would then move much more quickly along the ground. Then again, resting their axe at the top of the wine jar to soak up the alcohol fumes strengthened it enough to chop wood. If they hadn't been forced to submit to outside interference, if it hadn't been for the spread of science, Maqiao people perhaps would never have acknowledged that these were lifeless objects lacking the capacity to feel and think for themselves.

With these assumptions in mind, we've reason to feel sad at the death of a tree, even to cherish its memory. In places where trees are toppled one after another without provoking any sadness, the trees have never lived, have never been anything but an inert natural resource, a form of revenue. People from these places wouldn't use the word *ken* like they did in Maqiao.

When I was little, I also had lots of strange fantasies involving personifications and spirits. For example, I used to turn blossoms on trees into the dreams of the tree roots, or rugged mountain paths into a conspiracy plotted by the forest—all very childish, of course. After I got bigger and stronger, I used my knowledge of physics or chemistry to explain blossom or mountain paths—or should I say, rather, that because I could use my knowledge of physics or chemistry to explain blossom and mountain paths, I started to get bigger and stronger. The problem, though, is whether big and strong modes of thought are correct modes of thought. For a long time, men were bigger and stronger than women—does that mean that men were correct? The great imperial powers were bigger and stronger than the colonies—does that mean that the great powers were correct? If in an alien galaxy there exists a race of beings much more advanced and much stronger than mankind, should their mode of thought be used to exterminate and replace that of mankind?

This is a question, a question I can't answer, a question that pulls me this way and that. Because I yearn both to be big and strong, and to go back to my small, weak childhood, to tree-root dreams and mountain conspiracies.

***Dear Life** [貴生]: One winter's day, Zhihuang's snot-nosed son Xiongshi was playing with a few ox-herder lads on the hillside to the north. They'd dug out a snake hole, planning to extract a hibernating snake to roast. They unearthed a heavy, rusty iron carbuncle but had no idea what it was; Xiongshi banged it hard with a sickle, saying he wanted to use the two ends of the carbuncle to hammer out a few kitchen knives for his mother to sell in the market.

His banging set off an explosion that blasted the lads, who were some distance away hunting snake holes, a good few feet off the ground, arms and legs flailing helplessly in mid-air. After falling painfully, they looked back, but Xiongshi, oddly enough, was nowhere to be seen—there was only a light shower of leaves and earth, along with a few icy drops of rain, floating down from the sky. The boys were surprised to discover that these droplets were red and seemed rather like . . . blood?

Having no idea what had happened, they still thought that Xiongshi was hiding somewhere, so they set about yelling for him at the tops of their lungs. There was no answer. One of them, frightened by the discovery of a bloodied, fleshy lump of finger, took it back to show the grown-ups.

Later on, people from the commune came and busied themselves for a while. People from the county seat also came and busied themselves for a while, before a conclusion was produced: a bomb dropped by Japanese planes in 1942 had detonated after a thirty-year delay. This meant that the Sino-Japanese War in Maqiao lasted right up to the year when it claimed the life of Xiongshi.

Zhihuang and his wife were utterly grief-stricken. Zhihuang took it particularly badly: since previously he'd always thought there'd been something between his wife and Wanyu, and that Xiongshi was most likely illegitimate, he'd never been terribly affectionate toward his son. After Wanyu died, the discovery that Wanyu was hardly a man dispelled this cloud of suspicion, and he turned a far more genial, fatherly face to Xiongshi, picking wild chestnuts and other things for him on his way home from the mountain quarry. Little had he imagined that from that time on, there would no longer be a pair of little hands to receive those chestnuts. Xiongshi wasn't at home, in the fields, by the stream, near the mountains; he was nowhere. His son had become a resounding explosion, before scattering and disappearing into eternal quiet.

Xiongshi's head was both unusually big and unusually round. He grew into quite a sturdy figure, his fluttering eyes as bright and beautiful as his mother Shuishui's. Just one of his sidelong glances dripped with feminine charm, reminding people of how Shuishui had been in her days as an actress. When people saw him, they couldn't help giving his bottom or his cheeks a pinch, vying with each other to squeeze his irresistible charms. He hated this kind of harassment, and unless offered something nice to eat would imperiously reject such advances, giving outsiders a steely once-over. With one roll of the eyes he could gauge whether you really had something to eat in your pocket, whether it was really worth trusting your smiling face, or whether he should act cool and calm for the time being and bide his time. He hated mushy talk from old people more than anything, it drove him mad, to curse then kick then spit—until, pushed to his limit, he would suddenly bite. His lion's jaws bit everything under the sun, starting with his mother's breast. No one who'd sat next to him at primary school, whether male or female, escaped his teeth. In the end, even the teacher's luck ran out.

He refused to produce a self-criticism in front of the headmaster for hacking at the table edge with his knife. "Self-criticize this, self-criticize that! I've had enough of doing things your way!"

As the head teacher dragged him by the ear to the teacher's room, he retaliated by biting the head teacher, then fled far, far away, holding up his pants and swearing his head off.

"I'll get you, you horrible brat!" raged the head teacher.

"You might beat me today, but just wait until you get old and come by my place with a stick, I'll push you into a great big pit!"

He was forecasting a victory many years in the future.

The head teacher followed him off into the distance, brandishing a carrying pole.

He couldn't catch up with him, of course, and soon the ball of flesh that was Xiongshi had rolled up to the house facing the mountains, and stood there, arms akimbo, keeping up the flow of abuse. "Hey, Li Xiaotang, you big old pig, your pubes are showing. . . ."

He was using the headmaster's full name to curse him, although I don't know how he found it out.

Going back to school was, of course, now out of the question. Other people said that Zhihuang had brought up a complete menace through lack of discipline. Him, a student? You'd train a dog before you trained him!

Later, he would often come down to look at the school, viewing from a distance the students reading aloud in unison, doing gymnastics, or playing ball. If his former classmates saw him, he would make as if he was playing horse, "Whoah there, chaaaaaarge," galloping off into the distance, acting as if he were having a grand old time, as if he were taking absolutely no notice of what was going on in the school.

One day, playing in the sands with a few kids, he started to antagonize the others by grabbing hold of a battered overshoe which he was using to shovel sand. A few of them resolved to take revenge by shitting into the village well and framing Xiongshi for the deed. Saying he'd done it, they went with great fanfare to where the adults were working to report him. The adults were all furious at this news and Shuishui wanted to hide her face in shame; turning red, then white in anger, she yelled at Xiongshi: "Can't stand it if you don't get into trouble, can you?"

"I . . . didn't do it."

"Still talking back! All these people saw you—d'you think they're blind, got beans for eyes?"

"I didn't do it."

"There's no water to drink, so you'd better go fetch some! You fetch water for every single family, go fetch it from the river!"

"I didn't do it!"

"Still won't own up?" Shuishui gave him a resounding blow to the face. Xiongshi swayed back, swayed forward; the impact instantly produced a deep red imprint of her fingers on his face.

Seeing that Shuishui was prepared to go further, a few women standing around stepped forward to calm her down, telling her to let it be, kids don't understand anything, they're always like that, knock them around a bit, okay, but you don't want to beat them too hard. . . . These mediations in fact only enraged Shuishui yet further, acting as a kind of pressure on her: if she didn't become more furious, more ferocious, she would have had no way of differentiating herself from everyone else. It wasn't worth anybody's while to try and calm her down—a bad end was already in sight. Under this kind of pressure, she had no option but to roll up her sleeves and plunge on. Pow, wham, two more slaps exploded; not with the sound made off a human face, more like the cracking of a wooden bucket.

Xiongshi bit his lip hard and stared fixedly at his mother. Tears gleamed unsteadily in his eyes; in the end they didn't fall, but paused then slowly retreated.

He didn't return home that evening, nor the next day, nor the day after that . . . still no Xiongshi. Zhihuang and Shuishui searched everywhere in the mountains, helped by the villagers. Just as everyone was pretty much despairing, an old herbalist from Zhangjia District found Xiongshi in a burrow in the mountains. Wild in appearance, he was asleep in a nest of thatch grass, and apart from the occasional flash of his eyes, all else was filth and grime, the clothes on his back ripped and torn into strips of tattered cloth. For a whole eleven days, he had survived on wild fruits, leaves, and tree bark; when he was taken back home and Shuishui boiled him two eggs, his face contorted into a terrible grimace after just one bite. He ate no more, and ran outside to sit under a tree, staring blankly at everyone, as he ripped up the grass around him in an automatic reflex and stuffed it into his mouth. The onlookers were all astounded: surely only animals prefer grass to boiled eggs?

Probably because of this history, Shuishui lost her mental grip after Xiongshi was obliterated in the huge explosion, and for some time refused to believe that her son was no more. She would run up to the mountains and shout herself hoarse calling her son's name—she still believed he was hiding in some hole in the mountains. This went on until people had no choice but to show her what they had all along held back: the finger, the half of the little foot and the two bowls containing splinters of bone and flesh. Her eyeballs bulged terrifyingly, then she fell into a dead faint.

When she came to, some of the women said to her, "You have to think of the bigger picture, in a situation like this all you can do is think of the bigger picture. Your Xiongshi left you early, but wasn't it a dear life? No worries about food, or clothes, messing about all day long, then when he'd messed about as much as he could, he left, no illness, no pain, he was lucky. Things could have only got worse for him."

"Dear life" refers to a man's life before the age of eighteen, or a woman's life before the age of sixteen. "Full life" refers to a man's life up to the age of thirty-six and to a woman's life up to the age of thirty-two. To live this long is to live fully, and anything after that is "cheap life," worthless. By this logic, an early death is of course better, of higher value.

Xiongshi's parents had no reason to grieve.

The village women gathered around Shuishui's bed, each producing a platitude more beautiful than the last. Ah, Shuishui, your Xiongshi never went hungry, isn't that much better? Much better that your Xiongshi never felt the cold. Much better your Xiongshi never saw his dad die, his mom die, didn't go after his brothers and sisters, never saw a cloud pass over him. If heaven brought him back to life, he'd have to find a wife, set up home on his own, fight with his brothers for a patch of land one day, fight with his sisters for a bite to eat the next, row with his mom and dad in between, where was the fun in that? You know what our life's like, harvesting in the boiling heat, sun baking overhead, water steaming up below, dark both ends of the working day, soon as day breaks, it's off to the fields, you can only feel with your hands whether it's rice or grass. You know what our life's like, fixing irrigation under a full moon, shoulders rubbed raw, tramping over ice in bare feet, so cold you wet yourself. What was so great about that, hey? Your Xiongshi left before trouble came knocking at his door, he was the cat that had all the cream, then went out with a bang. He's still got his dad to weep, his mom to wail, so many uncles to give him a good send-off, it's really better this way— you've got to think of the bigger picture.

They also started to talk about an old laborer in the upper village, a destitute old man whose children had all died before him and who now lived like a dog, lame in one leg, unable even to fetch water for himself— he'd had all the trouble he was going to have. Think about it, sister, if your Xiongshi were destined to have a long life, a cheap life, wouldn't he be much worse off?

They were unified around the belief that people should die young; it was just that they were trapped, unable to die. Only Xiongshi could die good and early, only Xiongshi had this stroke of luck.

In the end, Shuishui decided to stop crying.

***Cheap** [賤]: When old people met each other, they would always ask "Still cheap?" meaning how were they feeling. This word was often used when inquiring about old people, for example "Yanzao's ma is still as cheap as anything, she eats two bowls of rice at a sitting."

In Maqiao language, old age is cheap life, and the longer your life the cheaper it gets. Despite this, some people still hope to live longer, until their eyesight fails, their hearing goes, their teeth have fallen out, their spirit has left them, they're bedridden, can't recognize anybody—living is still living.

Probably thanks to the efforts of some well-intentioned types, the character for "cheap" (pronounced *jian*) is hardly ever used when this expression is seen written down. When recording dialect, "cheap" *jian* is usually changed to the homophonic character *jian* meaning healthy. "Are you healthy" has a much nicer ring to it and has passed into everyday usage, to alleviate the harsh pitch of human life.

By this linguistic reckoning, Maqiao's cheapest life was a destitute cripple, called Old Pa Zisheng. He himself had no idea how many years he had lived—in any case he'd outlived his sons, grandsons, great-grandsons. . . . Even though his grandsons had met a premature death, his life still limped on. His ability to stay alive was starting to make him rather anxious: when he made up his mind to hang himself, the rope broke; having made up his mind to throw himself into the pond, he jumped only to discover that the water was too shallow. One evening, as he called on the Zhihuang household to borrow a bowl, the door was opened by Shuishui. Raising the lamp in her hand, she first saw the face of the old man, then taking a closer look, discovered that behind the old man were two round, shining balls, like two lamps. Rather surprised by this, she raised the lamp even higher. Her whole body went weak: they weren't lamps! It turned out that a large, downy head was breathing raspily behind Pa Zisheng, its towering spine dimly swaying in the darkness.

Tiger! Those two lamps they're tiger's ayaaaaaaaes!

Shuishui couldn't remember whether or not she had in fact cried out; all she could remember was yanking the old man inside, then bolting the door tightly, sticking in a broom then two hoes for good measure.

When her breathing had once more returned to normal, she sneaked a look out of the window, but the field was completely empty except for a faint suspension of moonlight. The two lamps had already gone.

The tiger never reappeared; most probably, it had just come upon Maqiao by chance. Far from rejoicing at this event, Pa Zisheng was filled with sorrow. "You see how cheap I am? Even tigers reckon there's no meat on me, they follow me along but can't even be bothered to take a bite. Where's the good in someone like me staying alive, hey?"

☆**Dream-Woman** [夢婆]: Shuishui was from Pingjiang County but was married in faraway Maqiao, on this side of the Luo River. Her little sister, it was said, was a famous actress in Pingjiang, a good opera singer, whose dainty lotus-flower gait had won her quite a following. It was also said that in the past Shuishui had been even more beautiful and talented than her sister, it was just that once she'd given birth to Xiongshi, her back began to ache, and her voice cracked and broke; as soon as her mouth opened, it produced a sound of breath hissing through her bronchial tubes, and any words came out harsh and splintered. From then on, her clothes were always in disarray and her gown was never buttoned up right, neither at the top nor bottom. Her hair was wild, her face unwashed; her features were always ringed in black. She would often weave cloth, hunt out pig fodder, sift rice chaff with women much older than she was; listening to them coughing up phlegm, clearing their noses, she probably didn't have to worry about her own appearance, didn't need to mark in any special way the passing of those drab, gloomy days.

Once females moved to their husband's house, particularly after they had had children, they became women, wives, and stopped taking any great care of themselves. However, it did seem that Shuishui's appearance was excessively unkempt, as if it was some kind of drive to abuse herself intentionally, a drive to hold herself hostage in obstinate retaliation against someone or other. There were plenty of times when she went out to look for pig food, hips swivelling to both sides, tramping along in a worn-out pair of men's shoes, yelling out raucously "heya-heyaheya" to chase the chickens out of the vegetable patch, the deep red menstruation stain in the crotch of her pants on full display to all she passed. It would be hard to say this was workaday carelessness.

After Xiongshi died, Shuishui became a dream-woman, what's known in Mandarin as a mentally ill person: her face often wore a flickering smile and she developed an absolute intolerance of potato plants—one look and she'd want to rip them out by the roots, as if she believed that her son was hiding under the ground and all she had to do was grab the potato plants, pull them up, then she could pull her son out of the earth. Usually, she was rather better in the mornings than in the afternoons, better on clear days than on rainy. At these times, her gaze was clear, and the way she behaved toward people and things and bustled around inside and out wasn't that different from ordinary people. She was, at best, someone of few words. Her worst, most agitated times came at dusk on rainy days. As the clouds drew in ever more gloomily, her breathing became rougher and heavier, and anything—the sound of the water drip-drip-dripping off the eaves, a withered leaf flying in the window, catching sight of the base of a wall or foot of the bed permeated with damp, the gradual blurring of neighbors' faces into darkness, or the melancholy cackle of ducks and chickens suddenly coming out of any part of the house—could send her into a state of trance. Moonlight was even worse: one glimpse of moonlight outside the window sent her body into a fit of uncontrollable trembling, she would put on a flowered head scarf, take it off, then put it back on, repeating this countless times.

If Zhihuang hadn't roped her hands together, she could have carried on like this all night. She would always say that the head scarf wasn't hers, and rip it off. She'd then say that her head was cold, she had to wear the head scarf, and put it back on.

In the end, Shuishui and Zhihuang got divorced and her parents took her back to Pingjiang. When I revisited Maqiao many years later, I asked about her. People were very surprised that I didn't know what had happened to Shuishui, almost as surprised as if I hadn't heard of Chairman Mao. Haven't you heard about her? You really haven't heard? They found my state of ill-informed ignorance insufferable and pitiful at the same time. Shuishui was really famous now, they said, her parent's home was always surrounded by cars, motorbikes, and bicycles; peddlers and traders all relied on her psychic powers to do business. People sought her out from miles and miles around to ask her to guess winning lottery numbers. At that time, tickets for the welfare lottery, the sports lottery, and so on were all selling like wildfire; the main street in town was in a depression, no one browsed around, and customers in teahouses and restaurants were few and far between—everyone was converting their money into lottery tickets. The rural cadres were all furiously agitating: if things went on like this, with no one even buying pesticide or fertilizer, then how would production continue? Would business still keep going?

Predicting the winning number became the most urgent topic of conversation. At this time, the mass focus of attention lay not on officials or big businessmen, even less on intellectuals, but on the insane. Suddenly people everywhere were asking for and searching out these lunatics, bowing and scraping before them, willing to bribe them with bundles of money, begging them to indicate the winning lottery number so that when they came to buy tickets, money and victory would roll in with one stroke of the pen. Word spread that in these matters, children were more gifted than adults, women more gifted than men, illiterates more gifted than the educated, but even more important, the insane were more gifted than the sane.

Shuishui, it must be said, stood out particularly prominently amongst her fellow lunatics; her predictions were said to hit the mark repeatedly, none failed, and she had already made lots of lottery players rich overnight. Her fame, of course, spread far and wide.

In the county seat, I met an editor from a broadcasting station who, surprised to hear I knew Shuishui, said that he'd also gone to search her out. This man, who'd spent four years at college, went on and on about it, about how he'd dashed to Pingjiang by long-distance bus, had waited almost five hours before he'd met Shuishui. He hadn't gained any concrete indication from her—the dream-woman would never have so easily revealed Heaven's designs to anyone. Shuishui took one look at him, and simply pointed at a picture on the wall which showed the sun rising out of a mountain. The editor, of course, was an intelligent man, and readily took the hint; on returning, he immediately thought "the East is Red" (a famous revolutionary song of the Maoist era), took the numbers of the notation from the first line of the song *The East is Red* (5 5 6 2) and filled in his lottery card accordingly. A few days later, when the result was publicly announced, he almost fainted in surprise: the winning number was 1 1 6 2!

The chance of a fortune had rubbed shoulders with him and passed on!

He didn't feel resentful in the slightest, explaining at convincing length that you couldn't blame Shuishui for this, you could only blame his own mistaken understanding. He was too stupid, too, too stupid! It turned out he'd forgotten that the first line of *The East is Red* is "The East is red," but the second is "the sun rises"—its notation was 1 1 6 2 exactly!

As he was telling me this, his face darkened, his voice convulsed with groans.

Confronted with this editor who believed so deeply in Shuishui, I realized the significance of the term "dream-woman": although people normally seen as remote from learning and reason (children, women, the insane, and so on) were mostly regarded as pitiful weaklings, at key, fateful moments they would suddenly become the people who were closest to truth, who were the most trustworthy and reliable.

I'm perfectly ready to admit that knowledge and reason are certainly not able to resolve all life's problems. But I'm still surprised at how much stronger the forces that reject knowledge and reason are than we often think. A long time ago now, the Austrian thinker Sigmund Freud used his study of psychoanalysis to produce a precise and systematic theoretical account of this. He had doubts about the power of reason and little belief even in consciousness, placing greater emphasis on the role of the unconscious; he believed that the confusion, the triviality, the secrecy of the unconscious were not lacking in their own significance. Quite the opposite, in fact: as the source and impetus of consciousness, the unconscious concealed a yet more important truth requiring careful exploration.

Freud believed that the unconscious emerged most often in children, women, the insane, and even more frequently in dreams—namely, wherever reason is in a weakened or collapsed condition. An expert in the explanation of dreams, this psychoanalyst wrote *The Interpretation of Dreams*. In his opinion, dreams marked the veiled emergence of the unconscious, were the most important point of entry into research on mental illness. No doubt he would be happily surprised to learn of the term Maqiao people used for a crazy female: dream-woman. He would also no doubt be able to understand the contradictory attitude that Maqiao people adopted toward dream-women: one of pity, at times when logical behavior produced results, but also of veneration, at times when the secrets of heaven's will were unfathomable.

The word "dream-woman" concisely and accurately summarized Freud's discoveries: dreams are the deepest repositories of normal people's insanity, and mental illness is a state of awakened, daytime dreaming.

The particular status of "dream-women" in Maqiao seems to support the crucial standpoint of anti-intellectualism: in Maqiao, this most unscientific of places, was concealed an even more abstruse science.

I don't know whether other languages carry this implication too. The etymological root of the word "lunatic" in English is "luna," namely "moon." Crazy people, in other words, are moon people. The moon only comes out at night, which of course is already close to dream-time. Readers will no doubt recall that Shuishui's spells of mental illness invariably occurred between dusk and nightfall, always against the backdrop of oil lamps or moonlight. Perhaps knowledge or intellect requires clarity, can't survive so easily in hazy darkness. Perhaps moonlight is the natural inducer of mental illness (the first implication of dream-woman) and of divinity (the second implication of dream-woman). Someone who loves moonlight, who loves above all to stare at moonlight or walk under the moonlight, whose behavior is poetic or dreamlike, is already wandering at the margins of the familiar world, possesses abnormal mental tendencies.

By this reckoning, all mental hospitals should consider moonlight the most dangerous of contagions.

By the same logic, all religious institutions, all absolute faiths and forms of consciousness that transcend science should consider moonlight to be the highest form of enlightenment.

*Stick(y) [羇] (*Nia*): I searched through every dictionary I could find, including *A Dictionary of Modern Chinese Dialects* (Jiangsu Educational Publishing House), without managing to find the character I was looking for. The dictionary meaning of the character [黏] that in the end I reluctantly used for this word was "to tease or pester," which is not so *very* far from the sense I wanted to express. This character is pronounced "nian," only slightly different from the "nia" I was looking for—I hope readers can remember this.

Nia, meaning "to stick" or "sticky," is often used as a dirty word. Maybe it's because of this that dictionaries for gentlemen, dictionaries for campuses and libraries, dictionaries that adults keep in hardback in their sitting rooms, all based on lofty linguistic ethics, have to ignore it, or at best lightly pass over it, or stick to hazy generalizations. But in real life, where Maqiao people live, *nia* is a word in constant use. Very often, people would use the word tens, even hundreds of times in one day— they didn't live by the dictionaries in general circulation.

Nia has many different uses in Maqiao:

1. Pronounced in second tone, *nia* means to stick. For example, when sealing an envelope, they'd say "*nia* the envelope properly." Of the thick, sticky quality of glue or paste, they'd say "really *nia*" or "good and *nia*." Magnetic rock is "*nia* (sticky) rock." A snot-nose is "*nia*."

2. Pronounced in first tone, *nia* means intimacy, affection, pester-ing, skin pressed against hair—sticky. To "get *nia*" means to be actively intimate and affectionate with others. To "act *nia*" means to entice others, by expression or manner, to be intimate and affectionate, implying a passive mode of behavior. These phrases are often used for relations between parents and chil-dren, between men and women. When a young girl is in the passionate throes of a romance, she is always "very *nia*" towards her man; her tone of voice, the look in her eyes, and so on, all remind people of the quality of glue or paste.

3. In third tone, *nia* means to make fun of, tease, bother, and so on, not far in meaning from "provoke." For example, "don't *nia* trou-ble," "don't *nia* a quarrel." Maqiao people also have a saying about "Three People You Don't *Nia*": the young, the old, and beggars. They mean that these three kinds of people are very tricky to handle, that it's best not to have any dealings with them, let alone cross swords with them; even if you're in the right, the only thing to do is give in and run far, far away.

    This is the same attitude people have towards glue and paste: they're afraid that once stuck, disengaging will prove difficult and they'll find themselves in a very sticky situation. Despite the many ways in which *nia* is used, a common seam of meaning clearly runs through them all, they all share a linguistic point of intersection.

4. In fourth tone, *nia* (to stick) means the heterosexual sex act. Northern dialects contain similar words, such as *cao*, screw, for example. This word was brought down south, to Maqiao, by soldiers and itinerant workers men from the north.

In fact, this northern *cao* [傸] appears to be rather different from *nia*. Firstly, the shape of the character—a human radical on top, meat radical on the bottom—indicates that it's a male act; that it should have a crisp, brisk, forceful pronunciation is entirely fitting. *Nia*, however, is pronounced with slow, lingering softness, implying an act of gentleness. Bearing in mind the original meaning of *nia*, or at least the meanings linked with it, a state of *nia*, or sticking, naturally indicates a kind of adhesion, of close contact, intertwining, intimacy, teasing, a state reminiscent of glue or paste, lacking any violent, aggressive quality.

Almost all physiological surveys so far carried out confirm that females reach a state of sexual excitement much more slowly than males and that females often require a certain degree of tenderness before they can be aroused. This is a first-tone *nia*, second-tone *nia*, and third-tone *nia* kind of process, of which males need to be aware and to which they need to adjust. This leads me to a bold hypothesis: the word *nia* suits the particularities of the female physiology better than *cao*, is preferred by women. If such a thing as a female language exists in this world, the former word will be far more widely used than the latter in their sexual vocabulary.

A women's book has been discovered in Jiangyong County in Hunan Province, written in language that would only circulate and be used among women, thus attracting a great deal of attention from feminists. I do still strongly doubt that an independent female language could exist. But when you consider that even today many traces of matriarchal society still remain in the South, that historically the South developed into a male-dominated society one step behind the North, then female physiology and psychology may in fact find fuller expression in southern languages. I'd like to see *nia* as one proof of this bold hypothesis.

☆**Low (and X-Ray Glasses)** [下(以及穿山鏡)]: Low, low-down, low doings: the etymological origins of this word lie in sexual behavior of a deviant, or even perfectly normal nature. Since the 1980s, Hunanese dialect has referred to hooliganism by the phrase "lowlife," obviously an extension and expansion of the word "low."

In terms of the design of the human body, the head is positioned on top, and so human thought and spirit have always appeared uplifted, have enjoyed symbolic status as "lofty," "sublime," "metaphysical"; sexual organs, however, are positioned down below, and so sexual behavior has always been termed "low."

Thinking about it like this, it becomes very hard to say that it's merely an accident of choice that temples are built on high mountains, criminals are imprisoned in hell, aristocrats live in high palaces, commoners kneel at the foot of steps, the victor's flag is raised aloft in the sky, the loser's flag is trampled underfoot. . . . Surely all this must be the externalization, the product of some form of belief. I suspect all this started with cave-dwellers, with their sense of bemusement towards and earliest knowledge of their own bodies; from this time on, temples, aristocrats, and victors' flags all served as extensions of the heads of cave-dwellers, all became thus uplifted. And anything opposite to this was forever relegated down below, to the shameful ranks of the lower body.

Apparently, Maqiao used to be particularly low, and only became more upright after brutal rectification by the commune cadres. After arriving in the village, Mr. He the Commune Head not only took over any private land, manure, chickens, ducks, and so on that exceeded the permitted quota, he also at one large meeting produced a strange object made up of two long tubes with lenses inside: "What are these, you ask? X-ray glasses! With these, I can see every single low-down thing you get up to! If I catch someone, I'll punish 'em! Catch ten, punish ten! No mercy!"

These, in fact, were binoculars belonging to the Commune Forestry station, used to watch for mountain fires.

Hearing this, even Benyi started to look anxious, directing one troubled glance after another at the binoculars. Afterwards, people no longer dared speak or act indiscreetly, for months not one filthy word slipped from Wanyu's mouth—you could beat him to death before you'd get a *qoqo* song out of him. When evening came, everyone went early to bed and all fell perfectly quiet in the village, every lamp left unlit. Many people said they didn't even dare touch their wives during that time.

Wanyu had been deeply upset about the X-ray glasses: "It's unfair, it's so unfair," he once complained to me. "You city people have films to watch, zoos to visit, cars and trains to look at—what do we country people have? This is the only cultural life we have,"—he was referring to his *qoqo* songs and to goings-on between men and women—"using X-ray glasses, now, what's the world coming to! And another thing, if the Communist Party doesn't let everyone do low stuff, how's there going to be a little Communist Party later on?"

I won't consider right now whether or not Wanyu's complaints about Commune Head He were justified. I will say, though, that it isn't historically correct to view sexual conservatism, as represented by the binoculars, as a speciality of the Communist Party. When the Guomindang (GMD) ruled China, it so happened that the military governments of Guangzhou, Wuhan, and other places too prohibited ballroom dancing, regarding it as a form of licentiousness "harmful to social morals and mores." And earlier than this, when China was ruled by the Qing dynasty, *The Romance of the Western Chamber* was right at the top of the list of forbidden operas, and love stories and poems were all officially viewed as "works of evil filth," with pile after pile rooted out, confiscated, and burned. The word "low," still in use by Maqiao people, likewise has a long history as a moral prejudice against sexual behavior, and forms part of a single thread that has permeated Chinese linguistic thinking for several thousand years. As long as this name, "low," remains unchanged or unexpunged, people will always have difficulty in truly, totally, thoroughly walking out from under the shadow of prejudice. Even if Commune Head He had been an exceptionally open and enlightened individual, he wouldn't necessarily have been able to shake off a mindset that was as much a part of him as his own flesh and blood. He was just a traditional dictionary user, wielding his binoculars, coasting along the track of a given meaning; like a donkey on a halter, he could do nothing other than move forwards. In this sense, then, do people produce words, or words produce people? Was Commune Head He indeed responsible for his implacable strictness, or was it this word "low" that way back in the past had become a halter for Commune Head He—in that case, then, should all users of Chinese, including Maqiao people, be held responsible for Commune Head He? This, of course, is a question.

***He-Ground (and She-Field)** [公地(以及母田)]: When Maqiao people were working on the land, their favorite type of conversation, apart from food talk, was low talk. The endless variety of low talk would make your eyes pop, jaw drop, mind blow, thoughts wander, make the heavens spin, the earth turn, and the sun and moon darken. Nothing, not even the most ordinary of things—radishes, ploughs, carrying poles, caves, birds in flight, grain mortars, grassland, ovens—failed to invite low associations for them, anything could become an excuse or an analogy for lowness, could provide justification for the endless repetition (with minor alterations) of jokes and stories, could detonate rallies of raucous laughter. It was during the planting season in particular that their crude rantings got wilder than ever.

She pants to catch me
Runs to catch me—I'm like a wet loach,
Loaches love their rice gruel
Squeezing into slippery wet rice gruel . . .

At planting time, a song like this was counted as really quite refined. Singing this stuff wasn't normally allowed, it was prohibited by the government, but it was encouraged in the planting season and cadres turned a deaf ear. Wanyu said this was called "soiling the ground"—and the lower you went, the better. Unsoiled ground was dead ground, cold ground, ground that wouldn't produce shoots or allow seeds to take root.

Maqiao people saw "ground" as distinct from "fields": ground was "male," fields were "female." Ground had to be sown by women, whereas fields, of course, had to be sown by men. Both these stipulations had an important part to play in guaranteeing bumper harvests. Rice seedlings were to be planted in the fields, so the job of immersing them in water inevitably had to be done by men, and it was strictly taboo for women even to stand by and look.

By the same logic, a greater degree of sexual immodesty amongst women when they were on the ground was temporarily permitted and became entirely proper, enjoyed a kind of tacit approval. This wasn't just a type of diversion: it was a struggle for production, a sacred mission to be carried out with the loftiest sense of responsibility. Some female Educated Youth couldn't get used to it, couldn't hide their feelings of embarrassment and aversion on encountering it; their frowning and blocking of their ears so disheartened the local women that they couldn't get any "soiling" done; the men would then get anxious and make the team cadre transfer the female Educated Youth to work elsewhere.

I've seen with my own eyes the savagery of women on the ground, how they dragged a young man to one side, for example, how everyone pitched in to pull down his pants and throw balls of ox dung down his crotch to teach him a lesson, then scattered with roars of laughter. They wouldn't have treated Educated Youth like this, of course, but lesser instances of harassment were quite common, stealing and sitting on a grass hat, for example, followed by a volley of guffaws; or calling you over to make you guess the answer to a riddle, followed by a volley of guffaws. Ill at ease, you couldn't clearly make out what the riddle was, but you could tell from their mad laughter that this riddle didn't need to be answered, and could never, ever be answered.

☆**Menstrual Holes** [月口]: Fields were maternal, female, and so the holes where water flowed in the ridges between fields were called "menstrual holes." Humans have menstrual leaks, or menstruation as it's more standardly termed, so it's perfectly natural that fields should also have menstrual holes.

Depending on the irrigation needs of the seedlings in the fields, the water level needed to be adjusted whenever necessary by blocking up or digging open each menstrual hole; this was the duty of the water regulators. Normally it was old people who took on this job, solitary figures roaming around the ridges with a hoe on their shoulders; sometimes you heard the intermittent pad-pad-pad of their footsteps in the depths of the night, each one sounding out with a particular, crisp clarity, one clattering pebble after another rising up out of an insomniac night.

There were always small puddles by these menstrual holes where water sprang forth, sometimes there were even small fish struggling desperately against the water-flow; this was where people could easily wash and scrub themselves when work stopped for the day. If women couldn't face going to the river, which was a long way away, they'd stop to wash their hoes or sickles if they passed by one of these holes; while they were about it they'd wash their hands and feet, wash away the mud and sweat from their faces; one after another, they'd wash back into view a shining face and bright eyes before they walked off toward the cooking smoke of the evening. Once they'd passed the menstrual holes, they were transformed. Their brightness tarnished by a whole day of overwork, it was only on their way back home that the gurgling flow of water from the menstrual hole suddenly restored their radiance.

☆**Nine Pockets** [九袋]: As I used to imagine them, beggars had to have shabby clothes and haggard faces. It would have been absurd, impossible to link beggars with extravagant living. It was only after coming to Maqiao that I realized I was mistaken, that there are all sorts of beggars in this world.

Benyi's father-in-law was a beggar who lived off the fat of the land, who lived better than many landlords. But as he didn't have a single inch of land, he couldn't be classified as a landlord. He didn't have a shop either, so he couldn't be counted a capitalist. Forced to adjust to this, the first land-reform team reluctantly defined him as a "rich peasant beggar." The work team that checked and rechecked class status felt this term was neither one thing nor another, but since they couldn't actually find a policy clause that would furnish a better label, since they didn't know how to settle the question, they had to make do.

This man was called Dai Shiqing and used to live in Changle. The place was a communications center on land and water, a collecting and distributing center for rice, bamboo, tea-tree oil, tung oil, and medicinal herbs through the ages. It was, of course, full of life, of brothels, opium shops, pawnshops, taverns, and other similarly intricate enterprizes; even the water running in the sewers reeked prosperously of oil, and just one mouthful of street air turned the stomachs of country-dwellers used to nothing but maize gruel. Because of this, Changle was nicknamed "Little Nanjing," and for the local villagers became something to boast about to outsiders. People traveled dozens of miles bringing a couple of tobacco leaves or to break a few lengths of bamboo strips, just to strut down one length of the main street; this they called "doing business." In fact, there was no commercial sense at all behind their journeys, they were just an excuse to see some of the action or listen to people singing and reciting stories. I don't know when the numbers of beggars, with their emaciated bodies and long hair, small faces and big eyes, and ill-fitting shoes of every hue, gradually began to increase, endlessly multiplying the pairs of eyeballs intent on swallowing up the cooking pots on the market street.

Dai Shiqing, who came from Pingjiang, became the leader of these beggars. Beggars divided into various classes: One Pocket, Three Pockets, Five Pockets, Seven Pockets, and Nine Pockets. He was of the highest rank, a Nine Pockets, and was respectfully addressed as "Old Master Nine Pockets"—everyone in the town knew this. A bird cage always hung on his begging stick, inside which a mynah bird always called out "Old Master Nine Pockets is here, Old Master Nine Pockets is here." There was no need to knock on the door of whichever household the myna bird called out in front of, no need to say anything; no family would fail to come out and greet him with smiling faces. When they were confronted with ordinary beggars, one dipper of rice was quite enough. But Old Master Nine Pockets had to be appeased with a whole bamboo cup, sometimes even with large presents, his pockets stuffed with money or with cured chicken feet (his favorite food).

Once, a newly arrived salt merchant who didn't understand the rules around here sent him on his way with just one copper coin. He was so angry he hurled the coin onto the ground with a clatter.

The salt merchant, who'd never seen anything like it, almost dropped his glasses.

"What d'you think this is?" Old Master Nine Pockets glowered.

"You—you—you—what're you complaining about?"

"I, Old Master Nine Pockets, have been through nine provinces and forty-eight counties and have never met such a gutless bloodsucking houseowner!"

"This is all very odd—look here, who's doing the begging here? If you want it, then take it, if not then get out of here, stop holding up my business."

"You think I'm begging? Me, begging?" Old Master Nine Pockets opened his eyes wide, feeling he owed it to this idiot to teach him a lesson or six. "Mysterious winds and clouds float across the heavens, from morning to night man meets good fortune and bad. In these unlucky times of ours, the country faces calamities, drought in the North and flooding in the South; government and people unite in concern. Although I, Dai Shiqing, am but one insignificant mortal, I accept that it is right to lead a loyal and filial life, placing country before family, family before self. Is it right that I should stretch my hand out to the government? No. Is it right that I should stretch out my hand to parents, brothers, kinsmen? Once more, no! I walk everywhere on my two bare feet, the true man of honor, strengthening my character without rest or repose, neither robbing nor stealing, neither cheating nor deceiving, conducting myself with dignity and respect, helping myself. And you expect me to put up with a stuck-up, cross-eyed bully like you! I've seen plenty of your sort, I have, once you've got a couple of stinking coppers to rub together your morals go out the window, it's just money money money . . ."

The salt merchant had never heard such a stream of rhetoric: spattered into retreat, step-by-step, by showers of saliva, all he could do was raise his hands in self-defence, "okay, okay, okay, whatever you say, but I've still got business to do, off you go, off you go. Off, off."

"Off? I'm going to get something through to you if I do nothing else today! I want you to tell me, clearly now: am I begging? Have I come to beg from you today?"

Making a face, the salt merchant rummaged out a few more copper coins and pressed them against his chest with a kind of desperation that showed his resignation to defeat. "Okay, okay, you're not begging today, and you haven't come to beg from me."

Instead of accepting the money, Old Master Nine Pockets plonked himself down on the threshold, panting with rage. "Stinking cash, stinking cash, all I beg for today is justice! If you'd only acted reasonably, I'd have given you all my money!" He took out a big handful of copper coins, far more than the salt merchant's coppers, that glinted and gleamed, and attracted the eyes of lots of little urchins.

After that, if he hadn't suddenly needed to visit the toilet, the salt merchant would never have gotten him off his threshold. By the time he returned, the salt store had already been tightly bolted shut. He banged his stick on the door with all his might, but it wouldn't open; male and female voices shouted out filthy abuse from inside.

The formal opening of the salt store came a few days later, and a few courtesy tables of meat and wine were laid out for the town's VIPs and the merchant's neighbors. Just after the firecrackers had been let off, a raggedy bunch of beggars suddenly descended, a dense agglomeration giving off an unspecified rancid odor, and who surrounded the salt store, shouting and yelling. If they were given steamed rolls, they'd say they were spoiled and throw them back one after another. If they were given a bucket of rice, again they'd say there was sand in the rice and spit it out all over the ground and street. There was nowhere for passers-by to tread and the guests who'd come for the banquet were repeatedly splattered on the nose or forehead by rice grains. Finally, four beggars beating a broken drum scurried in amongst the feast to perform a small drum dance in celebration of this happy event, their bodies covered in pig and dog shit. The terrified guests fled in all directions, holding their noses. The beggars then took the opportunity one after another to spit on the fine fare laid out on the table.

It was only after a good half of the guests had fled that the salt merchant realized what a force Old Master Nine Pockets was to be reckoned with, and what a sticky situation he was in. He asked his neighbors to plead for mercy from Old Master Nine Pockets. Old Master Nine Pockets was asleep under a big tree at the quayside and took absolutely no notice. The salt merchant had no choice but to prepare two cured pig's heads and two vessels of matured wine, and go in person to apologize for his transgression; in addition, with help from his neighbors he shelled out to buy the favor of a Seven Pockets, second in rank only to Old Master Nine Pockets, to have him also intervene for him. Only then did Dai Shiqing raise his eyelid a tiny, tiny crack and remark bitterly that the weather was very hot.

The salt merchant rushed forward to fan him.

Dai Shiqing let out a yawn and waved his hand; I know, he said.

His words were very veiled. But for the salt merchant to get this much out of him was no mean feat, and when he returned home he in fact discovered that the beggars had already scattered, with only four self-styled Five Pockets beggars remaining, stuffing their faces around a table of wine and meat; they were just stoking up for later, nothing excessive.

The salt merchant smilingly told them to eat more, poured wine for them himself.

It was no simple matter for Dai Shiqing to achieve such strict, orderly control over the comings and goings of vagrant beggars. Apparently, the original Nine Pockets had been a cripple from Jiangxi, a man of astonishing courage, a man of iron who surpassed all others in the beggars' gang. But he was also a crooked individual, who'd collected in too many of the takings; when dividing up the beggars' land all the best land went to his nephews—the most fertile plots, in other words, were never fairly allocated. This was more than Dai Shiqing, at that time of the Seven Pockets rank, could bear, and finally one dark night, he and two other brothers under his leadership pounded this Nine Pockets to death with bricks. After he became the Nine Pockets, matters were managed more justly than under the previous dynasty: the beggars' fields were redivided, fertile land was balanced out with barren, and everything rotated at set times so that no one lost out and everyone had an opportunity to "rinse bowls" with prosperity. He also ruled that if members of the gang were ever ill and couldn't work in the fields, they could eat off common land and draw a guaranteed allowance from him; this, in particular, won him the unanimous gratitude of gang members.

Old Master Nine Pockets was a beggar not only of scruples, but also of talent. By the river was situated a Five Lotus Zen temple in possession of a relic that had been requested back from Putuo Shan (a Buddhist mountain in eastern China); the incense attendants were doing very well out of it and, from the looks of it, some of the monks were growing plumper and plumper. Afraid of offending the Buddha, no one had ever come to beg a bowl of rice, and likewise no one would dare take anything by force. Unafraid of evil spirits, Old Master Nine Pockets Dai was determined to get a slice of this pie. He headed off alone and asked to see the Master Abbot, saying that he didn't believe the relic was really stored in the temple and that he wanted to see it with his own eyes. The monk didn't put up any opposition, and with great care took the relic out of its glass bottle and placed it in his hands. Without another word, he swallowed the relic down in one gulp, at which the abbot began shaking all over with fury, grabbed hold of him by the collar and started to beat him.

"Terribly hungry, I was, just had to eat something," he said.

"I'll beat you to death, you scum!" The monks brandished their staffs in agitation.

"Don't you think that if you keep beating me like this, you'll make such a racket everyone in the street will come and see you bald coots have lost the relic?" he smartly, threateningly pointed out.

And so the monks didn't dare raise a hand against him, but simply stood around him in circles, on the verge of tears, so they seemed.

"How about this: you give me thirty silver dollars and I'll give you the relic back."

"How will you give it back?"

"That's not for you to worry about."

His antagonists didn't have that much faith in what he said, but having no choice in the matter they swiftly produced the silver dollars. After checking over each and every one, Dai Shiqing graciously pressed this small gift to his bosom, then produced a croton berry he was carrying on him—a kind of strong laxative.

After he'd swallowed the croton, with a roll of his eyes he soon released behind the Buddha Hall a large pool of diarrhea, the stench from which assaulted heaven itself. The Master and a few of his subordinates finally fished the relic out from amongst the mass of diarrhoea, washed it clean with fresh water and placed it once more in its glass bottle, giving thanks to heaven and earth.

After this, nothing lay beyond his skills in begging or cadging; his fame grew and grew, and his power spread to Luoshui, in Pingjiang County. Even colleagues of rank similar to Nine Pockets from the great port city of Wuhan came from all that way to call on him, to repeat over and over how they revered him as Master. He'd burn a piece of tortoiseshell to divine when was the best time and which direction was most auspicious for begging, and no one who went out following his directions failed to make money. When people in the town held weddings or funerals, the place of guest of honor at the banquet was always reserved for him. If he didn't appear, people would worry that the meal wouldn't proceed peacefully, that beggars would come and disrupt the feast. One Mr Zhu, someone who'd been in government, even presented him with a plaque inscribed with a couplet in black and gold characters, made of high-quality pearblossom wood and so heavy that several people were needed to carry it.

The two couplets ran thus:

Public opinion is as fleeting as the clouds and rain
Both rich and poor are the same to the beggar whose mind
   is vaster than the universe.

The horizontal inscription was: "a clear heart purifies the world," with Old Master Nine Pockets' name inlaid within.

After Old Master Nine Pockets had been presented with this plaque by the government official, he bought a luxurious, blue-bricked residence with four wings and three entrances, made loans and received visitors, and took four wives. Now, of course, he didn't need to go out begging every day, except for the first and fifteenth of every month when he would make an imperial obeisance and take a turn around the streets, behaving, in total earnestness, just as his subordinates did. This kind of behavior might have seemed a little unnecessary, but those who knew him well knew that he simply couldn't not go begging; if, apparently, ten days or a couple of weeks passed without him begging, his feet swelled up, and if three or five days passed without him going barefoot, his feet would break out in red itchy blotches that he'd be scratching day and night until he drew blood.

He attached the greatest importance of all to begging on the thirtieth day of the last lunar month. Every year on this day, he would refuse all banquet invitations and forbid any fires to be lit at home, would order his four wives each to take off their padded silks, each to put on tattered items of clothing; each would pick up a bag or a bowl and go out begging on her own. They could only eat what they brought back from their begging. When Tiexiang was only three years old, she'd been scolded and beaten, forced to follow him tearfully out the door and beg for food in snow and wind that cut right through you, knocking on door after door, kowtowing as soon as someone appeared.

If the youth of today didn't understand what suffering was, he said, what would become of them later?

He also said that it was a pity, a real pity that most people knew about the delicacies that came of the mountains and seas, but knew not that the fruits of begging tasted sweetest of all.

He was later classified by the Communist Party as a "Rich Peasant Beggar" because he both exploited his employees (he exploited all the beggars below the rank of Seven Pockets) and was a dyed-in-the-wool beggar himself (even though only on the thirtieth of the last month); and so this rather unsatisfactory term had to do. On the one hand, he possessed a fired-brick mansion complete with four wives, on the other he still went around often barefoot and dressed in tatters—this fact had to be acknowledged somehow.

This was most unfair, he felt. He said that the Communist Party were burning their bridges behind them—when they first arrived, they'd relied on him as an ally. At that time they were Purging Bandits and Fighting Local Tyrants, and the bandits were fleeing everywhere. Dai Shiqing had helped the work team out by dispatching beggars as scouts to keep an eye on the comings and goings of suspicious elements around the town, and to visit each house to "count bowls": this meant surreptitiously noting, under cover of begging, how many bowls each household was washing and gauging from this whether the household was feeding an extra guest, whether they were concealing a suspicious personage. This, of course, only lasted a short while, however. Dai Shiqing had never foreseen the revolution would turn on the beggars and transform him into Changle's Local Bully, have him tied up and paraded under escort to the country jail.

In the end, he died of illness in custody. According to the recollections of his fellow unfortunates, when close to death he said: "This is the way of things for great men. When my star was rising, a thousand people couldn't topple me; now that I'm down on my luck, ten thousand couldn't raise me up."

By the time he said this, he'd been unable to stand for some time.

His illness started from his feet up—first they swelled so much he couldn't get either shoes or socks on, even after he'd cut them open at the sides. The line of his ankle bones disappeared, and his feet became as wide and round as two bags of rice. Later, as was to be expected, erythema developed and within a few months the red patches turned into purple patches. After another month, they turned into black patches. He scratched at them until there wasn't a scrap of healthy skin left on his feet, until they were nothing but a mass of scabs. All night long in the cells you'd hear his shouts and cries. He was sent to the hospital to be cured, but the penicillin the hospital gave him had no effect at all. He would kneel in front of the iron gates of the prison, shaking and clanging them, begging the guard:

"Just kill me! Quick, just get a knife and kill me!"

"We're not going to kill you, we want to reform you."

"If you're not going to kill me then let me go and beg."

"Let you go and kneel on the street, you mean?"

"I'm begging for mercy, begging you to be kind masters, please, quickly, let me go and beg. See how my two feet are rotting away . . ."

The guard gave an icy smile: "Don't go playing your tricks on me."

"I'm not playing tricks. If you don't trust me, then send an armed escort in behind."

"Get going, you're supposed to be moving fired bricks this afternoon." The guard didn't want to waste any more breath on him.

"No—no—no, no good, I can't move any bricks."

"Doesn't matter if you can't, you've still got to: it's what we call labor reform. You still want to beg? Still want to live off the fat of the land, not lift a finger? This is the New Society—we're going to give your sort some backbone!"

And so, in the end, the guard wouldn't let him go and beg. One morning, a few days later, when the prisoners were eating breakfast they realized that Dai Shiqing was still shrunk down inside his quilt. Someone went to shake him awake but discovered that he'd already gone stiff. One eye was staring open, the other eye closed. Four or five blood-sucking mosquitoes flew out of the nest of straw by his pillow.

*Scattered [散發]: When people told me the story of Dai Shiqing, they used the word "scattered." If he couldn't beg, they said, Tiexiang's old man just scattered.

"Scattered," obviously, meant died.

This is one of my favorite words in this dictionary of Maqiao. Dying, expiring, snuffing it, croaking, passing away, going to the underworld, kicking the bucket, closing your eyes, breathing your last, giving up the ghost, and so on, all mean the same as "scattering," but all, by comparison, seem simplistic and superficial, none able to illustrate the process as precisely, vividly, or minutely as "scatter." Once life has finished, then all the different elements that hold life together disintegrate and disperse. Flesh and blood, for example, rot into mud and water, the rising steam turns into clouds and air. Or they are bitten by insects and channeled into autumnal chirping; absorbed by roots into green grassland and many-hued petals under the sunlight, stretching out into vast formlessness. When we fix our gazes upon the multifarious, diverse, unceasingly active wilds of the earth, we perceive all sorts of faint sounds and smells, such as at dusk, when dense golden mists, fresh and damp, seem to float restlessly under old maple trees. We know that life, that countless earlier lives are contained within—it's just that we don't know what they were called.

The moment that their heartbeat stops, their names and stories also disperse in fragments of human memories and legend, and after the passing of just a few years will end up utterly lost in the sea of humanity, never to return to their beginnings.

As the four seasons pass and clock hands rotate, the scattering of all matter is part of an inexorable linear progression, revealing the absoluteness of time. The second law of thermodynamics terms this a process of entropy: an ordered organism will slowly disintegrate into disorder, uniformly, homogeneously scatter into solitary, mutual isolation—once this state is reached, there's no qualitative difference between a corpse and the earth it's buried in, between Dai Shiqing's feet and his teeth.

To accumulate or cohere is, of course, the opposite of scattering. Cohesion is the basic condition of existence, of life. Blood and energy cohere to make people, clouds and mist cohere to make rain, mud and sand cohere to make rock, language and words cohere to make thought, days cohere to make history, people cohere to make families, political parties, or empires. A weakening of the power to cohere marks the onset of death. Sometimes, the more things expand and prosper, the more limited their power to sustain life becomes, the harder it becomes to maintain internal cohesion. Bearing this in mind, it becomes understandable that Maqiao people don't use "scatter" just to mean people dying, but also for any catastrophic predicament—and in particular, clouds that travel inside silver linings.

Many years later, listening to the old people considering the merits of television, I heard them remark in fearful tones: "If you watch television every day, till your head's full of it, won't you end up scattered?" They were simply expressing the anxiety that all the extra knowledge people picked up from watching television would stimulate more and more desires—and then how would they manage to cohere? And if they couldn't cohere, surely they were done for?

I can't say whether or not their terror of television was rational. But it did make me realize the connotations of "scattered" had by then extended far beyond what they had been twenty years ago. I also realized that Maqiao people retained their own sense of stubborn vigilance toward any form of scattering, toward the wild flights of fancy, the merging with the wider world one could experience while watching, for example, a color television.

*Bandit Ma (and 1948) [馬疤子(以及一九四八年)]: Guangfu, a physical-education teacher in the county capital, was one of Maqiao's few intellectuals and, as it happened, the only person from Maqiao who settled in town with a state-allocated job.

His father was the one great historical figure who came out of Maqiao. But for a very long time, Maqiao people were loath to mention this great man, would hedge vaguely about events from the past that involved him. It was only later that I found out this great man was called Ma Wenjie, and that his case was reexamined and he was rehabilitated only in 1982, after which the labels of "Bandit Leader" and "Reactionary Bureaucrat" were dropped in favor of "Performer of Outstanding Service in Uprising." At the time, Guangfu was on the standing committee of the County Chinese People's Political Consultative Conference (CPPCC), of which he later became the vice-chairman, a fact which was not, of course, entirely unrelated to his father's rehabilitation. It was also at this time, the time I paid my visit to Guangfu, that I found out a little more of the story behind Ma Wenjie taking up the post of County Head under the GMD.

As I said, this was in 1982. It was on a rainy, overcast evening that I found myself in a small streetside beancurd shop by the river—when Guangfu couldn't be sure of earning enough to live on even as a Phys. Ed. teacher, he opened this little shop. I took down what he said in a small exercise book, the smell of soya bean dregs tickling my nose. A thought suddenly came to me: as far as I was concerned, as far as all I knew about Ma Wenjie was concerned, 1948 wasn't actually 1948 at all. It had been postponed and postponed, had fermented and soured. In other words, it had been postponed until it reemerged on this rainy evening of 1982. It was just like the bomb that blew up Maqiao's Xiong-shi, that bomb from the Sino-Japanese War that had lain quietly in the mud, frozen for thirty years, this longstanding postponement waiting until a beautiful, bright spring to explode in a child's face.

In the case of something we don't know about, we can't say definitely that it exists, or at the very least we lack sufficient evidence to conclude it exists. Before 1982 came along, Ma Wenjie's 1948 was a total blank as far as I was concerned.

By the same reasoning, Ma Wenjie's 1948, Maqiao's 1948 was not, in fact, the 1948 of many history textbooks. The events that made up this year, the mass of developments and changes that made this year moving, significant, memorable—the GMD-CCP talks at Beiping, the battle of Liaoshen and the Battle of Huaihai, Mao Zedong's angry rejection of the USSR's suggestion to divide China at the Yangtze River, the intense struggles within the GMD between Chiang Kaishek's clique and Xiao Zongren's clique, and so on—neither Ma Wenjie nor any of his followers knew anything of this at the time. Thanks to the multilayered screen of the Jiulian mountain range, in addition to the chaos of war, a great drought and a few other factors besides, Maqiao Bow's contact with the outside world had been on the wane for some time. Maqiao people's understanding of the outside world extended no further than the fragmentary rumors of a few old soldiers returning to the countryside.

Most of these old-timers had served under Regiment Commander Ma Wenjie, messing with the Forty-second Army; they'd reached Shandong and Anhui before taking part in the Battle of Binhu, relieving the garrison of the Forty-fourth Army. They looked down on the Sichuanese Forty-fourth Army, the most ill-disciplined army of all, in which almost everyone smoked opium; when the Japanese army disguised themselves in mufti and infiltrated their ranks, the army's command was finished off in one fell swoop. Of course, Regiment Commander Ma didn't have an easy ride either: once, in an ambush in Yuanjiang County, the hundred-odd landmines he'd buried all turned out to be duds. Just brought over from Shaoyang, the landmines exploded into two, like the halves of a melon: the explosions made quite a noise but failed to kill anyone. As they stood amidst the gunpowder, the Japanese found themselves not a single man down, and every one of them charged with a great cry of "ya—ya—ya," slashing the Forty-second Army into pieces in no time at all. Seeing the way things were going, Commander Ma had no choice but to order his followers to dump all the remaining mountain explosives in the river as quickly as possible and to scatter into guerrilla units. The

Japanese were here to transport grain, and it was just a question of drawing things out toward winter, when the water in the holes and lakes would have dried up, when the Japanese boats would no longer be able to set out, and Ma's containment duties would be completed.

They recalled how Ma Wenjie led them on expeditions to capture prisoners. The reward for capturing a Japanese soldier was 10,000 yuan. Every company had to capture four prisoners each month; if they didn't manage it, the failing would be marked heavily against the Company Commander *and* the next month's quota would be doubled. If they failed to fill the quota again, the Company Commander would be dismissed and flogged, as laid down by army law. Three strokes with a carrying pole always left the buttocks bleeding. The buttocks of one luckless Commander, who didn't manage to stay out of trouble very often, were permanently dented.

When they found a position to defend, they'd change into mufti, take up their "Good Citizen" passes and, thus disguised, carry out punitive raids into enemy areas. The braver among them would latch onto the "tail" of Japanese troops. One company, made up entirely of Miao people from Xiangxi, all good swimmers and courageous too, captured the most prisoners, but unfortunately they all died in the line of duty when caught in a surprise attack in Huarong County. Those few fellow villagers of Ma Wenjie who'd served under him had been pretty lucky, it seemed, to survive with their heads left on; it was just that every time they captured a prisoner, they brought back either a Mongolian or a Korean, not genuine Japanese goods. Although they were grudgingly allowed to report for completion of duties, they didn't get any reward. Even after they returned home, these Maqiao people would still simmer with resentment at this. Bandit Ma was being unreasonable, they'd say: Mongolian Tartars were the biggest in size, too big even for three or four people to lift. We had it rough, they reckoned: how come everyone else got a reward, and we got nothing but cold water?

Bandit Ma was Ma Wenjie's nickname.

Their audience was sympathetically scandalized: that's right, that's right, Bandit Ma's a skinflint, he landed a big official job but no one ever saw him give his wife a gold bracelet. That time he returned to his home village and invited his relatives over for a meal, he cooked only five catties of pork, filled everyone's bowls with radish!

Their 1948 was full of such topics of conversation. To sum up, in other words, the outside world of the time, as defined by their own mental horizons, was: the opium-smoking Sichuan army, the Shaoyang landmines that exploded without killing anyone, the Mongolian Tartars in the Japanese army, and so on—they might, at best, have heard vague rumors of the Third Changsha Campaign, too. They had no idea even what "1948" was, they'd never used the Gregorian calendar. The term "1948" remained unknown to them right up until the time I came to know them. They used some of the following terms to refer to this year:

1. *The year of the Great Battle of Changsha.*

This was obviously incorrect. *Their* Battle of Changsha was a piece of news that came nearly six years late, and was mistaken by them for an event that took place in 1948. If someone from outside Maqiao who had no clue about the Third Battle of Changsha relied solely on what Maqiao people said to gain a sense of history, they'd end up with a very muddled chronology.

2. *The year Mao Gong was head of the Protection Committee.*

You could say this was correct, you could also say this was incorrect. Maogong was from Maqiao Upper Village, but that year he was in fact covering for someone from Zhangjia District, and it was his turn to act as Head of the Protection Committee, with jurisdiction over the eighteen bows around. There was nothing much wrong in marking 1948 by this event. The problem, however, was that Maqiao people didn't know the Japanese had already surrendered and that the Protection Committees set up under Japanese coercion no longer existed in most places, that the "Good Citizen" card was no longer in use; because they were cut off from news, they were still doing things by the old rules, still using the term "Protection Committee"; this might lead to later confusion.

3. *The year the bamboo in Zhangjia District flowered.*

There was a grove of fine bamboo in Zhangjia District and in 1948, when a terrible drought came and not a single grain was harvested from the fields, a kind of seed-yielding white flower bloomed on all the bamboo. When people picked these seeds and threshed off the husk, they found bamboo rice-chaff, a pale red in color, which produced a heady scent when steamed and which tasted pretty much like nonglutinous red rice. After a bamboo flowered, it immediately died, but this grove of bamboo enabled the people who lived nearby to get through the famine; the locals were deeply grateful for its generosity, and named the grove "the merciful bamboo." This event made a very deep impression on Maqiao people, who henceforth remembered the year by it. There was, in general terms, nothing incorrect about this, it was just that outsiders wouldn't have known about the event itself. When the census register was taken, or recruits drafted, or school entrance exams registered for, those born in "the year the Zhangjia District bamboo flowered" and their parents would need to spend ages gesturing and explaining before managing to communicate to an outsider the age of the person concerned.

4. *The year Guangfu got muddled in Longjia Sands.*

To "get muddled" meant to start school. Guangfu, the son of Ma Wenjie, didn't have that much natural aptitude for learning; when he was little, he loved playing around and it took him seven years to finish primary school. Year upon year he had to repeat, which he found terribly embarrassing, and even after he grew up he hated admitting to this poor record, so on his curriculum vitae he put the time he got muddled forward three years, to 1951. If someone who didn't know these details were to calculate time only by Guangfu's curriculum vitae or by what Guangfu said, he'd dislocate Maqiao's whole history forward by three springs and three autumns. So this, too, is a very perilous way of conceptualizing time.

5. *The year Ma Wenjie called an amnesty.*

Ma Wenjie's amnesty was a great event: news of it spread near and far, everyone knew about it; it served as a highly convenient temporal marker for Maqiao people and was the easiest way of explaining things to people from outside the area.

There are a few things to be said about this amnesty, of course.

The atmosphere had been very tense that year. In the twelfth lunar month, a lot of people in the countryside were busy weaving grass mats to send over to the county seat in preparation for the wrapping of corpses. Rumor had it that the men from around Pingjiang had sworn alliance to the provincial army, which was under the generalship of "Donkey Peng" and was claimed to have mustered ten thousand men and three cannon, all ready for a fight to the death with Ma Wenjie and the men on both banks on the Luo River. Reckoning his number was up, Ma Wenjie divided up his family's property amongst the crowds and prepared his own coffin. He asked only one thing of Donkey Peng: he didn't want to fight in the city. So as to avoid bringing suffering on the people, the white mud embankment on the lower reaches of the Luo waters was the best place for the battle. Not having any of it, Donkey Peng cut off the head of the messenger Ma Wenjie had sent, and hung it on the bridge outside the east gate of Baisha Town. When the locals went out they didn't dare cross the bridge, and could cross only by wading through the water under the bridge.

When the news spread around, the ordinary people in the county seat fled in panic. After a while, though, after there was neither sound of cannon nor sighting of Donkey Peng's army approaching the city boundaries, it emerged that Ma Wenjie had issued a proclamation that he wouldn't fight. He had a new title, too: County Head and Head Commander of the Provisional Fourteenth Company. When he took people out to eat dogmeat in restaurants in Changle, people spotted that his followers all wore National Army uniforms and that a sprinkling of foreign-style machine guns gleamed in their possession.

As later opinion had it, Ma Wenjie did an incredibly stupid thing in going over to the GMD in the year of the GMD's great defeat. With regard to this, Guangfu explained to me over and over again how his dad had in the first place wanted to surrender to the Communist Party, but with the *yin* in a bad way and the *yang* tied up in knots he ended up surrendering at the wrong door. With his few years' experience of traveling around in the army, his dad had learned a thing or two, and knew vaguely about the Communist Party; he'd heard that the Communist Party killed the rich and helped the poor, that they were good fighters; he had no ill feeling towards them. While under pressure from the provincial army, he dispatched his sworn brother Wang Laoxuan to go and seek out the Communist Party. Wang Laoxuan had a brother-in-law who worked as a carpenter in Liuyang and who was very thick with the Communists. But things worked out very unfortunately: as soon as Wang Laoxuan set out, he was struck down by evil spirits and a huge carbuncle erupted on his back. He applied herbal medicine but it was still so painful he ended up knocked out for two whole days at an inn. By the time he hurried on to Liuyang, his brother-in-law had just left for Jiangxi.

"Two days, two rotten, measly days! If Wang Laoxuan hadn't got a boil, if he'd carried out his orders on time, wouldn't my dad have joined the Communist Party?"

Guangfu took a gulp of beer, fixing his eyes on me as he spoke.

Guangfu had reason to be regretful, of course. It was just those two short days that changed the fates of Ma Wenjie and his hundred or so followers, and that changed Guangfu's fate, too. Instead of finding the Communists, Wang Laoxuan was later introduced at Yueyang by the boss of a theater troupe to the aide-de-camp of a GMD Section B warlord. The Section B warlord offered Ma Wenjie amnesty and enlistment, for which arrangements began at that meeting.

By this time, it was nearing the end of 1948, exactly when the GMD's political power was beginning to collapse completely in the Mainland—but country-dwellers cut off by winter conditions didn't know this. I'd guess that the Section B warlord knew then that the game was already up, that amnesties and weapon handovers were happening everywhere, but wanted to make things just a little more stressful and difficult for the Communist Army as it prepared to head south. Or, as historical documents later made clear, it so happened that the Hunan Provincial Government Army belonged at the time to Section H of the GMD, between whom and Section B there was a rift; strife was both open and covert, but the friction never ceased. Section B was trying to enlist itinerant bandits on Section H's territory to increase their own power and contain Section H. Either way, the amnesty and generous support offered by Section B pleasantly surprised Bandit Ma, who, as a simple country bumpkin, was overjoyed to receive a certificate of appointment from his opposite number, as well as eighty guns and the assurance of a period of peace on both banks of the Luo River. He knew nothing of the factional struggle within the GMD, nor of the motives of the Section B commanding officer (even now, we can't be entirely sure of all this); he just thought that as long as they wore a uniform they were government troops, that they were to be feared by him, that he should sue for peace from them.

When he and his followers went out drinking to celebrate, he didn't know that the very step he had taken would drag him down into hell.

On the dry, exposed sandbank of the Luo River, 1948 slipped by, quietly bringing with it a swathe of enormous historical changes to the south. But for Bandit Ma and his followers, the 1948 they spent in their isolated, mountainous area was very different from the 1948 that appears in the official documents of the GMD Section B or Section H warlords. And again, when in later years the red county militia recalled a 1948 of overwhelming victory for the revolution, in which they launched a sudden machine-gun assault on Bandit Ma's few dozen "failed insurgents," their 1948 was very different from the 1948 that passed in Bandit Ma's isolated, mountainous area.

This is a dislocation of time.

☆**Daoist Ritual** [打醮]: The bandits on either side of the Luo River each did things their own way. In relative terms, though, Bandit Ma stood out as the figure of greatest authority amongst these gangs: not only because his soldiers and horses were tough and strong, but also because he possessed mystical powers. He was a believer in the Blue Teachings, a sect of popular Daoism, and every day he'd perform the Daoist rituals, pay reverence at the incense table to the bodisattva Guanyin, make his subordinates sit cross-legged on mats and mumble incantations. Sitting like this for long periods would, apparently, pacify your heart, purify your spirit, deepen your understanding of the Dao, increase your strength. It was sitting like this that had cured him of his ten-year-long coughing trouble. And beyond this, there were regulations for sitting and standing wherever his cohort of followers found themselves; they'd abstain from food and drink for two days, then run, as if on winged feet, onto the battlefield to fight. Some told tales more incredible still of their fighting, that with their own eyes they'd seen them not bleed when cut, their flag resist piercing by bullets—all of which, of course, was thanks to their sitting on mats.

There was one more special thing about Bandit Ma's troops: they never wore shoes while on the march or in battle, and were exceptionally fleet of foot when climbing mountains or fleeing across ravines; nothing—neither sharp rocks nor iron nails—could hurt their feet. Ordinary people called them the "Barefoot Army" and said that every evening they had to chant the secret spells and incantations of the Thirteen Guanbao spirits before perfecting such art. This, Guangfu later told me, was exaggeration, of course. They went barefoot simply in order to be quicker on their feet: paper-mulberry juice and tung sapling were ground together into a paste, spread over the sole of the foot, reapplied after hardening and repeated several times over, until a crust tougher than the sole of any shoe had formed on the sole of the foot; his father had learnt this technique from the Miao people of Xiangxi, while traveling around in the army.

People marveled at this barefoot army. Wherever it went, there would be children or old women wanting to study their Daoist rituals and how to sit on mats. Naturally, some didn't sit in the right way and went insane after walking over fire or going into a trance. Bandit Ma urged ordinary people not to study from him, not to practice Daoism casually.

He said that a clear mind and temperate spirit were the most important elements in practicing Daoism, that you should follow the way of righteousness. At that time, grain was in critically short supply and everywhere gang members were turning to thievery. As soon as Ma Wenjie entered the city, he was waylaid by both men and women, young and old, all crying and complaining about injustices; some had had their money stolen, some had had their women stolen, and all looked to Boss Ma for justice.

In Changle, Ma Wenjie convened a meeting of the ringleaders of each gang; he'd let movable property go, he said, but human booty should be released, and grain and oxen had to be returned. When all the gang members saw this solitary figure tramp up in straw sandals to convene the meeting, without even a single soldier as bodyguard, not even a gun or a bullet on him, they were immediately struck by his aura of overpowering righteousness and had lost a good third of their nerve even before he'd started to speak. Some just stared until their vision clouded over, until a halo of white light appeared above his head, a purple cloud floating on top of that. Soon, everyone was nodding like idiots. Everyone sat at one table to drink, carved off a corner of the table as a pledge, then parted company and went home to enforce the agreement.

Bandit Ma also went by the name of Clear-Sky Ma. People said that Bandit Ma's troops asked for grain, not money, and didn't take anything away after they'd eaten their fill. In other words, wherever they went his followers were allowed to ask for food from ordinary people when they were hungry, but only for one meal; anything else they seized was viewed as harassment of the populace and would be punished once discovered. Once, having rubbed handfuls of tobacco ashes over their faces to avoid being recognized, two of his followers broke into the house of the head of the county middle school at night and robbed the head teacher's wife of two gold bracelets from around her wrist. A quick-thinking housekeeper in the head teacher's household scattered outside the threshold a bowl of wood ashes in which they left their footprints as they left; the next day, she asked Bandit Ma over to inspect the scene. Returning to examine soles of feet, Bandit Ma very quickly uncovered the two robber bandits and immediately imprisoned them in a cage. Both were locked in the metal cage for three days, their collarbones threaded through with metal wire, as an example to all, during which time the holes in their flesh where the wire had passed through rotted and began to smell foul. After this, one was burned alive, his body blazing yellow smoke, his skin crackling noisily. The other, who hadn't been the ringleader, received more lenient treatment: he was stabbed to death with a dagger, his corpse left intact—the daggers went straight in and out, without twisting. The blood spurted several feet high out of the hole the dagger made, dyeing red a large expanse of plaster wall nearby.

The two dead wrong-doers never begged for mercy, never cried out; not even a single groan.

That really was something! No one who witnessed it failed to be moved to admiration.

Even when the soldiers under Bandit Ma were avaricious, they were unflinchingly avaricious, and because of this, other gangs couldn't help viewing them differently.

From that time on, other gangs would never make trouble on whichever road Bandit Ma's soldiers took. If they guarded goods in transit, they wouldn't carry any arms, just walk alongside empty-handed. This was called "the guard of righteousness." When they came across members of other gangs, they'd exchange handshakes, mention the great name of Ma Wenjie, throwing in a bit of nomadic vernacular as they went, and thus turn bad luck into good, continuing peacefully on their way. Sometimes, people would be kind enough to leave food, to make a gift of a leg of beef or a couple of bottles of good wine, to establish friendship.

☆**On the Take** [打起發]: *The Modern Chinese Dictionary of Dialects* (Jiangsu Educational Press, 1993) defines this term as follows:

1. Petty thievery: in times of famine or flight from armies, people go on the take in abandoned cities.
2. Pulling a fast one: he's a sharp one, don't think about going on the take with him (don't think about pulling a fast one on him). Also: sponging off people is done overtly, while going on the take is a covert activity.

For Maqiao people, this term also implied a sense of something hugely diverting or enjoyable. It was specifically used in reference to the year Bandit Ma's troops drove Donkey Peng of GMD Section H out of town; as they broke into the county capital of Pingjiang, they were accompanied by a throng of more than ten thousand peasants drawn from a dozen or so of the surrounding villages in the Luo region, who ruthlessly set about finding themselves fortunes. Some stole salt, some stole rice, some put on something like a dozen women's gowns at once, ballooning ludicrously, overheating so much their faces ran with sweat. There were others who weren't so lucky and who didn't get a thing, save for a bucket or a wooden door they managed to carry off home. Benyi's dad, Ma Ziyuan, did quite the most incredible thing of all, hauling one hundred tiles out of the city, which exhausted him so much that, gasping for breath, he lagged behind everyone else. His fellow villagers laughed at how "awakened" he was: why didn't he haul a load of mud back while he was about it? Hadn't he seen there was mud at home? His family had no lack of salt or rice, nor clothes, he said complacently; all he needed was a few dozen tiles to finish off the pigsty. These fine Maozhou tiles he'd spotted were just the thing!

He didn't feel he'd lost out in the slightest.

He knew even less about those things they called electric lamps. Some young men had cut down light bulbs in the city, intending to take them back to hang on the roof beams of their own houses; this handy little thing lit up at night, they said, didn't go dark even when the wind blew. Totally mad, Ma Ziyuan thought they were; there was no way such a treasure could possibly exist the world over.

Going "on the take" was later listed as one of Ma Wenjie's "crimes." He hadn't foreseen that so many would follow him into the city, and in order to bring the chaos under control he ordered his followers to suppress the looters. Among those wounded was Benyi's dad: because the tiles on his shoulder were too heavy, he was right at the back of those leaving the city and the soldiers caught up with him.

Before he'd had time to turn round, he felt a cold wind whistle past him and half his head, including one eye and one ear, flew into the air, dispatched in the wake of a silver-white sword blade. Propped up by his shoulders, the remaining half bounced along for another ten steps or so. His body and limbs flailed and his carrying pole bobbed up and down until, only quite some while later, his body finally lay dejectedly prostrate. His assassin, standing beside him, was shocked speechless for some time.

When the corpse was being cleaned, Maqiao's elders said, someone luckily noticed that Benyi's dad's foot was still stirring, and after giving it a rub discovered his hand was still warm and there was still a puff of life coming from his mouth. When Ma Wenjie came over and recognized an acquaintance from his own village, he hurriedly found a doctor to save him, who mixed up a bowl of paste, applied it to the wound, and stopped the bleeding, as if tightly sealing the mouth of an earthen jar. The doctor also poured a little rice broth into his mouth, and seeing that, after a short wait, the rice soup had actually been swallowed down, pronounced, "he won't die."

After Benyi's dad was sent back to Maqiao, he lived another five or so years; although he only had half a head left and couldn't work in the fields or say anything, he could still sit under the eaves making grass shoes and chopping up pig fodder.

The man with half a head never went where there were a lot of people, so as to avoid frightening everybody, in particular to avoid frightening children. Hiding away in his house all day, he got a bit restless, so he had to find things to do. And so, in this way, he managed to get done more than most normal people.

I find all this very hard to believe, and the idea of a man with half a head bustling around everywhere is even more fantastic, but this was how all the old people told it, insisting they'd all worn straw sandals sewn by Benyi's half-headed old dad. I just let them talk on.

☆**Bandit Ma (continued)** [馬疤子(續)]: One rainy evening, a staff member from the Liberation Army sent out as an advance guard met with County Leader Ma Wenjie under an oil lamp, explained to him the national situation and Communist Party policy, and urged him to give up his rebellion. Ma Wenjie demonstrated his consent, accepted the post of deputy director of the "Advisory Committee," and agreed to begin persuading the armies of the enemy, the puppet regime, and every gang member to submit.

Ma Wenjie had been County Leader for a few months but had never sat in office; he didn't even know where his office was. He'd never received any salary, didn't even know where he should go to receive his salary. He still liked wearing straw sandals; he could write a little but didn't have any great fondness for writing letters: whenever he dispatched messengers to the gangs, he'd make them carry an arrow-shaped bamboo token with three of his blood-red fingerprints on the top as guarantee. The gang members usually recognized his fingerprints and complied with his orders. Generally speaking, wherever the fingerprints went, guns would be handed over. The Baima Group from Baini Bow handed over thirty-odd great swords, which were carried clatteringly all the way to the county seat.

Little did Ma Wenjie know that Baima Group's Big Brother "Dragon's Head," whom he himself had persuaded to surrender, would find himself in prison two months later, and in chains.

Astounded, he went looking for the County Military Team-leader, whom he subjected to a spluttering interrogation, only to be rendered speechless when the man brought out a great heap of irrefutable evidence drawn from case investigations. He discovered that the Baima Group had in fact only feigned surrender, while secretly storing up guns and gunpowder, and preparing to flee. Then there was a Xu Someone, whom he'd also persuaded to surrender, who had gallons of blood on his hands, who'd tyrannized the local area, raped countless local girls. . . . Finally, his own chief of staff was interrogated by the new regime and discovered to be a military spy sent in by the GMD on a secret mission to control Ma Wenjie, or even to carry out assassinations. Should someone like this just be set free to operate free and undisturbed outside the law?

Ma Wenjie was in a cold sweat, incapable of doing anything except nod continuously.

The streets were plastered with slogans demanding the suppression of counterrevolutionaries. The peasants on the outskirts of the city, it was said, were sending grass ropes into the county seat, in preparation for tying people up. Every day, it was said, people were being dragged out of the county prison to be shot; large cells, containing several dozen men, could be emptied in a night, without anyone knowing whether they'd been sent elsewhere or killed. Rumors both true and false finally converged on Ma Wenjie himself: that his "Advisory Committee" was a hotbed of phoney surrenderers and that he was the ringleader of the "Advisory Gang." He waited for his superiors to send people to seize him, waited several days without anything happening; quite the opposite, his superiors behaved entirely as usual, inviting him to come to meetings here and there, sending someone over with his khaki Liberation Army uniform. He wore this uniform when he went out into the streets; when people who knew him saw how anxious he looked, they kept to the other side of the road, gave him a wide berth.

It's hard to give a clear account of how things worked out, partly because there were so few parties involved and because they weren't willing to talk, but also because what little the parties involved did manage to say was so dubious, in so many places, and differed so enormously from one version to the next. Some said that Bandit Ma's old enemy Donkey Peng had also surrendered and gotten himself an official position higher than Bandit Ma's. Keen to make a show of loyalty to the new regime, Peng found the easiest method was to denounce lots of people for having falsely surrendered. There were also those who said that Section B and Section H in the GMD had never gotten along; when the Japanese devils had been there, each had played the Japanese against their opponent; now that the CCP had come, they were making use of the CCP to elbow out their adversaries. Seeing as Section B had used Bandit Ma to contain the H section, Section H could, of course, make use of the CCP to deal with Bandit Ma. How could Bandit Ma, a local yokel, possibly keep up with all these underhanded dealings and secret summonses?

Of course, there were also those who said this wasn't how things were. They believed that a lot of bandits only surrendered half-heartedly, that Bandit Ma was an incorrigible brigand and had secretly planned several defections and rebellions, that he was guilty of the most heinous crimes. It was only because he was already dead that the government later forgave him his past.

I have no way of distinguishing the true from the false amongst these accounts, so I'll have to sidestep them all and just tell briefly how the story ended. I can't necessarily even give a proper account of how it ended, all I can do is try my best to piece together the fragmented sources available. It would probably have been one day a couple of months later, when Ma Wenjie was on his way back home from a meeting at the prefectural commissioner's office, and he heard a terrible commotion of weeping coming from inside his house. When he pushed open the door, he was confronted by a gang of women who threw themselves upon him at this very same instant, their eyes glittering with tears, their mouths open wide. The sound of crying came to an abrupt halt. But it stopped only for a moment, before violently re-erupting. The few children present followed suit, their faces twisting with sobs.

He couldn't believe his eyes.

Director Ma! County Leader Ma! General! Third Master! Third Uncle
. . . The women cried out every imaginable name, as they jostled frenziedly to reach the front to make their kowtows, thumping out a terrible
din with their heads.

"Our lives are over!"

"Our lives are in your hands!"

"Give me back my precious love!"

"We only surrendered because of what you said! You're responsible!"

"His dad said he had to go, but what about the family, there's seven,
eight of them, they all need feeding, what am I going to do . . ."

One woman rushed forward, grabbed hold of his lapels, smacked him
right in the face, and yelled out, as if crazed: "It's all your fault! Give us
back our men, give them back—"

By the time Ma Wenjie's wife had come forward to coax the mad-
woman away, Ma Wenjie's jacket lapels were torn and his assailant had
clawed two bleeding scratches across his hand.

Ma Wenjie slowly worked out what had happened. While he'd been
having a meeting with his superiors, the "Advisory Gang" had risen up in
rebellion, killing first of all three members of the work team in Baoluo
Township; they'd planned a rebellion of even greater dimensions, but
failed to anticipate the government intercepting and seizing a secret mis-
sive; all the government then had to do was strike first, and hardest, exe-
cuting the ringleaders of the rebellion as soon as possible—the husbands
of these women numbering among them. They'd not seen their husbands return from a meeting called several days ago. In the end, the government informed them they should go to a place called Bramble Street
to pick up their effects; that's how simply things were managed.

As he listened, Ma Wenjie once more went into a cold sweat, pacing
up and down the room with his hands behind his back, staring up at the
heavens, his tears pouring out. He clasped the hands of every single
woman gathered in the room: "Your brother's let you down," he said,
"he's let you down."

Crying all the while, he pulled open some cases, took out all the shiny
silver dollars they contained—only fifty-odd coins altogether—and
stuffed them into the hands of his petitioners. His wife, wiping her eyes,
also produced her private savings, made up of the scattered coins that
Ma Wenjie normally left at his pillowside, on tables, in drawers, in the
stable or toilet. He was usually careless with his money, but luckily his
wife followed behind him, scooping it all up.

The two of them finally managed to send their weeping and wailing
guests home.

Ma Wenjie didn't close his eyes once all night; when he rose the next day and saw that the cockerel at the gate stretching its neck but producing no noise, he sensed something a little odd had happened. When, tapping the table absent-mindedly, he realized that still there was no noise, something, he felt, was even odder. Finding himself at an old Daoist temple, at the front of whose hall was an old bell, he walked up to the bell, tried to sound it and discovered there was still no sound; now unable to control his mounting anxiety, he swung the hammer and rang the bell with all his might; hearing its deafening chimes, everyone from roundabout ran over, staring at him with huge, terrified eyes. It was only then that he realized it wasn't the bell that was failing to make a noise—he had gone deaf. He put the bell hammer down without a word.

Having drunk a bowl of gruel that his wife had prepared for him, he heaved a sigh and got ready to go and see the doctor, but just as he reached the mouth of the lane, he collided with a flood of people on the streets, taking part in another demonstration march for the suppression of counterrevolutionary elements, a memorial meeting for the three revolutionary martyrs of Baoluo Township. Headed in the direction of the county prison, the people's militia and primary school students were shouting out slogans. What they were shouting with their mouths so wide open, he didn't know.

He stopped and, using the wall for support, slowly turned and went back home.

From his house to the mouth of the lane, it was fifty-one steps, from the mouth of the lane to his house it was also fifty-one steps, no more, no less; this happened to be his age exactly.

"How come it's exactly fifty-one steps?" It surprised him.

His wife handed him an umbrella, urging him to go and see the doctor.

"Tell me, how come it's exactly fifty-one steps?"

He couldn't hear whatever his wife had to say.

"What did you say?"

His wife's mouth once more opened and closed noiselessly.

He remembered again that he was deaf and didn't repeat his question, just shook his head. "Strange. Very strange."

That afternoon, a doctor friend came to have a look at his hearing problem. He asked his guest for a little coarse opium. You practice Daoist rituals and breathing every day, his friend gestured at him, aren't you supposed not to smoke? He tapped his forehead, meaning that he'd caught a slight chill, that he was feeling the cold badly, and that he needed something to smoke to drive out the cold, bring on a sweat. His friend gave him a pouchful.

It rained that night. After he'd performed his last ritual, he committed suicide by swallowing opium. He'd changed into a clean, neat set of clothes, shaved off his beard, even carefully cut his fingernails.

Going by what most people said, he hadn't needed to die. He was in no particular danger. Even though he was implicated in a few felonies—such as deciding to surrender to the GMD and allowing his followers to kill a few ordinary people on the take—he was, in the end, a big cheese and the arrow-tokens of his Advisory Committee had, in the end, achieved a great deal for the new regime. When he'd studied carpentry, moreover, he'd been apprenticed alongside some important senior officer in the Communist Party, whose family he'd protected, sending over rice to help them through. The day after he killed himself, a section chief arrived posthaste on a special trip across the province to deliver a letter written by the senior officer himself. At the end of the letter, the senior officer invited him, at his convenience, to come as his guest to the provincial capital to talk about old times.

He was already asleep in his grass mat shroud before he got to see this letter. After taking instructions from the prefectural commissioner's office and the province, the county government bought him a coffin, a pair of white candles, and a string of firecrackers.

*Bramble Gourd** [荆界瓜]: Most Maqiao people wouldn't know what Bramble Street, the place I just mentioned, was; most people from near Maqiao wouldn't know either—especially not the younger generation.

Bramble Street disappeared many years ago. If you left the county seat from the East Gate on Sanhuali Road, then crossed the Luo River, you'd see a flat stretch of bank, where cotton or sweet potatoes grew; on top of the northern face, which was slightly elevated, were a few scattered stones, some straggling grass, and a couple of thatched sheds built for night watchmen. If you came in a bit closer to look, you'd probably glimpse some ox droppings or the nests of wild birds in amongst the deep grasses, or a broken straw sandal. This was Bramble Street, now called Brambleland, or Brambleland Embankment. It would have been near impossible for younger generations to gain a sense of how this had in fact once been a "street," that it had actually been host to a hundred bustling, clamoring people and a huge, grand Confucian temple, famous for miles around.

Bramble Street had become a name without any links to reality, that had gone to waste.

Bramble Street only continued to figure, only carried any importance as a place-name, in stories relating to Ma Wenjie. Even so, its inevitable disappearance into oblivion was merely postponed for a few decades in the minds of one group of people—nothing more. The massacre of the "Advisory Gang" which took place that year started right here. In the last stage of their study meeting, the fifty-odd leaders of the surrendering bandits had been ordered to dig a pond. They dug and dug, hauled and hauled, dripped with sweat for three days; as soon as some kind of a pond had been dug, the rat-a-tat-tat of a machine gun hidden on a roof somewhere suddenly went off—a sudden noise, it was, that would have sounded very foreign, very distant to its hearers. The rain of bullets whistled over, rolled up into a whirlwind. None felt the bullets passing through his flesh, but as clouds of dust leapt up from the mud slope behind them and sand splattered in all directions, it became very obvious that *something* had exploded through one side of their bodies before blossoming out into a whole chain of dust-cloud blooms on the other side. Maybe they were just beginning to understand what kind of a thing metal is, what kind of a thing speed is, how freely and easily metal bullets passed through flesh and how hard this instant was to grasp. And finally, they fell, one after another, into the hole in the ground they themselves had just dug.

It was only after 1982, when the government pronounced the "Revolt of the Advisory Committee" to be a case misjudged for all sorts of complex reasons, that talk of this episode once more began to flash into conversation, that the strange name of Bramble Street began to be used once more. Some old people said that after that volley of gunfire, Bramble Street became the haunt of ghosts, that house after house had caught fire for no apparent reason, and that before two years had passed, seven houses had burned down. A lot of the children born there—three within two years—were born feebleminded. The fengshui man said there were ghosts at work there and that the fish in the pool couldn't keep them off, so of course houses were going to get burned down. Mr Fengshui also babbled something about these being *guan* ("government") ghosts, ghosts connected to catastrophes in government, *guan* being homophonic with the word coffin, which referred to souls which hadn't scattered after death, something like this—no one listening quite got what he said. People immediately started to dig inside and outside their houses, tunneled several feet down, and cleared out any suspicious broken bits of material which might have been rotten coffins. They also dug a new pond and planted a few thousand fishtail seedlings in a determined effort to increase the flow of water, to overcome fire with water. The strange thing was that the fish in this pond just wouldn't survive: all of them went belly-up within a month. Finally, an umbrella-maker's shop on the eastern side of the street caught fire and people slowly lost confidence in fire-fighting; one after another, they were forced to move elsewhere, a great many to the area around Huang Bay.

By the end of the 1950s, Bramble Street had become totally deserted, a stretch of wasteland; even the well had caved in, and mosquitoes and wigglers flourished in vast numbers.

In fact, it became a patch of good land, very fertile, so it was said, where cotton flowers and sweet potatoes would grow particularly well; it also produced a wonderfully sweet variety of melon that very quickly became famous. Sometimes, in an effort to drum up customers, the peddlers in the county capital would yell with particular vigor, "Get your Brambleland Embankment Brambleland Melons!"

Some people wrote this as "Baubleland Melons" on the signs for their melon stalls.

*1948 (continued) [一九四八年(續)]: I used to think that time was measured equally everywhere, that it was something that traveled at uniform speed, a transparent fluid equally, evenly, and precisely distributed, drop by drop. But no: this, in fact, is just the time felt by our bodies: being born, growing up, getting old, dying, for example, all according to the prescribed order. But people aren't trees, or stones. Perhaps, apart from material time, it is *felt* time that is most meaningful to people. A person's period of childhood is always very long, just as periods of upheaval, danger, and distress are very long. There can be no doubt that a sense of *longue durée* springs from a person's special sensitivity of feeling, clarity of memory, and depth of new knowledge. For those who pass comfortable, dull days, in whose lives one day is replicated by one hundred, and one year is replicated by ten, we see the opposite occurring: time isn't drawn out, it isn't expanded or enlarged, but becomes increasingly hurried, increasingly shrunken, until it finally turns into a zero, a blink, then it's gone without a trace. One day, they suddenly discover to their wide-eyed horror that the old person in the mirror is themselves.

By a similar logic, time we know very little about, the time of the ancients, the time of distant nations, for example, is always hazy and so close to being invisible that it can be practically ignored, just as anything far away, anything at the very extreme of our worldview shrinks into specks of dust, into something barely distinct from air. When I used to read American fiction, I found that I often got the 1920s and the 1940s in America mixed up, and the seventeenth and nineteenth centuries, even more so. I was frightened at myself: how could the entirely distinct, undeniable living and dying, and dying and living—several decades, even several centuries long—of all the generations that lay behind a novel, quietly escape me, why were they so frantically brief that they stimulated me only to skim quickly through a book, or even yawn?

The reason was very simple: I was too far away, I couldn't see every-thing clearly.

Time is a hostage to the powers of perception.

Human time only exists through perception, and people whose pow-ers of perception are weakened, or even totally lost, human vegetables confined to their sickbeds, for example, lack a truly meaningful sense of time. This transparent fluid, time, has never trickled down in equal quantities, at uniform speeds, it quietly changes form according to dif-ferent powers of perception, undetectably extending or shortening, con-centrating or scattering, protruding or collapsing.

The problem is, everyone's perceptions are different, and one person's perceptions will constantly alter as a situation changes. Standing amongst a huge pile of crushed sensory fragments, do we still have a reli-able, permanently fixed, abiding image of time? A unified time? When we discuss the year 1948, which perception of 1948 are we discussing? On that rainy, overcast evening, in that small beancurd stall, after Guangfu had had a cry about his dad, he got onto the subject of lotus root. He said the lotus root that year was incredibly sweet, unusually powdery after you'd boiled it—you couldn't get stuff like that to eat now. Lotus root nowadays, he said, grew from chemical fertilizer, was a hundred times inferior to lotus root back then.

What he said left me a little perplexed. I knew that nowadays some places did in fact use too many chemical fertilizers, that this did in fact affect crop quality. But most lotus root *was* still organic and not all that different from old Guangfu's lotus root of yore. I suspected it wasn't the flavor of the lotus root that had changed, but rather Guangfu's percep-tion of its taste that had changed, as he grew older and older, as periods of famine or liver trouble receded further and further back in the past. This is a very common phenomenon. We often gloss over things from the past, lotus root or a book, some neighbor of ours, for example, because we've forgotten the specific circumstances which produced our original warmth of feeling. We may even feel that a distressing experi-ence from the past was incredibly beautiful, because we've already become distant spectators, utterly removed from the danger of sinking back down into its mire. We're no longer in distress, we're simply enjoy-ing the memory of that distress.

And so time, that hostage to perception, in fact corrodes our percep-tions.

To what extent was the 1948 of which Guangfu spoke to me truthful, reliable, still uncorroded? To what extent were his unreliable recollec-tions of the flavor of lotus root distinct from his own unreliable beliefs?

On the subject of the government's recent decision to rehabilitate the "Advisory Committee," Guangfu said that what the CCP did was far from easy for them: rectifying your own mistakes, swallowing down your own phlegm, none of this is easy. As he said this, he discovered that the box of tobacco was empty and told his son to go and buy some tobacco, and get two bottles of soda for the guest while he was at it. His son was twelve or thirteen years old, and at the mention of soda his eyes lit up and he ran barefoot out the door. When he returned with tobacco and soda, he didn't leave things at that: he frenziedly pried off the cap of the soda bottle with the tip of a chopstick. Pop—he stood there, briefly dazed, before he began turning in every direction, climbing under the dark bed to grope around, his pointy buttocks sticking right up in the air. The tin bottle cap must have flown off somewhere.

He re-emerged with a spider's web on his head: I couldn't see it, he said, I couldn't see it, then brushed off his hands and took the other bottle of soda off outside to drink, humming a tuneless popular song.

"So that's that, hmmm?" Guangfu asked him angrily.

"I looked everywhere, I couldn't see it."

"Did it grow wings? Fly off into the sky?"

I didn't know why Guangfu was attaching so much importance to a tin bottle cap. Maybe the little tin cap could be returned for money? Or was he furious about his kid's devil-may-care attitude?

He made the child have another look, interrupting his conversation with me, helping move a pile of charcoal away from a corner of the wall, along with a wooden bucket and hoe and other tools, huffing and puffing as he did so, subjecting every single suspicious hiding place to a thorough investigation. "Where the hell are you hiding?" he threatened the bottle cap, "I know you're hiding somewhere! Where've you gone to?"

Of course, he didn't forget to scold the child: "Get looking, you good-for-nothing! Look! Getting a bit big for your boots, are you? Let me tell you, if it wasn't for the Communist Party rehabilitating your grandfather, d'you think you'd be drinking soda? Or wearing shiny leather shoes? Or going to high school with a fountain pen in your pocket? I nearly died doing labor reform, I was so hungry I even picked out the grass from ox dung to eat . . ."

The child pouted, kicking sourly at a piece of wood ash.

"Kicking, are you, you pig-sticker!" (see the entry "Stick[y]"). The Phys. Ed. teacher whacked him on the top of his head.

The child raised his arms to ward off the blow; maybe he used a little more force than was necessary, for his father had to take a couple of steps back, almost slipped over. "So hit back at me, would you? You'd hit back, you good-for-nothing?" He snatched the bottle of soda from the child's hand, "I'll bury you alive, I will!"

Panting with fury, the boy ran outside screaming like a mad thing: "You old bastard! You old bandit! You old counterrevolutionary! What kind of teacher are you, hitting people like that?" A torrent of abuse ensued: "Reckon this is still the old society? Reckon you can bully everyone else, make everyone's life miserable, humiliate the nation and forfeit its sovereignty, hmmm?" These two phrases he'd used sounded very scholarly. "Serves you right! Serves you right, picking over ox dung! My life'd be better if you went to prison. If I get to be premier when I grow up, I'll launch political movements! And tell you what, I won't be rehabilitating your type! . . ."

"I—I—I—"

Guangfu's angry response caught in his throat; even though he was a Phys. Ed. teacher, he still couldn't catch up with his son, but his whole body shook with anger; luckily, I was there to help him get back home and calm down. The boy's attitude toward him left me surprised and bewildered. Of course, the boy had spoken in anger, so his words shouldn't be taken too seriously. But the way he'd jabbed at his father's sore points proved at the very least that he had no acute sense of pain toward past events, and that no misjudgement of any case could compare in importance with his bottle of soda. It was at this moment that I was again made conscious of the ambiguities of time. Like a lot of people, Guangfu thought that most people would sympathize with his ordeals, that everything set in stone by Time should be forever preserved in its original form, universally recognized and admired like a precious cultural relic in a museum. Rooted in this belief as he was, he was like my parents or lots of people from earlier generations, always lecturing the younger generation by revisiting past events, talking about his time in prison, the famine, ox dung, or 1948.

What he hadn't realized was that time isn't a cultural relic, that there is no unified sense of time, existing for and appreciated by him and his son simultaneously. When the government returned to him a 1948 in which his father was pure as the driven snow, they failed to allocate one to his son as well. The boy's sullen kick at the pile of wood ash showed he was not only uninterested in, but resented all that came from the past, including 1948.

This, it would seem, was illogical. Despite having no personal experience of the past, he could at least be curious about strange events that took place in the past, just as children normally respond enthusiastically to classical legends, rather than kicking them angrily away. There was one plausible explanation for this: he didn't have any real hatred of the past, it was just that he hated the present past, which was to say the past of this overcast evening, the past that resonated with his father's scolding lectures and pomposity, the past that had snatched away his half-bottle of soda.

Guangfu's anger drove him to tears. This got me thinking about the policy that had made their whole family suffer injustice, a policy that had ruled that all personnel still serving in the old regime after 1947 at department and lieutenant-commander level and above were historically counterrevolutionary. This was applied across the board, to anybody, anywhere, in any temporal schema, the implication being: everyone lived within one, single time scheme, with no exceptions permitted. Years later, people finally realized that this policy was an oversimplification, and thanks to the revoking of this policy Guangfu's bitterness was replaced by sweetness. On the other hand, however, Guangfu was still trying to force his son to live in a single time scheme, again with no exceptions permitted. He was insisting on nothing less than a new timetable: the past that he detested so much, his son also had to detest; the present that he cherished, his son also had to cherish. The vast and momentous 1948 of his mind had to take on the same form and supremacy in his son's mind, it couldn't shrink, couldn't scatter, least of all disappear into nothingness. What he hadn't realized was that his son lived entirely outside his father's time—that in his son, a tiny little tin bottle cap could lead to a totally different conclusion:

"Served you right going to prison like that!"

"I'd be better off if you were in prison!"

Maybe, from this evening onwards, in this tiny little beancurd stall, an irrevocable chasm opened up between their pasts, a chasm that included 1948, and that was practically unbridgeable.

☆**Army Mosquito** [軍頭蚊]: A very small variety of mosquito, this was, and very dark in color; if you examined it carefully, though, you'd see there was a small white dot on its black head. Its sting produced a red bite, not that big but unbelievably itchy, that lasted about three days. Maqiao people called it the "army mosquito." People said Maqiao didn't used to have this sort of mosquito, only the vegetable mosquito, a large, greyish creature. Although the bites it produced were big and extremely itchy, they disappeared pretty quickly. Maqiao people also said that the army mosquito had been brought by the provincial army, the year that Donkey Peng's provincial army had fought their way up to Changle. They'd been stationed there for ten days, leaving behind piles of pig bristles, chicken feathers, and this vicious breed of mosquito.

That's how the army mosquito got its name.

It was during my time in the countryside that these mosquitoes taught me just how fierce they were. Particularly in the summer, when work finished very late, mosquitoes would swarm around your face and legs, making a deafening buzz, forming clouds so dense they could almost lift you off the ground. We were too hungry when we got home for our hands to take care of anything besides eating and drinking. And so, wolfing and gulping as we held our bowls, we had to keep our legs jigging about in a mealtime dance that we had to get used to: if you stopped for only a moment, a swarm of mosquitoes would mercilessly descend. If your hand happened to shoot out to rub your leg, you'd rub a few mosquito corpses off. People were quite used to rubbing rather than swatting mosquitoes, because in the end hands and feet were your own flesh and wouldn't put up with getting slapped all the time.

When it got late, the mosquitoes, too, seemed to get tired and rest, and the buzzing noise would grow fainter.

*Public Family [公家]: Maqiao's paddy fields were unusually shaped, interlocking like fangs, and lay on a strip of valley between two mountains, slowly descending, one step at a time, to the drifting chimney smoke or evening moonlight of Zhangjia District. This stretch of land was called the "Great Gully," a name which should tell outsiders there were a lot of gully fields in the area. These "gully fields" were a type of paddy field to be found in mountainous areas where residual water exceeded flowing water, thereby producing a cold, swampy mud that concealed a great many deep gully holes; once you'd stepped in one, you could be in up to your forehead. The gully holes weren't easy to spot from the surface, and only people often in the fields would get to know the position of each and every one.

Maqiao's oxen also knew where the gully holes were, and if they suddenly stopped short somewhere, the plougher would know to tread very carefully indeed.

Each of these fields had its own name, derived either from its shape—turtle patch, snake patch, melon strip patch, silver carp patch, wooden bench patch, straw hat patch, and so on—or from the quantity of grain it ought to produce—three-peck patch, eight-peck patch, and so on; some were named after political slogans—unity patch, leap forward patch, four purifications red flag patch, and so on. Even so, naming them thus still wasn't enough to identity all those scattered fields, and people's names had to be used, or placed in front of the field names, in order to tell them apart: "Benyi's family's three-peck patch" and "Zhihuang's family's three-peck patch," for example, differentiated these two pieces of land.

It should thus be apparent that these fields used to be privately owned, or had been allocated to private owners during Land Reform; it was thus very natural that they should be linked with the names of the landowners.

Considering that collectivisation had happened a good ten years before I arrived, I was surprised they all still remembered so determinedly what had once belonged to their own families. Even the children, once they'd reached a certain age, all knew where the fields that had originally belonged to their own families were and whether rice would (*ken*) grow there. When putting down fertilizer, they'd put a bit extra down there. If they needed to pee, they'd relieve themselves there. Once, a child stepped on a piece of china, almost carving his foot open, and hurled it angrily onto another field. A woman standing nearby immediately glared at him:

"Where d'you think you're throwing stuff, eh? Want a smack, do you? Or a poke with my chopsticks!"

That patch had originally been her family's—a long, long time ago.

This woman's continuing recollection of her family's private field proved that public ownership of land in Maqiao, right up to the early 1970s, was no more than a system, that it hadn't yet permeated to the depth of a feeling, or at least not to the depth of a whole-hearted feeling. Systems and feelings are, of course, two very different sorts of things, and all that seethes below the surface of a system is different again. Within the matrimonial system, a husband and wife could share a bed while dreaming different dreams, while having changes of heart. (Can this still be termed "marriage"?) In an absolutist system, factions can operate behind the scenes after great power has waned. (Can this still be called "absolutist"?) By a similar logic, for as long as many Maqiao people would hold in their urine in order to release it over what had previously been their own private fields, their grasp of the concepts of public ownership, of the "public family" had to be a little shaky.

Of course, neither was it the case that they were dead-set on private ownership. In fact, Maqiao had never had a proper system of private ownership. Villagers told me that even before the Republic (founded in 1912), their private rights extended only to three inches of swamp below the surface of the fields. Anything below three inches had always belonged to the emperor, to the state. Everything, the world over, belonged to the ruler, and officialdom did as they pleased, the landowner remaining powerless to prevent them. This explained, outsiders can perhaps understand that when collectivisation was later introduced in

Maqiao, although some private complaints were inevitable, once the government order was given, the masses meekly entered the public family without giving the matter much further thought.

On the other hand, though, when they talked about "public" and "private," they always attached the word "family" afterwards; this was quite different from usage in Western languages. "Private" in the West means private to the individual. Any talk of property between husband and wife or father and son brings with it clear demarcations of private rights. For Maqiao people, the term "private family" signifies something public within the private. There was never a division between this and that, you and me, within a family. In the West, "public" means public society; in English, "public" means a horizontal stratum of equal, private bodies, often with political and economic significance, distinct from private issues such as personal secrets. For Maqiao people, the "public family" signified things that were private within the public sphere: marital disputes, young loves, burying the old, children's study, women's clothes, men's bragging, hens laying, rats burrowing—all private matters came under the scrutiny of the public family, they all counted as the responsibility of the public family. The public family became one big Private.

Precisely because of this collective clan sentiment (public—family), people usually called cadres "parent officials." When Maqiao's Ma Benyi was only thirty, or thereabouts, and had just married, he was respectfully addressed by many as "Daddy Benyi" or "Public Benyi" (Benyi *Gong*), because of his status as Party Secretary.

This phrase, in fact, returned to the original sense of the word "public" in Chinese. The earliest usage of the word for "public," *gong*, in Chinese did not mean public at all; it referred to a tribal leader or to the king of a state, was synonymous with the word "lord." Strictly speaking, translating the Western word "public" as *gong* is not right at all. In transporting Western terms such as "private ownership system" and "public ownership system" wholesale to Maqiao, you run the risk, it would seem, of creating a chasm between name and reality.

Benyi was Maqiao's *gong* (in its sense in classical Chinese), at the same time as he represented Maqiao's *gong* (in its sense in English and other Western languages).

Taiwan [台灣]: In amongst the gully fields, there was one field called Taiwan, which to begin with I'd never taken much notice of. When we were fighting the drought by running the waterwheel, Fucha and I used to work deep into the night on a shift together, yawning as we climbed up onto the waterwheel, pedaling creakily away. Innumerable bare feet had already tramped the slow-turning wooden tread-weight into a radiant surface that gleamed with amazing brightness; one slip in concentration and my footing would be lost, my hands locked onto the handrail, and I'd be strung up yowling like a dog. At times like this, the waterwheel Fucha was turning under his feet could wreck your courage, the tread-weight spiraling unstoppably up over and over, pulverizing your feet black-and-blue or into a bloody mass. Fucha advised me not to watch my feet, as it was easy to miss your footing that way, but I couldn't allow myself to trust him, couldn't follow his advice. Time after time, he tried to get me talking, chatting, just to help me relax.

He loved more than anything else to hear me talk about things from the city, or things to do with science, stuff about Mars or Uranus, for example. He'd graduated from junior middle school and had a head for matters scientific; he understood how sticky (magnetic) rocks worked, for example, and said that if enemy planes should ever drop bombs again maybe we could make a huge sticky stone that enemy planes would stick to from out of the sky—wouldn't that be more useful than artillery guns or guided missiles?

Soberly pondering my objections, he very seldom expressed surprise at the various bits of scientific knowledge I boasted about, just as he was never usually miserable amidst great misery, or joyful amidst great joy, his baby-face retaining at all times its look of knowing sagacity. All his various emotions were filtered into a single expression of placidity, of shyness, his permanently limpid gaze radiating out at an unglimpsed angle. Once you'd met this gaze, you immediately felt it was omnipresent, that any move of yours would be apprehended and penetrated. There were eyes behind his eyes, a gaze behind his gaze, you felt you couldn't keep anything concealed from him.

He disappeared, then popped out again from somewhere, cradling a snake-melon, probably stolen from the garden of some house nearby. When we'd finished eating, he dug a hole in the ground and started carefully burying the melon skin and seeds: "It's midnight already; let's go to sleep."

There were a lot of mosquitoes around and I was slapping away at my legs.

He searched out some leaves from somewhere and rubbed them over my legs, hands, and forehead—to great effect, it turned out, as the buzzing of the mosquitoes lessened significantly.

As I gazed at the moonlight just burst out from among the mountains, listened to the croaking of the frogs, one *rebbit* after another rising up from the gullies, I felt a slight anxiety: "So we're going to . . . sleep?"

"When we work, we work, when we rest, we rest."

"Benyi *Gong* said he wanted the wheel to fill the field by tonight."

"That's his problem."

"Will he come and check?"

"Nope."

"How d'you know?"

"I don't need to know—he just won't!"

This I found rather strange.

He knew that I'd carry on asking him why. "It's superstition, peasant superstition, just forget it." He then collapsed at my side, turned his back to me, hugged his legs in tightly, and prepared to sleep.

I wasn't like him, couldn't sleep when I felt like it, couldn't not sleep when I didn't feel like it, all neat and simple. I really did want to sleep, but my eyes couldn't rest, so I asked him to tell me some more empty talk (see the entry "Empty Talk"), even superstitions would do. Eventually he capitulated, but insisted he'd heard it from elsewhere—whenever relating matters of great import, he'd first communicate the provenance of the story in order to absolve himself. He'd heard so-and-so say, he said, that the owner of this field had been called Maogong, a bitter enemy of Benyi. The year the lower-level agricultural producers' cooperative was established, Maogong stubbornly refused to join the cooperative until his was the only field still individually farmed out of all the surrounding fields. As head of the cooperative, Benyi wouldn't allow Maogong to take water from the fields above his. Maogong still refused to yield, preferring to haul his thick hide to the river to fetch water than beg for it. Finally, seizing the opportunity provided by Maogong's suffering an asthma attack, Benyi charged hollering onto the field at the head of a group of men, a bucket raised aloft, to claim his grain; this, he said, was "liberating Taiwan."

In the past, Maogong had been the head of the Protection Committee and owned a lot of land: he was a landlord traitor to the Chinese. That, of course, made his land "Taiwan." Come to mention it, though, that label of traitor was a little unfair. Before, this area had been the fourteenth district under the puppet regime set up by the Japanese, and it had a Protection Committee with jurisdiction over Maqiao and the surrounding eighteen bows; those with wealth or status took turns as Head of Committee for three months each; a gong was sent to the home of whoever's turn it was. As leader, you drew no particular salary, but the gong gave you the right to sound off about public affairs and you could pick up "straw sandal money" wherever you went; in other words, cream off a little profit for yourself under the cover of public duty. Maogong's turn came right at the last of the eighteen bows, and by the time it came around to him, the Japanese Army had already surrendered, so he didn't have to take the job; but because the locals didn't know what was going on outside, the gong was still passed to him.

Maogong was someone who enjoyed the limelight, and once the gong passed into his hands, he immediately dressed up in a long, white silk gown and took to wielding a staff, coughing and spluttering at great volume whenever he turned up on someone's terrace. Overly rapacious in collecting his straw sandal money, he demanded at least twice as much as his recent predecessors and took second helpings wherever he went. There was no end to the strange tricks he used. Once, while having a meal at Wanyu's house, he picked up, unobserved, a piece of string pecked at by chickens that Wanyu's dad had dropped under the stove, and hid it in his sleeve; when they sat at table and his host wasn't looking, he put it in the bowl of chicken. When he lifted his chopsticks and "discovered" the tape, he accused his host of tricking him and demanded five silver dollars off him. After his host had begged and pleaded with him, the matter was finally settled at two dollars. Another time, on a visit to a household in Zhangjia District, he first of all defecated outside on his own straw hat, so that a dog would come and chew it. After having sat inside the house for a while, reckoning that the dog would've chewed the hat to bits, he went back outside and made a huge fuss, accusing his host of deliberately antagonizing him, the Head of the Committee, and the imperial army, saying he couldn't even leave his straw hat alone, that he'd fed it to the dog behind his back. Nothing his host said was of any use, so he finally swallowed his anger and gave him an iron pot in compensation.

Everyone knew, in fact, that the straw hat had been tattered and broken from way back.

Seeing as he'd planted so many seeds of bitterness, it's not hard to imagine how the villagers responded to Benyi's cry to "liberate Taiwan" by the hundreds, charging onto the battlefield, particularly Wanyu's dad, who not only ran onto Maogong's fields to trample the crops, but also shredded the melon creepers planted at the side of Maogong's field. Afraid Maogong wouldn't hear them, some of the young men yelled and hooted in deliberate, ear-splitting unison, making a racket that terrified all the chickens and dogs in the village.

Not surprisingly, Maogong did hear and hurried over, wheezing away. Pounding the ground with a stick, he cursed: "You good-for-nothing Benyi, stealing my grain in broad daylight, I hope you die horribly . . ."

Benyi raised his arm and shouted: "Liberate Taiwan!"

Law-abiding members of the commune shouted with him: "Liberate Taiwan!"

"What happens to opponents of the cooperative?" he shouted.

Again came the deafening roar in response, "Reap their grain, eat their crops! Take what you can! Reap their grain, eat their crops! Take what you can!"

Maogong's eyes went bloodshot with fury: "Fine, fine, take what you want, take all you want, but when I starve to death and become a hungry ghost, I'll come and stab you to death!"

He turned to shout at his sons Yanzao and Yanwu to go back and fetch knives. The two brothers were just little kids, already paralyzed with fear by this scene, and just stood there on the hillside, not daring to move. Maogong cursed his sons a while, spittle flying everywhere, then went back himself, leaning on a bent stick; not long after, he returned carrying a bunch of firewood and set fire to the edge of the field. His fields had long been deprived of water and the crops were very withered; with just one gust of wind the fire crackled into a huge blaze. He cackled raucously as he watched the fire, cursing and stamping his foot: "I can't eat this, you bastards, so help yourselves, help yourselves, hahaha—"

In the blink of an eye, his own grain had turned to ashes.

A few days later, Maogong failed to catch his next breath, and died.

People said that Maogong's ghost didn't scatter. One full moon, after Benyi's family had been cutting millstones, the journey back home from the quarry took them past Maogong's gate. Benyi had put down his carrying pole and taken a few steps up the mountain in search of some wild chicken nests, when he was frightened out of his skin by a sudden great rumbling noise behind him. Practically everyone in the lower village heard the strange noise too, and first children then men hurried over to see what was happening. When they arrived on the scene, everyone was so astounded they just stood, stunned, like petrified chickens, completely unable to believe their eyes: Benyi's two new millstones were locked in battle with a stone mortar in the doorway of Maogong's house—

At this point in the story, Fucha asked me if I knew what a stone mortar was. I said that I'd seen one, it was a tool for threshing ordinary or glutinous rice, shaped a bit like a bowl. I also knew there were two sorts of threshing: hand threshing and foot threshing. Hand threshing was when someone held the threshing pestle and pounded it up and down. Foot threshing was slightly more labor-saving, a bit like a see-saw: someone stood on one end of the seesaw and stamped down so that the pestle on the other end rose very high; once the foot was released, the threshing end pounded down heavily on the stone mortar.

Fucha said *he* didn't believe a stone mortar could fight either, but the old-timers insisted they'd seen it with their own eyes, swearing on their eyes and noses. A stone mortar had pitted itself against the two mill-stones, jumping here and there, breaking out to the right, to the left, causing such thunderous collisions that the very stars seemed to tremble in the heavens, pounding a series of holes in the ground, as if tamping the earth down as densely as it could. At that moment, it seemed that all the birds from all around had flown over to spectate, forming a dense, cawing mass that filled every single tree.

Two or three of the strongest men came forward to intervene, trying to separate the bitterly embattled parties with a rod, but failed to separate them, their faces sweating profusely from the effort. The rod pressed against the stone mortar actually snapped with a crack and the stone mortar jumped up again in fury, lunging crazily at the millstone, while onlookers darted to either side to dodge its grinding. They were entwined in a blinding struggle: if one retreated, one advanced, if one dodged, one blocked; in the end they moved off the terrace, fighting on to the edge of the ditch, to the bridge, before twisting their way up the mountain, the din resounding across the grassland. Stranger still, a kind of yellowish blood actually flowed from these stones onto the ground and onto the blades of grass. When their corpses lay in pieces on the peak, with only the odd fragment stirring, struggling listlessly, blood flowed and burbled from the broken sides of all the pieces, winding its gurgling way down the mountain for half a *li*, before staining yellow a whole embankment of bamboo.

After gathering up the shattered corpses, which had scattered far and wide, people used them to block up a gully in a paddy field. The millstones filled the Three-Peck Field of Benyi's family, the mortar stone filled Maogong's field; thus the dispute was finally settled.

Because the owners' families had been enemies, the old-timers said later, the grievance extended to their stones, who also became enemies. In future, enemies had better be a bit more careful not to lay down their things any old how, any old place.

From this time on, although Benyi would badmouth and curse Maogong from time to time, he never again walked in front of Maogong's door or came to Maogong's field. Maogong's wife and two sons finally joined the cooperative, but Benyi said he didn't want the cooperative to have anything to do with their family ox, and took it away to be sold in town. There was also a plough and a rake that Benyi didn't dare keep either, and he got people to carry them off to the ironworks furnace.

I burst out laughing when I'd heard all this; I didn't believe such a thing had really happened.

"I don't believe it either, they're just spirit-talking (see the entry for

"Spirit"). They've got no culture." Fucha chuckled, then turned over, "but you just relax and go to sleep."

He turned his spine to me, and fell still; I didn't know whether he was asleep or not—he may have been asleep but his ears were still pricked up in all directions. I also kept my ears open, listening to my own breathing, listening to the sound of little water pockets springing out of the muddy porridge in Maogong's field.

*Gruel [漿]: This was a kind of thin porridge, pronounced *gang* in Maqiao dialect (*jiang* in mandarin). As Maqiao was a poor mountain village short of grain, "gruel" was a pretty commonly used word.

One of the "Odes of the small states" in the *Book of Odes* says: "It is better to serve guests wine than gruel," and the word gruel is generally used to refer to a drink one rung below wine, such as corn soaked in water. The biography of Bao Xuan in Chapter Seventy-two of the *Han History* contains the phrase "wine into gruel, meat into bean leaves," referring to those who live in extravagance and luxury, treating wine like gruel, meat like the leaves on beans. From this it becomes clear how the term "gruel" has since come to refer more generally to the food and drink of the poor.

When the Educated Youth first came to Maqiao, they often misheard "eating *gang* (gruel)" as "eating *gan* (dry grain)," thus confusing it with its exact opposite. In fact, the people around here always replaced the j sound with a hard g sound: the word for river (*jiang*), for example, was also pronounced *gang*. So "eating gruel" sometimes sounded like "eating river." When the harvest was late and the pot in every household held nothing but water thickened with only a sprinkling of grain, this phrase fit perfectly well.

*Traitor to the Chinese [漢奸]: Maogong's eldest son, Yanzao, was always the one who did the heavy work in the work team, hauling rotted ox manure, breaking up stones, burning charcoal, and so on. When houses were being built, he cast the earthen bricks, when there were funerals, he carried the coffins; his mouth used to hang open with exhaustion, unable to stay shut, and the blue veins on his calves bulged into great, terrifying nodules. Because of this, he'd always wear long pants, however hot the weather was, patched in layer after layer, to hide his ugly legs.

When I first met him, his old granny was still alive. His old granny was what was known in local legend as a poison woman, someone who hid deadly poisonous powder made from snakes and scorpions in cracks in her nails and tried to kill enemies or strangers by secreting it into their drinks. Such people normally used poison to avenge a grievance or, some said, to shorten other people's lives in order to lengthen their own life spans. People said that Yanzao's granny only became a poison woman after the cooperatives were set up, because of her class hatred for poor and lower-middle peasants, because she wouldn't let things lie with the Communist Party. Benyi's mother had died many years ago, and Benyi had always suspected she'd been poisoned by this devil-woman.

The wind had blown down Yanzao's thatched hut that day, and he entreated the villagers to come and help him mend it. I went along too, to help mix the putty. I caught a glimpse of this famous old woman's benign countenance as she stood over the stove tending the fire; to my amazement, it bore absolutely no resemblance to the picture of villainy painted by popular legend.

The thatch was fixed in a morning. As people were carrying their own tools back home, Yanzao ran up behind them: "Why aren't you staying to eat?" he shouted, "Why are you going without eating? What's the sense in that?"

Having smelled the fragrance of meat float out of the kitchen some time ago, I too felt there was no good reason for everyone to be going. Then I heard Fucha say that people not only wouldn't eat at his home, they wouldn't even dare touch the food bowls there. Everyone knew there was a poison woman in the family.

I moistened my lips, and slipped off home with quickened steps.

A short while later, Yanzao came pounding on the doors of houses to beg everyone once more to come and eat; he even pushed open the door of our house. Instantly thumping to his knees, he pounded out three crisp, resonant kowtows. "D'you want me to throw myself into the river? D'you want me to hang myself? Doing things for free, without getting fed, that's never been the way, not since the time of the three great emperors and five lords. You've walked over everyone in the Yanzao household today, I can't go on living, I'll just die here."

Frightened out of our wits, we quickly pulled him to his feet, saying that we'd cooked at home and hadn't planned to eat out. In any case, we hadn't done anything much, it was embarrassing to eat his food, and so on and so forth.

His face was sweating profusely with agitation; despite all this effort, he hadn't changed the mind of one single person, and was now on the verge of tears. "I know, I know, you're all afraid, afraid that old . . ."

"Not at all, not at all, rubbish, total rubbish!"

"Even if you don't trust that old woman, why shouldn't you trust me? D'you want me to cut out my heart, liver, and lungs, chop them into tiny pieces for you to see? Fine, if you're afraid, then don't eat. But right now, my little big brother's rinsing out the pots to cook all over again! If any of you are still worried, just go and watch her cook. This time I won't let that old woman anywhere near . . ."

"Yanzao, why are you so upset?"

"Generous, honorable people, please allow me to live." Saying this, he fell to his knees once more, his head pounding the floor as if he were crushing garlic with a pestle.

One by one, he begged everyone who'd helped; he ended up pounding his forehead so much it bled, and still he hadn't managed to persuade anyone. It was just as he said: he really had thrown out three whole tables of already prepared food, thrown them into a ditch, and made his sister wash rice and borrow meat again to make another three tables—by this point, it was already time to start the afternoon's work. Some time ago, he'd tied up his granny with rope, a long, long way from the cooking area, under a big maple tree in the village, making a public example out of her. Out of curiosity, I went to have a look. The old woman was wearing only one shoe and seemed to be somewhere between sleep and consciousness, her eyes slanted downwards, focused on some spot on the upper face of a stone, her toothless mouth opening and closing, listlessly producing a few indistinct sounds. She'd wet her pants and stank of sourness. A few children watched her from far-off, not without fear.

The tables of food were once more laid on the terrace in front of his house, but still there was no one to be seen. I saw Yanzao's elder sister sitting by the tables, wiping her eyes.

Finally, we Educated Youth were unable to contain our greed—and didn't much believe in evil spirits, in any case. With one of us taking the lead, a few of the lads went and enjoyed a few pieces of beef each. One of them muttered, as his mouth ran with grease, that he hardly knew what the meat tasted like: he didn't care whether he was poisoned or not, he'd quite happily die of overeating.

Probably because of this act of face-giving, Yanzao henceforth felt exceptionally indebted to us. We practically never chopped our own firewood—he'd always carry it over before it was needed. He had a unique capacity for carrying heavy loads. As I recall, his back was almost never empty: if there wasn't a carrying pole of rotted manure then there'd be a carrying pole of firewood, or the whole, sprawling mass of a threshing machine. In winter, in summer, his shoulders could never be empty, neither on fine, nor rainy days. It looked strange and awkward if he wasn't carrying something on his shoulders: like a snail without its shell, it just didn't look right. It was like a deformity that made him uneasy, that made his heels slip up when he walked—when he wasn't carrying things he really did stumble along, stubbing his toe so much that the blood throbbed inside it.

If he carried cotton, he carried so much that it covered his entire frame, so much that from a distance it looked like two mounded snowy mountains were moving of their own accord along the road, bobbing up and down as they advanced—very strange.

Once, he and I went to deliver grain, and on the way back home he actually put a big rock in his two empty baskets. He said that if he didn't have a bit of pressure like that, he couldn't walk properly. As soon as the carrying pole was twisted by downwards pressure over his shoulders, it became intimately fused with his body, the swishing movement of every muscle took on a dance rhythm, his step became elastic, and he bounded along the road out of sight, transformed from only a moment before, when ashen-faced he'd been carrying empty baskets, his steps unrhythmic and erratic.

He too was a traitor to the Chinese. It was only later that I found out that, in Maqiao terms, as his father was a traitor to the Chinese, he couldn't escape the label either. This was how he saw matters himself. When we Educated Youth were newly arrived in Maqiao, when we saw how much rotted ox manure he carried, how energetically he worked, we naturally nominated him as a model worker; momentarily aghast, he waved his hands in agitation, "That's awakened, impossible: I'm a traitor to the Chinese!"

The Educated Youth all jumped in fright.

Maqiao people felt that policies from above stipulating that lines should be drawn between enemies and their children were really rather *de trop*. By a similar logic, I expect, after Benyi became Party Branch Secretary and when his wife went to the supply and marketing cooperative to buy meat, the other women would remark with envy, "She's Secretary—who'd dare short-change her?" When Benyi's kids misbehaved at school, the teacher would actually scold them, "Secretary! Stop talking in class! And peeing!"

Yanzao later became a "Dumb-ox"—a mute, in other words. He hadn't been a mute to start with, it was just that he'd never had that much to say for himself. Being a traitor *and* having a poison woman in the family meant he couldn't find a wife, even by the time his forehead was starting to get wrinkles. His elder sister had once tried to trick him, people said, by finding him a blind girl; when the wedding day came, he scowled and refused to enter the house, spending the whole evening hauling pond silt outside the village. The next day, and the day after that . . . still the same. The poor blind girl wept for three nights in the empty bridal chamber. In the end, his elder sister had no choice but to take the blind girl back home and give her a hundred catties of grain as compensation for the retraction of marriage. When his elder sister yelled at him for being so hard-hearted, he just said he was a traitor to the Chinese and he shouldn't bring anyone else down with him.

His elder sister was married in faraway Pingjiang County, but every time she went back home to visit, she saw Yanzao didn't have one good thing to wear, that the cooking pot was always half full of freezing gruel, without a hint of warmth in it. Out of the few dozen catties of unhusked grain allocated to him by the work team, he had to save enough to give his little brother Yanwu, who was in school, to throw into the rice-pot at school; it left his elder sister's eyes continually red with tears. They were so poor they never had extra quilts and every time the elder sister went back home she always squeezed up with her younger brother in bed. One evening, when it was raining hard, the elder sister woke up in the night to discover the foot of the bed was empty, that Yanzao was sitting there, bowed over, not having slept at all, making a sobbing noise in the darkness. His elder sister asked him what was wrong. Yanzao gave no reply, and walked into the kitchen to twist grass rope.

Also sobbing, his elder sister walked into the kitchen and extended a trembling hand, reaching for the hand of her younger brother: if you can't bear it, she said, don't treat me like a member of the family, just treat me like I'm someone you don't know. . . . I want you to know what women taste like.

Her hair was in a mess, her underclothes already undone, as she offered her jade white breasts up to her younger brother's stunned gaze. "Take me, it's not your fault."

He whipped his hand back and retreated a step.

"It's not your fault." His elder sister's hand moved down to her own trouser string, "We don't count as human anyway."

He fled as if for his life, his footsteps disappearing into the wind and rain.

Weeping noisily, he ran to his parents' grave. When he returned home early the next morning, his elder sister had already gone, leaving a bowl of steamed sweet potatoes and a few socks, washed and darned, laid out on the bed.

She never returned home again.

It was probably from this time onwards that Yanzao would talk even less, as if his tongue had been cut out. Whatever people told him to do, he did it. If people didn't tell him to do anything, he'd go off and sit squatting to one side; when people stopped issuing orders to him, he'd silently return home. As time went on, he just about became a real mute. At one point he, along with all the other members of the commune, was called up for road-mending work. Discovering on the construction site that his rake had disappeared, he began to search everywhere, his whole face flushed bright red with anxiety. The People's Militiaman who was supervising them asked him suspiciously, what the hell was he doing, darting in and out like that? He could only howl in response.

The People's Militiaman interpreted his incoherent mumbling as a form of trickery, and feeling a thorough investigation was required, pointed his rifle at his chest with a click: "Tell the truth now: what the hell are you up to?"

Sweat beaded on his forehead, his face reddened up to his ears and down to his neck, the muscles in his rigid face pulled half-askew, trembling and quivering like jelly, his eyes widening ever farther with every tremble; his mouth—that mouth on which bystanders were waiting so anxiously—was wide open all this time, but its expansion in vain, as not a single word was spat out.

"Talk!" The bystanders were also sweating with anxiety.

Panting, wheezing, after repeated efforts that locked his faculties and features into a terrifying, tortured, life-and-death struggle, a sound finally erupted forth: "Wah—rake!"

"What rake?"

His eyes bulged, but no further words came out.

"You a mute, hmm?" The Militiaman was getting increasingly irritable.

The muscles in his cheeks erupted into repeated bursts of twitching.

"He's a mute," someone standing nearby told him. "He hasn't got much to say for himself; he said everything he had to say in a previous life."

"Won't talk?" The Militiaman turned back to glance at him. "Say 'Long Live Chairman Mao!'"

Yanzao got so agitated he howled even louder; he raised an index finger, then an arm, and made a gesture of cheering, to convey "Long Live." But the People's Militiaman wouldn't let it go, insisted that he say it. His face took a few punches that day, and his body a few kicks, but still he didn't manage to get this whole sentence out. Finally, at the very last gasp, he shouted out a "Mao."

Seeing that he was a real mute, the People's Militiaman punished him by making him haul another five carrying-poles of earth and left it at that for the time being.

From this time on, Yanzao's status as a mute was formally certified. There was of course nothing bad about being a mute: too much talking saps the strength and catastrophes start at the mouth, so less talk meant fewer arguments, or at least that Benyi no longer suspected him of saying bad, reactionary things behind his back, that he could ease up a bit on his watchfulness. When someone on the work team was needed to spread pesticide, Benyi thought first of him: maybe this spawn of a poison woman wasn't afraid of poison, he said, and now that he was a dumb-ox he wouldn't say anything to anyone, couldn't easily make a fuss, so they could send him off on the job alone.

The mud in the Great Gully was freezing cold, and there'd never used to be many bugs living there. But according to what the locals said, the bugs were all driven out into the open by the noise of the diesel engines; once the engines started up, the rushes on the mountain all swarmed with them. Where there were insects, of course, there'd have to be pesticide spread. When Fucha tried it out for a day, just for novelty's sake, he came back vomiting and foaming at the mouth; face green and legs swollen, he stayed in bed for three days, saying he'd been poisoned, after which no one dared touch the sprayer again. People were afraid that if the landlords and rich peasants were sent to do this unpleasant job, they'd poison the commune's cows, pigs, or cadres with pesticide. Having thought it over several times, Benyi decided Yanzao was the most honest, law-abiding traitor around, that he'd do.

When Yanzao started out, he also suffered from poisoning: his head swelled up like a melon and was kept wrapped up in a piece of cloth all day, however hot the weather got; he looked like a masked bandit, with only his eyes, blinking away, exposed to the outside. As the days went by, he probably slowly acclimatized to the poison and took the scarf off; he wouldn't even wear the mouth and nose scarf the Educated Youth gave him, or wash his hands first at the waterside before going home to eat. The most poisonous pesticide, 1059 or 1605, something like that, was absolutely nothing to him: the hand that had just spread the pesticide could a moment later be wiping his mouth, scratching his ear, grabbing a sweet potato and stuffing it into his mouth, cupping cold water to his mouth—all of which was astounding to onlookers. He had a ceramic bowl that was plastered with pesticide residue, that was specially used to spread pesticide. Once, in the fields, he caught a few mud loaches and chucked them in the bowl; a moment later, the loaches were writhing in agony. He lit a fire to the side of the field, roasted the loaches and gobbled them down one by one, suffering no ill effects whatsoever.

After various discussions about all this, the villagers decided he must have become a poisonous being and the blood flowing through his veins could no longer be human blood.

People also said that from this time on, he no longer needed a mosquito net while sleeping, that all mosquitoes gave him a wide berth: simply touching his finger meant instant death. For a mosquito flying over him, exposure to just one breath of his would send the little creature crashing to the ground, its head spinning. His mouth was more effective than the pesticide sprayer.

*Resentment [冤頭]: Some words undergo a bizarre transformation once they pass into actual usage: their opposite meaning gestates and grows within until it bursts out of them, until they end up annihilating, totally negating themselves. In this latent sense, such words always carry within them their own antonyms—if only people realized it.

They harbor shadows that are very hard to glimpse.

The hidden meaning of "expose," for example, is in fact "hide." At first watching, the *exposure* of sex in a pornographic film can shock and stun viewers. But when films like this become commonplace, a dime a dozen, when they're coming out of your ears, their "exposure" will have no effect at all beyond leaving viewers increasingly numb, unmoved, and indifferent; show them endless pornography and they'll just yawn and yawn. Excessive sexual stimulation results in the exhaustion, even in the total annihilation, of sexual feeling.

Criticism is the hidden meaning of "praise." Criticizing someone is most likely to win that person more sympathy. Criticizing a film is most likely to lower audience expectations before people view it, so when they do watch it, it will make an unexpectedly favorable impression on them. Anyone experienced in the ways of the world can't fail to acknowledge the logic behind linking praise and criticism, can't fail to realize the terrifying potential of what Lu Xun called "being clapped to death." Praise can pile too much glory and honor onto the shoulders of enemies, attract envy, make the general public deliberately faultfinding in a way they might not have been otherwise, vastly increasing the risk of widespread resentment. Praise may also go to an enemy's head, encourage sloppiness, result in unforced errors in the future; his reputation will end up in tatters without anyone else needing to raise a finger in reproach. More often than not, the best way of dealing with enemies is in fact to praise and not criticize.

Then what about "love"? What about Yanzao's love for his grandmother? Did that also have a reverse side lurking behind it? After the feeling of love had ebbed away, had some unexpected residue been left behind?

Yanzao's grandmother was a very peculiar character. She'd sleep during the day, then climb down from her bed in the evening to chop wood and boil tea, sometimes even humming a song or two. Yanzao would help her over to the toilet hut, then she wouldn't relieve herself; then just as Yanzao had helped her to bed, she'd start to reek of piss and shit. She'd yell and shout about wanting to eat garlic bulbs, but when Yanzao had busted a gut to borrow some, she'd yell and shout she wanted to eat crispy rice and push the garlic heads out of her bowl, all over the floor. Then, when she'd eaten up all the crispy rice, she'd announce she'd had nothing to eat at all, that she was so hungry her stomach was stuck to her spine, she'd curse Yanzao for starving her to death, for being a disloyal, unfilial good-for-nothing. For a good many years now, Yanzao had been at his wits' ends over this old woman he looked after, this old woman who'd brought him and his brother up.

Yanzao howled and roared, feeling a particularly distressed kind of love for his grandmother. As soon as he saw her going on some irrational hunger strike or other, he'd whirl around and around in agitation, blue veins bulging out of his forehead, snarling and grimacing, shouting so loud that people in the upper village could hear. The small dining table in his house had already needed repairing several times, each time thumped to pieces by him in a fit of temper. I knew, of course, that this howling and thumping stemmed from his distress. Unfortunately, I also knew that every time he became distressed, his grandmother got more and more used to his distress and valued it less and less, until finally it became valueless to her, or she insensible to it. She'd just roll her eyes and mumble wistfully about Yanzao's younger brother Yanwu. It was indisputably Yanzao who'd made her cloth shoes, but she'd insist it was Yanwu who'd made them. It was indisputably Yanzao who'd carried her on his back to the clinic to see the doctor, but afterwards she'd insist it was Yanwu who'd carried her. No one could set her bizarre recollections straight.

Yanwu was at school in distant parts, studying painting or Chinese medicine; he'd never stayed at home to look after her, hadn't even gone to see her in the hospital when she'd been seriously ill. But whenever he happened to return home for a visit, the old woman would bend his ear enumerating Yanzao's faults one by one; sometimes, her face covered in smiles, she'd delve from out of her pocket a glutinous rice cake that she'd been keeping warm for the last few days, or a couple of shriveled grape-fruits, and surreptitiously press them on him.

Yanwu's great talent was for blaming and criticizing, through express-ing annoyance at his brother's howling, for example, "She's an old woman, old young old young, what's the difference—you've got to treat her like a kid, what's the point in getting mad at her?"

Yanzao silently accepted the criticism.

"When she wants to make a fuss, just let her make a fuss. Her spirit's up, too much *yang* in there, making a fuss'll release her energy, give her back her balance, make her sleep better at night."

A true man of learning, he was, who spoke with so much erudition he barely made sense.

Still no sound from Yanzao.

"I know she gets you down. There's nothing to be done. The more you argue, the more she gets you down, there's still no way out, she's still a person, isn't she? Even if she were just a dog, you couldn't just kill her like that, could you? How could you lay a finger on her?"

He was referring to the time, not long ago, when Yanzao had lashed out at his grandmother's hand—the hand that, at that moment in time, had been stuffing a ball of chicken shit into her mouth. After the event, Yanzao didn't know himself why he'd exploded like that, why his hand had fallen so heavily—after only two blows the old woman's hand had swelled up very badly and a few days later shed a layer of skin. People said Yanzao'd had too much contact with pesticide, that he was poisonous all over, that one blow from him would burn anyone's skin off.

"Her quilt needs washing, it reeks of urine. D'you hear me?" The man of learning said his piece and left. It was like this every time he came home: he'd have a meal, wipe his mouth, dictate a few instructions, then leave. Of course, he'd leave as much money as he could. Money—he had money.

I can't say that Yanwu's chiding and his money weren't a kind of generosity—even if he was reacting from outside and after the fact, generosity was still generosity. But the prerequisite for this generosity was precisely that he'd spent very little time at home, that he'd suffered very little torture at his grandmother's hands. Neither can I say that Yanzao's use of violence wasn't a kind of callousness—even though he was confronted with a masochist who refused to listen to reason, callousness was still callousness. This callousness was the desperation that resulted from the failure of all other methods, from the failure of love. In a situation like this, love and hate swapped places, just as when a negative is developed the black is filtered into white, and the white filtered into black. When confronted with this old poison woman of Maqiao, one person's generosity was filtered into callousness, and one person's callousness was filtered into generosity.

Maqiao people had a special word, *yuantou*, meaning "resentment," also a little like "grievance," which carried the double implication of love and hate. "Resentment" generally developed thus: after one party has lost all lovable qualities, a torpid feeling of love for them is drained of all emotion, becomes no more than an intellectual test of endurance. Imagine what it's like: when love is totally exhausted, burned out, withered away, when one party has squandered it and stamped it flat into the ground, when only the bones and dregs of love are left, full of bitterness, full of day-after-day of torture. This is "resentment." He who loves receives some reward, gets to keep the touching, personal memories that remain after giving out love. But he who resents gets no reward, is left with nothing, he's given out and given out until he's lost everything, including anything that implies or is reminiscent of love. By this stage, he who resents has lost his right to a clear conscience before the judges of morality and ethics.

Yanzao *resented* his grandmother.

In the end, his grandmother died. When they buried her, Yanwu rushed back home to weep in the most heartbroken way, kneeling in front of the coffin, refusing to let other people pull him away. Anyone could see from his crystalline tears that his grief was genuine. But Yanzao was just wooden: if someone wanted him to do something, then he'd do it, his gaze remaining cavernously blank. Perhaps what with all his bathing the old woman, dressing her in her longevity clothes, and buying her coffin over the last few days, he'd just been too busy to have time to cry, and now he had no tears left.

Because of the class status of Yanzao's family, not many people attended the old poison woman's funeral, and no one was asked to sing filial songs. The whole business was desperately bleak. The few relatives on her mother's side who came couldn't stop themselves venting their grievances toward Yanzao: at least Yanwu had some filial piety, they said, at least his eyes were red from crying, he could bring himself to kneel, but that Yanzao had no sense of decency, had treated the old woman badly, so they said, fighting with her every other day; he didn't have a word to say even now, his eyes were dry as a bone. You'd be more upset if a dog had died, wouldn't you? Should be struck by lightning, that rotten old curmudgeon, shouldn't he?

Yanzao remained silent before this sea of voices.

☆**Scarlet Woman** [紅娘子]: There were a lot of snakes in the mountains. Particularly on the evenings of hot days, snakes would burrow out of clumps of grass to enjoy the cool, length after length stretched out across the road, their exquisitely patterned bodies shimmering, presenting a vision of lush greenness to passers-by, their forked tongues shooting out, quivering, glimmering, fresh and bright. At such moments, they weren't in fact necessarily dangerous. Once, as I sleepily returned home late at night, staggering dazedly to the left, then to the right, one momentary lapse of concentration led to me treading barefoot on something fresh, cool, and soft, that had suddenly come to life; before I'd had time to work out what it was, my instincts had me leaping around like a madman, trying to kick both feet above my head. Without pausing for breath, I ran ten or twenty meters, with only one word squeezing its way out of my brain: Snaaaaaake! Mustering all the courage I could, I took a look at my feet but found no wound. When I turned to look, I could see no snake's tail in pursuit.

Around here, the mountain people said, there were "Chessboard snakes": their bodies, when coiled up, happened to look just like a chessboard. There was the "Bellows-wind" too, also known as the Spectacles snake, which moved faster than the wind; when its hiss rang out, even the mountain pigs were frozen in their tracks.

The mountain people also believed that snakes were lecherous. For this reason, snake-catchers always drew the image of a woman on a piece of wood and smeared on rouge—if a woman could be made to spit on it, better still—then stuck it at the side of the road or on the mountain-side for a night; when they went back to look, a snake would very likely be found coiled up, stock-still on the wood, as if dead drunk. The snake-catcher could then at his own leisure entrap his prey in a snake basket. By the same logic, they said, people walking at night who were nervous around snakes were best off carrying a stick or a piece of bamboo. It was said that bamboo was lover to the snake, and snakes, generally speaking, wouldn't dare do anything rash to someone with bamboo in hand.

If they met a venomous snake on the road, poised to attack, the mountain people still had one escape route: shouting "scarlet woman." Shouting this, apparently, confused snakes and gave you enough time to make your getaway. What history lay behind these words, that they had to be spoken and no others? No one had a convincing explanation.

Once, while spreading pesticide on the northern slope, Yanzao was bitten by a snake and ran back, howling. His number was up, he thought, but after running a while he discovered that his feet were neither swollen nor painful, that he was suffering neither cramps nor shivers. He sat down for a while, and managed to stay alive quite successfully, could still drink water, still see the sky, still pick his nose. Puzzled and perplexed, he turned back to look for the sprayer, but gaped, dumbstruck, when he reached the place where he'd left it: a clay-skin snake, a good three feet long, the very one that had just bitten him, lay stiff and dead on the cotton-flower field.

He'd become more poisonous than a snake.

Curious, he ran to the tea plantation to rummage around by the roots of the tea trees, where a good number of clay-skin snakes always lurked. He held out his hand for the snakes to bite, then watched them one by one lie writhing and twitching at his feet, until finally, as if miraculously, they stopped moving.

When dusk came, he tied a great armful of them together with a dead snake and carried them back home; people who spotted him from a distance thought he was strolling back home with a bundle of cut grass.

☆**This Him (*Qu*)** [渠]: Up until this point, whenever I've spoken of Yanzao or other people, in the Chinese version I've always used the word *ta*, meaning "he" or "him." In Maqiao, a close synonym of *ta*, is *qu*. The only difference is that *ta* refers to someone faraway, meaning "that him over there"; *qu* is people you can see, nearby people, meaning "this him over here." Maqiao people, I imagine, must think it ludicrous the way Mandarin-speakers from outside their area don't differentiate between "that him" and "this him."

They use these words in jokes: for example, "Master there (*ta*), Servant here (*qu*)," to ridicule someone who's humble to a person's face, arrogant behind a person's back—in this context, although the *ta* and *qu* refer to the same person, they mean two very different things and couldn't be mixed up.

The ancients also used *qu* as a demonstrative pronoun. *The Record of the Three Kingdoms* contains the phrase: "My son-in-law came yesterday, he (*qu*) must be the thief." The ancients often used this word, which can also mean a small channel or stream, in poetry too: "For a spring (*qu*) to be as pure as this, there must be running water at its source"; "when the mosquito tries to bite an iron ox, there's nowhere he (*qu*) can sink his teeth . . ." (meaning not being able to get a word in edgeways). But these lines of poetry don't illustrate the distance-related meaning of *qu*. Privately, I've always felt that this stubborn fixation on differentiating spatial relationships linguistically perhaps stems purely from the meddlesome nature of Maqiao people—there's no particular need for it.

Until now, neither Mandarin Chinese (felt by those who use it to be quite adequate), nor English, French, Russian, and so on have made this distinction.

Returning to Maqiao all those years later, I felt my ears filling up once more with this *qu*, saw face after face of *qu*, both familiar and unknown to me. I didn't see Yanzao as *qu*. I started to remember how he'd often helped us carry firewood all those years back then, how we were forever fooling around with him, for example how we'd often steal his pesticide when he wasn't looking and mix it with grain to poison rats, ducks, and chickens, or just take it to the supply and marketing cooperative to exchange for flour, making him suffer endless injustices and abuse from the village cadres.

The picture that particularly stuck in my mind was what he looked like when anxious: his face would flood scarlet, the blue veins on his forehead would bulge out extravagantly, he'd flare up at whomsoever he saw, howling even more savagely at us to show his suspicions about our involvement in the conspiracy. But none of this fury prevented him from continuing to carry firewood or other stuff for us later on. All it took was for us to spot his shoulders were looking bereft, smile, gesture, and he'd head, muttering away to himself, toward the heavy object.

I didn't manage to find him. The villagers said someone in Longjia Sands had called him over to help out with some work. There was no need, in fact there was no way I could visit his home. His wife was completely awakened, couldn't even cook; when she was pulling up crops in the fields she'd just pull and pull until she fell over onto her great big behind into the mud—that's the sort of person she was!

But off I still went, off toward that pitch-dark door, while other people snickered away. Hanging on the walls I saw a few gourds holding seeds, along with several terrifying dried snakeskins, like multicolored wall-carpets. As anticipated, the lady of the house looked a complete mess, her cranium bizarrely outsized, as if everything she ate went straight to her head; an eye-catching scar, the cause of which I never discovered, shone on her forehead. She failed to laugh when she was meant to, then would suddenly let out a great guffaw when she shouldn't; I was a little confounded by the air of intimacy she struck up toward me, as if we were great friends of old. She brought me a bowl of tea, but I couldn't touch it; one glance at the greasy ring of black dirt round the edge of the bowl left me nauseated for some time afterwards. The floor inside the house of such a mistress would never be flat, would be more potted and bumpy than anything outside, and any slip in concentration when walking over it might leave you with a twisted ankle. Clothes of all different colors had merged into just one color, a kind of confused, murky grey, piled chaotically on the bed. When the mistress of the house suddenly pulled something out from under there, I almost jumped out of my skin. The thing turned out to have a nose and eyes: it was a child. It never actually made a sound, wasn't frightened by guffaws, remained oblivious to the flies climbing over its face, its eyes kept screwed shut.

I almost wondered if it were dead—had the mistress of the house brought it out just for show?

I hurriedly gave her twenty yuan.

This was rather stingy, of course, and rather hypocritical. I could have produced thirty yuan, forty yuan, fifty yuan, but I didn't. According to my unspoken calculations and assessment, twenty yuan was enough. What could this twenty yuan achieve? It wasn't quite sympathy for Yan-zao; rather, it was payment for my own sense of yearning, a financial exchange for some kind of apology from me, buying back mental peace and contentment, buying back my own high self-esteem. If I imagined that twenty yuan could do all this, then that would be cheap indeed. If I imagined that twenty yuan could in an instant have me humming a ditty, fiddling with my camera, could immediately release me from this sickening, run-down slum, into the sunlight and birdsong, then that would be very cheap indeed. If I thought that twenty yuan could fill my subsequent memories with glorious rose-tinted poetry, then that really would be very cheap indeed.

I put down the bowl of tea, its cover unlifted, and left.

That evening, I stayed in a room in the county government guest house. There was a knock on my door; when I opened it, I could see no trace of anyone in the pitch-darkness outside, but a single, solitary log charged headlong into my room. I finally made out that Yanzao had accompanied it in: he was even thinner than before, the angle of every joint in his body very acute, his whole body the strange juncture of a mass of acute angles. His Adam's apple protruded with particular sharp-ness, as if it were about to decapitate him. When he smiled, his fleshy gums bulged everywhere, revealing more red than white inside his mouth.

His shoulders, as ever, hadn't been empty: they'd carried this log for about ten *li*.

He'd clearly come in pursuit of me. From his gestures, it looked like he wanted to give me this log as a gift, in repayment for my sympathy for and remembrance of him. I expect his home contained nothing of greater value.

He still wasn't a great talker, stammering out a few brief, random, and rather indistinct syllables. Most of the time, he responded to my ques-tions with nods or shakes of the head; this kept the conversation moving along. I later realized that this, still, wasn't the principal obstacle to our conversing; even if he hadn't been a mute, we still wouldn't have found anything to talk about. Apart from elaborating for a time on the weather or on today's harvest, apart from politely refusing this log that I had no way of carrying off with me, I didn't know what to talk about, what would light up his eyes, what would move him to expression beyond a nod or a shake of the head. He fell silent, making me sense yet more acutely the superfluity of words. Lacking for words, I still groped for words: you went to Longjia Sands today, I've been to your home today, I saw Fucha and Zhongqi today too, and so on, like that. I talked this meaningless babble, struggling to piece stretch after stretch of silence into something resembling conversation.

Fortunately, the guestroom had a black-and-white television which was just then showing an old kung-fu film. I put on a show of enthusiasm, repeatedly shifting my gaze onto the boxing high kicks of the kung-fu warriors, young ladies, and old monks, as an excuse for my silence.

Luckily, some snot-nosed kid I didn't know pushed on the door a few times, giving me something to do: I asked his name, moved a stool over for him, chatted with a woman standing behind him about his age and rural family planning.

Something like half an hour passed. In other words, the minimum required duration for reunions and reminiscences had been achieved, and we could part. Half an hour isn't ten minutes, or five. Half an hour isn't too hasty, or gushy, too empty or indifferent; it enabled us to remember each other as friends. In the final analysis, I'd tolerated, endured the nameless, strong, grassy smell Yanzao's body gave off—the kind of smell that a certain kind of bamboo gives off after it's been cut— for this effortfully, unendingly long stretch of time; my mission would soon be accomplished.

He got up to say goodbye, and at my emphatic request once more picked up onto his back that heavy piece of wood, and reiterated his "uh-uh" noise at me, the noise that sounded as if he was about to vomit. There were a lot of things he wanted to say, I'm sure, but everything he said reminded you of vomiting.

As he went out the door, a tear suddenly glimmered in the corner of his eye.

The footsteps in the black night gradually grew distant.

I'd seen that teardrop. Despite the dimness of the light at that moment, that teardrop sank deep into my memory, so deep that I had no way of wiping it away with a blink of the eyelids. It had gleamed gold. When I quietly released my breath, when I relaxed my face from its frozen smile, I was unable to forget it. I had no sense of release. As I watched the kung-fu movie on the television, I couldn't forget it. As I ran a bowl of hot water for washing my feet, I couldn't forget it. As I squeezed onto the long-distance bus and yelled at a big fat man in front of me, I couldn't forget it. When buying the newspaper, I couldn't forget it. While going to the food market, umbrella in hand, and breathing in fishy smells, I couldn't forget it. While under gentle but unremitting pressure from two members of the intellectual elite to edit with them teaching materials on traffic regulation and go to the Public Security Bureau to buy the head of traffic's obligatory distribution rights, I couldn't forget it. When getting out of bed, I couldn't forget it.

The footsteps had disappeared into the night.

I knew this teardrop came from somewhere very distant. Distant people, separated by time and space, are often filtered in our memories into something cherished, touching, beautiful, become multicolored hallucinations in the imaginings of our souls. Once they come near, once they turn into a *qu*, a this him, standing before you, then everything changes completely. They may well morph into a hazy, uninteresting strangeness, swathed in layer upon layer of totally different experiences, interests, and types of discourse, swathed so tightly, so immovably that no breath of air can break in, a strangeness with nothing to say to me—just as I, perhaps, am totally different in their eyes, am totally unrelated to their memories.

I was looking for *ta*, that him, but could only find *qu*, this him.

I had to get away from this him, but I couldn't forget that him.

The clear distinction in Maqiao language between *ta* and *qu* highlights the great difference that exists between near and far, between fact and description, between fact at a distance and actual fact itself. That evening I saw very clearly that between these two words, as that strangely conjoined mass of acute angles, as that wood-bearing *qu* strode off to become *ta*, a silent teardrop gleamed.

***Confucian** [道學]: I gave Yanzao's wife twenty yuan. She was overjoyed to receive it, and, of course, immediately began spewing out politenesses:

"Yanzao often talks about you all."

"How come you're so Confucian?"

And so on.

Confucian, in Maqiao dialect, referred to a sense of etiquette, of morals, to lofty intellect, to a slightly wordy seriousness. Generally speaking, this word carried no pejorative connotations.

But when you start thinking about how much hypocrisy has been dressed up over the years in the cloak of Confucian orthodoxy, it wasn't a word that made you feel too comfortable. What seemed to be philanthropy—that twenty yuan I just mentioned, for example—stemmed not from a deep sincerity, nor from natural instinct, but merely from cultural indoctrination. This is inevitably a rather depressing thought.

Beyond the framework of "Confucianism," can the sympathy and affection of genuine feeling exist between humans? Did Maqiao people replace "good," "decent," "warm-hearted," and other close synonyms with "Confucian" because they couldn't rid themselves of grave doubts over human nature? What feelings of fear or shame might these doubts produce in alms-givers?

*Yellowskin [黃皮]: "Yellowskin" was a dog, an incredibly ordinary dog who lacked any other characteristics from which we could devise a name for it. No one knew where it came from and it seemed to have no owner. Because the Educated Youth had rather more grain to eat than other households, thanks to parental supplements, the Educated Youth's cooking pot gave off more appetizing smells. They hadn't managed totally to shake off wasteful habits, and dirty rice or spoiled vegetables would be flicked carelessly onto the ground or into the ditch. As day after day Yellowskin fed royally, it seemed to set down roots here, its ever-hopeful gaze fixed permanently on our bowls.

It also got to know the voices of the Educated Youth. If you wanted to call it from far off, or set it onto some target, you had to talk in the Changsha city dialect. If you used Maqiao dialect, it'd gaze to left, to right, in front and behind, before it made any kind of a move. Maqiao people were furious when they discovered this.

It'd even gotten to know the sound of our breathing and footsteps. Sometimes we'd go out in the evening, to pay visits in nearby villages or to the commune to make a phone call; by the time we returned to the village the night would already be well advanced. We'd climb up over Tianzi Peak, with Maqiao down below, sunk into the gently flickering, hazy blue moonlight, still at least another five or six *li* away from us. And then, without us needing to say anything, still less to whistle, there'd be a movement in faraway Maqiao, a sound of breakneck pattering would rise up from somewhere deep within the moonlight, skirting along the twisted path, closer and closer, faster and faster until it finally loomed into a silent black shadow that threw itself at our sleeves or collars in an expression of welcome.

It was like this every time. Yellowskin could catch and distinguish any sound from more than five or six *li* away, sparing no effort in its mad dash to meet us, always providing a source of warmth for us nocturnal travelers, offering the embrace of an advance party from home.

I don't know how it managed to survive after we left Maqiao. I only remember that after Uncle Luo was bitten by a mad dog, the commune launched a huge dog-catching campaign. Benyi said Yellowskin was the most vicious dog of all, the one most needing to be destroyed, and took action with a rifle himself, but failed to hit his target even with three shots. Left with a bleeding back leg, Yellowskin scurried off yowling into the mountains.

At nighttime, we'd hear a familiar cry, a dog barking on the hillside near the house, calling for nights on end. Probably it found it all very puzzling: it could hear our footsteps from far off on the horizon, so why couldn't we hear its nearby cries for help?

At that time, we were busy looking for jobs to take us away from Maqiao and paid no attention. We didn't even notice when its cries stopped.

When I revisited Maqiao, however many years later it was, I did actually recognize it, recognized its three-legged limp. It threw a completely expressionless look at me, closed its eyes once more and went back to sleep at the foot of a wall. It was old and scrawny, able to do nothing but sleep for more than half the time; neither could it understand Changsha dialect. When I extended a hand to stroke its head, it twitched with a violent start, then unceremoniously turned its head to take a great bite; it didn't really bite, of course, just clamped its teeth heavily around my hand, to express menace and hatred.

This taciturn dog took another look at me, then went off, its head hanging.

☆**Streetsickness** [晕街]: Although standard Mandarin has words like "seasick," "carsick," and "airsick," it doesn't have Maqiao's "streetsick." Streetsickness was an illness with symptoms similar to seasickness, but which struck sufferers instead on city streets, causing greenness of face, blurred eyesight and hearing, loss of appetite, insomnia, absent-mindedness, apathy, weakness, shortness of breath, fever, irregular pulse, sickness and diarrhoea, and so on; female sufferers would tend to get irregular periods and run out of breast milk after giving birth. A whole swathe of quacks in Maqiao had special decoction prescriptions for curing streetsickness, including wolfberry, tuber of gastridia, walnuts, all manner of things.

So although Maqiao people would visit nearby Changle, they very seldom spent the night there, even less lived there for any length of time. The year Guangfu from the upper village went to study in the county seat, he was seriously streetsick after a month or so, lost an enormous amount of weight, and returned to the mountains on the brink of death. Terrible, terrible, he said, the city's no place for humans! That he later read for a diploma and managed to feed himself by his teaching job in the city constituted a feat that, in Maqiao eyes, was no less than miraculous. His experience of dealing with streetsickness had taught him one thing: to eat more pickles. Only with the help of two big jars of good pickles and often going barefoot did he manage to stick it out in the city for ten or so years.

Streetsickness was a frequent cause of disagreement between me and Maqiao people. This wasn't a real illness, I suspected, or it was at least a deeply misunderstood illness. The city didn't rock like cars, boats, and planes; there was, at worst, more smell of coal smoke, of gasoline, more chlorine in the tap water and more noise than in the countryside—hardly enough to make anyone ill. In fact, there were millions of city people who'd managed to escape this illness. After I left Maqiao, I read a few journals which increased my suspicion that streetsickness amounted to nothing more than a particular form of psychological suggestibility, rather like hypnosis. Providing you're psychologically suggestible, when you hear someone say sleep, then quite possibly you will really go to sleep; when you hear someone say ghosts and goblins, then you'll probably see them. By the same logic, someone who's received years of education in the principles of class struggle and identification of enemies will probably see enemies everywhere in life—then once his forecast of enmity has incurred hostility, affront, and even retaliation in kind from others, this state of actual enmity will continue to affirm his expectations in fact, giving him even more grounds for his feelings of enmity.

This range of examples has revealed a further range of facts; or rather, not facts in a strict sense, but second-degree facts, facts that are linguistically manufactured or regenerated.

Dogs have no language, and so dogs are never streetsick. Once humans become linguistic beings, they attain possibilities that other animals lack completely—they can harness the magical powers of language; language becomes prophecy, a mass hysteria that confuses true and false, and that establishes fictions, manufacturing one factual miracle after another. After I'd thought of this, I conducted an experiment using my daughter. I took her on a car journey, having pronounced beforehand that she wouldn't get carsick; and, as predicted, she was perfectly happy for the whole journey, didn't feel a trace of discomfort. The next time we traveled by car, I predicted she *would* get carsick; as a result, she became incredibly anxious, unable to sit still, until in the end her face went ashen, her brow creased over, and she leaned onto me, half-sick before the car had even started moving. I can't claim my experiment has been exhaustively tested, but it serves as proof that language isn't something to be sneezed at, it's a dangerous thing we need to defend ourselves against and handle with respect. Language is a kind of incantation, a dictionary is a kind of Pandora's Box capable of releasing a hundred thousand spirits and demons—just as the inventor of the word "streetsick-ness," someone I don't know, manufactured the physiology peculiar to generation after generation of Maqiao people and their long-held aver-sion to the city.

And what about "revolution," "knowledge," "hometown," "director," "labor reform criminal," "god," "generation gap"? What have *these* words already manufactured? What else will they manufacture?

Maqiao people wouldn't accept any of this.

I later learned that Benyi missed out on a job with the state because of his streetsickness. When he returned from the Korean War, he looked after the horses in the prefectural commission and could very likely have become a cadre later on; a glorious future stretched out before him. But, just like other Maqiao people, he felt that life in the city was no life at all. You hardly ever saw ginger salted bean tea, heard no sound of flowing water under the starry sky on summer nights, there was no roasting of knees and crotch by the fireplace. . . . He had difficulty making his Maqiao dialect understood. Neither could he get up as early as city people. His colleagues were constantly snickering at his forgetting to button up his fly. He couldn't get used to calling the toilet hut "lavatory," or whatever it was, nor to differentiating between men's and women's toilets.

He did learn some of his colleagues' habits, using a toothbrush, using a fountain pen, for example, even messing about at basketball. The first time he played, he ran around so much his face streamed with sweat, and he didn't even manage one touch of the ball. The second time, when someone on the opposite team had grabbed the ball and was about to score a basket, he suddenly cried out: "Stop—." All eyes turned to him, no one knowing what had happened. Slowly, unhurriedly, he left the court, picked a booger, then returned to the court, waving at the players as if nothing had happened: "Slow down, slow down, easy there."

He didn't know why the people on the court burst out laughing and perceived some malice in the laughter. What was wrong with him pick-ing his nose?

On hot summer days, it was much hotter and drier on the streets than in the countryside—mercilessly hot. Roaming the streets at night, he spotted some girl students run past in front of him, wearing really *low* clothes, shorts that revealed their thighs and legs. He also saw row upon row of bamboo beds in the shade of trees, on which unknown women lay fanning themselves and sleeping. A smell reminiscent of cooked meat floated from their chins, bare feet, the tufts of hair in their armpits or the rounds of snow-white skin accidentally exposed by their collars.

His whole body burned, his breathing quickened, his head was swaddled in insupportable agonies—it had to be streetsickness. He tried rubbing in half a jar of balm, to no effect; he had someone pare a few bright red pimples off his back, but his brain was still fried, bubbles still foaming out of his mouth. Hands in sleeves, he took a few deeply discontented turns through the streets and back, then kicked a rush basket about ten feet:

"I'm off!"

A few days later, he came back from the countryside, his fire somewhat cooled, his face covered in smiles. He took out a *baba* cake from the mountains and divided it amongst his colleagues to give them a taste of something new.

What had happened was a *ligelang* of his in Zhangjia District, a widow twelve years older than him, as big as a bucket, had quelled his fires—and then some.

The prefectural commission was a good two days' journey from Maqiao and he couldn't often go back to cool his humors. He reported to his senior officer that he had streetsickness, that everyone from Maqiao got this illness, that it stopped them enjoying the good life. He hoped he could return to the mountains to work on his two *mu* of paddy fields. The senior officer just thought he wasn't happy looking after horses and changed his job for him, making him custodian at the Public Security Station. In the eyes of his colleagues, he was a little unappreciative of this favor from his superior, as on the second day he reported for duty he was actually rude to the department chief's wife. At the time in question, the wife had been examining a sweater on the bed, her buttocks sticking up very high as her hands gripped the sides of the bed. Rather pleased by this, Benyi gave those arresting buttocks a pat: "What're you looking at?"

The astounded woman went bright red and started to yell at him: "Where did you crawl out from, you filthy turtle's egg? What d'you think you're doing?"

"Why're you laying into me like that?" He asked a secretary standing by: "Why doesn't someone wash her mouth out? All I did was have a little pat . . ."

"Still full of it! Shameless!"

"What did I say?"

As soon as he got upset, Benyi started to talk in Maqiao dialect; he could talk till he was blue in the face and still no one would be able to understand him. But he saw that filthy woman move off to cower in a corner and heard her clearly, distinctly enunciate one word:

"Bumpkin!"

Afterwards, the leader came looking for Benyi to have a word. Benyi had no idea what the leader could possibly have to talk to him about. How absurd—did this count as a mistake? Was this taking liberties? All he'd done was pat with his hand, he could pat where he wanted, in his village whose buttocks couldn't he pat? But he controlled himself, didn't wrangle with the leader.

The leader declared he wanted him to examine the roots of his own criminally erroneous thinking.

"There are no roots, I'm just streetsick. Once I get onto those streets, my fires rise, my scalp hurts, when I wake up every morning it's like I've been beaten upside the head."

"What're you talking about?"

"I said, I'm streetsick."

"What d'you mean, streetsick?"

The leader wasn't from Maqiao and didn't understand what street-sickness was, neither did he believe Benyi's explanations and snapped back that Benyi was stalling him with gibberish. But this cloud's silver lining brought Benyi great joy: that one pat absolved him from further punishment, lost him his commission and meant he could go back home! From now on, every day he could drink ginger salted bean tea, every day he could sleep in! When he received the order to return to the countryside, he had a very satisfactory yell at his wife, then went alone to the tavern to wolf down a bowl of shredded pork noodles and three ounces of wine.

Years later, on a visit to the county seat to attend a cadre meeting, he bumped into a certain Hu, one of his own old colleagues from the prefectural commission, a junior reporter in days gone by. This Hu was now an official who'd discussed at the meeting "the three crux issues," "the four links," and "the five implementations," all of which were completely lost on Benyi. Hu's way of smoking, of arranging his hair up and to the right, of gargling after meals and peeling his apples with a small knife all seemed very alien to Benyi, and filled him with amazement and envy. He felt all at sea in the guestroom at the hostel where his old colleague lodged, unable to look at the bright electric lamp with his eyes open.

"Hey, you were unlucky, you know, way back then, they shouldn't have punished you so hard for such a small thing." Hu mused on the past in the light of the present, passing him an apple he'd already peeled.

" 'Snot important, not important at all."

His old colleague heaved a sigh: "You're no good now, your cultural level's too low, it wouldn't be right for you to come back on the team. D'you have kids?"

"A boy and a girl."

"Good, good; how's the harvest?"

" 'Bout the same as you, still got food in the pot."

"Good, good; are your folks still alive?"

"Been sent up to the yellow earth commune work team in the sky."

"You still like your little joke, I see. Where's your wife from?"

"She's from Changle, she's nice enough, bit of a temper though."

"Good, good—good to have a bit of a temper."

Benyi didn't know what this "good, good" was supposed to mean; after these careful inquiries into his situation, he thought Hu was going to arrange something for him, do him some favor, but he never heard anything about it in the end. That was a happy evening, though. He was grateful to his old colleague for not having forgotten him, for being polite to him still, for giving him ten catties' worth of grain coupons. Thinking back to the good, round rump of that section chief's wife all those years back still sent him off on a happy spirit journey. The day the meeting broke up, his old colleague wanted to keep him there for another evening. Benyi wouldn't agree. He said he was getting on now, that his streetsickness was even worse, that he'd better go back; his old colleague wanted to send him back on his way in his jeep, but still Benyi waved his hands in refusal. He was afraid of the smell of gasoline, he said, if ever his path took him by a gas station, he usually had to make a long, twisty detour; there was no way he could sit in a car. A cadre standing nearby affirmed that he wasn't just being polite, that a lot of people from round Maqiao were afraid of gasoline and would rather walk than go by car. The County Automobile Transportation Company had, not long ago, extended the long-distance route to Longjia Bay, intending to make life more convenient for the masses, but since, contrary to all expectations, barely a handful of people had taken the bus in the past month, they'd had to cancel the regular bus service.

Only then did Old Hu believe him, waving as he watched Benyi's silhouette set off down the road.

☆**Colored Tea** [顏茶]: When Benyi was looking after the horses at the prefectural commission, city tea was the thing he found hardest to swallow. Normally, Maqiao people drank ginger tea, also known as pounded tea. Using a tiny bone pestle and mortar, they pounded chopped ginger, added salt, then poured on boiling water from a hanging kettle until it was brewed. The fairly affluent would use a copper kettle rather than a ceramic kettle, always polished till it dazzled with an extraordinary metallic gleam. Housewives put flavorings such as beans and sesame seeds into iron pots and stuck them in amongst the wood fire to roast. None of them was afraid of getting burned, and while firewood was burning under the cooking range, they'd often grab hold of the iron pot with their bare fingers to give it a shake, to prevent the flavoring ingredients inside from getting scorched. The rustling of the shaking, the exploding of the beans, and the cracking of the sesame seeds soon released a piping hot fragrance that coaxed smiles from the faces of guests.

Red dates and eggs could also be added, to make even grander sorts of tea.

Benyi could never understand why it was that city people, who weren't short of cash, insisted on drinking colored tea, tea with no spices in it, the lowest grade of tea. Colored tea wasn't freshly boiled, it was usually heated up in a big pan and stored in a big pot, one batch lasting two or three days, its only function being to quench thirst. Often enough, tea leaves weren't used for colored tea; instead, it was boiled up out of a few tea-tree twigs till it was as dark as soy sauce. Maybe this was where the name "colored tea" came from.

How could you fail to laugh at, to pity city people who drank only this and not pounded tea?

*Barbarian Parts [夷邊]: Around here, the dialect changes three times every ten *li*. People from Changle all call any faraway place "over there," people from Shuanglong all say "over the way," and people from Dongluodong all say "over to the west"; but Maqiao people say "barbarian parts," whether they're talking about Pingjiang County, Changsha, Wuhan, or America. Whether they're cotton-pickers, hide-trappers, or sent-down youth and cadres, they're all people from "barbarian parts." The Cultural Revolution, fighting in Indochina, Benyi looking after horses in the prefectural commission—all these events took place in "barbarian parts." I reckon they must have always felt they were in the center, must always have had a deep sense of self-satisfaction and confidence. What justification did they have for regarding these places outside their own poor village as "barbarian"?

This word "barbarian" was used by the ancient people of the central plains to describe the small, weak, surrounding races. The Chinese character for this word combines the characters for "bow" [弓] and "people" [人]: [夷]. What justification did Maqiao people have for believing that the inhabitants of those flourishing, developed cities that lay beyond the horizon still lived by hunting? Or that they were tribes who hadn't yet mastered agricultural techniques?

A professor of cultural anthropology told me that in ancient China, among the hundreds of disputing philosophies of the Warring States period (770–221 b.c.), only one tiny school of thought contradicted the belief that China was the center of the world: the School of Logicians from the Spring and Autumn period (777–476 b.c.). Finding the ideas of this school rather hard to stomach, some thinkers later expressed doubts over their nationality: their names, such as "Gongsun Longzi," sounded rather odd, very much like the kind of name that would be given to a foreign student or visiting scholar in China. When translating the oracle bones, the modern poet Guo Moruo came to believe China's Ten Heavenly Stems and Twelve Terrestrial Branches revealed an influence from Babylonian culture. Ling Chunsheng also conjectured that the tribe of the "Queen Mother of the West" written of in China's ancient historical annals was just a translation of the Babylonian word *Siwan* (moon spirit), thus inferring that foreign culture had flowed into China long before the Silk Road, and that the sources of ancient Chinese culture were perhaps very complex. All this increased people's suspicions about the origins of the Logicians. Of course, with an enormous entity such as Chinese culture, even if the disciples of Gongsun Longzi really were a group of foreign scholars, their voices were still very feeble and they never managed to shake the confidence of the Chinese race in its belief that it inhabited the "Middle Kingdom"; it would have been pretty difficult to weaken the Chinese sense of cultural complacency. This use of the word "barbarian" in Maqiao clearly displayed its ancient Chinese pedigree, containing within it contempt for and dismissal of anything that hailed from distant parts. Maqiao's forefathers never gave a moment's thought to the heartfelt warnings of Gongsun Longzi, and this obduracy has survived in its language up until the present day.

*Speech Rights [話份]: Benyi said that people in the provincial capital didn't drink pounded tea, didn't know how to weave cloth shoes, that many families—imagine how pitiful!—hadn't enough cloth for pants and wore shorts no bigger than a palm, like the girdle that women wore on horseback, pulled in agonizingly tight at the crotch. Because of this, Maqiao people brimmed over with sympathy for city people and whenever they saw us Educated Youth about to return to the city, they'd always be urging us to buy more local cloth to take back and make up a few pairs of pants for our parents.

Thinking this very funny, we told them there was no shortage of cloth in the cities, and if shorts were made on the small side, it was to fit better, to look good, or for convenience when playing sports.

Maqiao people just blinked and looked doubtful.

As time went by, we discovered that it didn't matter what we said, that we couldn't dismiss Benyi's rumors as false—because we had no speech rights.

There isn't really a close synonym for "speech rights" in standard Mandarin, but it was a word of particular importance in the Maqiao vocabulary, signifying linguistic power, or in other words the right to claim a very definite portion of the sum total of linguistic clout. Possessors of speech rights bore no particular external marker or status, but everyone was aware of their existence as linguistic leaders, was aware of the force that sprang from their shadowy authority. They had only to open their mouths, or cough, or direct a look, and those standing around would immediately shut their mouths and listen respectfully, not daring to interrupt randomly the flow of words, even if they disagreed. This kind of hush was the most usual manifestation of speech rights, the most tacit, coordinated, voluntary submission to linguistic dictatorship. The words of someone without speech rights, by contrast, were as dust and nothingness: anything they said was wasted breath, no one cared what they said, didn't even care whether they had the chance to speak. Their words were inevitably scattered and lost in a wasteland of indifference, never to gain any response. When such occurrences became frequent, it wasn't easy for someone to keep up their vocal confidence, or even to preserve an ordinary kind of competence in speech production. The way that Yanzao ended up practically a mute represented an extreme example of loss of speech rights.

The topics of conversation covered by the possessors of speech rights were taken up by the general multitude; their expressions, sentence structures, tones of speech, and so on fell into common usage; power was constituted in this linguistic diffusion, was realized and affirmed by these processes of linguistic expansion and outward radiation. The term "speech rights" exposes the linguistic basis of power. A mature governing regime or a powerful faction will always have its own powerful linguistic system, is always accompanied by a series of official documents, meetings, ceremonies, lecturers, key texts, memorials, theories, propaganda slogans, works of art, even new place-names or new reign titles, thus acquiring and establishing its own speech rights throughout all society. Power sources that fail to acquire their own speech rights are the rabble who follow those with wealth or might, bandits who manage to cut down the government troops a few times on their progress toward the capital city: even if they briefly gain the upper hand, their success is inevitably short-lived.

This point is neatly illustrated by the great stock the holders of power set by documents and meetings. Documents and meetings are both the key to safeguarding power and the best way of reinforcing speech rights. Mountains of paperwork and oceans of meetings are a fundamental or integral part of, and genuine source of excitement within, the bureaucratic way of life. Even if meetings are river upon river of empty talk, even if they haven't the slightest real use, most bureaucrats still derive a basic level of enjoyment from them. The reason is very simple: it's only at these moments that the chairman's podium and the mats of the listening masses will be placed in position, that hierarchies will be clearly demarcated, giving people a clear consciousness of the existence (or lack thereof) and degree (large or small) of their own speech rights. Only here do the speech rights of those with power and influence, on passing through the ears of the masses, through notebooks, megaphones, and so on, enjoy support from coercive forms of dissemination and broadcasting. Only in this kind of an environment do those with power and influence, immersed in the language with which they themselves are familiar, become aware that their power is receiving the warm, moist, nurturing, nourishing, safeguarding protection of language.

All this is often far more important than the actual aims of the meeting.

And by the same basic principle, those with power and influence are filled with a natural sense of vigilance and animosity toward language they are not themselves used to or familiar with. During the Cultural Revolution, Marx and Lu Xun enjoyed the highest respect in China, became the only two out of a few last, great figures who could still be found in the empty, deserted bookshops. And even so, reading Marx and Lu Xun then was still extremely dangerous. A book of Marx's that I had in the countryside nearly became proof of my "reactionary" crimes— "That Educated Youth's reading a book by Marx," the commune cadre said, "not a book by Chairman Mao! What on earth is he thinking? What on earth is he feeling?"

I realized that the commune cadres neither meant nor dared to oppose Marx; neither did they know what that book by Marx (*The Eighteenth Brumaire of Louis Bonaparte*) said, whether it subverted their controls over forestation or family planning or evening out resources. No, they had no idea about all this, and neither did they much care. They glared and raged at any language they didn't understand very well, feeling their speech rights implicitly challenged and threatened.

Throughout the twentieth century, as modernism broadened its influence, abstract painting, absurdist theater, stream-of-consciousness novels, and surrealist poetry disrupted the status quo, bringing antiorthodox cultural phenomena such as hippies, feminism, rock music, and the like in their wake. Interestingly, as these new phenomena emerged, almost every single one was viewed as a sinister political conspiracy. Bourgeois newspapers attacked Picasso's abstract paintings as "evil Soviet trickery aimed at the downfall of Western democratic society," as "propaganda for Bolshevik ideology," while Elvis Presley and John Lennon, the representative member of the Beatles, were suspected by churches and governments alike of being "underground spies for the Communist Party," of aiming to "corrupt the younger generation, to destroy them before the battle with communism had begun"—their music was continually prohibited on US army bases in Europe. All Red regimes, meanwhile, do pretty much the same thing, and over the last few decades all modern art, whether high or low, has been officially denounced, defined in official documents and university textbooks as the "avant-garde of peaceful evolution," as "the declining and degenerate ideology of the Western bourgeoisie," as "spiritual toxins aimed at poisoning youth," and so on.

These reactions represent, of course, a defensive excess. This fact was later gradually recognized by both sides, which, to greater or lesser degrees, relaxed their levels of surveillance, even became willing to make use of the expressive power of these various new cultural forms for their own purposes, using rock music to praise Yanan (Mao's revolutionary center in Northwest China) or Nanniwan (a barren area of Northwest China where the Communist army struggled for self-sufficiency), for example; or using abstract paintings to promote the export of clothes.

Of course, it would be overly ingenuous to regard these reactions merely as forms of defensive excess. Any unfamiliar form of language, in fact, is an uncontrollable form of language, and hence an uncontrollable form of power. Regardless of its external political markers, it will exercize a real centrifugal force, creating obstructions and interruptions within information channels, resulting, to varying degrees, in the weakening, in the dissolution of the speech rights of power-holders.

Maqiao people, it seemed, had achieved a penetrating understanding of power-holding, had seen through it all a long time ago, in summarizing power thus as speech rights, as talking.

Let's see who in Maqiao had speech rights:

1. Women didn't generally have speech rights. They were used to not interrupting when men were speaking and just stayed on the sidelines, breast-feeding a child or stitching shoe soles. The

cadres never asked them to join in the big Village Meetings of the People.

2. Young people didn't have speech rights. From a very young age, they got used to hearing age-old admonitions such as "children listen as grown-ups talk," and would always let older people have their say first. Even if they disagreed or, more often than not, muttered behind their backs, it would have been an unthinkable heresy to talk back to their faces.

3. Poor families didn't have speech rights. The wealthy could huff and puff, while the poor could only wheeze: feeling they lacked dignity, poor people were usually unwilling to show their faces where there were a lot of people about, and so inevitably missed out on a great many opportunities for talking to others. And there was another custom in Maqiao: those in debt, even if they only owed half a pint of unhusked grain, weren't allowed to take important roles at village weddings and funerals, such as master of ceremonies, master of sacrifices, matron of honor, so as not to bring the host family bad luck. The place nearest the tea cabinet, by the brazier in each household, was the most prominent place to sit and was called the head place; no guest except the creditor could casually sit down there, unless an insult to the host was intended. All these regulations ensured that speaking power was amassed in the wealthy fists of those with lending power.

It appears from the above that speech rights were decided by a combination of factors, such as sex, age, and wealth. Even more important, of course, were political factors—Benyi, as the local Party Secretary, was Maqiao's highest power holder, and whenever he spoke his voice would boom out with gravitas, with solemn pledges, as if he meant what he said, as if no protest would be brooked. As time went on, bellowing became something of a habit with him; his throat would often be worn out, producing more wheeze than voice, but still he'd be blathering all over the place. Even when walking alone, hands behind his back, he couldn't keep his mouth shut and sometimes ended up talking to himself, posing questions he answered himself. "Could beans grow here?" "Go fuck a dragon, the ground's so wet the roots'd go rotten." "If we mixed in some silt that might do the trick." "What're you doing hauling stuff all over the place? If you've got time to haul mud, you'd be better off growing a bit more grain on the hill." "Awakened son of a . . ."

All this, in fact, was a solo performance by him, and him alone. If you ever walked behind him for any length of time, you'd discover that he never shut up, that he argued indefatigably with himself, that he was capable of conducting entire debates single-mouthedly.

People called him "Big Gong Yi" and knew that things would be noisy wherever he went. The commune cadres were all rather deferential toward "Big Gong Yi." At one commune meeting, Benyi rolled up as if he were running the whole show, as usual going off first to poke his nose into the kitchen to check up on the smells being produced. Looking for a cigarette light from the stove, his face immediately fell when he spotted the foot basin, full of nothing but cut-up radish, without a single meat bone in sight: "What's this, then? Where's your feeling for poor and lower-middle peasants! Hmm?" Boiling with rage, he pushed up his sleeves and strode off, ignoring the meeting, straight to the butcher's in the supply and marketing cooperative to ask whether they had any meat. The butcher said the meat had just all been sold out. He lifted up a broadsword: grab me a pig, grab a pig over here, he said, chop chop! Commune regulations only permitted one pig to be killed every day, said the butcher. So, when the commune said we could eat for free from now on, did you believe that too? said Benyi, referring back to one of the unreliable promises made by the Communist state during the Great Leap Forward.

Wanyu, who just happened to be sitting nearby, sniggered: "Goody, goody, count me in for a bowl of pork soup today too."

Benyi glared: "What're you doing, sitting here?"

Wanyu blinked: "Good question, what am I doing sitting here?"

Short-tempered at the best of times, Benyi banged the broadsword: "Look at you, you useless loafer, what're you doing around here, when it's not New Year's or a holiday? You'd better come back with me, and look sharp about it! If you haven't hoed those acres of rape plants on the north hill by the end of today, I'll get the masses to struggle you to death!"

Wanyu wet his pants in terror at the sound of the broadsword and slipped out the door as quickly as he could; but a while later, his shiny scalp timidly poked back in: "You—you . . . what was it you just wanted me to do?"

"You deaf or something? I want you to hoe the rape plants!"

"Got it, got it. Keep your shirt on."

His shiny scalp retreated once more. Benyi finally calmed down and had rolled up a twist of tobacco when he heard a movement behind him; there, as he turned to look, was Wanyu's face again, smiling into contortions, "Sorry, I was in too much of a flap just then to hear right, you wanted me to hoe . . . hoe . . ."

I reckon he must've been so frightened he couldn't hear a single thing properly.

Only when Benyi roared the words RAPE—PLANTS into his ear was he finally rid of him.

After a series of oinks were heard from behind the shop, Benyi's color finally improved somewhat. He loved slaughtering pigs more than anything else and was very expert at it. After another round of oinks, he returned to the stove for a smoke, his face covered in splotches of mud and hands stained with blood. That same broadsword had just cleanly, neatly dispatched the pig. He kept careful watch at the butcher's shop, until it was time to invite a few of the lads from the supply and marketing cooperative to gather around the sizzling-hot cooking range; he ate some pork and drank some pig's blood soup before contentedly wiping his greasy mouth and belching with repleteness.

Despite his nonattendance at the meeting, the commune cadres didn't dare criticize him. When he returned to the hall, all red in the face, the cadres still felt obliged to invite him onto the stage to speak—a sufficient demonstration of the prodigious extent of his speech rights.

"I'm not going to talk for long today, just a couple of points I've got," he said.

This was the routine public announcement with which he prefaced every speech. Whether he in fact spoke on two, or three, four, five, or even more points, whether he produced two or three words or a lengthy disquisition, he would always declare in advance that he only wanted to speak on two points.

He talked and talked, blasting out smells of meat soup, then talked about his past experiences in the Korean War, made reference to his military prowess in fighting American soldiers as evidence that tasks such as irrigation repairs, crop planting, pig raising, and family planning would, could, must be achieved! He was always calling American tanks "tractors." On the 38th Parallel, he said, the earth shook when the American tractors arrived, scared the crap out of you, it did. But the volunteer troops were all heroes, real men: at 300 meters, no one fired, 150 meters, still no one fired, 100 meters, still no one fired, then finally, when the American tractor was right in our faces, one round of fire blew the fucker up!

He looked all around, very pleased with himself.

Once, Commune Head He corrected him: "It's not a tractor, it's called a tank."

He blinked: "Isn't it called tractor? I didn't get much education, I'm illegitimate."

What he meant was he was illiterate, that it wasn't surprising he couldn't distinguish clearly between tanks and tractors. He studied the word tank with some application but by the next meeting, once he'd got through the stressful 300-150-100 meters bit, he slipped as usual into saying tractor.

His confusion about such terms had no effect whatsoever on the respect listeners paid to his comments: "People only die of illness, not of work"; "Great natural disasters, bumper harvest; small natural disasters, small harvests"; "Everyone should work on their thinking, on making progress, on the world"— none of this made much sense, but because they were said by Benyi, they gradually entered into common usage, were passed on. His hearing, too, was rather poor. Once, listening to the commune cadres, he heard "We must grasp the key to the road ahead" as "We must grasp the tree on the road ahead," which was obviously wrong, but since "tree" came straight out of Benyi's mouth, Maqiao people trusted it implicitly and instead laughed at us Educated Youth, saying we had to grasp the "key" to the road ahead—what was that supposed to mean?

*Light the Sky Red [滿天紅]: The 1960s and the 1970s were the decades of "Light the Sky Red." "Light the Sky Red" was a kind of big kettle lamp, with two long kettle spouts sticking out, from which protruded candlewicks as thick as a little finger and that burned cotton or diesel oil, spewing forth rolls of black smoke as they did so. During these decades, one of these lamps would often be hauled on a long bamboo pole to alleviate the heavy darkness when we were breaking in virgin mountain land, sowing grain in the fields, assembling the masses for a meeting, rallying a team for a march. These were decades during which there weren't enough hours of daylight and frenzied activity spilled over into nighttime. The blacksmiths produced batch after best-selling batch of "Light the Sky Red" lamps. Whenever cadres discussed a commune's or a team's revolutionary performance, they'd talk in these terms: "Just look at them, they use up at least ten Light the Sky Reds when they get going!"

When I was sent down to Maqiao, I was just in time for the "demonstrate loyalty" craze. In showing loyalty to the leader, one indispensable daily activity consisted of going to Fucha's living room every evening. Only his room was that bit bigger, big enough to contain the entire production team workforce. One dim Light the Sky Red was hung up too high, leaving the people beneath as no more than hazy black shadows, impossible to make out. If you bumped into someone, you couldn't tell if it was a man or a woman.

After everyone had stood before the portrait of the leader, the cadres issued a chorused order, at which the workforce suddenly emitted an ear-shaking, deafening roar, reciting from memory and in one breath five or six quotations from Chairman Mao. This gave us sent-down youth a real shock. None of us had thought that Maqiao people could memorize so much, and their revolutionary theory left our heads reeling.

After a while, when we discovered that they recited the same ones, just those few, every time, we relaxed.

As the sent-down youth had had some education, they very quickly and easily memorized far more of the leader's quotations and could roar them straight out in one go, keen to outdo the villagers' ferocious zeal. After the battle had been lost, the villagers became rather more subdued; whenever they reached for their cigarettes they'd first ask the sent-down youth if they wanted any; their voices when they recited, too, were rather tired, weak, and lackluster.

After the bellowing was done, it fell to one of the cadres, usually Benyi or Uncle Luo, to give the Chairman Mao on the wall a brief, concise report on that day's agricultural events, after which they'd timidly add: "Sleep well, hey, old man."

Or they'd say: "It snowed today, have you burned more wood, hey, old man?"

Chairman Mao, it seemed, had tacitly given his blessing. Only then would everyone disperse, their hands in their sleeves, bundling one after another out the door into the whistling winter wind.

Once, Zhaoqing lurked at the back taking a nap, and after everyone else had gone, he was left squatting in a corner. Not having noticed either, Fucha's family shut the door and went to sleep. Only when it got to midnight did they hear someone shouting and yelling: you villains, you! D'you want to freeze me to death?

Not knowing whether to laugh or cry, all Fucha could say was, blame the Light the Sky Red for being so low on oil you couldn't see in the dark.

From this it should be clear that after daily study of this kind, everyone was pretty well versed in revolutionary theory. What was rather more particular to Maqiao people, however, was the way they produced some more unusual quotations from Chairman Mao: "Chairman Mao says this year's rape plants are really coming along," for example; "Chairman Mao says we should economize on grain but we can't eat porridge every day"; "Chairman Mao says if landlord elements are dishonest, then we should string 'em up"; "Chairman Mao says Shortie Zhao isn't sticking to family planning, he only talks about quantity not quality of children"; "Chairman Mao says whoever pours water into the pig dung should be investigated and fined a mouthful of grain!" and other such phrases. Even after I made very wide inquiries, no one knew the source of these higher instructions, neither did anyone know who first broadcast such remarks. But people treated them with a deep seriousness and used them endlessly in conversation.

There was nothing strange about this, of course. When I later read up on Chinese literary history, I discovered that Maqiao people had done nothing that several Confucian masters hadn't done earlier. These individuals would insist on "consulting the sages," but in fact would as often as not just fabricate sagelike words as coming from the mouths of Confucius, Laozi, Xunzi, or Mencius to frighten people. Yang Xiong of the Han Dynasty used a great many quotations from Confucius, but when people later came to check them, hardly any were found to be genuine.

*Form [格]: "Form" was a word in common use, close in meaning to words such as "character" and "quality," without being limited to these alone. Whether or not a person had form, or had lost form, was the basic yardstick by which Maqiao people judged others. A person's qualifications, study record, background, position, reputation, authority, courage, insight, ability, wealth, good or bad conduct, even reproductive capability and so on, could all cause his "form" to change. Form and speech rights were linked together in external-internal, cause-effect relations: people with form naturally had speech rights; people with speech rights definitely had form.

Fucha's same-pot uncle Mingqi, widely known as Uncle Mingqi, had studied professional rice, bread, and cake catering in Changle. When the commune had a big meeting, they'd often ask him to make the steamed bread; this gave him great form. Whenever such an opportunity came up, Uncle Mingqi would change to Father Mingqi, and it was not only Mingqi himself who felt he had face, all the villagers in Maqiao felt they had face; if they bumped into people from other villages passing by their village, whether these people knew him or not, Maqiao people would always, consciously and unconsciously, reverentially invoke his name. If the listener's face drew a complete blank, or didn't show any particular interest, Maqiao people's faces would instantly fall and their eyes drip contempt: you don't even know about Father Mingqi? they'd say. If they'd been about to treat you to a cup of hot tea, their hospitality might well turn into a bowl of stone-cold colored tea, simply due to your ignorance or indifference. After Mingqi had finished making the steamed bread and returned home, he liked to take a turn around the village, his hands behind his back, and point out things that didn't please his eye. Even naughty children would be rather awe-struck at the steamed-bread smell that enveloped his body, and meekly hang their heads in silence. Once, a few quiet words from Mingqi intimidated a lad named "Three Ears" out of catching mud loaches: we Educated Youth were amazed to see him simply pick up his bucket and slosh them back in. Three Ears wasn't normally afraid of anything at all. "How come you're so well-behaved today?" I leaned over and whispered in his ear. A look of forebearance on his face, he muttered, as if his nerve had deserted him by the time it reached his mouth: "He's got form, you know, I'm not going to go asking for trouble today."

It was only then that I began to realize, although they were all Maqiao people, they lived very differently, according to whether or not they had form.

Old Uncle Luo had an adopted son who sent him money from barbarian parts—which amounted to sending him form. Otherwise, if he'd only had his age going for him, he'd have had barely enough form for Benyi to give him the time of day.

Zhaoqing couldn't make steamed bread, nor did he have an adopted son who sent him money, but he produced six sons almost without blinking, which gave his form a bit of a boost. When dividing sweet potatoes or beans in the village, the scales controlled by the cadres would always be tipped a bit when it got to his share, as a marker of respect to him.

Of course, some temporary varieties of form could produce comic results. For example, when the Educated Youth nicknamed Master Black returned from the city, he swapped a mountain chicken with Zhongqi for the bottle of Dragon soy sauce he'd brought back. This kind of soy sauce was a brand-name, tribute soy sauce, people said, that was sent every year to Beijing to make Chairman Mao's red braised pork; in the provinces, you had to be at least a county-level magistrate before you'd get a taste of it. When the news broke, Zhongqi enjoyed half a month's form, for half a month his coughs and throat-clearings enjoyed a new depth and authority. But even though he used the soy sauce drop by half-drop, in the end he couldn't withstand the almost daily requests from his neighbors on all sides, the endless visits from the commune cadres and Benyi; as the bottle emptied by the day, his form fell like a boat on subsiding waters, until it sank back to its original level. He begged Master Black to swap him another bottle of Dragon brand soy sauce, this time prepared to pay two mountain chickens. Master Black was full of promises, but he never produced the goods; there was probably something of a premium on tribute soy sauce in the city too.

Zhongqi also thought of asking Father Mingqi, to open up an alternative path to finding Dragon brand soy sauce, to finding form. But Father Mingqi's form was so vast and Zhongqi so overcome by stammering that he failed repeatedly to find an opportunity to sidle up and talk to him. It was round about this time that Mingqi was busy in the commune making steamed buns, and directing all sorts of things in the village. If the team cadres were holding a meeting and saw him come in, they'd make room for him without even thinking about it. Listening to Benyi allocate work, he didn't feel in the least bit superfluous, nodding or shaking his head, expressing approval or disagreement; sometimes he'd interrupt before someone had finished talking, most of what he said totally unrelated to public affairs in Maqiao, related only to how the weather at the moment was too cold and the dough wasn't rising, to the shoddy workmanship at the yeast factory, to how the yeast wasn't working and so on—all steamed-bun-related matters. The team cadres would listen meekly, making an occasional contribution to his discussion of professional catering techniques. If one day he got carried away and held up the cadres for one or two hours, it didn't matter and no one ever asked him to leave—because he had form.

The great pity of the matter was that form easily went to a person's head; in the case of someone like Mingqi, who got form not through his own strengths but through a lucky chance, it was particularly easy to go mad with the success. The fame of his steamed buns spread far and wide, and when there was a big meeting in the county he'd sometimes be called upon to go and do the catering. On whichever occasion it was he went to the city, he met Widow Li, a floor-cleaner at the county government guesthouse, and the two of them became entangled in the course of various encounters. To cut a long story short, the widow had grown up in the city and knew how many beans made five, knew a few tricks in bed; in the meantime, the white steamed buns that Mingqi brought from the kitchens kept hunger at bay for the widow and her son; and so, as time went by, a pact of true love was forged. In the end, Mingqi finished what he'd started, sneaking out to the Li family a whole bag of special batch "Wealth and Power" flour (reserved exclusively for the head of the County Committee) and taking a pig's head with him while he was at it.

When the news got out, Widow Li was stripped of her post as floor-sweeper, and afterwards lived by scavenging rubbish. Mingqi (minus the title "Father") returned dejectedly to Maqiao, never again to enjoy the opportunity of making steamed buns in the county seat or in the commune. His status in the village, moreover, went into dramatic decline: his appearance gradually became more and more wretched, his neck always shrunk down into his hunched shoulders whether it was hot or cold, as if he wanted to bury his face. He was, of course, stripped almost entirely of his speech rights. Whether it was a meeting for cadres or for every member of the commune, it was never his turn to speak. If there was some matter on which everyone had to express an opinion, he would stick his head out in panic, his voice about as loud as the buzz of a fly or mosquito, provoking Benyi to holler: "Speak up! Speak up! It's not like you haven't been fed!"

He was often assigned the hardest, most exhausting work, and his work points were lower than other people's.

Maqiao people hated iron that failed to become steel, they hated Mingqi for his greed and lust, for cutting the whole village off, just like that, from its gleaming portion of glory; it was as if everyone in the village had stolen a bag of flour and a pig's head. So they dealt with him by unwritten rule: they'd hiss "lost form" at him, just the once, driving him into chronic dejection and depression; before we left Maqiao to return to the city, his accumulation of melancholy had turned to illness and his soul had returned to the underworld. This rather brutal process taught me that "form" could also be collectivized. Mingqi's form took on the importance it did precisely because he was such a rare treasure for Maqiao, precisely because it'd become a source of capital shared by all the villagers in Maqiao. His casual throwing away of his form constituted a crime committed against everyone in the village.

Returning to Maqiao many years later, as I walked along the ridges between the fields I heard a child singing a folksong under a tree:

Mingqi bagged a wild bird,
Caught in the act he was,
They took him to Crotch County
Pulled off his pants, ripped his clothes
The police beat his bottom,
If you blow your own trumpet,
Once the trumpet's blown,
You'll be left with a bright red bum . . .

My heart skipped a beat. I'd never imagined that even all those years later Mingqi would still live on in Maqiao, in the folksongs of Maqiao's next generation, that such an immortal oral monument would have been erected to his bag of flour, to his loss of form, to his decline and fall. I expect this monument will be passed on from mouth to mouth, generation to generation in Maqiao, until Benyi, Fucha, or others, and I, and even the child singing under the tree, are no longer in this world.

As long as language still exists, perhaps he will always live on, deep into the future.

*Clout [煞]: Maqiao women's form usually came from men. For women who were already married, if their husband's family had form then they themselves had form, if their husband's family lost form then they themselves lost form; for women who weren't yet married, form was determined mainly by their fathers, after they no longer had a father, their form depended on their elder brothers.

There were, of course, exceptions. One I encountered once at the road-works construction site. A real free-for-all it was there, with laborers from every village come to help out, all fighting for tools, for earth, for rice and vegetables. The whistling winter wind billowed up wave upon wave of scree, muddying the sky and the heavens into a great yellowed expanse. Those hauling earth, tamping the ground, and pulling wheelbarrows were all blown around by the wind like dancers, like a shadow play without sufficient light, the old and young indistinguishable from each other.

There were no women on the construction site and the laborers took a piss or a crap whenever they wanted. I'd just finished shaking off the last couple of drops when I spotted some people who looked like cadres come to measure the earth and draw up lines of lime, among them someone wearing an old army uniform, a cotton cap over the head, a scarf over half the face, at that moment using a bamboo pole to direct two other people to run back and forth pulling the rope. Against interference from wind-noise and the high-pitched loudspeaker, this person was yelling something at someone, but seeing they hadn't heard, threw down the bamboo pole and ran over, hurling down the hillside a big stone that had been lying across the lime. I was pretty impressed by this cadre's show of strength: if it'd been me, I'd have had to call at least one other person over to give me a hand.

As soon as Fucha saw this person, he started to look worried: "What we've done, will it . . . do?" he asked, twisting his hands.

The person stuck the bamboo pole a few times into the land by the landfill area, then took out the pole, measuring how deep it'd gone into the ground. "Still needs tamping down a layer."

Fucha's tongue hung out.

"What about the people Commune Head He asked you to send?" the person asked.

Fucha pointed at me, then at another Educated Youth.

The person walked over and stuck a hand out at us. This was clearly a gesture that came from outside Maqiao; I stood there, stupefied, until I realized this was called shaking hands and we should also stick out our hands.

I was slightly surprised. This person's hand was not as bony and sinewy as I had anticipated, it was even rather soft. I took another look at that face the size of a palm, at its eyes with their extraordinarily big black pupils, which possessed an air of delicate prettiness as they fluttered open and shut, and which struck me as somewhat out of the ordinary.

We followed this person to the command office to help edit a quick report. On the way, we heard people address this person as "Teacher Wan," "Brother Wan," but on the whole this person wouldn't reply, would at most nod in the direction of the speaker, or give a faint smile. "This guy's got top form," my companion Educated Youth muttered to me, not expecting Teacher Wan/Brother Wan, a few meters away, to catch what he said. Wan turned, came to a halt, fixed shiny black eyes on my companion as a silent warning, scoured me with a sharp, knifelike stare, as a punishment to warn me off future transgressions, then steadily walked away.

We hadn't imagined this person's ears would be so sharp, nor that the return fire would be so swift or fierce. This struck us as a bad omen: you had to be extra careful around someone like this.

It wasn't until that afternoon that we discovered this Wan person was actually a woman. When he went off to relieve himself, my companion saw that as Wan took off the cotton cap, a head of long black hair rolled out. My companion was so surprised he didn't even visit the toilet hut but ran straight back to report, holding in his urine. Amazed by this, I also went to have a look and saw that Wan Whoever-it-was, squeezed in among a table of men, really had started out life a baby girl. According to local rules, women didn't eat at the table. As time went on, we got used to this rule, to the way things should look, and we actually found the discovery of a woman's face in front of a dining table surprising, even discomforting, as if someone had rubbed sand in our eyes.

It was only later that I discovered Wan was from Zhangjia Mill. Her full name was Wan Shanhong, and she'd taught in a locally run school for two years but hadn't wanted to stay there, so she returned to the village to study agriculture for two years—she could even plough just like a man. She was a proper high school graduate and a member of the commune youth group propaganda committee; whenever there was anything important to be done in the commune, they'd generally ask her to come and help write or add things up, people said they even wanted to train her to be a successor to someone or other. Because of this, people still respectfully called her "Teacher Wan" or "Propaganda Committee Wan." She didn't like the young men calling her "Brother Wan" but her objection was only one voice against many and popular feeling couldn't be resisted, so as time went by she had to put up with this name. I must admit that Brother Wan without her cap was not half bad looking: she had a good figure and there was a strong line to her jaw, from ear to chin. She walked back and forth through crowds of men like a sharp scythe cutting back and forth through the grass. But she didn't seem to be much of a talker: during a winter spent with us repairing the highway, she did little more than fling instructions at us in her slightly raspy intonation, a few "okays," "no goods," "let's eats"; and when she spoke, her face was as expressive as a papaya.

Strange to say, the brusquer her words, the more authoritative they became, and the harder it was for anyone else to put up any resistance. As Maqiao people would put it, this was called having *sha*, or "clout." *Sha* implied authority or extreme competence, a homonym for the word meaning "kill"; it also meant completion. People with "clout" could be understood as those who had the last word, the ones who had the deciding vote in conversation. Brother Wan's was the only female face with clout that I came across down in the countryside.

In the presence of such clout, any interaction was pretty much no interaction at all; however well you knew her, you still seemed to be separated by 108,000 *li*. If she bumped into us, she acted as if she'd bumped into thin air; the gleam in her black eyes instantly skimmed over the tops of our heads, landing on some unknown spot in the distance. To begin with, we found this hard to get used to: offering an awkward greeting didn't feel right, but neither did offering no greeting at all; as time went on, however, we saw she acted the same toward everyone, so we accepted it as normal and didn't take it to heart. When I mentioned her name to people from Zhangjia Mill I came across, they'd smile: it's not just Maqiao Bow, there's no one even in the same village, the same stockade who's made friends with her, no one can make her out. She lives near us, but it's like she doesn't exist.

So: it seemed she couldn't get close to anyone.

She just represented official business, a concept, a symbol called Brother Wan that lacked any flicker of a smile, of emotion, warmth, or understanding, and so to many people she had an unreal quality; if you shut your eyes and thought about her, she was no more than an illusion, as if there, but not there. Some said she had a complicated past, that she was the illegitimate child of an important official, the seed of a work team leader planted during land reform; ten or so years later, her mother had brought her to the city, wanting to have a blood test and to voice her grievances. This had left her distinguished father with no choice but to keep her in the county seat and send her to high school, secretly providing for her living and education costs. I don't know how much truth there is in this. Some also said that when she'd been making noisy "Cultural Revolution" a few years ago in the county seat, she'd been a famous student leader who'd got to Beijing and Shanghai, who'd carried a rifle and gone to prison, who'd even been taken to a meeting in a car sent by the provincial military organization, who'd had her picture taken with some big cheese from the Central Committee. I don't know how much truth there is in this, either. Others said although there'd been no talk of marriage for Sister Wan even by the time she was twenty-five or twenty-six, in fact she had a long-term boyfriend, a former classmate of hers who'd joined the army. Every year she'd go to Guangdong for a time to see her boyfriend, people said. Unfortunately, the young lad had been misguided enough to join Lin Biao's clique in the 1971 coup d'état; after it failed, he was thrown into prison and for several years no word of him was heard; his family and Brother Wan (who'd never been carried over the threshold) only received news after he'd died from illness in prison. Again, I don't know how much truth there is in this.

To me, she'd forever be the stuff of stories and rumors. Her youth washed away amidst such stories and rumors, gradually acquiring the darkened complexion of middle age.

Once, seeing her walking along the road, some uncouth young men decided to pick on her, to provoke her by singing low songs. Seeing that she was turning a deaf ear, they took revenge with filthy catcalls:

"Hey, why so stuck-up? Reckon you're so chummy with the higher-ups, don't you?"

"What kind of a flower d'you think you are, anyway? You must've been knocked up by that army guy ages ago, broken by that dead devil, or else how'd your tits get that big?"

"Forget her missy-prissy act, I don't believe she doesn't want it. Look at how she walks, bum sticking out up to the sky, isn't she just asking for it?"

A wave of laughter.

She acted as if she hadn't heard.

When Maqiao's Zhaoqing heard about this, he laughed at the lads, said they must've been really woman-crazy to pick on Brother Wan. They didn't even think who she was. D'you think you'd be able to stick (see the entry "Stick(y)") a woman with as much form as that?

His underlying message being that form is a male thing; once a woman's got it, she no longer counts as a woman, or at least no longer counts as a pure woman, and lowness from young men becomes inappropriate. Taking this one step further, form is a kind of scourge that eliminates gender; excessively high form can wound a person, even jeopardize the birth of later generations.

I don't know how much truth lay behind Zhaoqing's comments. But Brother Wan—no, Sister Wan actually—really did preserve her chastity and never married; when I left Maqiao she was still a powerful, lofty, single unit. But she didn't stay on in Maqiao for long: a year or so later her natural father's wife died and he was reinstated in his post, back from the May 7 Cadre School, so he had her recalled to the city.

People said she was sent to a big state-owned factory in Gansu Province.

*Jackal-Fiend[豹猛子]: In the layered folds of Tianzi Peak was hidden a small stockade, called Chazi Bow, to reach which you had to cross a small stream. The water wasn't deep and a few stepping-stones poked out of the surface; with three steps and a couple of jumps, you were across. The stones crouched among the clumps of waterweed, often draped with moss; there was nothing special about them.

I crossed over here several times on my way to Chazi Bow to paint Chairman Mao's quotations or to carry seedlings. Once, my traveling companion asked me if I'd noticed anything different last time I crossed the stream. I paused to think, then said I hadn't. Think again, he said. I thought again, and still said I hadn't. D'you remember a big, long rock in the water? he asked. I couldn't remember, and only his repeated promptings brought back a vague recollection. The last time I'd crossed the stream, there seemed to have been a long rock, probably near a clump of water willow in the middle of the current, that I'd stepped on, even squatted down on to drink a couple of mouthfuls of water. Maybe.

My companion smiled. That wasn't a rock, he said. Oh no. The last time the river was up, a few young oxherders on the mountain had spotted that long rock suddenly stand erect, stir up a murky whirlpool in the stream, then travel downstream with the floodwater—turned out it'd been alive: a jackal-fiend.

A jackal-fiend was a jackal fish, another name for which was jackal mute. Maqiao people said this fish didn't eat plants but other fish; it was the fiercest of all fish, but could also at times be the most stoic: people could tread over it for months on end without it moving.

After this, whenever I saw big rocks or big lumps of wood, I'd always feel a tremor of anxiety or apprehension. I was worried they'd suddenly start writhing, come alive, scurry away. Anything covered in moss might suddenly crack open a cavernous black eye and wink nonchalantly at me.

*Precious [寶氣]: Benyi had a nickname: "Dribbler." It was Zhihuang who picked out this nickname. While working on the construction site, during one mealtime he noticed Benyi's eyeballs bulging, his chopsticks scraping noisily against the side of his bowl, locked in life-and-death chopstick-to-chopstick combat with everyone else's in the plate of meat. In a tone of surprise, Zhihuang suddenly asked: "How come you're dribbling so much?"

Discovering that everyone's gaze was fixed on him, Benyi wiped his mouth a couple of times, "what dribble?" He wiped off a string of saliva, but failed to wipe off the rice grains and drops of oil on his stubble.

Zhihuang pointed at him and laughed, "You dribbled again!"

Everyone else laughed too.

Benyi tugged at his cuff to have another wipe but still didn't manage to wipe himself clean; he muttered something and looked a bit hangdog. By the time he'd picked up his bowl and chopsticks again, he discovered that in the blink of an eye the dish of meat had emptied. He couldn't stop himself peering around at the mouths surrounding him, as if with his own eyes he wanted to track down the whereabouts of those lumps of fat meat, as they sank into those rotten guts.

He cast a somewhat baleful look at Zhihuang afterwards. "Eating is eating, what were you fussing about?"

In general, Benyi wasn't unused to ridicule, he wasn't that good at protecting his own prestige outside public affairs. When confronted with less than respectful comments, sometimes he could only pretend to be deaf—he was actually rather deaf. But his sense of hearing was unusually sharp that day and he was very anxious about face because there were people from outside the village on the construction site: Commune Head He and Sister Wan from Zhangjia Mill. Zhihuang was just being precious, making a big thing of his dribble on an occasion like this.

"Precious" meant stupid; "preciousness" meant stupidity. Zhihuang's preciousness was renowned throughout all Maqiao. For example, he didn't understand you had to give up your seat to cadres, he didn't understand how to fake when tamping down earth, it took him a very long time to figure out that women have periods every month. That he used to beat his wife so violently showed how precious he was. His wife later divorced him and went back to her family home in Pingjiang, but from time to time he'd send the dream-woman food and clothing—this showed he was even more precious. The three quarries on Tianzi Peak were gouged out by him, one by one, hammer blow by hammer blow. You could've built a mountain out of all the rocks he'd hammered out, and people bought them, hauled them away, used them who knows where. Even so, as soon as his thoughts began to wander, he'd start viewing all these rocks as his own property. A lot of people just couldn't make him come to his senses, couldn't do anything about how precious he was on this point. All they could do was rain curses down on him, and that was how he got the name "Precious Huang."

Once he went to someone's home to clean the millstone, to recondition the old stone. While the two of them were idly chatting, the conversation got around to operas; the householder's opinion differed from his and they ended up arguing till they were red in the face. Just go, go, said the peasant, I don't want my millstone washing. Zhihuang gathered up his tools, got up, and had gone out the door when something occurred to him, and he turned back to add: "Whether you have it washed or not, this millstone still isn't yours. Just as long as you understand that."

The peasant pondered this for some time, but still didn't understand anything at all.

After Zhihuang had walked another few steps away, he turned around again in a fury: "Got that? It's not yours!"

"Well, it's not going to be yours, is it?"

"It's not mine either, it's my dad's."

What he meant was, the millstone had been hammered out by his dad, so it was his dad's.

There was another time when someone from Shuanglong Bow came to the quarry weeping and wailing, saying his uncle had died and he had no money for the funeral; his great fear was that his uncle wouldn't have a decent burial, and he begged Zhihuang to sell him a tombstone on credit. Zhihuang saw how pitifully he was sobbing and said, don't worry about credit. Just take it, give your uncle a decent burial. Having said this, he hauled out a piece of top-quality blue-and-white stone and chiseled out a stele, even tied it up with some rope and helped him carry it down the mountain, taking him back part of the way. By this time, the quarry had been reclaimed into the collective. When the accountant Fucha discovered that he'd given a memorial stone to someone for nothing at all, he insisted that he chase after him to get the money back, saying he just didn't have the right to take pity on people like that. The two of them had a big row. Zhihuang's face darkened: "I dynamited the rock, I broke it, I carried it, I chiseled it, so how come it belongs to the team leader now? What's the sense in that!"

Fucha just docked him some work points and left it at that.

Zhihuang didn't actually care about work points, even if he was being docked by a team cadre. He didn't care about anything apart from rocks, nothing that hadn't been produced by his own two hands had any great importance for him; he just couldn't find any reason to care. The year he and Shuishui got divorced, Shuishui's people came and almost cleaned his house out of stuff, but he didn't care a bit; he just watched them move things out, and even made them tea. He lived in the upper village, and on the mountainside not far away there was a grove of good bamboo. When spring came, the bamboo roots spread like wildfire underneath the ground, the shoots running everywhere: sometimes, as if by magic, a thick bamboo tip would sprout up in someone's vegetable garden, or under their bed, or in their pigsty. According to the general rule, the bamboo shoot belonged to whichever household it had run to. Zhihuang understood this, it was just that he had difficulty remembering to put it into practice. Once, when he went to his vegetable patch to build a melon hut, he saw a stranger there, a passer-by most likely, who fled in panic as soon as he saw him. He obviously didn't know the way, and jumped into the ditch instead of taking the main road; Zhihuang shouted out but couldn't get him to stop and watched, wide-eyed, as he stepped onto nothingness and then fell into the deep ditch, sinking up to his waist in sludge. He yowled at great volume, a big fat bamboo shoot rolling out of his shirt.

It was obvious that this bamboo shoot had been dug up from Zhihuang's garden. But making as if he'd seen nothing, Zhihuang hurried over, deftly cut down a sapling with a wood knife he produced from behind his back, and lowered one end down into the ditch for the person in the ditch to grab hold of and slowly climb out.

Seeing the knife in Zhihuang's hands, the passer-by blanched and started trembling all over. Seeing as Zhihuang didn't seem to be making any move, the man took a few tentative pigeon steps toward the main road.

"Hey! Your bamboo shoot—" Zhihuang yelled out.

The person almost tripped and fell.

"Your bamboo shoot, don't you want it?"

He threw the bamboo shoot over.

The person picked the bamboo shoot up from the ground, stared at Zhihuang in stupefaction, but as he couldn't actually spot any trick, any danger, off he pelted like a madman and soon afterwards disappeared. Zhihuang watched his back view with some amusement, and it was only a good while later that the expression on his face turned to puzzlement.

All the villagers laughed at Zhihuang afterwards, laughed that he hadn't just failed to catch the thief, he'd even cut down a tree and rescued the thief from out of the ditch. And the funniest thing of all was that he'd worried the thief would've had a wasted trip and made a gift of what was his own property. Zhihuang blinked at these comments, and just smoked his tobacco.

Precious (continued) [寶氣(續)]: I've got a couple more things to say about "precious."

I once saw Zhihuang bring a few people to the supply and marketing cooperative to put up two buildings. When the last piece of tile had been lowered into place, Benyi sprang up from somewhere or other to check on the quality of work, giving it a kick here, a prod there. His face suddenly clouded over: the stone wall hadn't been built level, he declared, and too little mortar had been used—everyone would have their work points cut.

Zhihuang went to reason with him, to ask what on earth he was talking about. "I'm a stonemason, d'you think I don't know how much mortar to use?

Benyi sniggered icily: "Are you Party Secretary or am I Party Secretary? What's more important: what Awakened Huang says, or what the Party Secretary says?"

It looked like he had it in for Zhihuang.

Bystanders tried to smooth things over, pulling Zhihuang to one side, placating Benyi. Zhaoqing tailed the Party Secretary everywhere: if he saw him going to the toilet hut, he'd wait outside the toilet hut; if he saw him going to the butcher's, he'd wait outside the butcher's. When he finally saw him leave the butcher's smoking a cigarette, he accompanied him on an inspection tour of the cucumbers and peppers along the side of the road, but still couldn't get so much as a backward glance out of him.

The mealtime bell sounded in the cooperative. Benyi rubbed his hands in glee, "Good, good, off to Director Huang's to eat a nice bit of turtle!"

The delight was written all over his face.

Just as he was about to set off, a rat-a-tat noise suddenly erupted from somewhere around the just-completed granary, a rather irregular noise. People hurried over to report: unbelievable, unbelievable, Precious Huang's out there pulling down the building. Momentarily stunned, Benyi quickly propelled himself over to have a look and discovered that old Zhihuang had indeed worked himself into a lather; this solitary figure, swearing and cursing away, was savagely thwacking the wall with his double-ball hammer.

The new wall was like beancurd. One piece of stone had already warped on one side, another piece had started to bend, and powdered debris cascaded in fine trickles. Old Huang of the cooperative was at his side, unable to get him to stop. Old Huang spotted Benyi: "What's going on here? What's going on here? What's the point in pulling down a good building? Even if you don't care about your labor, eh, I care about my bricks. Four cents a brick, doncha know?"

Benyi cleared his throat, to announce his arrival on the scene.

Precious Huang didn't grasp the significance of the cough.

"Huang, you fartbrain!"

Huang threw him a glance, but took no notice.

"Why're you acting so precious!" Benyi had reddened to the base of his neck, "Whether we pull it down or not, you've got to wait till the cadres have looked into it . . . and then we'll see. You've got no speech rights. Go back home! All of you, you're going back with me!"

Zhihuang spat into the palm of his hand, then picked up the stone hammer again. "I broke these stones off the mountain, I brought them here in my cart, I built the wall. If I pull 'em down, what's it to you?"

Once he'd gotten onto the subject of stones, no one could reason with Zhihuang, no one could do anything about his baleful glares. Zhongqi stepped forward to give the Party Secretary some verbal support. "Huang, m'boy, that's no way to talk, the stone isn't the cooperative's, it isn't yours either. You belong to the team leader, so the stones you break belong to the team leader."

"What kind of logic is that? Old Dribbler belongs to the team leader too, and his old lady too, so everyone can sleep with her, can they?"

Everyone snickered quietly to themselves.

This got Benyi so angry he couldn't speak, and his jaw hung out of place till he pulled it back in again. "Fine, you smash away! Give it a good smash! I won't just dock all your work points, I'll punish you till you howl! I won't give you another chance, you'll know that nails are made of iron and eggs are eggs when I'm through with you!"

When they heard they'd be punished, the situation started to turn; the expression on several people's faces changed and they came forward to tug at, to intervene with, Zhihuang. Some stuffed cigarettes into his hand.

"What's the point? Calm down a bit, calm down."

"Don't ruin things for other people."

"Let them cut our work points, but why pull the thing down?"

"Part of this wall's mine too: why should it be smashed just because you say so? . . ."

Zhihuang was quite a bruiser, and one shake of his shoulders to the left, then to the right, threw the people on both sides off. "Don't worry, I only want my stones, I won't lay a finger on any of yours."

This was, in fact, nonsense. The stones he'd laid today were all at the base of the wall. If he pulled out the bottom, could the wall above hang in thin air?

Benyi threw up his hands and walked off into the distance. But Zhao-qing, who'd tailed him all the way, quickly ran back, his face covered in smiles, saying that Benyi had changed his mind, that not one of the work points would be cut—or not for the time being, that he'd settle accounts later on. At this the tension finally, simultaneously vanished from everyone's faces. Seeing that Precious Huang's hammer had stopped, everyone piled in to stuff back into place the rocks he'd just smashed out.

On the way back to the village, a lot of people fought for the privilege of helping Zhihuang carry the tool basket: if Precious Huang hadn't been around today, they said, wouldn't everyone have been done over good and proper by Old Dribbler? Wouldn't they have been dead meat on the chopping block? They thronged Zhihuang on all sides to sing his praises, Precious Huang this, Precious Huang that, on and on it went. In my opinion, the word "precious" here was now no longer derogatory but had recovered its original meaning: something to be treasured.

☆**Lion Dance** [雙獅滾繡球]: Zhihuang had been the hand-drummer in the old opera troupe, the head drummer in other words. He drummed beats like "Phoenix Nodding," "Dragon Gate Leaping," "Ten Vows Redeemed" and "Lion Dance," whirlwind blasts that made the blood surge, the spirit soar, a string of terrifying thunderbolts that fell like axe-blows. There were a lot of bar breaks and dotted notes, all kinds of dangerous and unexpected sudden halts. It stopped and started, died away then picked itself up, snatched itself back from the jaws of death, dramatically recovered from the brink of collapse. If it pulverized your every bone, dislocated your every muscle, made your sight run to your nose and your sense of smell run to your ears, smashed up every part of your brain—then it had to be Zhihuang's "Lion Dance."

You needed a full half hour to beat a set of "Lion Dance." Many drums were smashed under this lion's thunderous feet—Zhihuang's rock-chiseling hands were too heavy.

A lot of the lads in the village wanted to learn from him, but no one mastered his art.

He very nearly got to drum in our Mao Zedong Thought arts propaganda team. He accepted the invitation with great excitement and set about fixing up oil lamps, making gong hammers, writing Propaganda Team System, or something like that, on red paper in higgledy-piggledy characters, throwing himself into absolutely everything. He smiled at everyone: because he was too thin, when he smiled all that remained of his lower face were two rows of bright, clean, snow-white teeth. But he only drummed for a day, then never came back; the next day he went back to the mountain to break rocks. Fucha went to call him back, even promised to give him twice as many work points as the others, but he wouldn't budge.

The main reason, apparently, was he felt the new operas were dull, they had no scope to give free play to his percussion. Spoken poems, short songs, the bumper harvest dance—none of these needed the added excitement of a Lion. When a scene from a Model Opera—*The New Fourth Army Convalescing in the Homes of the People*—came along, his lion finally showed its muzzle, only to be slain by one wave of the director's hand.

"I haven't finished!" he yelled in outrage.

"How can people sing when all we can hear is you drumming?" The director was from the County Cultural Institute. "This opera's for strings and wind, when it finishes just tack on a finale and that'll do."

Zhihuang's face darkened, but all he could do was keep waiting.

When the Japanese devils had come on and the scene had livened up, was Zhihuang allowed to play a good hand? The director, it turned out, was even worse than he'd thought, and only allowed him to beat some running water sounds and bang a few small gongs at the end. He didn't get it, so the director grabbed the hammer and banged it a couple of times to show him, "just like that, got it?"

"What tune is it?"

"Tune?"

"There's no tune for the percussion?"

"No tune."

"So, just let it out any old how, like a kid having a crap?"

"The problem with you, you know, is you only know the old stuff, it's always Lion Dance this, Lion Dance that. What lion's dancing when the Jap devils come on, eh?"

Zhihuang had nothing to say to this and had to take what he was given. After one whole day of rehearsal, after drumming odds and ends with no pattern or order, he had no choice but to resign in massive disappointment. He had total contempt for the director and refused to believe there were any good operas in the world apart from Bi Rengui, Yang Silang, Cheng Yaojin, Zhang Fei, and the like; in fact he found it very hard to believe there was all that much else full stop in the world that could impress him. If you told him about special effects in opera films, how many people the world's biggest steamer could seat, how if you always walk forward you'll return to your starting place because the earth is round, how in gravity-less space a child's finger could lift 108,000 catties, and so on and on, he'd summarize his opinion of it all in four utterly cold, indifferent words:

"You're putting me on."

He wouldn't argue, or get angry, sometimes he'd even give a thin little smile; but he'd lick his lips and summarize, always, with perfect confidence: "You're putting me on."

Normally, he'd be really quite civil to us transferred youth, and had some respect for knowledge. He wasn't uncurious or unquestioning, quite the opposite: whenever there was an opportunity, he liked to approach those of us who'd been to middle school and ask questions he'd never been able to think of an answer to. It was just that he had his doubts about anything new—including Marxist writings—and was too quick to judge our answers, too absolute, he'd always be denying things without leaving any room for discussion.

"You're putting me on again."

For example, he'd seen films but categorically refused to believe that the kung-fu in revolutionary model operas was rehearsed. "Rehearsed? What rehearsal? These people've been having the bones knocked out of them since they were children, there's only flesh left in 'em; they get the living daylights thrashed out of them onstage, offstage they can't even pick up an empty water bucket."

At times like these, persuading him, convincing him the bones of those kung-fu fighters were still in place, that carrying water would be absolutely no problem at all, was harder than flying to the moon.

*Boss Hong [洪老板]: After stopping work one day, I spotted by the side of the road a small calf, too young to have grown horns, its furry muzzle round and well-formed, snuffling down under the mulberry tree eating grass. I felt like giving its tail a tug and had just extended a hand when, as if it had grown eyes in the back of its head, it slipped away, head tilted to one side. I was just about to go after it when a moo sounded out from a flatland in the distance and a big, glaring ox pointed its horns at me and charged ferociously, leaving the ground and mountains trembling in its wake; I dropped my hoe in terror and ran.

It was only some time later that, still with lingering fear, I came to retrieve my hoe.

While retrieving the hoe, I tried to ingratiate myself with the calf by feeding it some grass, but just as I'd waved the blades of grass near its mouth, the ox in the distance charged at me again, mooing like a banshee, with maddening obtuseness, intolerant of treatment either good or bad.

The big ox's desperate fierceness toward me meant it must be the calf's mother. It was only later that I found out this animal was called "Boss Hong": because it had been born with a bit of its ear missing, people identified it as the reincarnation of someone who'd come from near Luo

River. This person, Boss Hong, had been a great bully with seven or eight wives and had also had a bit of his left ear missing. People said he'd done so many bad things that Heaven had condemned him to a lifetime as an ox, pulling ploughs, drawing harrows and being whipped to atone for the sins of his previous life.

People also said that Heaven must really have eyes in its head to have sent Boss Hong to be reborn in Maqiao. The year the Red Army came to incite the peasants to attack local bullies, Maqiao people hadn't dared make a move at first; but when they saw a tyrant in Longjia Sands had been brought down, had had his head cracked open, and that nothing had come of it, they itched to have a go themselves. Unfortunately, by the time they'd got the peasants' association together, drunk the chicken's blood wine and made a red flag, they discovered their moment had already passed: all the certified bullies in the vicinity had already been struck down and all the granaries emptied, bar a few rats. None too happy about this, they made a few inquiries back and forth before finally heading across the Luo River, spears and blunderbusses in hand, to make revolution in Boss Hong's village. Little did they expect that the peasants there would also be making revolution: Boss Hong was their bully, they said, only they could revolutionize him, not people from other villages, and the Hong family's grain could only be divided between them, not between people from other villages. You don't go watering other people's fields, do you, now? The peasants' associations of the two villages negotiated without reaching any agreement and in the end it came to blows. The people from around Maqiao (not just Maqiao itself) thought the people from over the way were protecting the bully, that they were a fake peasants' association, making fake revolution, and built a pine tree cannon to bomb the village. The people from over the way showed no signs of weakening either: banging an almighty racket out of their gongs, they took down the wooden doors of the whole village, moved a few threshing windmills, and blocked the road that led into the village. They also fired at will, until the leaves hidden deep in the forest trembled and fell to the ground in a tattered flurry.

Two men from round Maqiao were injured and a good bronze gong was lost in the struggle, the whole squadron of men and horses was swimming in sweat and grime and no one had had anything to eat all day. Unable to believe that the revolutionary consciousness of their peasant brothers over the way could be so low, they gave it some thought and seized on the idea that it was all down to Boss Hong's plotting. And this was how their deep feelings of animosity and hatred toward Boss Hong were sealed.

Now they were perfectly satisfied, with everything fair and just:

Grandfather Heaven had sent Boss Hong to shoulder the plough for Maqiao, to be used to death in Maqiao—this settled the debt. One summer, after the higher-ups had transferred some of the oxen to plough the tea fields, only two were left in Maqiao. After having ploughed the last paddy of late summer rice, a panting and wheezing Boss Hong lay down to sleep in the mud, never to clamber up again. When it was sent to the slaughterhouse, it was discovered its lungs had completely filled up with blood, that almost every bubble in its lungs had burst; they lay abandoned in a wooden basin, like a pile of blood-dyed melon pulp.

*Three-Hairs [三毛]: There's another ox I want to talk about.

This ox was called "Three-Hairs," a fearsome character over whom, in all Maqiao, only "Precious" Zhihuang had any jurisdiction. People said it hadn't been born of a heifer, it had burst out of a stone like Monkey Sun in *Journey to the West*. It wasn't in fact an ox at all, it was a stone come to life. As Precious Huang was a stonemason, of course it followed very naturally that he should look after this lump of stone. This line of reasoning was universally accepted by all.

Cited in connection with this line of reasoning was the fact that the cry Zhihuang used for calling oxen was quite different from everyone else's. When most people wanted to catch oxen, they all went "chuh–chuh–chuh"; only Zhihuang used "slippy–slip slip" to catch Three-Hairs. "Slip" was a word often used by the stonemason. "Slip the son of heaven" meant hit with the iron hammer; therefore, all stones must, will fear getting the "slip." If Three-Hairs got into a fight with other oxen, however hard people tried to calm things down, the usual methods would never persuade Three-Hairs to let things lie. Only after hearing Zhihuang shout "slip" would it leave off, head hanging, panicked, and meek as a bale of cotton.

As I recall, Zhihuang's ox-handling skills were excellent: his whip never touched the ox's body and even after a day of ploughing the fields, he'd be clean as a whistle, not a speck of mud on him; he'd look just like he was returning, immaculately dressed, from a visit to some relatives, not like he was coming from the fields. In the fields that he'd ploughed, the churned black mud was like page after page of a book, lying smooth, glossy, flawless, elegant, neat, and even, amidst the rising currents of warm air; they exuded an air of natural smoothness that was both perfectly controlled and relaxed, in possession of both spirit and form, that made you feel you couldn't bear to touch or destroy it. If you looked at them closely, you'd discover his furrows had hardly any botched lines: regardless of how irregular the shape of the paddy field, how difficult it was for the ploughman to place the furrow, he still proceeded without skipping over ridges, very rarely intersecting or repeating a furrow; his were the sparing brushstrokes of a grand master, with never a drop of paint wasted. Once, I noticed he'd ploughed the final circuit with a tiny dead end remaining before him which, from the looks of it, would have to be abandoned with regret. Suddenly, to my total astonishment, he leapt with a great cry into action, seizing the plough, tilting it to one side, and in the blink of an eye the dead end was neatly turned over.

Unbelievable.

I would swear that dead end hadn't been turned over by a plough. I can only believe he possessed some kind of magic power, a kind of invisible force that he'd spread, via his palms, through the whole iron plough till it burst out of the snow-bright plough tip, springing, leaping, scattering deep into the mud. At any given moment, any distant dead end he wanted to turn over—in the places his strength reached but his plough couldn't, his energy reached but his strength couldn't, his intent reached but his energy couldn't–would turn itself over.

As I recall, he didn't have much confidence in the ox-herders and their little tricks, and always wanted to let the oxen out himself, taking them far, far away in search of clean water and grass that would suit their palates; he'd only take care of himself after he'd settled the oxen. For this reason, he was often the last to get off work, a lonely black spot on the mountainside, sometimes moving, sometimes still against the blazing reddish-purple backdrop of the sky, as the sound of cowbells merged in and out of the silence, scattered in amongst the fiery clouds that soared through the sky. It was about this time that star after isolated star would be coming awake.

Maqiao would have been unimaginable, dusk would have been unimaginable without the sound of oxbells. Dusk without these muted bells was like a river without flowing water, a spring without flowers, would have left only a magnificent wasteland.

The ox at his side was always Three-Hairs.

The problem was that sometimes Zhihuang had to go to the quarry—particularly after autumn, when things got pretty busy there. After he'd left, no one dared use Three-Hairs. One time, though, I decided to try my luck at copying Zhihuang's way of "slipping" it. It was spattering rain that day, with lightning lashing the dark recesses of cloud layers; two bare metal broadcasting wires shaking in the wind had been struck by lightning and were spitting out great rounds of shooting stars. The naked wires strewed themselves across the patch of field I'd just been ploughing, over where I had to pass whenever I returned, my nerves jangling away as I did so. Every time I approached underneath, my legs would turn to jelly, time and again I'd hold my breath, twisting my neck upwards to keep watch, watching my fate rocking and swaying back and forth on a thread in the sky, spluttering handful upon handful of sparks, as I dreaded an earth-shattering blow hitting me smack on the head.

Seeing that other people were still braving the rain to plant seedlings out in the fields, I felt embarrassed at going inside without permission, felt that it'd look like I was running scared of death.

Three-Hairs seized this opportunity to have some fun with me. The farther away we were from the live electric wires, the more the animal tripped and gamboled, the more unresponsive and unstoppable it became, however hard I pulled. The nearer we got to being beneath the electric wires, the slower it went, either to crap or to pee, or to nibble the grass at the side of the field, as if greatly enjoying my discomfort. In the end, it stopped moving altogether, completely oblivious to how you "slipped," to how you cracked the whip—even if you pushed its behind forward. Its body leaned, slanted forward, but its four hooves had set down roots into the ground.

It just so happened to halt right under the electric wire. Sparks were still spluttering out in all directions, crackling, exploding, splitting, a string of them dancing along the electric wire, sounding off into the distance. My willow whip had been beaten to a straggle, breaking ever shorter at every crack. Then Three-Hairs suddenly, unexpectedly produced a great roar, yanked the ploughshare so that it shot out of the mud in a silver streak, and galloped crazily toward the cliffside. A tumult of terrified exclamations resounded somewhere off in the distance as the wrenching motion left me staggering, almost toppled over into the mud. The plough handle flew out of my hands, the pointed ploughshare swung forward and, like the merciless falling of an axe, stuck itself straight into one of Three-Hairs' back legs. Perhaps not yet feeling the pain, it leapt onto a mound of earth a good meter high and swayed briefly, dislodging great lumps of mud that collapsed with a crash; it didn't fall back off in the end, but the ploughshare behind it lodged, with a violent clunk, into a seam of rock.

I didn't know who was yelling in the distance, neither did I have any idea what was being yelled. It was only a long time after the event that I figured out this person was yelling at me to hurry up and pull out the ploughshare.

It was already too late. The ploughshare, stuck in the seam of rock, broke with a clang, and the entire plough frame twisted off into pieces.

The rope halter also snapped. Awash with the excitement of winning freedom, powered by a vast, unstoppable force, Three-Hairs headed bellowing for the mountains, its stride often lapsing into lop-sided leaps, surging with a never-before-experienced happiness.

That day, its nose was ripped through and it almost hacked off its own leg. In addition to breaking a plough, it also mowed down a telegraph pole, flattened a low wall, stamped to pieces a large bamboo basket, and barged over a manure shed in the village as it was being repaired—if the two people putting up the shed hadn't dodged quickly out of the way, they might not have escaped with their lives.

After this, I no longer dared use this ox. When the team leader decided to sell it, I gave my enthusiastic approval.

Zhihuang didn't agree the ox should be sold. His reasoning was somewhat singular: he'd fed this ox grass and water, he said, he'd got the doctor over to give it medicine when it was ill, if he said not to sell it, who had the right to sell it? The cadres said, you use the ox but you can't then say the ox's yours, you need to distinguish clearly between public and private. The ox was bought with the team leader's money. Zhihuang said, the landlord's fields were bought with money, but after land reform, weren't the landlord's fields all divided up? The fields went to whoever used them—wasn't this the same principle?

Everyone felt there was nothing much wrong with his reasoning.

"Accidents will happen. When Guan Yunchang threw Jingzhou away, did Zhu Geliang kill him, or sell him?" Even after everyone had finished talking and dispersed, Zhihuang was still wandering along making new points to himself.

Three-Hairs wasn't sold, but died at the hands of Zhihuang, in a finale that no one would have predicted. He staked his own honor on Three-Hairs: if this beast injured anyone again, he declared, he'd take the axe to it himself. He couldn't go back on what he'd said. One spring day, when everything in the world was sprouting back to life, sounds and colors shifting under the warm sunlight, a secret disquiet pervaded the air. Just as Zhihuang was driving Three-Hairs down the field, suddenly the animal's whole body shuddered, its eyes fixed straight ahead, and with a yank of the ploughshare it charged forward insanely, tramping the mud, smack-smack-splatter, into a rising and falling curtain of water.

Caught unawares, Zhihuang eventually identified Three-Hairs' target: a red dot at the side of the road. It was only afterwards that he found out it'd been a woman passing by from a neighboring village wearing a jacket with red flowers on it.

Oxen are particularly sensitive to the color red and often react to it aggressively—nothing strange about that. What was strange was that Three-Hairs, who'd always been led by the nose by Zhihuang, went mad like it did that day, became deaf, oblivious to the shouts and screams of its master. Not long after, a woman's high-pitched scream carried over.

In the evening, definite news came back from the commune clinic to Maqiao: the woman's star must have been in the ascendant, as she'd hung onto her life, but Three-Hairs had tossed her up into the air, smashing a bone in her right leg, and her fall to the ground had left her with a concussion.

Zhihuang hadn't gone to the clinic; dazed, alone, he sat at the side of the road fingering a half-length of ox rope. Three-Hairs was not far off, timidly eating grass.

When he returned to the village at dusk, he set Three-Hairs under the maple tree at the mouth of the village and searched out half a bowl of yellow beans to stuff into Three-Hairs' mouth. Three-Hairs probably sensed something was up and kneeled down before him, murky tears dropping from its eyes. He'd picked out a thick, coarse hemp rope and knotted it into a noose, looped round each of the beast's four legs. A good, long axe was grasped in his hand.

The village herd of oxen produced an anxious lowing chorus that merged into wave upon wave of echoes, swirling round the mountains and valleys. The setting sun sank, all of a sudden, into gloom.

He kept watch in front of Three-Hairs, waiting and waiting for it to finish eating the yellow beans. A few women thronged round, Fucha's mother, Zhaoqing's mother, Zhongqi's wife, wiping their noses, their eyes reddened. They said to Zhihuang, he's got himself into trouble, you know, you're sparing him, really, by settling things now. They then turned to Three-Hairs: it's no one's fault but your own things have turned out like this. Weren't you in the wrong, X number of years ago, when you hurt that ox in Zhangjia District? D'you admit you did wrong, Y number of years back, when you killed that ox from Longjia Sands? There was that time you almost kicked Wanyu's boy to death, you should've been killed long ago. That other time, though, that got people really mad, when you ate the yellow beans, you ate the eggs, and still you wouldn't stir yourself, wouldn't take the plough, then finally when it was on, you wouldn't move a muscle, even with four or five people beating you, and we nearly had to lift you onto a sedan chair—people don't forget these things, you know.

One by one they enumerated the black marks on Three-Hairs' history; finally they said, your sufferings are all over, go in peace, don't go blaming us Maqiao people for being cruel, our hands are tied, y'know.

Her eyes moist, Fucha's mother said everyone's got to go, sooner or later—don't you remember how Boss Hong suffered much more than you, he even died with the plough still on.

Three-Hairs was still shedding tears.

Zhihuang, his face totally expressionless, finally picked up the axe and walked over—

A dull thump.

The ox's head split into a rivulet of blood, followed by a second, a third. . . . Even when the fountain of blood had spurted a foot high, the ox still put up no resistance, didn't even call out, still kept its kneeling position. Finally, it swayed briefly, leaned to one side, then collapsed heavily, like a mud wall splaying over the ground. Its legs flexed weakly a few times, while its body lay straight and stiff over the ground, looking as if it had been stretched much longer than normal. The light grey skin covering its stomach, which you couldn't usually see that much of, lay completely exposed. The blood-red head twitched violently in repeated convulsions, the shiny black eyes wide open, fixed on the onlookers, fixed on Zhihuang, who stood before it covered in blood.

Fucha's mother told Zhihuang, "It's going; call out to it."

Zhihuang called out: "Three-Hairs."

The ox's gaze flickered.

Zhihuang shouted again: "Three-Hairs."

The ox's broad eyelids finally fell shut; its body slowly stopped twitching.

All night long, Zhihuang sat before those eyes which would never reopen.

***Born-to-the-Pen** [掛欄]: Each of Maqiao's oxen had its own name. People had lots of different words for oxen: for example, there were oxen that "understood," meaning oxen with intelligence; there were oxen "born-to-the-pen," meaning oxen that had been brought up like family, oxen that ox-rustlers found hard to steal away. Although Three-Hairs had something of a foul temper, it was still an ox born-to-the-pen.

Two months before it died, nothing had been seen of it for two days, the team leader had sent people searching everywhere with no result, and everyone thought it'd never be found again, that it'd already been slaughtered or sold by ox-rustlers. But on the evening of the third day, while I was playing chess at Zhihuang's, Zhihuang unexpectedly turned back from relieving himself and said his ox whip was twitching on the wall, there was definitely something up, definitely. Maybe Three-Hairs had come back. No sooner were we out of the door than we heard Three-Hairs' lows and saw a familiar black shadow in front of the oxpen.

Right at that moment it was butting the wooden oxpen with its horns—clunk, clunk, clunk—wanting to get inside. Half a length of ox rope was hanging from its nose, its tail had been cut to half its length for some unknown reason, its whole body was covered with dozens of bloody scars, its whiskers were in a real state and it had clearly lost a lot of weight. After escaping from the ox-rustlers it must have meandered all over the mountains on its long, long tramp home.

☆**Qingming Rain** [清明雨]: There was nothing I could say—seeing wave upon wave of misty rain sweep toward me over the fields on the mountainside, dousing the mud wall of the cow pen, wrinkling the surface water on the fields into wind-driven concertinas, dying away in round after round among the clumps of reeds on the ridge opposite, out of which two or three mute wild ducks would then flap furiously. The harmonies from the brook grew ever louder, ever more fragmented, until there was no way of differentiating precisely between each of the various original noises; nor did you know where they came from, there remained nothing but the vast expanse between heaven and earth that had converged into a roaring whole so turbulent that the very surface of the earth seemed to tremble. I saw in a doorway a dog soaked through, howling in wide-eyed terror at the storm.

Under the eaves of every house dripped a column of stagnant water, overflowing under the gaze of those avoiding the rain with nowhere to shelter themselves, overflowing with the bitter waiting of the Qingming season, in early April.

Every leaf on the mountain was being pattered to pieces.

Spring rain is enthusiastic, self-confident, it rushes and flows, it gushes from deep, long-held stores. Summer rain, in comparison, is more like an occasional absent-minded splatter, while autumn rain is an occasional, distracted about-face, and winter rain is simply indifferent. I reckon it'd be hard to find anyone who looked forward to rain as much as Educated Youth did, who knew so well the sound and smell of each type of rain and the temperature it left the skin. Because it was only on rainy days that we could haul our weary, aching bodies inside our houses, draw breath, and enjoy this precious opportunity for rest.

My daughter has never liked the rain. For her, spring rain means inconvenience, slippery roads, the terror of thunder and lightning, and the cancellation of sports matches or excursions. She'll never understand my feeling of uncontrollable excitement at the sound of rain, she'll never understand why it's bucketing down in every single one of my dreams about my time in the countryside. She has missed out on a decade of longing for the sound of rain.

Maybe I should rejoice at this.

It's started raining again, now. The sound of the rain always gives me a certain feeling: over there in the rain, way, way over there in the rain, there's still a trail of muddy footprints left by me, that floats up on rainy days, sinking into a dazzling white abyss on a mountain path rocked by the waves of rainfall.

☆**Rude** [不和氣]:The first time I heard this word was when crossing the Luo River in flood season, when the river was a few times wider than usual. On the same boat were two unfamiliar women, probably from distant regions, who covered their faces with bamboo hats once they'd boarded the boat, exposing no more than a pair of eyes. The boatman sized them up briefly, then waved at them to get off. The two women had no choice but to get off and smear their faces with mud till they looked like painted actors; doubling up with laughter at the sight of each other, they finally got back on the boat, still convulsed with giggles.

I was quite amazed: why did they have to paint these funny faces?

"Even ten Chairman Mao's can't control Sixth Master Dragon and his floods," said the boatman. "I can't be held responsible for the lives of a boatload of people, now can I?"

People on the boat immediately concurred: that's right, that's right, floods and fire take no prisoners, best be careful. They started talking about some time back in the past, when some woman had been so rude the boat capsized, the people fell in the water and couldn't reach the bank however hard they swam—must've been demons at work.

It was only afterwards that I found out "rude" meant "pretty." A very particular rule held on this crossing: in times of high winds or turbulent waters, women who weren't ugly weren't allowed to cross. Legend had it that a very long time ago an ugly woman from around here who could never get married had ended up throwing herself to her death off this pier into the river. The ugly woman's soul didn't then scatter: she only had to spot an attractive woman on a boat to whip the wind into jealous waves, causing endless accidents in which boats were destroyed and lives lost. Any remotely good-looking female on the crossing could only avoid bringing disaster on the whole boat by dirtying her face.

I don't pay much heed to or have much faith in this sort of legend, neither have I done any concrete research on the links between beauty and catastrophe: for example, does beauty tend to make people lose their minds, drive them wild, deranged, or crazy? Does it easily lead people into carelessness, into abandoning responsibilities? It's this word "rude" that I'm interested in. It conceals within an assumption that provokes an involuntary shiver: beauty is a form of evil, good is a form of danger, beautiful and good things will always bring disunity, instability, dissatisfaction, disputes, and animosity—rudeness. A "precious jade" (a beautiful woman) once provoked the State of Zhao to go to war with the State of Qin, Greece embarked on a ten-year war with Troy because of a beautiful woman called Helen—probably a useful footnote to all this. Ordinary people can only drift with the tide, turn to dust in the sunlight, stick to the bottom of the pile, and smear mud over their faces to maintain peace on earth.

"Rude" in Maqiao language was also widely used to mean excellence, to tower above others, to stand out from your peers, surpass the norm, and so on. Given that this word was used to describe Benyi's young wife Tiexiang, readers from outside Maqiao should now break into a cold sweat at the very mention of her.

☆**Spirit** [神]: Maqiao people believed that pretty women had a particular kind of smell—a fragrant but harmful kind of smell. When Benyi's wife Tiexiang came over from Changle to be married in Maqiao she brought this smell with her. Two months after her arrival, every single one of Maqiao's daylilies were dead. You could pick flower after dazzling gold flower into your basket, but before you got them back home they'd have collapsed into soggy black blobs which refused to respond to any amount of primping. The old people said this was why Maqiao people would never grow daylilies again, why they could only grow malformed melons, eggplants, bitter gourds, pumpkins, walnuts, and so on.

Tiexiang's smell also disturbed all sorts of farm animals. The moment it saw Tiexiang, Fucha's family dog went mad—there was no choice but to shoot it. Zhongqi used to have a "foot-pig" (or breeding pig): from the moment it saw Tiexiang, it just couldn't be kept quiet anymore and had to be castrated; it was later slaughtered for its meat. Some people's chickens and ducks were struck down by epidemics, which their owners all blamed on Tiexiang's influence. In the end, even Three-Hairs the ox charged at Tiexiang while under Zhihuang's supervision. She screamed in terror, and if it hadn't been for Zhihuang's sharp eyes and quick hands pulling its halter up smartly, she might have been butted all the way down the hillside.

The women were all rather sniffy about Tiexiang, but Benyi's face as Party Secretary stopped them from coming straight out with it. Some of them weren't so easily put off and would search out some needling comment as soon as they saw her. They'd go on about how extravagant, how elaborate their obeisance ceremonies or pot-placing had been when they'd arrived in their husband's house in Maqiao, how everything had been just so. *Of course* there'd been First Uncle carrying the dowry, Second Uncle blowing the trumpet, Third Uncle firing the blunderbuss, Fourth Uncle holding up the red parasol—and so on and so forth went the exaggerations. There were bales of Hangzhou silk brocade, hundreds of Japanese mandarin jackets, the bracelets on wrists were this big, the rings on ears were this shiny—as they never tired of saying.

Tiexiang's face turned livid as she listened to all this.

Once, one of them feigned surprise: "Aiya, all you grand ladies, all so lucky, you just make me want to die of shame. When I was left in this rotten dump, I was carrying nothing but a parasol, just a lump of flesh I was, dressed in a mandarin jacket!"

Everyone laughed.

This woman was obviously referring to how poor Tiexiang had been when she first arrived. Unable to bear it, Tiexiang fled back home to have a good cry and pummel her pillow and quilt.

In fact, Tiexiang had grown up in a wealthy household, a house with nursemaids and servants, where food would always be accompanied by soy sauce, aniseed, or sesame oil; she knew what biscuits and cakes were, not like Maqiao people, who called everything "candy." But when she arrived in Maqiao, her father had died in prison and the family finances were in decline. When she scurried across Benyi's threshold, she really was carrying nothing but a parasol.

Aged sixteen at the time, with a bit of rouge smeared on, a big stomach sticking out in front, she'd rushed alone into Maqiao in a great fluster and asked who the Party member was around here. People eyed her curiously and finally gave her a couple of names only after repeated questioning on her part. She then asked who, out of these Party members, was still a bachelor. Benyi, people said. She asked for directions to Benyi's home, walked straight up to the thatched hut, and quickly sized up house and man:

"So you're Ma Benyi?"

"Mmm."

"You're a Communist Party member?"

"Mmm."

"D'you want to get married?"

"Whassat?" Benyi was cutting up pigfeed and hadn't been listening properly.

"I asked, do you want a wife or don't you?"

"Wife?"

She drew a long breath, put down the parasol she'd brought with her: "I'm not bad-looking, am I? I can have children as well, you can see that. If you're happy with that, then I . . ."

"Uh?"

"That's what I'm here for."

"Here for what?" Benyi still hadn't quite got it.

Tiexiang stamped her foot, "I'm yours."

"My what?"

Tiexiang twisted her neck and glanced over the door: "To sleep with!"

Benyi jumped in fright, too stunned to produce a single sentence, "You you you you where did you spring from you spirit woman . . . Bloody hell, where's my basket?"

He fled indoors. Tiexiang pursued him inside: "What's there to complain about? Look at my face, look at my hands, my feet, all there, all present and correct. Look, I'll be frank with you, I've even got some of my own money. You can relax, I've got an educated man's baby inside me, if you want it, you can have it. You don't want it, then get rid of it. I just wanted to show you I can have children, there's nothing wrong with my body . . ."

Before she'd finished, she heard someone slip out the back door.

"You must've stored up lots of secret good deeds in an earlier life to land someone like me—" Tiexiang stamped her foot in fury; a noisy sob followed shortly.

Later, Benyi dispatched his same-pot brother Benren to send this spirit woman on her way. When Benren came to the door, he discovered the woman was already chopping up pig grass; wiping her hands, she got up to bid him sit down and took out the kettle to boil some tea. She really wasn't bad-looking, either. Seeing that her full, round buttocks and thick legs were the properly child-bearing sort, he went a bit tongue-tied and failed again and again to come up with the words required to send her packing. He later told Benyi: "She may be a bit of a spirit, but she looks pretty healthy. If you don't want her, I'll have her."

That night, Tiexiang didn't go home—she stayed at Benyi's place.

Things worked out pretty simply: Benyi didn't get a matchmaker, didn't buy any betrothal gifts, he got it all on the cheap. Tiexiang also got what she wanted: as she put it later, she'd been fed up with government surveillance and with her four mothers weeping and wailing all day long, fed up with the daily threats and nags of the handyman next door. So she made up her mind, walked out of the door with nothing but a parasol, and swore she'd find a member of the Communist Party to look after her. As things turned out, she succeeded at the first attempt and a few days later really did take a demobilized revolutionary soldier and Party Branch Secretary back home with her. The neighbors on both sides eyed her with more respect and, after one look at the medal pinned on

Benyi's chest for resisting America and helping Korea, the cadres became a few degrees politer to her family.

The two of them went to the government office to register. The government office said she was too young, she should come back in two years. When it became clear that nothing she said was having any effect, her apricot eyes hardened and she told the secretary who handled official seals: "If you don't register us, I won't go, I'll have the kid at your place and say it's yours. How'd you like that?" The secretary jumped in terror and scrambled to sort everything out, the sweat running down his face. He watched their back-views—hers and her bridegroom's—recede far off into the distance, his mind still unhinged with fear: that spirit woman, he said, d'you think she'll stay like that?

Bystanders also shook their heads and tut-tutted: she truly was Master Nine Pockets' daughter, they said, she'd eaten the food of every family in town and the skin on her face was thicker than shoe soles. If she was like this now, what would she be like later?

As Benyi afterwards slowly came to realize, it would be hard to say this marriage business had turned out well for him. Tiexiang was about ten years younger than him and so reserved the right to flare up into tempers at home; sometimes, when her spirit got quite carried away, it only took the slightest thing not to go her way, the tiniest provocation, and she'd be yelling about how god-forsaken Maqiao Bow was, how could anyone live there? She cursed Maqiao's roads for being uneven, cursed Maqiao's mountains for being too steep, cursed the gully holes for burying people alive, cursed the rice for having too much sand in it, cursed the firewood for being so wet you choked on the soot, cursed the way you had to run seven or eight *li* to buy a needle or soy sauce. What with her cursing this way and that, her curses inevitably ended up directed at Benyi. If she just cursed and left it at that, it would've been all right, but once in a particularly violent screaming fit she actually chopped off the head of an eel. What'd happened to patriarchal law? For better or for worse, Benyi was still her old man, for better or for worse a Party Secretary; how'd he gotten himself into this mess with eels' heads?

While Benyi's old ma was still alive, she too was helpless before her daughter-in-law, whose rages spared not even the old: "Are you never going to die, you old crock, I don't care how old you are, how heavy you are, will you never end? Just go and die! Why don't you just go and die?"

Generally speaking, Benyi turned a deaf ear to such remarks—he was, in fact, a little deaf. Even if sometimes, at the end of his tether, he yelled "I'll do you in!" all it took was for his wife to shut her mouth just for a moment and no real action would be taken. His moment of greatest authority was when one slap of his hand sent Tiexiang rolling into the middle of a flock of terrified ducks who scattered into the air in all four directions. That, as he put it, was the time that good overpowered bad, the east wind overpowered the west wind. When she clambered up again, Tiexiang would have thrown herself into the pond if she hadn't been stopped by the villagers. She had no choice but to run back to her parents' house, and nothing was heard of her for three months. Once again, it was Benren who, with two catties of potato flour and two catties of *baba* cakes, finally went to make peace with Tiexiang on behalf of his same-pot brother, and who drove her back on a dirt cart.

In the foregoing narrative, the reader may have noticed that the word "spirit" came up a few times. Maqiao people, it should by now be apparent, used the word "spirit" to describe any kind of unconventional behavior. People from around here were anxious above all else to affirm human ordinariness, to affirm that humans were conventional beings. Any unconventional behavior was, essentially, inhuman behavior, derived from the mysterious shadows of the netherworld, from superhuman forces of heaven or destiny. If the problem wasn't a spiritual (i.e., mental) matter, then it had to be a matter of spirits (i.e., ghosts or divinities). Maqiao people used the word "spirit" for both these two meanings, probably considering the difference between the two to be of little importance. Any story about spirits began with fantasies of a spiritually abnormal nature. People always babbled and danced insanely in front of altars to spirits. Maybe spiritual disorders were just spirits in worldly, vulgarized form. A whole bundle of expressions—"spirit-fast," "spirit-brave," "spirit-good," "spirit-weird," "spirit-pretty," "spirit-smooth"—referred to achievements that temporarily transgressed ordinary human limits, often witnessed in people close to the obsessive derangement of spiritual disorder, close to the spirits, and who were putting their mental state to positive use, either subconsciously or unconsciously.

A spirit like Tiexiang's, everyone said, just had to be possessed by evil forces.

☆**Rude (continued)** [不和氣(續)]: Tiexiang didn't much like spending time with Maqiao women, and after getting off work she'd hustle her way in amongst the men and really let herself go. Benyi didn't like this much, but there was nothing he could do. So although going to the mountains to cut down trees was men's work, she wanted to join in the fun too. When she got to the mountain, she grasped the axe as she would a chicken, gritted her teeth, but still didn't manage to chop even so much as a toothmark; the axe ended up ricocheting off to who knew where, while she collapsed onto her bottom in laughter, her body dissolving into waves of giggles.

After this fall, things got busy for the men. She ordered this one to beat dust off her, asked that one to extract the thorn from her finger, instructed this one to go look for the lost axe, commanded that one to hold the shoes she'd just trodden in the wet without realizing. Under the spell of her gaze, the men all hovered around in raptures. Her piercing cries, the tragic convulsions of her body, the possibility that at careless moments a wider expanse of dazzling white . . . something would glint out of her neckline or cuffs got the men (and their roving eyes) buzzing around.

Her fall had been far from heavy, but having tried a couple of steps on tiptoe she insisted it hurt too much to walk and demanded that Benyi carry her home on his back—never mind that Benyi was just then in conversation on the mountainside with two cadres visiting the forestry station.

"You spirit! Can't you get someone else to lean on?" Benyi's patience was low.

"No, I want you to carry me back!" she stamped her little foot.

"Just walk, you can walk."

"Even if I can walk, I still want you to carry me!"

"Firstly, there's no blood, secondly you haven't broken anything."

"My back hurts."

And so Benyi had no choice but to submit once more to his young wife, abandoning the forestry station to carry her down the mountain right in front of everyone. He knew that if he hadn't carried her off then, she might have announced her period had come, or something similar. She was someone who just wouldn't shut up, who'd publicize women's secrets at any opportunity, making her body a subject of general understanding and concern, a topic of conversation, the intellectual property of all men. Her periods were, in short, a great ceremonial event for the Maqiao collective. She wouldn't of course advertize them directly. But she'd say her back hurt, then remark meaningfully on how she hadn't been able to go near cold water for the last few days, then dispatch some man to the clinic to buy her some angelica, even yell at Benyi while they were in the fields to go back home and boil her some angelica or an egg—all this, of course, was quite sufficient to notify people of the phase her body was entering on, to underline her femininity, to excite male imaginations, to attract knowing smirks.

Whether in terror or delight, she made an extraordinary number of exclamations. Even if she was only expressing surprise at a caterpillar, the dulcet tones of her "aiyas" led men to suspect there had to be another context or background to them, to daydream about her pose in that context or background—and all sorts of other things besides. She wasn't responsible for these fantasies, of course, she was responsible only for the caterpillar. But that caterpillar of hers could triumph over the other women's ginger-salted-bean pounded tea and all their other distractions, could wrest men away, have them trot over obediently to shower her with attention, to perform any physical task she demanded of them. Every time this happened, shoulders back and head held high, she'd walk beneath the gaze of other Maqiao women, glowing with the undisguisable joy of victory.

I later heard Maqiao people whisper among themselves that this woman's dizzying, bewitching cries were really rude and got the better of at least three men.

First of all was a director from the County Cultural Institute, who came once to check on cultural work in the village and who stayed in her house; a secretary he brought with him was palmed off on Fucha. From that time on, the Cultural Institute director took a particular interest in Maqiao, and his fleshy face, grinning from ear to ear, would often pop up—here and there, in her kitchen, as if it had set down roots and started to grow. People said he'd give out free agriculture manuals, as well as free fertilizer quotas and disaster relief funds; whatever Tiexiang wanted she got. Getting the institute director to do things was even easier than ordering a child around—the director (a commissioned official) even helped her haul the toilet bucket, lurching over to the vegetable garden to empty it onto the manure heap.

Later on there was a handsome young lad, Tiexiang's nephew (allegedly) who worked in the photography institute in Pingjiang's county seat and who'd come down to the countryside to serve poor and lower-middle peasants. Tiexiang took him on a tour around nearby villages, explaining how good his photography was, getting people interested and fighting to have a look at the photographs the young lad was already clutching, which were, of course, a dozen or so photographs of Tiexiang in all kinds of different poses. This was the first time Maqiao people had seen a camera, so naturally they were curious. Something else they were curious about was an old watch belonging to the young lad, which for some months was fastened round Tiexiang's wrist. Some said that people cutting firewood on the mountain had spotted the two of them walking together hand-in-hand along the mountain road. Was this the sort of thing an aunt and a nephew did? What was going on between them?

Finally, people even said that Tiexiang had seduced Precious Huang, that Precious Huang had lugged to her house a made-to-order stone feeding-trough and drunk five whole cups of cold water without stopping, knots of flesh all over his body rising and rolling. This had sent Tiexiang into raptures of lust and she'd insisted that Precious Huang help her cut her fingernails—it was really hard to cut her right hand, she said. Afterwards, she secretly made a pair of shoes and delivered them over to Precious Huang's. Unfortunately, Precious Huang was too precious to understand her feminine wiles: he returned the shoes to Benyi saying they were a little bit small, they pinched his feet; he reckoned they'd fit Benyi better. Benyi fell silent, his face darkening immediately, his neck twisting to one side.

Not a shadow of Tiexiang was seen over the following few days. When she reappeared in public, she had a cut on her neck. When people asked about it, she said she'd been scratched by a cat.

That wasn't the truth—her old man had beaten her.

The Tiexiang with a cut at the base of her neck stopped horsing around with the men and quieted down. But then she suddenly got friendly with Three Ears.

It would've been stretching a point to call Three Ears a man—in most women's eyes he had no significance as a man—so of course there was no harm in him and Tiexiang getting friendly. Three Ears was Zhaoqing's second child, but he'd run wild as a boy and had turned out so disobedient and unfilial that Zhaoqing chased him out of the house with a hoe; he then joined up with Ma Ming, Master Yin, and Hu Erce from the House of Immortals and became one of Maqiao's Four Daoist Immortals. The nickname "Three Ears" came from an extra piece of flesh shaped like an ear that had come up in his left armpit. People said he'd been too stubborn in his previous life and the King of the Underworld had given him an extra ear this time around to make him listen harder to what his elders and the government said. He kept this under wraps like some kind of treasure—he wouldn't exhibit his precious third ear to just anyone. Whoever wanted to have a look had to hand over a cigarette first. If you wanted to have a feel, then the price doubled. He could also turn his right hand over, bring it around past his backbone, and grab hold of his right ear; anyone wanting to see this miracle had at the very least to buy him a bowl of wine in the supply and marketing cooperative.

He showed Tiexiang his third ear for free: seeing Tiexiang happy made him especially happy. He was very proud of his superfluous ear; in fact, he thought his nose, eyes, and mouth were pretty good, too. A few years earlier, he'd ascertained by looking in the mirror that he was not Zhaoqing's real son and had insisted his mother reveal the current whereabouts of his real father. He'd made such a fuss about this that his mother wept and wailed and he came to blows with his father (both of them drew blood). This, of course, further confirmed him in his conclusions: was this the behavior of a father? Chasing him out of the door with a rake? He wasn't awakened yesterday, Three Ears, he wasn't going to believe what this sonofabitch told him. He went looking for Benyi, politely offered him a cigarette, cleared his throat, set his expression, and made as if to discuss with the Party Secretary some matter of great import such as national family planning. "Uncle Benyi, as you know, the current revolutionary situation throughout the nation is indeed excellent, under the central leadership of the Party all cow demons and snake spirits have shown their true faces, those that are false are proved false, those that are real are proved real, the revolutionary truth is becoming clearer and clearer, the eyes of the revolutionary masses are brighter and brighter. Last month, our commune held a Party Representatives meeting and will next decide how to deal with the question of water conservation . . ."

Benyi's patience was, as ever, low: "Stop beating around the bush, if you're gonna fart, then do it quickly."

Three Ears stammered and meandered his way to the question of his natural father.

"Don't you ever look at yourself when you're having a piss, you scrawny wimp, what sort of dad d'you think you should have? Shortie Zhao's already too good for you." Benyi ground his teeth.

"Don't be like that, Uncle Benyi. I don't want to bother you or anything, I'd just like you to tell me something."

"Tell you what?"

"How was I really born?"

"Ask your mother! How should I know?"

"You're a Party cadre, I'm sure you know what really happened."

"What're you talking about? It was your mother who gave birth to you, you piece of trash, what would I know about it? I haven't even looked hard enough at her to see whether her eyebrows go straight across or straight up."

"That's not what I mean, all I was saying . . ."

"I've got work to do."

"So that's your final answer—you won't tell me?"

"Tell you what? What d'you want me to say? Hmm? Sticking a toad in a dragon's bed's easy enough to do, so what'll it be? D'you want a regiment commander or a director for a dad? Just say the word and I'll take you to find one. How about it?"

Three Ears bit his lip and said no more. No matter how much Benyi swore at him, his expression remained determinedly calm and even vaguely supercilious, watching the Party Secretary perform, as if he had some well-planned strategy all thought out. He waited urbanely while the Secretary finished swearing, then turned his head and walked off with a melancholy air.

He walked to the mouth of the village, quietly watched two kids playing with ants, then went back to where he lived. He'd work all his shifts as arranged—he wasn't about to be thrown off balance by Benyi.

He went looking for Uncle Luo, Fucha, and Precious Huang too, he even went looking for the Commune Head. In the end, he actually ran all the way into the county seat to inquire where Long Stick Xi had been sent for labor reform, because he strongly suspected he was in fact the seed of Long Stick Xi and wanted to see for himself what Long Stick Xi looked like before he dragged him off for a blood test. If Long Stick Xi was his natural father but wouldn't recognize him as his son, he'd smash his own brains out in front of him. He'd asked for nothing all his life, just this, all he wanted was to unravel the riddle of his own birth, to pay his respects to his real father, never mind if it was only for a day—just one moment would be enough.

Twice he went into the county seat, without managing to find Long Stick Xi either time. He didn't lose heart. He knew this wasn't a simple matter; perhaps it would be his life's destiny, but he was fully prepared in any case. He wasn't like the other Daoist Immortals, lying around all day sleeping, or wandering the mountains, or enjoying the waters. He was busy every day until late, busy searching and surveying, and—while he was at it—busy with all the interminable things in the world that make you busy. He was lazy by nature, but not outwardly: he often went off to the supply and marketing cooperative, the clinic, the granary, the forestry station, the school, as if he went to work there every day. He helped the quack pound the medicine, helped the butcher blow out the pig's bladder, helped the teacher carry water, helped the granary kitchen grind bean curd. He'd help out a friend on any important matter. Because his family's class status was too high, Maqiao's Yanwu was sent back home from school in Changle and refused entrance to the commune middle school. Determined to campaign on behalf of this victim of injustice, an indignant Three Ears dragged him, huffing and puffing, to the middle school, donated his entire collection of cigarettes to the headmaster, and asked the man to give him some face, to take in Yanwu.

The headmaster said it wasn't that he didn't want to take him, the problem was he'd been expelled from the county middle school and—how should he put it—there were political . . . problems.

Without a word, Three Ears rolled up a sleeve, took out a sickle, and drew it across his bare flesh; a stripe of blood immediately swelled out.

The headmaster gaped.

"Will you take him?"

"You—you—you threatening me?"

With another horizontal cut, another wound split open.

Both Yanwu and the headmaster blanched and rushed at him to grab the knife. The three of them became one great wrestling mass, the clothes of each spattered with blood, even part of the headmaster's mosquito net was stained red. Three Ears held the knife aloft and rasped: "You decide, Headmaster Tang: d'you want to see me die?"

"Calm, please calm down," the head-teacher begged him through his sobs. He ran out to find another two teachers, and following a brief discussion Yanwu was asked there and then to complete the formalities for entering the school.

Three Ears' arms were covered all over in knife wounds, but he also had a lot of friends. One thing about him, though, was that he'd never return to work in Maqiao. He'd rather shed blood elsewhere than shed one drop of sweat back in Maqiao. He wore an old army uniform he'd gotten hold of from somewhere or other, to make him look a bit more dignified. He said he was busy selling his blood, and when he'd gotten enough money for his blood, he'd go to the county seat to buy some bits and pieces, some leather belts and electric wires, some screwdrivers and spanners, then he'd make a mountain drill and open a copper mine on Tianzi Peak. His copper mine would make the people of Maqiao rich, and afterwards they wouldn't have to work in the fields any more, they wouldn't plant grain, cotton, sweet potatoes any more, they'd just eat and enjoy themselves every day.

No one expected that ugly little runt Three Ears would ever dare shit on Benyi's doorstep, would stir up all the trouble that was to come. That day, returning to Maqiao from the construction site at Bajingdong Reservoir, and wielding a Japanese-made 38-gauge rifle, Benyi forced Three Ears, tied up like a turkey, onto the grain-drying terrace. In his blinding rage, Benyi was making just about enough of a racket to frighten all the chickens and dogs out of the village: tired of living, was he, the smart-ass bastard? Must've been, to think of raping someone from the Party Secretary's family. If it hadn't been for Party policy on prisoners of war, he'd have cut off his dragon by now, wham, bam, gone. He hadn't been afraid of American imperialism in the Korean War, so was a lazybones like Three Ears going to scare him?

While he was saying his piece, people noticed that blood was coming out of Three Ears' nose, his clothes were torn to pieces, he had nothing but a pair of shorts on his lower body and his legs were black and blue. He'd lost the strength to keep his head up and it slumped weakly to one side; neither was he strong enough to talk and his eyes had shrunk to slits of greyish-white.

"Has he had it?" People were terrified by the very sight of him.

"Be good if he died, one less bastard for socialism to deal with!" Benyi said rather ungraciously.

"How could he do something like that?"

"He'd stab his own father with a rake, is there anything he'd stop at?" He yelled at Zhongqi to give him a hand hanging him up on a tree, then scooped up a great dipper of dung and held it up over his head. "D'you admit you're guilty? Speak up, d'you admit it?"

Three Ears shot a glance across at Benyi, blew a blood bubble out of his nostril; remained silent.

The dipperful of dung tipped over.

Tiexiang was nowhere to be seen. Some said she'd fainted from fright some time ago, some said she was hiding inside the house crying, repeating over and over he shouldn't be let off the rape charge, how her thighs and waist had been almost broken, spelling everything out very clearly. The men on the terrace put their heads together and whispered, once more drawn into concern over her body. Given that she hadn't attracted attention like this for some time, then, you could say, Three Ears was now doing this job for her again. Was she anxious her body had faded from people's memories?

It was already late at night by the time anyone released Three Ears down from the tree. He limped along, using walls or trees for support, and in the end it took him a full two hours, gasping and panting as he went, to walk a tiny stretch of road, stopping to rest all the time, his body aching from head to toe. Every step was an effort, as the most serious wound was between his legs; his "dragon bag" (scrotum) had been cut to pieces, one testicle had almost fallen off and it all hurt so much he could hardly see straight. But he didn't dare go to the clinic, afraid he'd be spotted there by people he knew, afraid it would feed the gossips, that people would kick up a huge fuss. Neither did he want to go back home: his mother would take him in, but he didn't want to go asking for more trouble from that damned Zhaoqing. He had no choice but to go back to the House of the Immortals, ask his housemate Ma Ming to help him find a needle and thread, and crouch round an oil lamp making a few crude stitches in his dragon bag. By the last stitch, the space between his legs was smeared with blood and his own hand shook so much he couldn't hold the needle steady; his whole body bathed in sweat, he fainted before he could gather up the thread.

All night long, the village dogs howled.

When Ma Ming woke, there wasn't a trace of Three Ears in his grass nest.

Nothing was seen of him for months on end.

One day in early autumn, some of the women were turning creepers on the sweet-potato patch when one of them cried out; sensing there was something there, everyone turned to discover someone standing on the road, two great big eyes staring out from under a mane of long hair. Someone finally made out that it was Three Ears, his face livid with rage. No one knew where he'd sprung from, nor how long he'd been standing there, staring silently.

The mane of hair walked over, a bag on his back, right up to Tiexiang.

Tiexiang took several steps backwards.

Thump—before anyone had seen what was happening, a wood knife was thrown at Tiexiang's feet and the mane knelt before her, neck stretched out as far as it could: "Kill me!"

Tiexiang shouted at the other women, "Help, someone! Help!"

"Are you going to kill me or not?"

Tiexiang went ashen, turned, and ran.

"Don't move!" Three Ears shouted at the top of his lungs; Tiexiang swayed briefly but didn't dare move any farther. He stood up, a thin, cold smile protruding sharply out of his face, "Lady, if you don't kill me, how're you going to have any peace? You poured a bowl of shit over my head, did you reckon I could swallow that?" Before Tiexiang could grasp what was going on, he suddenly pulled out a thick vine whip from his waist, and— crack—dealt Tiexiang a blow which left her staggering—another crack— she fell to the ground. She screeched and lifted her arms to ward off the blows, but when the women standing near saw how terrible the expression on Three Ears' face was, none dared intervene and all they could do was hurry back to the village to report as quick as they could.

"You filthy woman, you filthy whore, if you don't kill me, how's this thing going to end? . . ." Three Ears swore then whipped, swore then whipped until she rolled and writhed around everywhere. An observer looking on from afar would have seen and heard nothing, no one, nothing but grey, foggy waves of dust and sand, a pile of green potato leaves rolling here, turning there, making a rustling sound, a few shredded leaves flying up now and then. In the end, when her cries weakened and the leaves stopped moving, Three Ears finally stopped and dropped the whip.

He opened the cloth bag he'd brought with him, took out a new pair of leather shoes and a new pair of plastic sandals, and dropped them in the pile of now motionless potato leaves. "I'm still aching for you, you've seen that now!"

Then he stalked off.

At the intersection, he turned and shouted at the women: "Tell that piece of trash Benyi that I, Ma Xingli, stuck his wife twenty-five times, stuck her till she screamed—"

The people of Maqiao had almost forgotten he was called Ma Xingli.

***Nailed Backs** [背釘]: Benyi's first thought was to seize Three Ears, right there and then. When he returned from the construction site and heard the news from Zhongqi that his wife had had an affair with Three Ears, he was overcome with a murderous rage. But in the end the little bit of brain he had left made it clear to him this was a major loss of face; what would it achieve to kick up a huge fuss putting Three Ears on display? Thinking it over, then over again, the only thing to do was lock the door and thrash his wife to pieces. He broke a clothes-washing pestle on his adulterous wife, who rolled all over the floor under his blows until she tremblingly admitted everything. She still had a bit of fight left in her, though, and went along with Benyi's plan of dragging Three Ears into the mêlée. While the two men were slugging it out, it looked like Benyi was getting the worst of it, and he yelled at his wife to come and help out. Her loyalty was still with her old man, and an inspired lunge mid-fracas at Three Ears' crotch area almost knocked him out cold.

With this, Benyi finally got his hands free, fetched the hemp rope he'd prepared long in advance, and tied Three Ears up as tightly as a *zongzi*— a glutinous rice dumpling wrapped in bamboo leaves.

But Benyi had never imagined that his adulterous wife would suddenly disappear the following year. Three Ears didn't cross his mind once: even if she'd eloped or been abducted, only the director of the Cultural Institute or the photographer came under suspicion. He thought he'd lost a simply inhuman amount of face and completely ignored public business for days on end, locked and bolted the door, stuck two plasters on his forehead, and slept right through. Murderous gall rose deep inside him again: Party Secretary or no, wherever he next found that devil woman, he'd finish her off with one knife-stroke.

Most of the villagers hadn't considered Three Ears either, would never have imagined that a woman as attractive as Tiexiang would abandon two kids still in school and go off with a lazybones like him. People merely supposed something was going on in the Cultural Institute, and even sent someone to the county seat to make inquiries.

The following autumn, a piece of very surprising news came over from Jiangxi. This news proved that Tiexiang had in fact eloped and that she'd robbed a grain truck on the highway with Three Ears; out of the bandits hunted down by the army and the People's Militia, one had been beaten to death and ten or so arrested. The final two had been tough nuts to crack, evading arrest by hiding here and there in the mountains. Afterwards, making use of information provided by a local peasant, the People's Militia searching the mountains finally pinned them down and forced them into a mountain cave. The militia encircled the mouth of the cave several times over and shouted out: having got no response, they finally hurled in a hand grenade and blew them to smithereens. The militia discovered afterwards that the two dead were a man and a woman, so thin they only weighed seventy or eighty catties each. The woman's stomach stuck out, several months into pregnancy. An official seal was discovered among their clothing and bags for starting a copper-mining cooperative, or something of the sort. There were also two blank prescription letters, two sheets of special lesson preparation paper, and a few envelopes for official letters on which were written the name of this county and this commune. It was only thanks to this that Public Security contacted the area to send someone to identify them. Commune Head He went and identified, from the photographs left at the police substation, the blurred mass of flesh and blood that had been the faces of Tiexiang and Three Ears.

Commune Head He paid two of the local peasants twenty yuan to bury them.

According to Maqiao's ancient rules, as Tiexiang was unchaste and Three Ears was unrighteous, as both had contravened family rules and national law *and* been disloyal, in death they had to have "nailed backs." In other words, after their deaths, they had to face downward in their graves and nine nails had to be hammered into their backs. Facing downwards meant they had no face to look other people in the face. Nailing their backs meant they would be forever locked in the netherworld, that they could never again be reincarnated or reborn to bring further disaster upon others.

As Maqiao people hadn't taken charge of their corpses, they couldn't nail their backs. When they mentioned this, the old people in Maqiao couldn't conceal their great sense of anxiety at not knowing what further trouble from them might lie in store.

☆**Root** [根]: Three Ears' elopement with Tiexiang aroused a sense of moral outrage in Maqiao. In the past, it'd always been the women, particularly the women, who'd carped at Tiexiang behind her back, who'd poked their noses into her relations with the director of the Cultural Institute, with the young lad from the photography institute, who'd flared their nostrils and pursed their lips as her backside sashayed back and forth. Now, they suddenly felt these relationships were perfectly acceptable, could be overlooked. They even thought there was nothing much wrong in stealing someone—the important thing was, who stole whom. Although none of Tiexiang's affairs had been quite proper, this affair with Three Ears was definitely the worst thing she ever did. On this point, a great sense of injustice, a kind of protective group feeling suddenly welled up on behalf of Tiexiang, it agitated, moved, warmed them, as if Tiexiang was an athlete they'd entered for a competition, who'd lost the day at some sports meet due to some chance misfortune. It made them hopping mad. And Three Ears was just too undignified, simply beneath contempt, he'd never even washed his neck properly. Although he'd behaved properly toward his fellow villagers, he had no moral character to speak of, no family fortune, no decent education, no nothing, even his parents were the sort of people who'd end up lugging carrying poles all their lives; it was a joke, how *could* Tiexiang go off with him? And—as it turned out—get pregnant by him?

For a few months, they took this as a collective insult.

However much they thought it over, they couldn't figure Tiexiang out.

Only one thing could explain it: fate. In Maqiao dialect, people didn't much use the word "fate"; more often they'd use the word "root," as if they were comparing themselves to plants. They also read lines on the hand and on the foot, believing these marks were the precise embodiment of fate, the very image of roots. An old man passing by once read the roots on Tiexiang's hand: he said with a sigh that she was a threshold root, her ancestors had been beggars perhaps, had hung around the doorways of a thousand houses. This root was so long it hadn't been broken in her.

Tiexiang had giggled away disbelievingly. True enough, her father Dai Shiqing had been a beggar chief, but she'd married a Party Secretary, and the spouse of a Party Secretary *was* practically the Party Secretary— what doorway was she going to be found hanging around? Little did she realize that, all those years later, the words of that old man would turn out to be her fate when she followed Three Ears, a man so poor he had no choice but to hang around doorways, that she'd end her life wandering around destitute in distant parts. She was like a tree, desperately seeking sunlight and rainwater from up above, but after a thirty-year search, she discovered finally that no matter how much her own leaves grew, they couldn't escape their roots, couldn't flutter off into the sky.

Her palm was crossed with low-lying roots.

The phrase "return to your roots"—also related to the word "root"—signified not a wandering elder returning home, but "fatalism." This was how they put it: as mud is three inches deep, so man has three branches. During youth, everything remains in flux, but after completing the three branches of age—three dozen years, that is—people start to return to their roots, whether they're noble or base, wise or stupid, good or bad, all becomes clear after the age of thirty-six. *Que sera* and each to his own. It was during the very year of her thirty-sixth birthday that Tiexiang—as if possessed by the spirits—went off with a lazybones; this was her inescapable, inexorable doom. Or so they deeply, unshakably believed.

*Riding a Wheelbarrow** [打車子]: "Riding a wheelbarrow" was a phrase that Tiexiang used to refer to what went on between her and Three Ears in bed. This was something Zhongqi had secretly overheard; people laughed for days after it'd spread about, and it subsequently became a Maqiao idiom.

Chinese has no lack of food-related vocabulary. For cooking methods, there's steam, boil, fry, stir-fry, quick-fry, sauté, shallow fry, stew, cure, pickle, casserole, braise, and so on; for the action of the mouth there's eat, sip, suck, slurp, swallow, lick, gnaw, bite, chew, gulp, and so on; for the sense of taste, there's sweet, acrid, salty, bitter, hot, sour, fresh, spicy, crisp, slippery, numbing, clean, mellow, crumbly, powdery, and so on. But although sex is also a human need, there seem to be in comparison far fewer words relating to sex. As Confucius said: "food and sex are human nature." But our linguistic heritage has wiped out half of Confucius's venerable opinion.

There is still, of course, what's called low talk, mainly low-quality, perennially popular expressions, oral excretions you hear everywhere. Though there's no lack of them, their deficiencies are only too apparent. Firstly, they echo, they duplicate each other, they add nothing new; secondly, they lack content, they overgeneralize, they're all talk and no action, like politicians' speeches on state affairs, like cultural bureaucrats slapping each other on the back. Even worse, they're mainly borrowed words that don't even cover the meaning, that don't express the sense, that rely on tacit, contextual understanding; the effect produced is as ludicrous as putting Mr Zhang's hat on Mr Li, or calling a donkey a horse. "Clouds and rain," "grinding bean curd," "cannon firing," "steaming buns" . . . All these expressions sound like mafia codes. And so, left thus with no alternative, people begin to act like shifty mafiosi, while linguistic ethics equate sex with mafia crimes, with conspiracies that evade clear, precise expression.

This sexual vocabulary necessarily springs from the transformation of sexual feeling into something crude, formulaic, utilitarian, and furtive. The surging excitement of exchange between the sexes springs from a delicate, shimmering trembling from deep within the body, from anxiety, obduracy, sympathy, and an unnerving joy, all of which both clash with and support each other, from secret, storm-tossed explorations that, at dizzying emotional heights, sit poised on the cusp of destruction, infatuation, and hurtling descent, bringing every single part and process of one's being to life. . . . It's a great pity that all this has for so long been driven underground into a deep, linguistically unreachable blind spot.

A linguistic blank is a human abandonment of self-knowledge, an ignominious defeat, hinting at some form of enormous, lurking danger. Language serves as the link between humans and the world: once this link is broken or lost, people have as good as lost their control over the world. In this sense, it can perfectly justifiably be said that language equals the power to control. To chemistry experts, a complex chemistry laboratory is like their own backyard; to someone ignorant of chemistry, it's a terrifying minefield, covered in death traps. To those who've grown up in the city, a bustling city is their home territory, there's nowhere more convenient or comforting; but to people from the countryside with no knowledge or experience of the city, it's a thorny jungle where enemies, obstacles, and nameless, unshakable terrors lurk everywhere. There's a very simple reason for all this: a world hard to describe in words is a world beyond your control.

Sociological research has identified a kind of "marginal person," someone who leaves one culture and enters another, such as country people who go into the city, immigrants who leave their native country for distant lands. Language is the chief problem encountered by such people. Whether or not they have money, whether or not they have power, if they haven't grasped the new language, as long as they haven't yet gained a proficient linguistic grasp of their new environment, they'll never manage to shake off the feeling of rootlessness, of insecurity. When rich Japanese go to France, some of them suffer from "Paris syndrome." When courageous Chinese migrate to America, some suffer from "New York syndrome." Their limited foreign-language skills prevent them from blending into the unfamiliar turf of a foreign land. Neither their money nor their courage can protect them from their nameless anxiety, tension, terror, palpitations, rising blood pressure, paranoia, and the delusion they're being spied on. Any incomprehensible dialogue with neighbors or people on the street, any foreign object or vista they can't put a name to imperceptibly increases the psychological pressure on them, leaving them highly vulnerable to illness. Many people, in this kind of situation, closet themselves in desolate residences, continually fleeing from the outside world—just as people having sex seek to avoid the eyes and ears of others.

People have little fear about revealing their own bodies. In the bathhouse, the gym, swimming pool, even—in some Western countries—on nudist beaches, people feel no great discomfort or terror. People only feel the need to shut curtains and doors when having sex, like rats trying to burrow into a hole in the ground. There are a lot of reasons for this crucial distinction, of course. But in my opinion, one reason that's always been overlooked is that people have a complete linguistic grasp of activities like washing, exercising, swimming, and so have effective control over themselves and other people, sufficient to exercize their sense of reason. It's only when people drop their pants and face the unbounded linguistic blind spot of sex that ignorance and confusion create insecurity, and the human subconscious slinks back into its lair. What are people afraid of? Not just moralizing public opinion: subconsciously, they're far more afraid of themselves, afraid of losing themselves in the unnamed darkness of sex. Once they drop their pants, they too experience anxiety, tension, terror, palpitations, a rise in blood pressure, paranoia, and the delusion of being spied on, just as if they'd been thrown into the Paris or New York they have yearned for, only to burrow themselves away in their apartments.

Statistics show that crime levels for "marginal people" are high, as is the occurrence of mental illness. Everything foreign that lies beyond the linguistic grasp of marginal people, beyond the power of their intellect, amounts to primal chaos, dissipating with the greatest of ease their consciousness and competence. By a similar logic, the linguistic blind spot of sex easily brings human irrationality to the surface. Perhaps this is the unspoken condition by which sexual adventures achieve their charm, and also, of course, the condition by which sexual desire leads to catastrophe. Schemes involving beautiful women can often bring down great political plans, economic strategies, and military structures. Common sense can often melt away in one night of dissolution, hurling people carelessly into the wilds of passion—just as it did with Tiexiang.

Maybe this was how things were:

1. Tiexiang was perfectly aware of how poor and inferior Three Ears was, but after the two locked in carnal embrace she was suddenly seized by a kind of charitable urge, a kind of passionate interest in using her body to achieve miraculous ends. If she'd

already been bedded by several men of standing, a repeat of this experience would have held little interest for her. In Three Ears, she saw a new battleground, a more challenging mission. Poverty and inferiority held no terrors for her: quite the opposite, the idea of poverty and inferiority intoxicated her; the thought of rebuilding a man's sense of pride made her heart thump uncontrollably.

2. Three Ears did a great many truly terrible things, coming to blows with his parents, for example, fighting with his brothers, never working in the village, stealing a bag of chemical fertilizer from the team leader, even climbing the wall of the women's toilet in the clinic, and so on; Tiexiang, too, snorted with contempt at these past offences. But she later decided to attribute all this to her own magical powers. Maqiao's melons all rotted because of her, Maqiao's animals all went mad because of her—could it not be that Three Ears had committed all these outrages because of her? Three Ears—no, she now preferred to call him Xingli, her own Xingli—was brave, chivalrous, a man who could put up with a lot: the way he'd stuck his neck out over Yanwu's schooling was proof enough. If he hadn't secretly adored her all along, if he hadn't been driven wild with unrequited love, he wouldn't have run headlong into all those disasters with quite such abandon. All this produced a sudden burst of realization that filled her with an enormous sense of well-being: a stream of warm, compassionate emotion flooded through her heart, sending her body into uncontrollable spasms of trembling.

3. Even after the so-called rape, Xingli often returned to the village looking for her, his face set into a mask savagery, and he would beat her till her nose went blue and her face puffed up, till she screamed for her parents. This made everyone in the village furious. Even though some suspected the rape hadn't been everything it seemed, that maybe there'd been an injustice, a real man shouldn't fight with a woman, the vendetta couldn't go on and on like this. Surely only a madman, a bandit would go on beating a person like this? Only Tiexiang, out of all Maqiao, failed to sense any malice in Three Ears' revenge: quite the opposite, she tasted sweetness in her own pain, tasted the immutable love of her adversary. She believed that only the person who loved you most could be pushed beyond desperation to such deep resentment and hatred. In their past life together, Benyi hadn't been exactly happy with her, but he'd hardly ever beaten her; more

often than not, after he'd had a drink, he'd head out the door, hands behind his back, to a cadre meeting. The director of the Cultural Institute and the photographer had also been let down by her, but they were even less likely to strike out at anyone, they just rubbed their hands and slipped away without a trace. This tolerance and irresolution quite simply enraged her, prevented her from discovering her true position and power over these men. But she was addicted to the crack of the vine whip and rod, to men who left souvenirs of their wild obsession and crazed desire in the form of scar upon scar of heart-stopping pain. Several times (incredibly enough, even to her) orgasm would suddenly wash over her as she was being beaten, her cheeks burning bright red, her legs writhing uncontrollably.

Her pleasure intensified even further when Xingli passed on to her devices for feminine use. She secretly hid these things away, turning them over, looking at them when there was no one around.

In the end, she left in the night, casting back among Maqiao people the enormous linguistic blank represented by this code name, "riding a wheelbarrow."

☆**Hey-Eh Mouth** [呀哇嘴巴]: This word appears in the *Annals of the Ministry for the Suppression of Rebellion,* in the confession written by the rebel leader Ma Sanbao after his arrest: "I was very scared, but I was tricked by that Hey-eh Mouth Ma Laogua who said the government troops wouldn't come." Reading this, I thought to myself: someone who hasn't lived in Maqiao might not know what a "Hey-eh mouth" is.

"Hey-eh mouth" is still used in Maqiao today, meaning people who argue a lot, who like spreading rumors and secrets; also, unreliable blabbermouths. People like this probably use a lot of interjections like "hey" or "eh" as they talk, which would explain the word's provenance.

Zhongqi, from the lower village, who often reported to Benyi about rapes and other village matters, was a famous Hey-eh mouth. No secret in the village could get past his jug ears. Never mind how hot the day, he'd always stomp around in his shoes. Regardless of what he was working on, he'd never take off those suspicious, battered shoes—even if everyone else was going around barefoot, even if that day there'd be no work for which shoes could be worn, he'd just idly keep watch on the ridges between fields, wasting his time looking on as other people earned work points. No one knew what unspeakable visions hid within those shoes of his. He fiercely guarded the secret of his shoes, just as he tirelessly probed all the other villagers' secrets, and his face always wore an expression of secret satisfaction, deriving from a sense of profiting at others' expense.

Or perhaps I should say: *because* he himself had two shoefuls of secrets, he had to ferret out other people's secrets to make things even.

He'd creep stealthily up on me, prepare himself for a good long time, finally arrange his features into a smile and say: "Enjoy your sweet-potato flour last night, did you, hmm?" then shrink coyly back into himself, waiting for me to plead innocence or make excuses. Seeing I'd failed to react even slightly, he'd beat a deeply cautious but still smiling retreat from such personal matters. I didn't know how he'd found out about that sweet-potato flour last night, neither did I know why he considered this matter so important that he'd kept it in mind and made pointed reference to it. Even less did I know which part of him inside rejoiced at this ability of his, at his record of achievement in ferreting out the tiniest details.

Sometimes, he'd rouse himself into irregular passions: he'd be digging away at the ground, then suddenly heave a resonant sigh, or howl terrifyingly at some faraway dog, look to see if we'd reacted at all, then finally, his face a picture of misery, burst out with: "Yayaya, terrible." What's terrible? people would ask in surprise. Oh, nothing much, he'd say, shaking his head repeatedly, nothing much, a thread of self-satisfaction hanging from the corners of his mouth, smiling coldly at other people's indifference and disappointment.

Then, after a while, he'd go all miserable again, ah terrible, again. When other people asked him what was wrong, his tongue would loosen slightly, there was low stuff going on, he'd say, someone's got big, big problems, don't you know. . . . Once he'd gotten bystanders interested, he'd promptly slam on the brakes and reply with a complacent question: "Guess who it is? Guess who it is? Can you guess, eh?" He'd clam up, then repeat the performance five or six times, till no one asked anymore, till everyone was totally indifferent to, was exasperated by, his alternating melancholy and complacency; only then would he chuckle jubilantly and return to concentrating on his digging, as if he didn't have a care in the world.

*Agreed—Ma [馬同意]: Zhongqi was always a great supporter of the government, and a red Mao button, big as an egg, would usually be pinned conspicuously on his chest and a quotation bag always slung over his shoulder at meetings, long after they stopped being fashionable. Generally speaking, he was pretty handy at using political jargon, watched what he said, didn't let his tongue run unwisely away with him.

And there was always a fountain pen stuck in his breast pocket. He hadn't bought it, of course—one look at the slightly mangled shaft told you it'd been cobbled together from scrap remnants, it'd been through a tough refining process. As I recall, he'd never been a cadre or even held any kind of position in the Peasants' Association. But he loved using this pen, and he'd endorse anything that moved with "Agreed—Ma Zhongqi." Almost every team invoice, receipt, work-point book, account book, newspaper, and so on, carried this three-word mantra of his. Once, Fucha picked out a receipt for the purchase of some baby fish and was about to write it into the accounts when he spotted that, following a momentary lapse of watchfulness, the receipt had fallen into Zhongqi's hands; before he'd had time to shout stop, it'd already been inscribed with "Agreed," the nib being sucked in preparation for the final, solemn blow.

"Writing your funeral speech, are you?" Fucha snapped. "What's your agreeing got to do with it? What right d'you have to agree? Are you team leader, are you Party Secretary?"

Zhongqi laughed, "What skin's it off your nose? These fish were bought honest and above board, what's the problem if people agree? You tell me—did you steal these fish?"

"I don't want you to write on it! I just don't want you to write on it!"

"Did I write it wrong? How about if I tore that bit off?" Zhongqi was in a humorous mood.

"Damned pain he is," Fucha said to the people standing around.

"D'you want me to write 'Not agreed' then?"

"I don't want you to write anything at all, you shouldn't write anything on it! You want to write something, wait a couple of lives to see if you've turned into something human."

"Fine, then, I won't write anything. Mean little devil."

Feeling he'd got the upper hand, Zhongqi sedately stuck the fountain pen back in his pocket.

Somewhere between amusement and exasperation, Fucha fished another receipt out of his pocket and fluttered it about in front of everyone: "Hey, everyone, look, I haven't settled accounts with him. That catty of meat for the kiln yesterday, I can't charge it to the expense account, he's signed for it too."

Zhongqi reddened and glanced at the rustling receipt, "Don't charge it then."

"What were you doing writing 'agreed' on it? Got cold feet now?"

"I didn't see . . ."

"You sign something, you take responsibility."

"Well, I'll change it, okay?" He walked back over, hurriedly taking his pen out again.

"Can you change your crappy words? When Chairman Mao writes something, it's set in stone, the whole country follows every thousand-ton word. When you write, it's like a dog peeing, lifting its leg wherever it goes—what's it going to achieve?"

Zhongqi had reddened all the way down his neck, a small patch of light reflecting off the tip of his nose. "You're the dog round here, young Fucha. I reckon the higher-ups'll still pay—you work, you get to eat meat."

"If you've got the money, then get it out and pay! You're going to pay this back if it's the last thing you do today!

What with everyone being there, Zhongqi couldn't easily wriggle out of it. He stamped his foot: "Well, just charge it to me then, see if I care!" He swung off, his shoes clacking away. Shortly afterwards, he returned, rather out of breath, to slam a silver bracelet on the table. "Who's afraid of what a catty of meat costs? Young Fucha, I gave my agreement! Give it here, I'll pay for it!"

Fucha blinked silently; no one else knew what to do either, at that moment. A second ago, we'd been roaring with laughter, just winding Zhongqi up—none of us'd thought he'd be held to what he'd written, that he'd be forced into producing a silver bracelet.

But Zhongqi wasn't so easily put down, and he subsequently started to stamp his approval around even more recklessly. If Benyi or a commune cadre happened to take out a page of anything, he'd rush over and scribble "agreed," straight off. Agreeing had become a habit with him and no sheet of paper could escape his fountain pen, could escape his unfettered powers of ratification and approval. Fucha, who liked things to be neat and tidy, who preached orderliness, could only try desperately to avoid him: as soon as he heard the clacking of his shoes, as soon as he saw his face, he'd gather up all material of a papery nature, so as to avoid giving him the slightest opportunity to interfere. He had to pretend not to have seen, and would angrily turn and wander off somewhere else, looking for something else he could agree to, grabbing letters to us Educated Youth from out of the postman's hands, for example. As a result, every letter of mine carried his stamp of agreement to the recipient's name and address, sometimes they even carried his bright red fingerprint.

I found him as intensely irritating as Fucha did and resolved to find an opportunity to deal with him. One day at noon, as he napped, we stole his fountain pen and threw it into the pond.

Two days later, a ballpoint pen appeared in his pocket, its metal clip glittering away—it looked like there was nothing anyone could do.

☆**The Ghost Relative** [走鬼親]: Many years later, it was rumored someone in Maqiao had recognized a relative from a past life. When I was in

Maqiao, I'd heard stories like this and after returning to the city I heard that incidents of a similarly bizarre nature had taken place in other parts of Hunan. I didn't place much credence in them. A friend of mine, a scholar of folklore who's done specialized research on the subject, has even taken me off to places he's investigated and pointed out to me example after example of living proof, making each and every one of them relate their past lives. I still felt such occurrences lay beyond my comprehension.

So, of course, you can imagine my amazement when something like this happened to people I knew.

By then it was the 1980s: a young man from Maqiao, working at a bean curd shop in Changle, found himself destitute, had lost everything—even down to his underpants—at cards. He tried calling on some acquaintance of his, but as soon as they saw him they bolted the door fast, gesticulating vigorously at him to leave.

He was so hungry that black stars were appearing before his eyes. Fortunately, one person still had a heart—a girl from the Golden Happiness Tavern, only thirteen years old, called Hei Danzi. While her boss was out, she secretly pressed a few buns on the young man, and two yuan besides. "And what d'you call this?" the young man boasted to his gang of confreres. "This is the magic of Brother Sheng!"

Shengqiu was his name, and he was the son of Benyi, Maqiao's former Party Branch Secretary.

In time, the boss of the Golden Happiness Tavern found out what was going on, that Hei Danzi was often helping Shengqiu out, and suspected that she was abusing her position, giving away things from the tavern. After carrying out a very careful stock check, the boss failed to discover any deficit or goods missing from the shop; but it still struck him as strange: why should a mangy, unemployed vagrant be worth such care and attention from Hei Danzi? As a distant uncle of Hei Danzi's, he felt he should cross-examine her about it and called her to him for questioning.

Hei Danzi lowered her head and wept.

"What are you crying about, what are you crying about?"

"He . . ."

"What about him?"

"He's my . . ."

"Spit it out, is he your boyfriend?"

"He's my . . ."

"Spit it out!"

"He's my son."

The boss's jaw—and almost a cup of boiling tea—dropped.

And that was how this surprising piece of news got out. People said Hei Danzi—Hei Danzi from the Golden Happiness Tavern—had recognized her own son from a past life. That was to say, she was the reincarnation of Maqiao's celebrated Tiexiang. If her boss hadn't pressed her, she would never have dared say it out loud. For days on end, people thronged the tavern, pointing and peeking. To cadres from the municipal committee and police substation, this was no trifling matter: this was the revival of feudal superstition—what was the world coming to? Betting was back, prostitutes were back, highwaymen were back, and now, to top it all, there were ghosts too. There was certainly never a dull moment around here.

The cadres did their utmost to deflate this talk of ghosts and to educate the masses, summoning her down to the police substation for cross-examination—drawing a crowd of idly curious onlookers in the process. On and on they went, till the policemen's heads throbbed and ran with sweat, but still the case couldn't be settled; finally they had to agree to take her to Maqiao for further investigation. Even if she could recognize her son from a past life, surely she couldn't recognize other people from a past life? If she couldn't recognize them, then that would put an end to her corrupting claptrap, and about time, too.

Six people went: in addition to Hei Danzi, two policemen, a vice-director from the municipal committee, and two meddlesome cadres who tagged along. When they were still a good distance away from Maqiao, they got out of the car and made Hei Danzi go in front, leading the way, to see whether she truly remembered the scenery of her past life. The girl said that she only vaguely, approximately remembered this past life, and she might go the wrong way. But looking around her after each stretch she walked, she made straight for Maqiao, with a directness that made the people trailing behind break out in goose-pimples.

When her path took her across a stone quarry in the mountains, she suddenly stopped and cried a while. The stone quarry was by now abandoned: a few lumps of dried-up ox dung lay on the fragments of rubble all over the ground; puffy clumps of wild grass poked out that would perhaps, before too long, inundate the rubble. When the cadres asked her why she was crying, she said her husband in her previous life had been a stonemason, had cut stone here. The cadres, who'd made some inquiries in advance, secretly rejoiced, knowing this to be completely untrue.

After entering Maqiao she hesitated a little, saying that there hadn't been this many houses before, she couldn't recognize much of it.

The vice-director was delighted. "Had enough, eh? Don't want to play any more, eh?"

One of the policemen didn't agree with the vice-director and was unwilling to start back to the office: seeing as they'd got there, why not let her keep trying—they weren't going to get anything else done today in any case.

The vice-director thought for a moment, looked up at the sky, and didn't put up any opposition.

It was at this point that the person telling me the story started to get carried away—this, he said, was when things really took a turn for the weird. He said that as soon as she stepped into Benyi's house, Hei Danzi seemed possessed by some spirit: not only did she know the way there and the door, but also where the kettle was kept, the piss bucket, the rice cupboard, everything; she also knew at one glance that the semiprostrate old man on the bed was Benyi. Her tears immediately welled up, and she fell to the ground in obeisance, crying out brother Benyi's name, sobbing away. Even deafer than before, Benyi widened his eyes with a great effort and was utterly bemused to see the room full of strange faces. His bemusement only lessened slightly when his second wife came back from the vegetable garden and roared a few sentences at him. It was just too much for him to take, this little girl, still wet behind the ears, standing before him, and his eyes bulged up as big as copper coins: "If you want money, ask for money, you want food, ask for food, just what kind of ghost are you? She's not even grown-up, how can she be a ghost?"

Terrified into tears, Hei Danzi was hustled outside.

A lot of villagers came to inspect this bizarre novelty, to pick over Hei Danzi's appearance, thinking back to what Tiexiang had been like, subjecting every part of her to comparison. The majority conclusion was: how could this possibly be Tiexiang? Tiexiang had been bewitching, dazzling—what kind of a pickled cabbage dumpling was this? On and on they went, until Hei Danzi, squatting on the stepped eaves, weeping and warbling, suddenly raised her head and asked an unexpected question:

"What about Xiuqin?"

The Maqiao people squinted at each other—this was an unfamiliar-sounding name.

"What about Xiuqin?"

One after another they shook their heads, mystification shining from their eyes.

"Is Xiuqin dead?"

The little girl was once more on the verge of tears.

An old man suddenly remembered something: yes, yes, yes, he said, I think there's a Xiu-something-Qin, she's from Benyi's same-pot brother, Benren's, family. Benren had fled to Jiangxi many years ago and had never come back. Xiuqin had married into Duoshun's family, she was the third wife now, yes, she was still alive.

Hei Danzi's eyes shone.

With effort, people figured things out for themselves: if this girl before them was Tiexiang, then she'd have been the sister-in-law for a time of Third Wife—no wonder she was asking about her. Swept along by enthusiasm, a few people took her off to find her. "Third Wife lives on the bamboo hill, you come with us," they said to Hei Danzi. Hei Danzi nodded her head, then hurried to follow them over a hill and through a bamboo grove, before far off in the distance she saw a house flash out from among the bamboo.

Her rather meddlesome guides had already run off ahead into the yellow mud house, yelling and calling, had passed through the few empty rooms but discovered no one home. Someone then went to the lotus pond, and shortly after shouts came over from that direction: "She's here, she's here!"

An old woman was at the side of the pond, washing clothes.

Hei Danzi flew over and threw herself before the old woman: "Brother Xiuqin, Brother Xiuqin, it's me, Tiexiang . . ."

The old woman carefully looked her up and down, to left and to right.

"Don't you recognize me?"

"Tiexiang who?"

"When I was in the hospital, it was you who sent me food and water. The evening I ran off, it was you I came and kowtowed to!"

"Why you're—you're—you're—you're . . ." Whatever thought had just come into the old woman's head, she never verbalized: her words choked in her throat, her eyes glinting with tears.

They said nothing else, just wept so bitterly in each other's arms that the bystanders didn't know what to do, didn't even dare come closer, just watched from far off. A clothes-washing pole fell into the water and slowly spun in circles. A twisted bundle of clothing also rolled into the water, scattered, then slowly sank.

☆**Flame** [火焰]: It's very hard to define this word precisely, as it's both abstract and ambiguous in sense. If you said you didn't believe in ghosts, you'd never seen ghosts, Maqiao people would flatly declare it was because your "flame" was too high.

So what *is* flame, then?

If this question is a slightly tricky one to answer, then I could try rephrasing it as: what sort of people have a high flame? Maqiao people would say: city people, educated people, rich people, men, people in the prime of life, who've never been ill, state employees, people in daylight, people unplagued by disasters and difficulties, who live by highways, people on sunny days, in open country, people with lots of friends and relatives, people who've just eaten their fill. . . . And, of course, people who don't believe in ghosts.

This covers practically the full gamut of life's problems.

I'd surmise, then, that what they mean by flame is a general life view: in situations where humans find themselves in a weakened position, a person's flame goes low, is snuffed out, and ghosts and demons start to appear. The popular saying, "poor people see more ghosts" probably refers to the same sort of thing. Writing this reminds me of my own mother, who'd received a modern education, had been a teacher, and had never believed in ghosts. In the summer of 1981, because of a big septic boil on her back, an affliction that frequently reduced her to a state of semi-stupor, she started to see ghosts. Time and time again, she would cry out in terror in the middle of the night, shrinking, trembling back into the corner of the bed, claiming there was someone behind the door, a woman called Wang, come to assassinate her own ghost, and asking me to kill her with a vegetable knife. It was then that I was reminded of this word "flame." At that moment, I thought, her flame was definitely too low, she'd seen things I had no way of seeing, had entered a world I had no way of entering.

Afterwards, she hadn't the slightest recollection of what had happened.

The power of the intellect is without doubt the most important ingredient in flame: it's the mark of the strong, advancing revolution, science, and economic development; wherever it touches, ghostly shadows will disappear like smoke, ghostly talk will scatter like clouds, and dazzling sunlight will reign triumphant. The problem is, if you understand flame as Maqiao people do, then it's only relative: since the strong become weak before the even stronger, fear of ghosts may never be utterly, triumphantly dispelled. There are also times when the power of the intellect is thwarted, when it is insufficient, and disintegrates. My mother doesn't believe in ghosts. But when her sense of reason was sufficiently weakened so as to be rendered incapable of resisting a septic boil, on came the ghosts. Modern people don't place that much credence in ghosts, but when their sense of reason becomes incapable of overcoming difficulties such as war, poverty, pollution, indifference, becomes incapable of shaking off the weight of inner anxiety, then specters and superstitions of every shade and description will rear their heads once more in even the most scientific and developed cities of the twentieth century. Even those who categorically deny the existence of ghosts, even highly educated, modern people will still, perhaps, use ghostly imagery (think of modern painting), ghostly sounds (think of modern music), ghostly logic (think of modern surrealist poetry or fiction). . . . In a sense, modernist culture is the covert breeding ground for the biggest ghost town of this century, a scholarly cacophony of ghosts and spirits that derives from those members of modern society with the lowest flame: peasants, the uneducated, the poor, women, children and old people, sick people, people plagued by disasters and difficulties, refugees, people who live far from highways, with few friends and relatives, people at nighttime, on rainy days, who don't live in open country, people suffering from hunger . . . and people who believe in ghosts.

If you look into the biography of any important modernist writer or artist, you'll soon discover the shadowy forms and flashing eyes of people with low flame, people like those I have just listed.

I'm not arguing for the existence of ghosts. As I often remark, the ghosts Maqiao people discovered, including those ghosts which came from outside Maqiao, could only ever speak Maqiao dialect, they couldn't speak Mandarin, much less English or French; they obviously hadn't transgressed the intellectual bounds of their discoverers. This leads me to believe that ghosts are manmade things. Maybe they're just a kind of hallucination, a kind of imagining that springs forth at times when the body is weak (as in my mother's case) or the spirit is weak (like the despairing modernists)—the same as what happens, more or less, when people dream, get drunk, take drugs.

Facing up to ghosts amounts to facing up to our own weaknesses.

This is one way of understanding the term "flame."

And so I suspect that what's known as the Hei Danzi story never happened in Maqiao (see the entry "The Ghost Relative"), that Tiexiang wasn't really reincarnated. When I returned to Maqiao, Fucha categorically denied there was any truth to this story, rejected it as devil talk that misled the masses, as groundless gossip. I believed Fucha. Of course, I don't in the slightest suspect those who claimed to have seen Hei Danzi with their own eyes of deliberately deceiving me, no, they probably felt no compulsion to do that. It is simply the case that I see, in their scattered and contradictory narrative fragments, the dubiousness of this story. I once tried pursuing the story to its end: where was Hei Danzi now? Will she ever come back to Maqiao? They hemmed and hawed. Some said that Hei Danzi had eaten red carp—people who'd eaten this variety of fish no longer remember things from their past life, so she wouldn't come back. Some said Hei Danzi had followed her uncle down south to a city on the coast to make money and couldn't be found. Others said Hei Danzi was afraid of Benyi—which meant: she had neither the face nor the courage to come back. And so on, and so forth.

There was no neat ending. Of course, it didn't need a neat ending, I could weigh each version for myself. I had absolutely no doubt the whole story resulted from general confusion at a time of low flame, that it was a shared illusion of theirs, just like everything my mother saw while ill.

When people hope to see something, that something will always pop up one day or another. People have two possible means of making this something appear: at times of high flame, they use the techniques of revolutionary, scientific, or economic development; at times of low flame, they use illusion.

People can't be made identical to each other. If I can't raise the flame of most Maqiao people, I don't think I have any reason to rob them of their right to illusions, to prevent them from imagining that their Tiexiang returned once more to Maqiao, that she overcame the boundary between the living and the dead and wept in the arms of her sister-in-law by the side of the lotus pond.

*Red Flower Daddy [紅花爹爹]: Uncle Luo wasn't originally from Maqiao: he'd been a long-term hired hand all the way up to land reform, after which he became village head for a few years, making him a veteran cadre in Maqiao. Various people had proposed marriage to him at various times, but each time he'd refused. He was a confirmed bachelor: when he'd eaten his fill, there was no one else in his household to go hungry. When just he worked, everyone in his household toiled. Sometimes people called him "Red Flower Daddy"—"red flower" meant virgin.

People later discovered that the reason he wouldn't get married wasn't because he lacked money, it was because all his life he'd kept his distance from women, had been afraid of women; whenever he saw a woman approach he'd do his utmost to take a detour off elsewhere; you'd never, ever find him anyplace where there were a lot of women around. His nose was very sensitive, peculiarly so: he could always sniff out a fishy smell on women's bodies. He thought the only reason women used face powder was to cover up their fishy bodily smell. In spring in particular, the air was always full of this fishy female smell (which was particularly strong on women of about thirty), mingled with a smell of rotting melons; it could travel one hundred paces on the wind and his head would swim as soon as it hit his nostrils. If he remained in contact with this smell for any length of time, it would do terrible things to him: his face would go yellow, his forehead would break into a cold sweat, he'd retch over and over again.

He'd ascertained, moreover, it was this very fishy smell that had spoiled his fruit. Behind his house were two peach trees which, despite blooming luxuriantly every year, never produced much fruit; even when fruits appeared, they would rot away one by one. Some said these trees were diseased. He shook his head: those rotten women and their wild goings-on make *me* ill, he said, so how's a tree to bear it?

He was referring to the fact that the two peach trees were next to a tea plantation, where every year women would go to pick tea and generally let their hair down; as he saw it, it would've been strange if the trees *hadn't* gone rotten.

Some didn't give much credence to what he said and wanted to test his nose, test whether it really was different from everybody else's, whether it really had this implacable hatred for women. So, at the end of one working day they stole his straw coat and offered it to some women as a cushion to sit on, before returning it back to its original place to watch what kind of reaction there would be.

Everyone was astounded: when he picked up the raincoat, his nose wrinkled and face darkened instantly:

"You low-life lowlifes, who touched my raincoat?"

The men present glanced at each other, pretending to know nothing.

"What've I ever done to you? When did I do you wrong? To make you do this to me?" He made a face and stamped his foot in genuine anger.

The raincoat thieves quickly slipped away in alarm.

Uncle Luo threw away his coat and huffed and puffed his way back home. Anxious to make peace, Fucha washed the coat in the pond. But the coat never again reappeared on the old village head's back—people said he'd burned it immediately.

No one dared play another joke like this on him. If you invited him to dinner, there could never be any female guests at the table, nor any women's clothes drying nearby. And when arranging his work assignments, you had to be careful not to send women off with him. Once, Benyi sent him off on the tractor to the county seat to buy some cotton flower seeds, a trip that took him a whole two days; when he got back, he said when he'd set out his leg had suddenly started to hurt, but he hadn't been in time to catch the tractor and had had to go on foot, so he'd lost a day. It was only afterwards, when villagers happened to bump into the tractor driver in the commune, that they discovered he *had* been in time to catch the tractor, but just because there were a few women catching a lift on the vehicle he'd absolutely refused to get on, insisting that he preferred to walk by himself. There was no one to blame but himself.

He walked very slowly: the thirty *li* from the county seat back to Maqiao took him a whole day. And not only that: he did everything slowly, nothing rashly, as if he knew full well there were days beyond days, and also days beyond the days beyond the days, there was no need to shit your breakfast as soon as you'd got it down. The young men all liked to work with him, as he'd make the day fairly relaxed, not overly pressured. One day, the young men went with him to Tianzi Peak to repair the aqueduct over the mountains. The weather was terribly cold that day and an ice crust had frozen over the ground; even though everyone's feet were tied up with grass rope, they still slipped at every step, and at every fall, wails and laughter rose and fell in waves. By the time everyone arrived at the construction site, they were all dreading the work ahead of them, and seeing as even the cadres hadn't arrived and Uncle Luo was the only person who had any speech rights to speak of, they begged him to agree to let everyone wait a while, at least until the sun had come up and melted the ice, before starting work. His drowsy eyes full of sleep, Uncle Luo dug his tobacco out of his cloth bag saying: "Who's to say otherwise? Dragging everyone out from under their quilts on such a cold day, as if you were going to bury your nearest and dearest . . ." Whatever he was saying wasn't all that clear, but everyone caught what he meant. A roar of delight went up, then everyone dispersed, each looking for a corner to hide from the wind and warm himself up. Uncle Luo had searched out from who-knew-where a few withered, fallen leaves and had squatted down around a mounded fire, winning himself several jostling companions.

"Maybe you'd like to bring over a couple of baskets of charcoal, eh? Set up a few stoves, eh?" Benyi cleared his throat before producing these two enigmatic conversational gambits: everyone jumped with fright. No one knew where he'd popped up from, wielding a bamboo measuring pole.

Uncle Luo, his eyelids stuck up with sleepy dust, remained sedate: "The road's too slippery to stand up on, how d'you get that pole here? Didn't you see? Even the dogs won't go out on a day like this."

That's right, that's right, everyone else seconded him.

"Well, that's great!" Benyi gave a cold laugh, "So I came here to supervise your sleeping: Party members and People's Militia can take the lead sleeping, poor and lower-middle peasants can overcome hardships sleeping, you can all sleep everything into its fundamentals. D'you all know what sleep is?"

He was making use of the Marxist "externals/fundamentals" philosophy he'd just studied. When he'd finished talking, he took off his jacket, rolled up his sleeves, spat into his palm, heaved a brick boulder onto his shoulders, and headed off towards the aqueduct. This was quite an impressive performance, and everyone present watched in silent embarrassment; seeing as some of the others had also started to stir, a few at a time they reluctantly abandoned their corners of warmth, bracing themselves against the freezing wind.

Uncle Luo swallowed his anger, and when he'd finished smoking his ball of tobacco he too picked up a boulder of brick and followed Benyi, muttering as he went. Then something unexpected happened. Just as he'd walked up to the aqueduct, a shrill cry came from Benyi out in front: his body swayed back and forth, his feet failed to steady themselves, and he slid down the slippery face of the aqueduct. It looked as if he was going to slide over the edge of the mountain, right down into the mountain valley where water rushed and freezing air billowed. Everyone's hearts leapt into their mouths. But way before they'd realized how critical the situation was, Uncle Luo's eyes and hands were already on the case: he yelled out, hurled the brick boulder off his shoulder, and immediately flung himself forward; unable to grab hold of the torso before him, he managed a foot instead.

Fortunately, Uncle Luo's own foot was lodged behind a steel girder in the aqueduct and, though pinned against the ice and hauled along by Benyi's considerable weight, he ground to a halt at the edge of the aqueduct.

He couldn't really hear any of Benyi's yells—buffeted here and there by the valley wind, they sounded like a handful of mosquitoes buzzing from a very, very distant valley floor.

"What—did—you—say?" All Uncle Luo could see was the other foot flailing about wildly.

"Quick, pull me up, quick . . ."

"Let's not be hasty about this," Uncle Luo was also out of breath, "You're the one who's studied philosophy: now, would you say weather like this is an external, or a fundamental?"

"Quick . . ."

"There's no hurry, it's nice and cool here, nice place to have a chat."

"You son of a . . ."

By this time, a few of the young men had arrived on the scene: with some pulling the rope, some stretching out their hands, they finally, perilously managed to rescue the Party Secretary from his suspension under the aqueduct.

After Benyi got back on his feet, face red all over, he was no longer so proud, or so philosophical; he even needed to lean on people as he made his way pigeon-toed back down from the aqueduct. After returning to the village, he cut off a catty of meat and invited Uncle Luo over for a drink to thank him for saving his life.

From this time on, Benyi would spare only Uncle Luo—out of all Maqiao—his curses. Whenever Benyi had some decent wine, he'd take it over to Uncle Luo's thatched cottage and invite Uncle Luo to take a drop with him. Some said that later on, when Benyi was arguing with Tiexiang every other day, the main reason was that he was always hanging around Uncle Luo's place. They not only drank and chatted together, they also did some other things that people found rather puzzling, for example, washed together, even went under the mosquito net together, making the bed-plank creak under the pressure—no one knew what they were playing around at. As they were same-pot brothers, was there any reason to say they couldn't sleep under the same quilt? Once, someone in Uncle Luo's back garden stealing bamboo shoots happened to take a glance inside through a hole in the window paper. It was incredible:

They weren't sticking (see the entry "stick(y)") each other's bottoms, were they?

Meaning: irregular goings-on between men.

Maqiao people didn't concern themselves too much about such things. There was someone in Zhangjia District, and also some redflower daddies and red-flower uncles in neighboring villages who got up to similar stuff—it wasn't that uncommon. In any case, seeing as Benyi was always busy being angry during the day, no one dared make any further inquiries, so nothing was ever proved.

☆**Old Man (etc.)** [你老人家(以及其他)]: This term doesn't actually mean anything much, it's just a turn of phrase which can be used for old people, young people, even children. When overused, it gradually loses its meaning, becomes equivalent to the interjection of coughs or yawns into speech, camouflaged between phrases; no one whose ears were attuned would take any notice, would sense it was there. For example, someone might ask whether the supply and marketing cooperative had slaughtered a pig. The reply would be: "It's been slaughtered, old man." Or then again: have you bought any meat? The reply would be: "Bought some, old man." Here, the listener should hear but not heed "old man," should just pass it by, shouldn't take it the wrong way. Once, Uncle Luo cheerily greeted a female Educated Youth carrying rice seedlings whom he came across on the road: "Carrying seedlings, old man?" The girl, who'd just arrived in the village and wasn't much of a looker, spun on her heel and stomped off in a great rage. She later said to everyone else: "That old guy's so rude! Just because my skin's a bit dark doesn't mean I've become an old man, does it? I don't look older than him, do I?"

This was what happened when outsiders hadn't yet got the hang of local expressions; it also showed how Educated Youth didn't always understand the Maqiao tradition of prizing age far above youth: it was a compliment to call you old, it was, in fact, a form of flattery.

Careful investigation has shown that linguistic development and distribution are not even, uniform processes. There are actions that lack words, and words that lack actions—this is how things have always been, without any system or balance. It's rather like how some people die in droughts, some in floods, while inhabiting the same world. When the floodwaters are high, perfectly serviceable words will bloat up to distorted dimensions, then even when the high waters recede the effects of the flooding remain. When foreigners visit Japan, they never fail to notice all the superfluous "convention words" that exist. If a Japanese person were to praise a commodity you produced and approve your plans, without discussing with you any concrete steps toward a joint venture, you really mustn't take it seriously, you mustn't stay at home, waiting like an idiot for him to place an order. Foreigners have to be careful in Paris, too: if someone invites you to visit them at home, no matter how great their enthusiasm, no matter how much they slap your back, shake hands, even embrace you, press their face against yours, while they haven't actually given you their address, haven't actually fixed a time, you should just smile and read their behavior as a form of social nicety, as a common, standardized false token of friendly feeling, to be broadly ignored. You should *not* phone them and ask, "When should I come?"

It isn't that the Japanese and the French are particularly hypocritical; Chinese people are also extremely proficient at producing words that lack actions. For a long time now, Maqiao phrases such as "the revolutionary masses" / "the state of the nation is excellent, and is improving all the time" / "the warm, loving concern of our brilliant higher-level leadership" / "say what is in our hearts" / "elevate thought progressively" / "don't withdraw troops before victory is complete," etc. haven't stood up to serious scrutiny, either. Take, for example, the death of Uncle Luo, the old village leader. He'd been an old poor peasant, a pillar of Land Reform, even a sometime Red Army soldier—of course he had to have a proper funeral. At the wake, Benyi spoke as representative of the Party's deep sadness: "The golden monkey twirls a staff of a thousand tons, the jade roof is cleared of a myriad *li* of dust. The four oceans seethe, clouds and rain rage, the five continents quake, winds and thunder rise. In the mass upsurge of study of Mao Zedong philosophy and thought throughout the entire county, in the entire excellent circumstances of national revolutionary production, under the brilliant leadership and loving concern of the higher level Party organizational leadership, in the upsurge in our production brigade's complete implementation of deployment of the serial strategy from the Commune's Party representative meetings, our comrade Luo Yuxing was bitten by a mad dog . . ." A young cadre from the county civil administration wrinkled his brow and nudged Benyi, "What was that? What's that got to do with the brilliant upper-level leadership?" Taken aback, Benyi blinked: "Did I say leadership? I just said mad dog." The civil administration cadre said: "What about before? What did you say before that?" Benyi said: "Nothing much, just a bit of padding—shouldn't I have said it?"

Once he'd opened his mouth, the civil administration cadre had ruined the whole meeting: it wasn't just Benyi who was put out, the gathered crowds also felt their spirits dampened. As I saw it, no one had understood that people hear things in different ways, that everything Benyi had said before "mad dog" had long been automatically applicable to things like irrigation, manure collection, logging, struggling landlords, school commencements, had been so overused that it went in one ear and out the other, had already merged so completely with the linguistic scenery that only an outsider would take any notice of it. This outsider was still too young, didn't understand the potential of language to create verbal flourishes, to misfit reality, to diverge from facts.

As the encrustations of linguistic camouflage, superfluous words— which include terms of respect—can rarely be speedily purged and buried. In certain circumstances, they can suddenly, dramatically proliferate and expand, like a linguistic amplification of human morality, a sort of linguistic collagen implant within the austerity of human truth. Anyone with any knowledge of the world ought to realize this.

Having knowledge of the world means having the ability to make use of superfluous words—or rather, developing the functions cultivated by the vast quantities of ethical and political superfluous words in the world.

I know of a foreign writer who venerated slang, who described slang as the most powerful, the most precious language there was. These views of his are a little overstated, of course, a little inaccurate. But there's one reason, there's one point on which I can empathize with this writer: this writer wrote in the most refined and elegant of countries. That he shocked his world and transgressed its norms in this way must be because he had been so long suppressed by the oceans of incomparably refined, affable, courtly superfluities used in his sophisticated interpersonal relations that irritation finally gave way to torrents of obscenities. He must have been suffocating so much under the weight of linguistic falsity that he couldn't stop himself from spewing forth filth: it was as if he'd ripped off everyone's pants, exposing the anus of language to one and all. The anus is just like the nose, ears, and hands: it doesn't matter whether it's pretty or not, it isn't born pretty or ugly. In a world congested with falsity, the anus becomes the final unimpeded outlet to truth, the last bastion of rebellion where life force is stored and preserved. It thus becomes only too understandable that after Benyi had closed his grand, stately mourning meeting, as soon as he walked out into the night, he couldn't stop himself from yelling out:

"Stick your fucking, fuck, fucker—"

He'd stubbed his toe on a stone, seemed to be swearing at the stone.

His swearing done, he felt the blood begin to flow much more smoothly around his body.

☆**Eating (as Used in Springtime)** [茹飯(春天的用法)]: Spring brought with it an unperceived seasonal change in language. A nephew of Uncle Luo from far away had come to the mountains to haul charcoal and, on reaching Uncle Luo's doorway, was asked by the master of the house: "Have you eaten?"

To ask someone on meeting whether they'd eaten or not was a Maqiao custom, and a waste of breath: generally speaking, it was a convention that didn't need to be taken seriously.

Similarly speaking, "I've eaten," the set response, was not to be taken seriously. Particularly not in springtime, as it was then, in the time of shortage when every family ate porridge, when most people were so hungry their hands and feet went weak and their knees knocked.

But the nephew turned out to be a bit dim and adamantly replied: "No, I haven't," which caught Uncle Luo off guard. "You really haven't eaten?" he asked. "I really haven't," the young man said. Uncle Luo blinked: "Out with it now, if you've eaten you've eaten, if you haven't eaten you haven't eaten, now have you eaten or not?" The young man's features twisted under the pressure: "I really haven't." Uncle Luo started to get angry: "I know you, you never give me a straight answer. When you've eaten you say you haven't, when you haven't eaten you say you have, what're you playing at?! If you really haven't eaten, I'll go and cook something, the firewood's ready, the rice is ready, a lick of flame and it'll be done. Otherwise, I can go and borrow a bowl from someone, easy as pie, don't hold back now!" The young man was quite swept away by this verbal torrent, couldn't understand what he'd just held back on and started to sweat beads of embarrassment: "I . . . I really . . ." Uncle Luo fiercely intoned: "You, you, you really need a wife you do, still talking rubbish you are, don't leave things out, keep it plain, can't you tell me the truth? When you're here you make yourself at home. We're not strangers. If you've eaten, then you've eaten, if you haven't eaten, then you haven't eaten."

Under unbearable pressure by this point, the young man lost the will to defend himself and could only stammer out: "I . . . ate . . ."

Uncle Luo slapped his thigh in excitement, "Didn't I know it? I saw through it at once, didn't I? You were putting me on. Almost sixty, I am, and you've never said one honest thing to me. Wicked boy. You sit down."

He indicated a stool by the threshold.

Not daring to sit down, the nephew just hung his head, drank a bowl of cold water, heaved his charcoal back onto his shoulder, and left. Uncle Luo wanted him to rest a while before going on, but the nephew murmured that it would get late if he rested any longer.

Your sandals are falling apart, said Uncle Luo, you should change them before going.

The nephew said that new sandals would rub his feet, he wouldn't change them.

Not long after, while crossing the Luo River, the nephew went down to wash in the river and drowned, due to his own carelessness. Having no descendants of his own, Uncle Luo shared in the descendants of this brother of his who lived far away. Probably because his brother and his wife were afraid he'd be heartbroken, that he'd blame himself, they hid the truth from him, telling him only that his nephew had gone to the city to look for work and that he'd been in too much of a hurry when he went to say goodbye. As a result, for a long time afterwards Uncle Luo would still mention his nephew every now and then, with a great big smile on his face. When someone wanted to borrow a log, he'd say, I want to keep the wood to make a bed for my nephew when he gets married, my nephew eats out of the state rice-bowl now, he knows all about foreign city things, he'll have to ask a city carpenter to make his new bed. When someone bought a mountain chicken for him, he'd smile and say, good, good, and set it over the fire to smoke, keeping it until his nephew came to eat it.

As time went by, rumors slowly spread to Maqiao: everyone heard his nephew had died young and began to suspect that Uncle Luo was still in the dark. When they heard him mention his nephew, they couldn't help but sneak looks at him. He seemed to pick something up from these looks, to have an uneasy flash of realization—he'd be about to say something, then suddenly become agitatedly forgetful.

The more people expected him to correct himself, the more, by contrast, he stuck to his stubborn guns: he wouldn't even allow people around him to turn his nephew into a taboo subject to be skirted carefully around. Sometimes, when he saw other people's children, he would suddenly, voluntarily blurt out:

"Don't wish their lives away. That nephew of mine, there he was one moment, playing in the chicken shit, then the next moment he's working for the state, isn't he now?"

"That's right, that's right . . ."

The people standing around would fidget and mumble.

But Uncle Luo was very demanding. He wouldn't allow vagueness like this, he needed to draw even more attention to his nephew: "Stick-a-pig, haven't seen as much as a letter from him. You tell me, what use is it bringing up kids? He can't be that busy, can he? I've been to the city myself, what's to be busy about there? They just mess around from morning till night."

Still his listeners wouldn't take up the subject, exchanging covert glances among themselves.

He rubbed his chin, "But that's all well and good, I don't want him to come back to see me. What's there to see? If there's meat, don't I know how to eat it on my own? If there's cotton, don't I know how to wear it on my own?"

After having said enough, finally, about his nephew, having put on enough of a show as an elder uncle, having demonstrated enough of an elder uncle's happiness and headaches, he'd walk toward his thatched cottage, his head lowered, his hands behind his back. His spine, buckling under all those doubting gazes, hunched over as he walked.

☆**Model Worker (as Used on Fine Days)** [模範(晴天的用法)]: The commune wanted every team to nominate a model worker to study philosophy and attend meetings in the commune. Benyi was away, so it fell to Uncle Luo to take charge. After eating breakfast, he made his leisurely way to the terrace, took a few leisurely turns around it, escorted a snail that had climbed onto the terrace onto a clump of grass and that he was afraid everyone would tread on, and then assigned everyone work. He blinked the eyelids he never could completely open, bent his head to roll a cigarette out of tobacco ends and said Zhihuang, Wucheng, and Zhaoqing should go and tend the oxen, Fucha should go and lay rotted oxen manure, Yanzao, hmm, Yanzao should spread pesticide; the women and the sent-down kids should go and hoe the rape plants; model worker, ah, Wanyu'll do that.

I couldn't help laughing: "Shouldn't choosing a model worker . . . be put to a vote?"

Uncle Luo was surprised by this: "If Wanyu doesn't go, who'll go? His back's like a woman's, he's no good with oxen, not strong enough to lay manure, and yesterday he said his finger was swollen, to set him hoeing the rape plants'd be like setting a dragon to play the lute. I've thought about it, and there's no one else. Only he'll do."

Everyone else present felt making Wanyu the model worker was perfectly reasonable. What about Fucha? If it'd been raining, then Fucha could go and that would be that, he had a high cultural level. The problem was that the weather was fine today and there was work that had to be done. If Fucha were to go, who'd spread the manure? It was a no-win situation: if the manure wasn't spread on shoal patch (see the entry "Public Family"), how could it be ploughed tomorrow?

Pair after pair of perplexed, uncomprehending eyes stared at me. Only then did I understand that the term "model worker" meant one thing on fine days, and another on rainy days. I agreed: it had to be Wanyu.

☆**Speaking the Dao** [打玄講]: After Wanyu died, the hat of philosophy-studying-model-worker fell onto Uncle Luo's head. The team leader arranged that I should write the speech about his past experiences for him, and after having written it I'd read it to him sentence by sentence, get him to memorize it, then send him off to meetings in the commune or in the county to do philosophy work. The cadres said that when Wanyu had gone to the commune, he hadn't done that good a job talking philosophy; Uncle Luo, however, was elderly, had a long service record, had speech rights, had even carried out a courageous rescue at the aqueduct: the higher-ups would certainly be pleased to have him.

But Fucha also told me in confidence that although Uncle Luo was famous around here as an old revolutionary, he was a bit fuzzy in the head, and he was illiterate. As soon as he started talking, he'd mix up his sixes and sevens, his sheep and his goats—precautions would have to be taken. I had to get him to memorize the speech inside out.

It was only later that I discovered it was in fact very difficult to prevent Uncle Luo mixing up his sixes and sevens while making his philosophy report. He'd talk and talk, leaving the speech way behind him, clean forgetting everything he'd gone to so much trouble to memorize, digressing onto radishes, cabbages, tables, stools, onto who knew what. Sometimes, I considered waiting for him to find his own way back, only to discover that the more he ran on, the further he went; the further he went, the more fun he had. He'd never taken a wife, never even gone near the female sex, but this didn't stop him coming out with all sorts of risqué local expressions: "like my little sister looking at a prick" (meaning "by accident"); "like making my little sister drop a baby" (meaning "to bully someone")... All this "little sister" business didn't really mesh that well with philosophy.

From the look in my eyes, he could tell there was a problem: "stick-a-pig (see the entry "Stick[y]"), have I said the wrong thing again?" he'd blink.

The more he practiced, the more anxious he got, and in the end he began to mess up as soon as he opened his mouth: "Senior officers, comrades, I, Luo Yuxing, am fifty-six years old this year ..."

This didn't actually count as a mistake as such, but on instructions from the Party Branch I'd raised his age to sixty-five, so that he could be the even more outstanding embodiment of a Red old man. The philosophical significance of a sixty-five year old braving the rain to gather in the collective's harvest early was, of course, different from that of a fifty-six year old braving the rain to gather in the collective's harvest early.

I reminded him it was sixty-five: remember, the six at the beginning.

"Just listen to me talk! Ai, what use is a man when he gets old?" Ignoring my suppressed laughter, his face taking on a tragic expression, he looked around at the sky, set his concentration, then began again: "Officers, comrades, my name is Luo Yuxing, this year I'm fifty—"

"Wrong again!"

"My name is Luo Yuxing, this year ... fif ..."

I was on the point of despair.

He started to get a bit angry, "I'm fifty-six! Philosophy's all very well, but what's the point of changing my age? What's age got to do with philosophy?"

"Don't you want to make your deeds more moving?" I carefully explained to him the reasoning I had already explained, pointing out that an old man of seventy from Longjia Sands had made a broadcast speech about the philosophy of pig-rearing, and that fifty-six was chicken-feed compared with seventy, that it wouldn't convince anyone.

"I always knew that philosophy was a load of old garbage, just hey-eh mouths, sticking old stuff in new bottles. The Communist Party just likes sticking radishes up my little sisters' fannies—fake men, that's what that makes."

All this reactionary talk gave me a fright.

Just then a commune cadre arrived and spotted us. Going out to greet him, Uncle Luo started talking about what we'd just been doing, blinking away as if he hadn't woken up properly: "Study philosophy! Study! How could I not study? I studied half the night yesterday, the more I studied, the better it got. When the puppet government was in power I wanted to study but couldn't get as far as the school gates; the Communist Party, now, they really care about the poor and lower-middle peasants, they actually invite you to study. Studying this philosophy is studying understanding, reasoning, strength, studying at the right time, in the right way!"

The cadre beamed all over to hear this: Uncle Luo really was a poor old peasant, he said, his thinking really was on a higher level, see how well, how deeply he brings things together? Studying understanding, reasoning, strength.

I secretly admired how Uncle Luo adapted to circumstances, how his phrases came out so fully formed: though he always looked drowsy and sleepy-eyed, he produced sentence after sentence that directly hit the spot for his listener. I later found out that was the sort of person he was, never angry with his fellow villagers, never stuck for words: if he saw a person he'd speak to them, if he saw a ghost he'd divine them, and always come out with what they wanted to hear. If he bumped into someone who bred pigs, he'd say breeding pigs was good: "You can eat your own pigs wherever you want, whenever you want, no need to go and push in the line at the butcher's, eh?" If he bumped into someone who didn't breed pigs, he'd then say *not* breeding pigs was good: "When you want to eat meat, you take your money to the butcher's and cut some off, that's it, as much as you want, no short-changing! No need to wear yourself out breeding pigs, eh? Three slops every day, you've got to make sure the pig's full before you are, wears a person ragged, that does!" When he bumped into someone who'd had a little boy, he'd say boys were best: "You can rely on a boy to get on with things, hauling stuff, looking after the oxen, you're really lucky." When he bumped into someone who'd had a little girl, he'd say girls were best: "Take a daughter-in-law, lose a son, marry a girl, gain a bridegroom. When d'you last see a boy that's good to his parents? All well and good, they are. But it's always girls who care about their moms and their dads, you'll have *baba* cakes to eat, shoes and socks to wear, congratulations, congratulations."

Backwards and forwards he'd talk, not necessarily in a phoney way: his sincerity, honesty and forceful eloquence would show in every sentence, the earnest solemnity written all over his face. Maqiao people said he "spoke the Dao." The Dao was Daoism, the Way of *yin* and *yang*. First yes then no, now this then that, the Way is essentially a flexible whole lacking any tangible extreme, always expressible with clarity, and with no clarity at all.

He had no male offspring himself, only an adopted boy from Pingjiang County. According to local custom, the first guest to enter the house after the birth of a child was the "birth-meeting godfather" or "birth-meeting godmother." Many years ago, when Uncle Luo had gone to Pingjiang to peddle fir-tree resin, he'd turned up at someone's house by the roadside to beg for a mouthful of water and just so happened to barge in on the birth festivities; he thus became a godfather, and every time after that he went to Pingjiang he'd remember to bring his godson a bag of sweet-potato pieces. He'd never imagined this godson would later enter the Red Army and rise to the rank of general, and after he moved to the city he even invited Uncle Luo over to live in Nanjing. This was no blessing, Uncle Luo said: as soon as he set foot on the great quayside at Nanjing, he was taken into a little car by the general and his wife; as soon as the car started moving, heaven and earth started spinning and he'd had to scream to be let out. In the end, the general had no choice but to accompany him on foot, the car following slowly behind.

Neither could he get used to the way the general's home didn't have a fireplace, or a toilet bucket. You could've grown a fine garden of vegetables on the patch of land behind the house. With great effort he dug it over, leveled it out, but couldn't find the toilet bucket. But when he took to collecting dung in a bucket and enamel jar, the general's wife and her two daughters felt moved to hold their noses, and wail and moan about his lack of hygiene, of civilization. In high dudgeon by this point, he refused to eat for a whole day until the general was forced to buy an airline ticket to send him back to Maqiao.

"Lazy!" he shook his head, referring to his two god-granddaughters, "Too scientific (see the entry "Science") they are, just useless lumps of flesh; they can't feed pigs, can't spin silk, how'll they ever get to place a pot for their husband's family?"

I'd heard that the general sent him money at New Year's and on other festivals, and couldn't help asking enviously about it.

"What d'you mean, a lot of money? Stingy, very, very stingy." He dug his tobacco out of his cloth bag and blinked energetically as he mombled: "It's just . . . just . . . three or four yuan."

"So little?"

"Would I be telling lies, at my age? By my little sister's earwax—I swear that's how much!"

"I won't get anything out of you at land reform!"

"You come and search my home, search my home!"

I was really quite interested in him at the time, as I felt he truly embodied the essence of his simple, hardworking, poor old peasant class (unwilling to enjoy the easy life in the city) and possessed a glorious past (as exemplified by his close relations with the Red Army) that I hoped I could write into his speech. Little had I imagined that as soon as we got into details, he'd suddenly start speaking the Dao, until I was utterly lost in a fog of incomprehension. He'd praise the Red Army, would always be praising the Red Army, on and on until he changed tone and said the Red Army was totally rotten: there'd been a platoon leader who'd had local connections, sworn brothers, and whom the newly arrived company commander had killed as a counterrevolutionary. The company commander was only sixteen, and not too tall, so when he cut the head off, he'd had to jump up to do it, hacking so much that the blood spurted up to the sky, and *then* he stuck his face into the neck to drink the blood while it was hot—terrifying stuff. When he got onto the subject of class enemies, he even wept reactionary tears. "What'd Bandit Ma done wrong? A decent, honorable farmer, he was, salt of the earth. Such a pity, he went to all that trouble to surrender, and you all wanted him to surrender, then when he surrendered you said he'd surrendered falsely and made him swallow opium, a terrible business that was . . ."

He wiped his nose with the palm of his hand.

I had to restrain him: "What're you crying about? You're all mixed up, that was a revolutionary operation when the Communist Party purged bandits and tyrants, what was unfair about what happened to Bandit Ma?"

"I . . . shouldn't cry?" He was a little uncomprehending.

"Of course you shouldn't cry. You shouldn't cry. You're a poor peasant. Think about it, who were you crying for just then?"

"This head of mine's no use anymore. I can't say what I do say, but you tell me I've got to talk!"

"Now that's not quite right, some bits you said very well."

When he went to relieve himself, he was gone half an hour, which struck me as a little strange. When he returned, I guided him onto recalling some of the crimes of the Guomindang reactionaries, got him to drink some water, calm himself, then begin again. It was only then that he recovered his identity as a poor peasant. He spoke of the extermination of Communists by the GMD, a vicious business that was. Even women and children had been killed together, three-year-old kids grabbed and hurled at walls, their heads shattering before they managed even a groan. Some were thrown into kilns and burned, their skin and flesh stinking for three whole days and nights. He spoke of Pock-marked Lu, who'd probably been a GMD ringleader, the most treacherous double-dealer of them all: he'd take Red Army livers and lungs, secretly mix them up in a big pot of beef and make everyone eat. He, Luo Yuxing, unaware of this at first, only found out after he'd eaten, when he vomited till his guts almost turned over. . . .

He'd done a month in the Red Army as well, then returned home after dropping out. Pock-marked Lu'd almost had *his* liver and lungs, but fortunately he sold a coffin he'd prepared for his grandmother, held a three-table banquet in atonement, and begged two people to be his guarantors—even so, he only just escaped with his life.

"That Pock-marked Lu, I'd run his ancestors through! Son of a tiger and a pig-sticker, stupid he was, evil too, even if his death took seven days and nights it still wouldn't settle these scores!" When he reached the bit about his grandmother's funeral, he couldn't stop himself howling and yowling. Out came the snot and tears again, once again he wiped his nose with the palm of his hand.

This wipe set my mind more at rest.

"If Chairman Mao and the Communist Party hadn't come, I, Luo Yuxing, wouldn't be here today!"

"Well said! You must say that when you get onto the stage, you must cry."

"Cry? Of course I'll cry!"

To my everlasting regret, he didn't actually cry. But still, it wasn't too bad: though he stammered a little from nerves, he basically produced the memorized speech, going from history to reality, from the individual to society, using philosophies like the "externals/fundamentals" theory, spoke of his own outstanding achievements, and praised socialism. He didn't wander too far off the point, thanks to my repeated earlier warnings to him, didn't end up blabbing about having been a porter for the GMD and having eaten American flour. The worst he did was to extemporize a little when denouncing revisionist philosophy: revisionism was really bad, he said, it plotted against Chairman Mao and harmed the meeting we were having now, held up work. Although this wasn't quite the point, it still went along with the general idea.

So, as it turned out, the three days I'd spent getting him to memorize it weren't wasted.

Afterwards the commune nominated him a few times to go and speak in other communes. By then I'd been given a temporary transfer to the County Cultural Institute to write theater scripts and didn't have much to do with him. All I heard about was that one time when, returning from philosophy work, he passed a mad dog on the road that attacked him and took a bite out of his leg; medical treatment came too late and he was bedridden for about six months. Later on, he scattered—died.

I remember the last time I saw him: a plaster stuck on his forehead, hardly anything left of him apart from his two eyes, he was watching oxen from the side of the field. A golden yellow butterfly was nibbling at the oxen's backs.

When I asked about his sickness, his eyes widened in surprise: "Strange, isn't it, I've never been bitten by a dog, and now one comes and bites me here."

This remark struck me as odd.

He lifted up his leg to show me. What he meant was, there'd been a scar on this leg where a sickle had cut him, where he'd fallen, and in the end a dog bit him here as well. He'd reflected on this replication a hundred times without ever figuring it out.

"Be better soon, eh?"

"How's it going to get better then?"

"Had an injection?"

"Doctors can cure illness, they can't cure fate."

"You should have faith, old man, it'll get better."

"What's the good in getting better? Won't I still have to slave like a beast of burden? Planting rice, digging the hills, what's so great about that? Much better to watch oxen like I am now."

"Don't you want to get better?"

"What's the good in not being better? It hurts me to take just one step, I can't even squat in the toilet hut."

He hadn't lost his way with words.

He had a small, pink radio in his hand, probably brought to him recently by his godson, a rare treasure indeed for country people.

"Here's a good friend," he pointed to the radio, "from morning till night, never stops talking, never stops singing, don't know where he gets his energy from."

He held the radio to my ear. I couldn't hear very well since the sound was too soft; probably the batteries were too low.

"Everyday I know whether it's raining in Beijing," he said smiling.

It was only later that I found out the illness had already reached his vital organs, that he'd put his funeral shoes at the head of the bed, afraid that when the moment came he wouldn't have time to put them on. But still, calmly as ever, he got out of bed to watch the oxen for a couple of days, to put down a layer of fresh grass in the ox pen, to twist two lengths of ox tether; he even smiled and discussed the rain in Beijing with me.

*Mouth-Ban (and Flip Your Feet) [嘴煞(以及翻腳板的)]: The team leader had asked the bamboo carpenters to mend the bamboo baskets and winnowing baskets, but there was no money for meat. Fucha, who, in his capacity as public accountant, was responsible for getting hold of meat to treat the carpenters, reckoned that Uncle Luo would be flush, that maybe he'd have his remittance from his godson in Nanjing, and decided to try borrowing a couple of yuan to tide things over.

Uncle Luo said he didn't have any money; what godson? he said, he spends all his salary on Party fees, he'd long forgotten all about his birth-meeting godfather.

Fucha didn't really believe him and said he'd return anything he borrowed, he wasn't going to keep what was his. What good was the money doing moldering in a crack in the wall?

This needled Uncle Luo: "Slanderer, you slanderer! Fucha, my boy, I'm eight years older than your dad, where's your conscience? Where's your conscience?"

That day Fucha had been frazzled by the sun, traipsing everywhere—with no success—to borrow the money, and as he walked along the road afterwards he couldn't stop himself swearing: "Flip your feet!"

You couldn't help saying things like this when the sun was just too hot.

Little did he realize that "Flip your feet," the most taboo oath that Maqiao people knew, the most poisonous curse imaginable, was practically equivalent to digging up someone's ancestral grave. As soon as the words were out of his mouth, two bamboo carpenters standing nearby jumped in surprise and looked Fucha over twice. Fucha was probably just like me, having no idea about the phrase's history, nor much time for mouth-bans, and the words just slipped out of his mouth when his guard was down.

The next day, Uncle Luo was bitten by a mad dog and set off for the underworld.

Uncle Luo's death became a source of terrible heartache for Fucha. There were, besides, some private mutterings in Maqiao that held Fucha responsible. According to local custom, a curse could still be retracted even after it'd been set loose: all it would've taken was for Fucha to stick incense into his doorframe in time, cut off a chicken's head, wash the threshold with chicken's blood, and Uncle Luo's life would have been protected. But Fucha had been busy that day and he forgot about this set of procedures. Afterwards, he explained to a lot of people that it'd been an accident, he hadn't at all meant to curse Uncle Luo to death. Nor had he known how serious the curse was. Why did a mad dog happen to come along so coincidentally? He tended particularly to address such remarks to Educated Youth, because Educated Youth came from barbarian parts and didn't care much for Maqiao rules; they all told him to give himself a break, that he shouldn't pay any credence to it being a mouthban, or whatever. Some Educated Youth even thumped their chests in fraternal spirit: curse me, then, curse as hard as you can, they'd say, let's see what demons you can bring out!

Quite overcome, Fucha would wend his uncertain way back home.

Not long after this, whenever he was talking about the drought or grain rations with other people, he'd meander distractedly onto the business of Uncle Luo, how he hadn't really meant it, it was just that the sun had frazzled his brain and his mouth had run away with him for a moment, and so on and so forth. This started to get on people's nerves, started to become a problem.

A "mouth-ban" is a linguistic taboo. Words are, in fact, just words, no more than a whoosh of wind past the ears, unable to harm a single hair on anyone's body. But Fucha quickly shed a layer of flesh, the white hairs on his head noticeably increased, and even when he flashed a smile it would lack depth, it would be a facial exercise without roots in his inner being. Previously, he'd generally been a neat dresser, would even glance in the mirror and comb his hair, would always pin his collar down straight and smooth with a few clips. But now his clothes were a mess: there was mud on his shoulders, his concentration easily wandered, had him doing his buttons up wrong, or losing his pen, his keys. In the past, he'd only needed a day to do the end-of-year accounts; now he had to sweat over them for three or four days, the accounts sheets heaped into a confused pile. His mind was decidedly not on the job, he'd search for ages, up and down in the pile of account books, until he'd forgotten what he was looking for. In the end, after he'd managed inexplicably to lose five hundred yuan of cotton money in the supply and marketing cooperative, the team committee no longer felt he could stay on as accountant.

He himself no longer felt he could stay on as accountant; he handed over the account books and they found someone else. Afterwards, he kept ducks for a while but they were struck down by duck plague. He studied carpentry for a time but couldn't get the hang of it. Basically, nothing worked out for him, and he ended up rushing into marriage with a woman whose hair was a permanent bird's nest.

I was amazed that a mouth-ban could affect a person like that for decades. Couldn't he make up for it in some way? Couldn't he begin again?

In the opinion of most Maqiao people, he couldn't. The matter was already past, and just as you couldn't cry over spilt milk, Fucha's mouth-ban would be there forever; the longer it was there the bigger it got, the longer it was there the tougher it got, it would never quiet down and dis-appear.

The power of language infiltrates our lives deeply. Language is the source of human superiority: humans can pity animals for their lack of language and therefore for their lack of knowledge, for their inability to form societies, to acquire the enormous power of cultural accumulation and scientific progress. But the other side of the coin is that animals, unlike Fucha, will never, ever, after having shouted something improper, go into terminal decline until they've practically lost their capacity for survival. On this point, language makes humans more vul-nerable than dogs.

A "mouth-ban" is a manmade convention, a framework for keeping feelings of fear and awe in place. Humans, who have used language to separate themselves from the animal world, still need to find some kind of framework for emotional expression, to give structure and solidity through commonly accepted psychological props. The way that Maqiao people laid down linguistic taboos is exactly like the way people else-where need rings when they marry, like a country needs a national flag, religion needs idols, humanitarianism needs stirring songs and enthusi-astic speeches. As these things are passed on and inherited, they then become sacred, inviolable. Any violation on the part of their inheritors and users ceases to represent simply abuse of a piece of metal (a ring), a piece of cloth (a national flag), a piece of stone (an idol), or a few sound waves (songs and speeches), but instead becomes an insult to people's feelings: they have, to be precise, been set into some kind of emotional framework.

A totally rational being who seeks out logic and functionality alone, should consider not only Maqiao's mouth-ban, but also the sanctifica-tion of metal, cloth, stone, and sound-waves absurd—no objective logic dictates these strange psychological constructions should be thus. But this is how things have to be. People just aren't dogs, they can't regard material items as simply material. Even a totally rational being often bestows a spiritual aura on certain material items: he will, for example, separate one piece of metal (his lover's, his mother's or his grand-mother's ring) from a big pile of metal objects, view it differently, imbue it with particular emotions. At this moment, maybe he's started to verge on the absurd, is no longer so rational—but he's started to act like a proper, normal person.

When a ring is no longer simply a lump of metal, rationality has ceded the field to faith, to all forms of unreasoned reasoning. The absurdity and sanctity of life join together in a bizarre fusion.

Confucius's dictum that "the true gentleman stays far from the kitchen" is, of course, a kind of emotional framework. He couldn't bear to witness the scenes of bloody slaughter that took place in the kitchen, but this didn't in the least prevent him from wolfing down meat (he had a particular fondness for lean, dried meat). The prohibition among Buddhist disciples on killing living things, even from eating meat and fish, is another kind of emotional framework. But they've failed to register that plants are also living organisms, and that, according to modern biology, although a tree can't let out a cry for help, it feels pain, has nervous reactions, and can even make quick physical actions in exactly the same way. But can we laugh at their emotional frameworks? Put another way, in what sense, to what degree, can we laugh at their forms of absurdity and hypocrisy? If we viewed things differently, if we encouraged every person, every child even, to carry out the large-scale slaughter of chicks, piglets, kittens, cygnets, and every edible living thing, if seeing children revel in such blood-letting, we felt no disquieting discomfort within, then absurdity and hypocrisy would no longer exist, to be sure, but at the same time wouldn't we have lost something else?

What should we do, then? Stop children from eating meat, from eating anything at all, or laugh at and destroy their sympathy for any beautiful living thing? This sympathy that comes from Confucius, from Buddhist disciples, and from our other cultural forbears?

It was only thinking about this that I came to understand Fucha. He hadn't retracted the curse, hadn't cut off a chicken's head and washed the threshold with chicken's blood in time to save Uncle Luo, and so was engulfed forever by an inescapable miasma of guilt.

He was totally irrational.

And totally rational.

☆**Knotted Grass Hoop** [結草箍]: Fucha had been to high school and was one of the few intellectuals for miles around. Not only was he a good accountant, he could also play the flute and the *huqin* (the Chinese violin), was respectful and polite to the old, careful and thorough in managing affairs, and his fine, pale white face monopolized the attention of women wherever he went. He was oblivious to this and his gaze was never careless or unfocused but always projected straight out in front of him, directed at some safe, reliable target, such as fields or the faces of old people. Was it that he was unaware or that he pretended to be unaware of the whispering huddles of women, of their pretences of bashful surprise? No one had any idea.

Some women, seeing him arrive, would deliberately plant the rice seedlings sloppily, to see whether he'd take any notice. He was a cadre, of course he took notice, but—his face utterly expressionless—he'd say something like "Careful with your planting," then walk on without pausing. Another woman, seeing him approach, deliberately tripped over and scattered the basket of tea leaves on her shoulders all over the ground, crying out in pain to see whether he'd help her out. He was a cadre, of course he'd help her out, but poker-faced as ever he just lent a hand gathering the tea back into the basket, hoisted it onto her shoulder, then walked on.

He had no sense that there was someone still lying on the ground, still wiping her tears, that this was something of greater importance than tea leaves. He just said "Sorry, got to go"—this was not nearly enough, not by a long shot. Neither did he have any sense that, when women wore clothes more flowery than usual and stuck more cassia or peach-blossom flowers into their hair, this had anything to do with him.

"Use your eyes, can't you?" The women became less and less tolerant, and more and more indignant toward his cold arrogance. After a few of the locals had sought out Fucha's mother to ask about marriage and been brusquely rebuffed by Fucha, this indignation gradually took on collective proportions, spreading out from Maqiao to its environs, and became a common topic of conversation throughout the mass of unmarried girls in the area. Sometimes, when they met each other at the market, or at some mass meeting in the commune, there'd be times when they couldn't help huddling around to share their hatred of the enemy, to bad-mouth his flute, his *huqin*, his milky-white skin. They'd say Maqiao already had one Red-flower Daddy with Uncle Luo, looked like it had a second generation Red-flower Daddy now—no, more likely it'd produced a eunuch the emperor didn't want. They reveled in their outbursts of venom, laughed till the tears fell.

Maybe they weren't as angry as all that. But their emotions were always magnified in the collective: things changed as soon as the girls got together. They lost control of their cells and nerve-ends, felt pain where there was no pain, itched where they didn't itch, felt happy where they weren't happy, angry where they weren't angry, they had to make a huge fuss about everything—nothing else would do.

In the end, about ten of them secretly knotted grass as an oath that none of them was allowed to marry him, and whoever broke the oath would be condemned by the gods to change into a pig or a dog.

This was called "knotting the grass hoop."

Time went on, year by year. Fucha had no idea such a grass hoop existed, had no idea he'd provoked such a sacred covenant. In the end, he won no daughter of a dragon king, no princess of a jade emperor, he took a wife whose hair was always badly combed, who always looked as if she had a chicken's nest perched on top of her head. This chicken's nest was the bedraggled result of these women's decade-long vow of collective hatred. Of course, long before this time, one by one they'd left their parents' homes to become the wives of other men. Among them, three could have chosen otherwise, since Fucha's matchmaker came to each of their houses in succession to convey the wishes of Fucha's mom and of Fucha. But they had a prior agreement, they'd knotted a grass hoop that they couldn't go back on and be shamed before their sisters. They had a sense of loyalty toward their earlier oath, a sense of joy in revenge, a sense of collective excitement that forgot personal interests, and shook their heads resolutely.

In my opinion, a vow is like a curse, or a linguistic tyranny. One of the three girls mentioned above, Qiuxian from Zhangjia District, due to this coercive tyranny, later married a veterinarian. It can't be said this coercion had particularly dire results. She learned tailoring and the family ended up quite well-off—it was just that she wasn't a brilliant match with her husband. That was all.

One day, when it was about to rain, she was cycling back home, having finished her door-to-door business, harboring an unspecifiable feeling of discontent, and decided she didn't want to go back home, that she'd spend the night at the house of a same-pot uncle. On the way, she passed a man with a deeply wrinkled face hitting a child, and her heart suddenly thumped in her chest: the person inside this pair of shabby pants with one leg shorter than the other was none other than old Fucha! If this old man hadn't timidly ducked his head at her in something approximating a nod, she would certainly have thought she'd got the wrong person.

"Brother Fucha . . ." The words sounded unfamiliar to her.

"Humph . . ." The man's face bore the trace of a bitter smile, "This boy's driving me mad! It's about to rain, but he just won't move."

"Keke, want a ride on my bike?" Qiuxian's gaze was directed at the child.

The child's eyes lit up on seeing the woman and her bicycle.

"No, tell little uncle you don't, don't hold her up."

"It doesn't matter, I've got to pass through Maqiao anyway."

The child sneaked a look at his father, then a look at Qiuxian, and climbed on like a flash, scrambling with great expertise onto the front bar of the bicycle.

Fucha was at a total loss: since he couldn't very easily step forward to grab the child, he could only stamp his foot from where he was: "Are you getting off then? Are you getting off then? Asking for a spanking?"

"Keke, tell your dad it's no problem."

"Dad, it's no problem!"

"Ask your dad if he wants a ride too."

"Dad, d'you want a ride too?"

"No . . . I don't know how . . ."

"You want him to get on."

"Dad, little uncle wants you to get on!"

"No, no, off you go . . ."

Qiuxian hesitated a little, then, hearing the pattering sound of rain on the mountain over the way, pressed her own umbrella on Fucha, bestrode the bicycle, and rode off. The child was very excited to have the wind rushing right up against him and made horse-galloping noises for a bit, then made car noises for a bit—when they passed children who stared along the way, these noises got even louder.

"Keke, is your dad . . . nice . . . to your mom?"

"Very nice. Vrooooosh!"

"Do they argue?"

"Nope."

"They really don't?"

"My mom says my dad has a good temper, so he's no good at arguing."

"They haven't argued once?"

"Nope."

"I don't believe you."

"They really haven't . . ."

"Your mom's really . . . lucky."

Qiuxian's tone dripped with disappointment.

After falling silent for a while, she then asked:

"D'you . . . like your mom?"

"Yup."

"What d'you like about her?"

"She makes *baba* cakes for me."

"What else?"

"And . . . when I don't do my homework and Fucha's about to hit me, she shouts at him." Whenever he felt resentful, he used his father's proper name.

"Has your mom bought you games?"

"Nope."

"Or taken you to the city to look at the trains?"

"Nope."

"Can your mom ride a bike?"

"She . . . can't."

"That's a real pity, isn't it?" Qiuxian was clearly jubilant.

"No, it's not. I don't want her to ride a bike."

"Why not?"

"She might fall off. Her mom, Guixiang, was almost squashed to death by a tractor when she was riding a bike."

"What a bad boy you are—aren't you afraid your little uncle will fall off her bike?"

"If you fall off, that's nothing."

"That's nothing" meant that's nothing to worry about.

Qiuxian asked anxiously: "Why's it nothing?"

"You . . . you're not my mom. Peow—peow—peow." The child had spotted another slope and was happily making the signal to accelerate.

Dazed, Qiuxian suddenly felt a moistness well up and threaten to drop from her eyes. She set her teeth and pedaled forward. Luckily, a shower of autumn rain had already started to fall.

☆**Asking Books** [問書]: The next time I saw Fucha, his head full of white hairs, one trouser leg shorter than the other, he rubbed his hands and insisted I come over to his house for a bit. I didn't really have time, but seeing as he just stood there, waiting to one side, not about to give up, I had no choice but to comply. I found out afterwards that he'd wanted to grab this opportunity to show me a book he'd written, drafted in tiny letters on a pile of sheets from an account book, bound in a plastic fertilizer bag, with a few strands of grass mixed in. The ink quality, faded and unclear in many places, wasn't great. But this, I discovered to my surprise, was the most daring piece of research I'd ever seen.

He wanted to correct, to overturn the universally acknowledged theorem of pi.

As I didn't understand math, I had no way of volunteering any opinions on his research—I was, in any case, pretty doubtful about his ground-breaking theorem.

He smiled faintly, rolled out some tobacco, and filled a bamboo pipe. Different professions were as far apart as different mountains, he said, so I wouldn't understand. Did I know of someone more senior?

"Who?"

"Someone who does math."

"No," I said quickly.

A glint of disappointment shone from his eyes but his smile didn't falter: "No problem, I'll keep looking."

After I went back to the city, he wrote me a letter: he'd put aside pi and started on some linguistic questions. For example, he considered the characters for "shoot" and "short" to be the inverse of each other. The character for "shoot" [射] was made up of the characters for body [身 and inch [寸]: an inch-long body. The character for "short" [矮] contained the sign for "arrow" [矢], thus implying "shoot." He'd written this up in a letter to the State Council and the State Committee for Character Reform, and was asking me to find an acquaintance to pass it on to, "someone who does language stuff."

In another letter, he wrote that Maqiao people used to say that people who "read books" (a phrase which in Chinese also means, more generally, "study" or "learn") "asked books"—this was what his dad used to say. Read, ask, read, ask: if you don't ask, how can you read (and learn)? "Reading books," by comparison, was now a fairly meaningless term for learning, as it manifested a tendency to overemphasize mechanical memorizing and rote learning. He recommended that schools all over the country revive the phrase "ask books" as a phrase more beneficial to national modernization.

☆**Master Black** [黑相公]: One night, wails and screams suddenly rose and fell throughout the village, joined a moment later by a chorus of dogs—something serious must have happened. I climbed out of bed and opened the door to peer into the hazy moonlight out of which Wanyu's piercing voice was screeching terrifyingly. A big mountain pig, it turned out, had snuck into the village, been hacked at and walloped by the men, leaving a trail of blood and a few pig bristles in its wake, before running off into the darkness. The men all said it was a great pity and released another round of combative yells at the dim black mountain.

Every door had been flung open, all the men had ransacked their houses for weapons and run out; even Wanyu, with his watersnake waist and girl's voice, had wrapped his fingers around a wood axe and was looking everywhere along with everyone else. This was nothing unusual, Fucha said, somewhat out of breath. Whenever any Master Black, any wild thing came into the village, it took one shout and everyone's doors were flung open. No one could keep their door shut at a time like this, and keep face.

They called all mountain pigs "Master Black."

After a round of yells, followed by round upon round of billowing echoes, everyone concluded there was no hope that night and finally dispersed disconsolately back to their homes. When, half asleep, I'd reached the eaves of our house, I was frightened almost out of my wits by a big black thing I glimpsed lurking under my window. After I'd yelled out to a few of the other Educated Youth, I realized it hadn't moved in ages; when I plucked up courage to go in a bit closer, still it didn't move. A nudge with my foot revealed it to be not a mountain pig, but a creaking bundle of firewood.

I was covered in cold sweat.

*Master Black (continued) [黑相公(續)]: When Maqiao people said "chase the meat," they meant go hunting; "make shoes" meant bring down the sword; "invite guests" meant poison; "ride in a sedan" meant dig a traphole; "whistle to heaven" meant scattered gunfire, and so on. They suspected animals of being fluent in humanspeak and said that when hunting, even if you were inside a building, you had to use code language to guard against indiscretions on which your quarry could eavesdrop.

It was particularly imperative that direction words be rearranged: "north" actually meant "south," "east" meant "west" (and vice versa). That's why people banged gongs and shouted when they hunted Master Black, creating a man-made cacophony to conceal the direction of traps or guns, and used a prearranged code language, shouting out east while attacking west, mixing true with false, all to confuse the animal.

Mou Jisheng knew all this perfectly well but he didn't take it in properly and sometimes things didn't quite click into place in his head when it came to the crunch. He was in the middle-school class of 1982, one year above me, and we were sent down to the countryside together. Once, when we were coming back from the banks of the Luo River carrying rice seedlings we'd bought, he said he wanted to get back extra early to wash his shoes and rushed on ahead alone, disappearing in the blink of an eye. We grumbled at how annoying he was: what did he want to wash his shoes for? When'd he ever washed his shoes before? The thing was, we were worried in case someone couldn't keep going on the way back; as he was the strongest, he'd have felt obliged to lend a hand. In any case, whether he helped out or not, he didn't have to scurry off so fast, like a thief—it tired a person out.

Mou had, indeed, never washed his shoes: whenever he discovered his foot slipping on something inside his shoe, he'd tie his shoes together by the laces, dangle them in the stream that flowed between fields, then pull them out a few days later, dry them in the sun and start wearing them again. He said this was the automatic shoe-washing method. Needless to say, shoes washed in this way still stank horribly and whenever a host gestured he should remove his shoes, anyone standing by would exit at top speed after just one sniff.

Our conjectures weren't proved wrong: as we suspected, he didn't go and wash his shoes. Not only that, when we got home his seedling basket was nowhere to be seen—in other words, he hadn't gotten back yet. As the afternoon wore on, even the stragglers returned and we managed to plant out several paddies of seedlings, without sight nor sound of him. When it'd got dark, we heard heavy footsteps on the road, sounds of breathing like the wheezing of a bellows, before finally, thank goodness, he collapsed to the ground as if there were a stone in his stomach. Covered in mud, barely half the rice seedlings in his load left hanging precariously off the pole, he tripped and stumbled over himself, unable to put one foot in front of another. He was not amused: "This damned turtle place with these damned turtle people! They talk crap! Sent me on a wild-goose chase over the mountains! I almost stepped in a trap! I'll stick all your grannies!" (see the entry "Stick[y]")

I didn't know who he was swearing at.

We asked him what'd happened, what he'd been playing around at all day. His face clouded with anger, he ignored everyone and walked to his room to hurl things around. It took us ages to discover that what he'd done was forget the locals' habit of reversing directions. He hadn't really got used to the local accent, either: he'd be all right as long as he didn't need to ask the way, but as soon as he asked he'd be bound to go wrong. So he'd hauled a heavy load of seedlings to Shuanglong Bow to the north of Maqiao, then carried them to Longjia Sands to the south of Maqiao, finally tramped all over the mountains till it was almost dark. A local he passed finally suspected he hadn't caught on, and reminded him about the direction rule. He'd almost keeled over with rage.

We all laughed—a lot.

After the peasants found out, they laughed even more. "As he's just a big lump of flesh that can't understand human speech," said Uncle Luo, "we should call him Master Black."

Since there were fewer and fewer wild pigs on the mountains, the term Master Black had long fallen into disuse, but Mou Jisheng enabled it to stage an unexpected comeback by changing its meaning. Normally, when Mou Jisheng went out to work he didn't wear a bamboo hat and bared his upper body to the sun's violent rays, burning his muscular back deep black; when he ran, his upper body rippled in dark waves, so the nickname Master Black seemed to suit his appearance.

He had a strong physique and liked wrestling with anyone on hand: he particularly enjoyed giving the local "turtle people" a good thrashing. While the turtle people carried two baskets of grain, he'd carry four, divided between two or three carrying poles; once this had produced open-mouthed shock from bystanders, he'd set them down and preen himself, panting with the effort. While the turtle people wore cotton jackets, he'd wear shorts in snowy weather so cold it turned your lips purple; once bystanders had expressed shocked admiration, he'd finally yield (with a teeth-gritted show of reluctance) to general persuasion and go inside. He liked playing basketball and on hot summer days he wouldn't rest at noon but instead would brave the violent sun on the drying terrace to knock a ball around, working up a full sweat even without a basket. The weather was so hot even the crickets, toads, and chickens were silent and only the thump of his ball reverberated throughout the village. The peasants clicked their tongues in awe.

"I was still drinking breast milk at thirteen! My mom was always away at work but the wet nurse would still make me drink!" He'd always be making announcements like this to explain the reasons for his incomparable physical strength and drop hints about how he came from a family of revolutionary cadres.

Human milk was a good thing, to be sure, and the peasants were entirely convinced by this explanation.

Zhongqi very early on expressed a particular interest toward him. When winter arrived, Zhongqi would produce a steaming-basket that he carried around with him everywhere when he got off work. The basket was so small it could only hold two or three burning pieces of charcoal at a time and could only be hugged by one person between the legs or against the chest, but still it was an ember that brought heat. Zhongqi had never let anyone else enjoy the use of his basket: even when women came to warm their hands, he might chortle generously but would still impose time limits and give them frequent warnings about their charcoal consumption and their massive expenditure of heat. Master Black was the lone exception to whom, with a clackety-clack of his shoes, he'd voluntarily pass the basket. Unfortunately, Master Black wasn't interested in this object, since his health was good and he'd never felt the cold; he took one look, then walked outside with a snort.

Zhongqi had weaseled out a lot of the village's secrets, none of which he'd make public just like that. At times, one sentence would be the furthest he'd go and as soon as anyone inquired any further, the smug taunts would immediately begin: "Take a guess, go on, take a guess." So no one ever got much sense out of him. Only with Master Black was he willing to share his secrets: a scrap today ("There was a pile of chicken feathers in Fucha's house yesterday"), another scrap tomorrow ("Uncle Luo tripped over on the mountain two days ago"), the day after that, in even more hushed tones, "Someone visited Shuishui's mom and brought two piglets."

Mou Jisheng had no interest in these secrets and only wanted to hear the low stuff. Zhongqi looked embarrassed, hemmed and hawed, reddened, then decided to make an offering. He mentioned the time when Fucha's mother, however many years ago it'd been, had woken up in a daze from a midday nap and discovered there was a man pressing down on her who turned out not to be Fucha's dad. But she'd been too tired and weak to resist, had lacked the will to figure out who this person was, so she shouted into the other room: "Quick, come here, third son, your granny's boiling hot! Come and tell me what this idiot's playing around at!" Her son was asleep in the other room and didn't wake. But her shout managed to frighten this hazy human form away. She turned over comfortably and continued her deep, heavy-breathing sleep.

"Is that it?" Deeply disappointed, Mou Jisheng didn't feel this secret was worth knowing either.

As I later discovered, relations between Zhongqi and Mou Jisheng gradually grew in intimacy. In the past, as soon as evening came on, Mou Jisheng would make a big fuss about turning off the lamp and going to sleep, but now, unexpectedly, he often went out alone and sometimes only returned to bed very late. When asked where he'd been, he'd go all mysterious and hedge our questions, a wrinkle of self-satisfaction between his eyebrows, then carelessly let out a burp smelling of dates or egg that would drive us wild with incredulous jealousy. He wasn't about to let us share his gourmet's luck: we'd have to beat him to death before he'd spit the truth out, this we knew full well. Our later investigations revealed that his burps were linked to Zhongqi: we discovered that Zhongqi had made glutinous rice cakes for him and that Zhongqi's wife had washed his quilt and shoes for him. We couldn't make any sense of it: Zhongqi was normally such a stingy so-and-so, he wouldn't help out just any old Wang, Li, or Zhang, so why was he sucking up to that half-wit Master Black?

One night, some time after we'd all fallen asleep, we were startled awake by a violently angry shove at the door. Lighting the oil lamp, we discovered Master Black huffing and puffing on his bed, spitting with rage.

"What's up with you?"

"I'll do him in!"

"Who?"

Not a word.

"Are you talking about Mr Agreed?"

Still not a word.

"What's he done to you?"

"Go to sleep!" Master Black rolled around on the bed plank, producing a series of loud creaks that woke everyone else up—he was the first to start snoring, though.

On the afternoon of the following day, Zhongqi's shoes were heard approaching the door, a Mao button as big as an egg flashing and glinting on his chest. "Chairman Mao says debts should be repaid. Where does it say that debts can be left unpaid in socialism?" He coughed loudly, "I won't bother the national government with unimportant matters like this: if Mou Jisheng can't pay me back in cash, grain will do as well."

Mou Jisheng rushed out: "What money do I owe you? You old fool!"

"You know what I mean."

"It was always you who invited me. I didn't beg, I didn't ask for anything, everything I ate I've shat out, so go and look in the toilet hut!"

"Comrade, you must be truthful, you must keep studying. You intellectuals shouldn't try to run before you can walk, you're still being educated by us poor and lower-middle peasants, understand? Tell you the truth, I know everything about you, Master Black, it's just I don't tell anyone. I've been kind to you so far!" Zhongqi's words contained a veiled menace.

"Talk, then! Talk!"

"Me, talk? You really want me to talk?"

"I'd give my dragon to hear you talk!"

"Okay, then. When we were planting peanuts last year, there was a shortfall in the team's planting peanuts every day—d'you think I didn't see the peanuts in your shit? A few days ago, you said you were having a wash, but what were you actually doing? . . ."

His face flushed scarlet, Master Black dashed forward, dragged Zhongqi outside and clanged his head against the doorframe. "He's killing me! He's killing me!" Zhongqi whimpered.

Afraid things would turn murderous, we rushed over to stay Master Black's hand, trying desperately to pry the two of them apart. Availing himself of this opportunity, Zhongqi wormed his way out from under my armpit and headed for the drying terrace, his shoes clacking away as he went.

When the sound of his cursing had faded off into the distance, we asked Mou Jisheng what had really happened.

"What happened? He wanted me to do low stuff."

"What kind of low stuff?"

"Sleep with his wife!"

There was a moment of unutterably astonished silence, before we all started cackling with laughter. One female Educated Youth ran off screaming in fright and didn't dare show her face again.

It was only later that we badgered any sense of the matter out of him, that Zhongqi was sterile, and had earmarked Master Black to do the job for him. "It must be you're special, brother Mou." "You've got to stick for your supper" (see the entry Stick[y]). "You shouldn't look a gift horse in the mouth." We were enjoying ourselves enormously, determined not to let Master Black stand up for himself, determined not to let him escape the Zhongqi family bed.

"These turtle people!" He pretended not to hear.

"Who're you swearing at now? Tell us the truth: did you sleep with her?"

"Would *you* sleep with her? Have you seen what his wife looks like? One look at her takes your appetite away! I'd rather sleep with a pig!"

"If you don't sleep with her, will you keep eating their chickens?"

"What chickens are you talking about? They take a month to eat a chicken, one ladle of soup at a time—the bowl's empty before you've tasted anything. Just drop the subject, just talking about it makes me mad."

That afternoon in the fields, the Master Black affair became the principal topic of conversation. What surprised me was that apart from Fucha, no one else in the village thought Zhongqi had done anything wrong. Poor old Zhongqi, so set on making friends with Master Black, d'you think it'd been easy to keep him fed and watered? He was a sick man, he'd just wanted to borrow a seed to produce a descendant—nothing unreasonable about that. He hadn't forced Master Black to get married or anything, he'd just wanted to borrow a tiny little thing he wasn't bothered about, what was so bad about that? It was the choice of someone who had no other choice. Zhaoqing also said that in any case, whether Master Black agreed or not, he'd eaten so much it would be mean not to repay him.

Needless to say, the Educated Youth didn't agree with this strange logic and spent the whole afternoon arguing till we were blue in the face, going on and on about how we were going to go and report to the commune, how there was no way we were going to let our revolutionary Educated Youth be seduced by that old codger Zhongqi.

Most of the villagers jabbered away without taking much notice. As Party Branch Secretary, Benyi didn't have anything sensible to say either. He summoned the Educated Youth to a meeting, where he first of all asked one of us to read a few pages of newspaper editorials. When the reading, and his nap, were both over, he yawned and asked Mou Jisheng: "Did you steal the team's peanuts last year?"

"I—I took a few handfuls."

"One planted peanut seed will grow into a lot of peanuts, d'you know that?"

"Uncle Benyi, we're meant to be discussing Zhongqi today, the peanuts are a completely separate matter."

"What d'you mean, separate? It's in the small things that you show your attitude to the collective, show whether you have feeling for poor and lower-middle peasants. Wasn't it him (he used the distant, *qu* him, I remember) that hit Zhaoqing's kid and made him cry, last month when we were digging the pond?" Benyi glared at everyone.

No one said anything.

"When you look at a problem, you have to look at the whole thing, you have to look at it historically! Chairman Mao says that whatever happens, it's wrong to hit people."

"I just lost my temper . . ." Mou Jisheng defended himself weakly.

"You still can't hit people. What kind of behavior is that? Are you Educated Youth or street hooligans?"

"I . . . won't hit . . . anyone . . . again . . ."

"That's a bit more like it: when you're in the wrong you're in the wrong. You've got to be honest about things—why make a fuss when you're clearly in the wrong? We'll leave it at that: no self-criticism necessary, you'll just be docked thirty catties of grain."

Benyi had already moved off, hands tucked behind his back, looking wholly satisfied with his resolution of the problem. He wrinkled his nose as he went out the door, as if he'd caught a whiff of toad-and-green-pepper stir-fry from our kitchen. As for that business with Zhongqi, he'd sort it out, he said, he'd sort it out.

The matter was never raised again and was thus left unresolved.

When I call this incident to mind, I realize that logic is both useful and useless, can both clear and muddy the waters. Confronted with the unique logic of the Maqiao Party Branch and the general masses, our puzzlement and indignation were totally useless. Mou Jisheng continued to endure public censure: his refusal to repay Zhongqi (either in cash or in kind) and to pay the grain fine became ironclad proof of his lack of good faith. From this point on, he began to show signs of depression and deliberately performed bizarre and terrifying acts, such as swallowing shards of enamel or lifting a whole dirt cart on his shoulders, or working the oil press alone and telling all his companions to sleep; but by that point it was very difficult to provoke general astonishment and acclaim, or attract acolytes. His Miss Xia also left him—this female Educated Youth with her refined features can't have wanted to have her name linked with Zhongqi's wife; even if these links were entirely groundless, she couldn't escape the imaginings of other people. In the end, Master Black suddenly appeared before us one day with his chest covered in Mao buttons.

"What're you wearing those for, Brother Mou?"

"I'm going to liberate Taiwan." He smiled at us.

I stared, with surprise, hard into his eyes and discovered his gaze had become that of a stranger.

Master Black was diagnosed as hysterical and his residence registration was moved back to the city. He was still physically strong, apparently, and could still play basketball. He could also watch films, smoke cigarettes, ride a bike on the street—he had a full life in the city. It was just that he wasn't very good at recognizing people, would babble and have random mood swings—probably the early stages of hysteria. When an old classmate met him on the street and slapped him on the shoulder, he blinked, briefly hesitated, then turned around and walked off.

*Curse-Grinding [磨咒]: Maqiao people had a whole set of procedures for taking revenge on bad elements from barbarian parts: "curse-grinding." Take, for example, someone who shat indiscriminately on Maqiao's ancestral graves, or was rude to Maqiao women. Without changing their voices or facial expressions, Maqiao people would covertly circle three times around this foreign visitor. After this had been done, they'd quietly bide their time until the visitor had gone into the mountains or the forests. When this moment came, they'd mutter incantations under their breath, complex, tongue-twisting rhymes that broke all the mountain place-names up, then mixed them all together: this was called their mountain incantation. Usually, the words of the incantation were highly effective. Their evil-doing victims would turn this way and that, unable to tell east from west, walking and walking till they returned to where they'd started, aware of the ever-darkening sky over their heads and with no one to call to for help. In the mountains, they might be hungry and cold, might step on an iron trap, might stir up hornets or ants and get stung till their faces and bodies swelled up with blood. People even said that there'd once been an ox-rustler from barbarian parts who'd died on the mountain, who'd never re-emerged from the sparse fir grove on the north face of Tianzi Peak.

Then there was the soul-taking incantation. All you needed to do was take a strand of the offender's hair, "grind" the words of the incantation again and again, and the offender's mind would cloud over until he or she ended up a walking zombie.

After Master Black returned to the city on grounds of ill health, rumors started up. Some suspected Zhongqi's wife of "grinding" a curse at Master Black. Needless to say, I had no truck with such rumors. I'd seen that woman: she hated Master Black, but she didn't have an evil word in her. Sometimes she'd sigh idiotically in front of the women in her neighbors' houses, about how all her born days she'd never begged for wealth or sought long life, all she'd wanted was to give birth to two sons, big as horses, strong as oxen, dead ringers for Master Black. That way, at least, those two breasts of hers wouldn't have hung there all her life for no good reason.

*Three Seconds [三秒]: When Mou Jisheng was still in Maqiao, his energy levels were quite excessive, and after finishing work he'd still want to play basketball. When the Educated Youth were too tired to play, he'd get together some local lads, or sometimes even run a few *li* to the middle school in the commune and play on until midnight, the bouncing ball shimmering in the moonlight.

His demands on his students were very strict: sometimes he'd whistle, point to someone on court, and yell: "Tie your pants higher!"

Both referee and coach, he even monitored his players' pants.

He made his students master the strictest rules of the basketball court, including the "three seconds" rule. Before he arrived, Maqiao's boys had already played ball, just not with many rules: you could bounce the ball twice, when things got really hairy you could run with the ball, the only thing you couldn't do was hit anyone. Mou Jisheng trained his students by the standards of the county's top team and introduced them to the "three seconds" rule. When I revisited Maqiao many years later, the village had a privately run culture institute and half a basketball court, where a few young men—all faces that were utterly unfamiliar to me—were kicking up quite a ruckus as they played. Only one thing sounded familiar: my heartbeat quickened at the way they were always shouting out "three seconds."

None of these young men knew who the Educated Youth had been. They had no idea who these people were, these people who, a long time ago, had stayed in the village for a few brief years, these people from barbarian parts who'd been guests in the village and had no deep understanding of Maqiao; neither was there any need to express interest. I strolled through the village. There wasn't a trace left of our years in Maqiao, even the old, familiar scratches on the mud wall had gone. Out of the few friends I vaguely remembered, none were to be found, all had departed this world one after another, either last year, or the year before, or three years before, or three years before that. With their passing, the Maqiao of my memories sank stone by stone, soon to disappear without a trace.

I'd lived here for six years. One gust of wind had scattered the days of those six years, leaving behind one lone relic: "three seconds"—although its meaning had changed. From what I could glean from watching the lads on the basketball court in front of me, "three seconds" not only outlawed hanging onto the ball for more than three seconds under the basket, it extended also to the flouting of all rules: hitting, shoving, running with the ball. Anything "three seconds" equaled "against the rules." In his time here, Mou Jisheng could never, ever have imagined this would come to pass.

*Lettuce Jade [萵瑋]: In the winter, when the commune would be wanting to build a grain store here, a middle school there, they were forever sending instructions down from above that each person was to contribute five fired bricks. Maqiao didn't have money for buying bricks and the villagers had to go to the mountains to dig up graves—overgrown, untended graves, of course.

The mountain-dwellers lived mainly in thatched barns or wooden houses, but their graves were anything but slapdash affairs, using great heaps of fired bricks to build immortal structures that would withstand centuries and millennia. These graves had been through too much history: most of the mounds had collapsed and been covered over with dense brambles and grass, with nothing to mark them out from regular flat ground covered with vegetation—one cursory glance couldn't distinguish where the grave was. After we'd hacked away at the vegetation around the grave with sickles, and removed the topsoil with rakes, the blue bricks supporting the grave would slowly come into view, stone by stone. At this moment, the faint-hearted girls among the Educated Youth would scurry a long way off into terrified hiding. The men, each attempting to be braver than the next, would jostle to lodge the teeth of their rakes into the joins in the bricks, slowly heaving them to and fro until the bricks loosened and the first brick was pried off with a violent wrench.

If the grave had been fairly well preserved, it was like a pot well sealed against moisture: as the grave was broken open, a white mist would rise up, billowing in waves out of the pit and spreading in gusts a bitter stench of skeleton that turned the stomach. After the white vapor had slowly thinned into nothingness, we timidly crowded closer, peering at the black world within the grave through the gap opened up in the bricks. By the light of a quivering thread of penetrating sunlight, we could glimpse the once-human skeleton, its big empty eye sockets, or its broad pelvis. We could also glimpse random piles of earth and rotting wood. We grave-diggers wouldn't normally expect to find any treasures of gold and silver in the grave: we'd be doing well to come across one or two bronze or ceramic vessels. Many of the skeletons we saw had been positioned facing downwards: this meant our luck was definitely out. According to local custom, people like this had had bad ends, been struck by lightning, hanged, or shot, for example. Those who'd survived them hadn't wanted them to revisit the world of light and pass their bad luck on, had wanted at all costs to prevent them being reborn. Facing them downwards was a crucial step in ensuring they never revisited the light of day.

In death, as in life, different people receive different treatment.

There was one time when, digging out a female corpse, we discovered that although her bones were white, her hair was as glossily jet-black as if there was still breath in her and reached down almost to her waist. Her two incisors hadn't rotted either, and they gleamed and protruded out of her mouth in splendid isolation, a good three inches long, so it seemed. We fled in terror. In the end, after some inquiries, the team committee paid Master Black—who had no fear of ill omens—two catties of meat and one catty of wine to paraffin and burn the skeleton, to stop this female spirit making any further trouble. Years later, I learned from an academic that this is actually perfectly normal. Human death is a long, slow process, and given a congenial environment the hair and teeth will continue to grow. Foreign physicians had done plenty of research on the subject.

We started to carry down more and more bricks from the mountain. The skeletons, of course, were left, abandoned on the mountain. People said that wherever there was a concentration of eagles hovering and swooping back and forth in the sky over the mountains was probably where the strong, rank smell had stimulated their appetites. Others said that in the evenings you could hear the sounds of men howling and women crying on the mountain: surely it was the ghosts, cursing their grave-diggers as they froze with cold.

Nevertheless, we still went into the mountains every day to carry out our dastardly mission.

Normally, Zhaoqing was as cowardly as they came, but he never hung back when we were digging ancestral graves. I later discovered that the reason why he always pushed himself forward was because he hoped to find a rare treasure in the grave pit: shaped like an uneven parcel of vegetables and of a dazzling crimson color, growing on the tongue of the dead person, like human breath that had coagulated over a long period of time in the tomb and then bloomed forth with incredible beauty. The peasants called this thing resembling a parcel of vegetables "lettuce jade": it was the best tonic in the world, they said, an intense concentration of physical strength that could focus the spirit and enrich the blood, could add to the *yin* and strengthen the *yang*, could dispel wind, protect embryos, prolong life. There's a reference to it in *The Extended Virtuous Words*: "Just as there is no false gold, there is no true lettuce jade." The villagers also said not just anybody could posthumously exhale lettuce jade; only the mouths of the wealthy, of those who had tasted top-drawer delicacies, slept on cotton pillows, whose bodies had been nurtured in gold and jade while they lived, would bear fruit in one hundred years' time.

One day while digging in the ground, Zhaoqing suddenly let out a long, tragic sigh.

"It'll never happen, never happen. What's the point in going on?" He shook his head: "This rotten mouth of mine's never going to grow a lettuce jade."

Knowing what he meant, his listeners also turned mournful. They thought about the strips of sweet potato, the aged brown rice, and the blackened dried vegetables they swallowed every day: if even their bottoms couldn't produce any kind of a smell, what hope was there of growing a lettuce jade?

"Uncle Luo could grow one," Wanyu was very confident of this, "he's got a godson in barbarian parts who sends him money."

"Benyi's got a hope too, he's pretty sturdy, there's a lot of fat on him," Zhaoqing said. "The bastard, at those meetings he goes to every other day, they kill a pig every time, there's so much meat it bends their chopsticks."

"Cadre meetings are revolutionary work. You jealous, then?" Zhongqi said.

"What d'you mean, work? Aren't they just growing their lettuce jades?"

"You can't say that. If everyone grew a lettuce jade, lettuce jade would become too cheap, too common—d'you think it would've got into *The Extended Virtuous Words* like that?"

"I could've become a cadre during Land Reform." Shortie Zhao set full sail for a delicious, dreamy journey of remembrance.

"You—a cadre? You can't even write Shortie Zhao properly! If you ever got to be a cadre, I'd walk everywhere on my hands." Zhongqi thought this very funny and chuckled away for a while.

Zhaoqing said: "What about you, then, Zhong, you dragon you, carrying your quotation book around every day, wearing your Chairman Mao button, who're you trying to impress? D'you honestly think you can grow a lettuce jade?"

"I don't want one."

"You couldn't grow one."

"I'm not going to grow one, that way no one'll come and dig my grave."

"Reckon you're going to have a grave that people can come and dig?"

Zhaoqing's remark was rather below the belt. Since Zhongqi had no descendants, it was generally held that he ran the risk of having no one to bury him after he'd died; Zhaoqing, however, had produced five or six kids, so a remark like this from him was a blatant assertion of his superiority, and touched a raw nerve in his opponent.

"You stinking, farting scumbag, Zhao."

"You pig-sticker."

"Parents never washed your mouth out, did they?"

"No use if you did wash your mouth—your belly's so full of shit."

Their exchanges swiftly got wilder and filthier, before bystanders finally managed—with great difficulty—to intervene. In an effort to thaw the atmosphere a little, Fucha mentioned Secretary Zhou in the commune: what was Benyi compared to him? Benyi only got his mouth around some lard at his five meetings per month—that wasn't going to make much of a dent on a stomachful of sweet potato and brown rice. Only the commune cadres had it really good, touring here today, there tomorrow, always with a reception party at the ready, like it was New Year's every day. Just think about Secretary Zhou's juicy pink-and-white flesh, fattened on great vats of frying oil. His golden throat still sounded out clear as a gong even after a night of making reports, better even than Tiexiang's voice. He must be building up to an enormous lettuce jade.

Uncle Luo took over: "That's quite right: it's just as important to spot the big ones as to spot them at all. If Benyi's mouth grew a lettuce jade, it would be as big as a sweet potato at best, and even ten of them would be nothing to just one of Secretary Zhou's. You'd be far better off digging up Secretary Zhou's grave."

From Secretary Zhou, they moved onto Commune Head He, onto the bigwigs in the county, in the province, and finally to Chairman Mao. They all believed unanimously that Chairman Mao was the luckiest of all, his allotment of fortune the highest. His lettuce jade a hundred years from now would be something incredible, not just a panacea for all ills but a magical elixir of life. A national treasure like this, they reckoned, would need high-level chemical preservatives and a massive military guard day and night.

Having reflected on the matter, everyone concurred that was how it would be. By this time, the sun was already slanting to the west, so they hauled their rakes pensively onto their shoulders and headed for home.

A few days later, Secretary Zhou visited Maqiao to examine the brick recovery situation, and while he was about it asked me to help him write up some official materials on carbon paper, telling me again and again how elegant my imitation Song-style calligraphy was. Watching his beaming fat face, my thoughts kept on straying, as I imagined in his mouth a lettuce jade big as a parcel of vegetables that accompanied him everywhere he went. His voice was indeed resonant, always imitating the music in broadcasts, singing the newest song of praise for Beijing. He'd often ask me what I thought of his singing, listening to endless replays of my fawning compliments. He also asked me what sort of a Cultural Director I thought he'd make. Of course, I said, of course, you've got art in your bones, you're clearly the stuff Cultural Directors are made of. This made him even happier, kept him merrily humming away, and anyone he saw he'd greet warmly, ask them how their kids and their pigs were. The lettuce jade in his mouth began swelling to ever greater proportions, as if self-confidence dripped out of his very pores.

He got Benyi to take him to see the brick firing. I watched the lesser lettuce jade leading the greater lettuce jade—maybe soon we'd have baby lettuce jades carrying fired bricks. . . . I couldn't clear my befuddled head of these fantasies. I must've been digging too many graves lately, I thought, my head was full of bad stuff, full of the smell of corpses.

"Tell me, apart from imitation Song-style, what other calligraphy styles look good?"

"Lettuce jade."

"What did you say?"

"Er, what was it you . . ."

"I asked what other calligraphy styles look good."

I suddenly came to and hurriedly answered his question about calligraphy.

☆**Presenting the Vine** [放藤]: Yellow vine was a highly poisonous species of plant: women who wanted to commit suicide usually went up the hillside and dug up some yellow vine, as did men planning to poison fish and shrimps in shallow, stagnant, slow-flowing bends in the river. A length of yellow vine knotted three times, with a piece of chicken feather inserted, or drenched in a bowl of chicken blood, presented to the enemy, was the final diplomatic communication before two sides met in war. Once this step had been taken, it meant things had already gotten pretty bad, and the conflict was irresolvable without some loss of life.

It was said that in the early years of the Republic, Maqiao people presented the vine to Longjia Sands. Returning home one day with an ox he'd bought, a certain Father Xingjia of Longjia Sands passed by a relative's house and popped in for a bite to eat and drink, leaving the ox tied up outside the main door. When he was, say, seventy or eighty percent drunk, he heard the sound of an ox lowing outside the door and asked a child to go outside and have a look. After taking a look, the child came back and said an unknown black ox had climbed onto the back of their ox. Father Xingjia was furious: he'd just brought his ox back from the market, what kind of a brute was this other animal? Raping it before he'd got his breath back?

Everyone jostled their way out the door, but found the owner of the black ox was nowhere to be seen. Rather the worse for wear and in a fit of drunken bravado, Father Xingjia's nephew grabbed a flaming branch and lashed out with it, jabbing it straight into the black ox's shoulder joint. With a great bray, the animal cantered off, taking with it the flaming branch, swinging and lurching as it went. Plunged deep in, the branch had, it would seem, wounded it to the very heart; after running home, the ox died that same day.

The ox was from Maqiao. The following day, Maqiao sent someone over with a yellow vine soaked in chicken blood.

The battle raged for ten days and Maqiao had by far the worst of it. The Peng family from Longjia Sands had a huge ancestral temple and, aiming to defeat Maqiao straight off, called up namesakes from a surrounding radius of thirty-six bows to come and help the village. Hopelessly outnumbered, the Maqiao forces had no choice but to ask an intermediary to make peace. Following the mediation, not only did the people of Maqiao not recover the money for the ox, they had to pull down houses and sell grain to compensate Longjia Sands to the tune of a copper gong, four pigs, and a six-table banquet, before the matter was settled. The Maqiao representatives dispatched to present compensation to Longjia Sands went banging drums: four old and four young there were, eight altogether, all with pants tied around their heads, all carrying bundles of rice straw on their backs to express the shame of defeat. Although they received a jar of wine from their adversaries as a gesture of friendship, they returned to the village with tears streaming down their faces, and kneeled, one after another, rooted to the ground before the ancestral tablet, intoning over and over how they'd betrayed their ancestors, how they no longer had the face to live. All night they drank, till their eyes were bloodshot, before finally swallowing yellow vine. On the morning of the following day, eight stiff corpses were carried out of the ancestral temple as the villagers all joined together in unanimous lament. Some of the abandoned graves I dug a few decades later, it was said, belonged to these people. Zhaoqing sighed, saying their descendants either died, or fled. Zhaoqing also said that the year the vine was presented happened to be a year of famine as well: none of the dead had had much to eat, none of them had had their fill of gruel, so of course their graves couldn't grow any lettuce jades.

When taking a rest on the burial ground, Maqiao men would eye the tangled mass of skeletons, keeping as far away as possible, an odd blankness in their eyes. They'd all beg Wanyu to sing something—most likely as a way of bolstering their courage. Wanyu would curl himself up under an earthen step out of the wind, wipe a handful of snot from his frozen red nose and slowly sing this verse:

Four brothers each with four ox horns
Each goes their own way, carrying a horn
Five hundred years on, the leaves return to their roots
A palm can't leave the back of its hand.
The eldest takes the southeast peak,
The second over the northwest hills,
The third goes down to the Bright Pearl Sea
The fourth fords the River that Crosses Heaven.
Five hundred years, five hundred years more,
Waiting every day till the sun's gone down,
The road to the west is wide and vast,
When will the brothers' horns lock once more?

*Old Forder [津巴佬]: During the great road-works campaign, Zhaoqing was the least popular person in the workers' shed. People said when he turned up at the construction site, he brought nothing with him save his one naked dragon. He treated everyone else's belongings as common property. If, when mealtime was approaching, you discovered your chopsticks were gone, nine times out of ten he'd got there first and walked off with them, and was shoveling his food in with them right there and then. If you discovered your towel had gone, it would be him who'd got his paws on it and was wiping clean his bony chest or flat nose with it. The Educated Youth objected both to his flame-yellow teeth and to his long nasal hairs, but took particular exception to his stealing their towels. When you'd grabbed the towel back, even when you'd scrubbed at it violently with soap several times over, you'd still worry his nostril filth was left on the towel.

He was as thick-skinned as they came, and would just laugh it off, or even have a go at the other person for being mean. Sometimes he'd even be shamelessly vulgar: "I didn't wash my wife's crotch with it—what're you so upset about?"

Everything came back to crotches with Shortie Zhao. If someone's nose was bleeding: Has your period come? he'd say. If someone went for a pee: Bringing baldy out to see the sun? he'd ask. He could tell these two jokes a hundred times without getting tired of them, or sensing anything at all boring or repetitive about them.

He'd also bring up the subject of his son Three Ears, about how this unfilial son of his had seduced and eloped with Tiexiang, "Before I'd had a chance, he got right in there and screwed that city woman—furious, I was!"

It was the female Educated Youth who took the greatest exception to him. Whenever they came out to work, they never wanted to be put with him.

At home, he'd never used soap. But he wouldn't let other people keep anything special for themselves, wouldn't let there be anything in the world he couldn't try himself. His interest in soap didn't take too long to develop and when he stole a towel he'd always nab the soap while he was about it. He'd get well into his washing, foaming up a huge basin of bubbles for one mandarin jacket—infuriating for the soap's owner.

When Mou Jisheng got back from work and discovered the piece of soap he'd just bought had shrunk almost beyond recognition to a tiny lump, he couldn't stop himself getting angry. "You scumbag, Shortie Zhao, don't you have any sense of right and wrong? Stealing other people's property is against the law, don't you know that?"

Zhao pulled a long face: "What're you shouting about? I'm a grandfather, my grandsons tend cows and gather wood, is using a bit of your soda (see the entry "Rough") against the law?"

"But why're you using it? I want compensation! Compensation from you!"

"I'll give you compensation, if that's what you want! D'you think I can't afford a bit of soda? I'll give you ten bits. What a fuss!"

"Your dragon, you'll give him compensation," some bystander snickered.

Zhao's face went burning red: "Reckon I can't pay him back? My sow's just had piglets, they're eating a pot of slops every day—any day now, they'll be out of the pen."

His antagonist still wanted to seek truth from facts: "You wouldn't want to pay me back even if your sow shat gold."

"I'll pay, I'll pay! I'll pay him back with my pants."

Mou Jisheng sprang to his feet: "I don't want your pants, d'you think I can wear those pants of yours?"

"What're you talking about? I got them made less than a month ago."

"They're like women's pants, there's no opening to piss or shit."

Mou Jisheng had the utmost contempt for the pants the peasants wore: tied together with a piece of grass string, they had no leather belt or belt hoops, and absolutely no shape at all, just two baggy tubes they were, the back identical to the front. People were always swapping them from front to back, so the bottom often ended up at the front, ballooning out and making people feel as if their lower bodies were heading in the opposite direction from their torsos.

"Well, what d'you want to do about it then?"

Unable to think of anything even remotely appealing in the possession of Shortie Zhao, an exasperated Mou Jisheng had to postpone settlement over the soap till later.

It was then that we realized why Maqiao people called Zhaoqing "Old Forder." Old Forder meant old miser, or stingy devil. In Maqiao vocabulary, a "ford" is the opposite of a "rock." "Rock" implies stupid, or straight-as-an-arrow honest, something mountainlike, while "ford" implies cunning, shrewd, watery: both meanings echo the ancient saying "the benevolent love mountains, the wise love water." Bearing in mind that in ancient times communications, commerce, calculations, and plans only came with the presence of flowing water, the word "ford" quite logically came to describe those who are calculating.

During the few days I shared a bed with Zhaoqing, it was the grinding of his teeth, more than anything else, that drove me mad. No one knew what grudge he was bearing, or against whom, but all night, every night, he'd grind away, as if masticating on some stubborn, unyielding, unchewable mass of glass or nails, and the whole of the workers' shed shook with him. Even insomniacs several sheds away must've been ground down and chewed up by his teeth. I noticed that a lot of people got up in the mornings with red eyes, swollen eyelids, hair sticking up and limbs shaky, utterly weary, painfully exhausted, as if they'd been through a massive trauma.

But Zhaoqing acted as if nothing had happened, bouncing along with a quick, light step, sometimes even flashing a grinning mouthful of yellow teeth, no trace left of the grievance he'd been venting all night.

I raised the issue with him. He seemed rather pleased with himself: "You didn't sleep well? I wonder why I didn't hear anything? I didn't even turn over once, that's how well I slept."

"You must've had a stroke, either that or your stomach's full of bugs!"

"I should go see the doctor. Lend me a bit of money, three yuan, five yuan, whatever you have'll do."

Borrowing money again. After bitter past experience of lending money and not getting it back, I exploded at him: "Still got the cheek to ask? What d'you think I am, a bank?"

"Just lend it me for two or three days, two or three days, once the pigs are out of the pen I'll pay you back."

I couldn't believe him. It wasn't just me, I knew; almost all the Educated Youth had made this mistake with him: once the money was out of your hands it was very difficult to get it back. For him, borrowing money was almost a hobby, an interest of his, a form of entertainment with little link to any concrete purposes—he often borrowed when he didn't need money at all. Once he let himself in for a savaging by Master Black, having borrowed one yuan off him in the morning, but, persuaded by his fist, returned the original article to him in the afternoon, without having done anything with it. Of course, borrowing the money was something in itself: with a note warming his pocket for a few hours, his heart could rest happy and easy. "Is all money the same?" he once remarked in all earnestness. "There's nothing special about using money, anyone can use money. What kind of money you use though, and using it in a way that brings happiness—now that takes effort."

He also said: "Man lives a lifetime, the grass for an autumn, what does money count for? People should just try to be happy."

Quite the philosopher, he was.

As he kept grinding his teeth, I ended up pushed beyond the limits of endurance and had to chase him out into another shed. He didn't have anything much to move: no quilt, no trunk, no bowl, no chopsticks either, he didn't even have his own carrying pole and hoe. No one in any of the work sheds was willing to take him in, due to his calculating lack of possessions: even his same-pot cousin begrudged him not having a straw bed-mat and wouldn't share a bed with him. Several days passed without him finding a nest to shelter in. This was no great problem to him: by day, he scraped by just like other people. Once night fell, the black night intensified his ability to take advantage. He'd wash his face, feet, and hands as hard as he could, grin as winsomely as he could and call on work shed after work shed, quietly honing in on his target, searching, groping, and clambering into an empty bed whenever he saw one. Drop your defences for an instant and he'd burrow into a corner of the bed. One more hesitation and he'd be faking a whistling snore. However much you thumped and swore at him, however much you yanked at his hair and ears, he wouldn't open his eyes, wouldn't budge.

You could've beaten him to death.

He had a small frame, wiry as a shrivelled toad's. Asleep on the corner of the bed, he resembled a tiny clenched fist; with his spine curled and feet tucked up, he didn't actually take up much space.

If on any one day the resistance was universally stiffer than usual and he couldn't in fact find a crack through which to squeeze himself, then he'd lay a couple of carrying poles down somewhere sheltered out of the wind and pass the night fully dressed on the poles. This was a unique skill of his. He even possessed talent at sleeping on one carrying pole: he could sleep like this for hours on end, not moving a muscle, not falling off—that spine of his would have astonished even tightrope walkers.

He preferred to give his carrying pole skill a showing every night rather than return home to fetch a straw bed-mat. The funny thing was that he slept in frost and dew without ever getting ill—he remained, in fact, as perky and chipper as a little cockerel. Whenever I woke up, he was already busy as a bee, twisting some grass rope or sharpening a piece of hoe in the hazy early morning light. By the time I turned up at the construction site, sleepy and bleary-eyed, he'd always worked up a sweat. When the sun came out, burning up the boundless expanses of mist that lay over the ground, it gilded Shortie Zhao's whole body with a reddish-gold glow. I remember his digging action as having a particular grace: it was as if the heavy harrow wasn't lifted by him but flew up voluntarily, descending in line with his steps, rising and falling with precision. The instant in which the harrow fell, a flick of the wrist deftly turned it, the head shattering the clods of earth with instantaneous economy. His feet stamped in perfect rhythm, in an action that lacked any trace of sloppiness, that wasted not a moment of time nor ounce of energy. His actions couldn't be analyzed separately, the one from the other: all his actions, in fact, were indivisible, were as one, were realized as a unity in which form followed thought, followed a smooth and easy progression, like a dance with no trips. Head lowered, he performed his dazzling, sublime dance in the gleaming orange mist.

This work machine, of course, got the most work points of all: if tasks were being timed, he'd often do in one day what took me two or three days, leaving envious incredulity in his wake. And yet he spent his nights on a carrying pole. I found out afterwards he often slept like this at home—with the seven or eight kids he had to raise, the tattered quilts on the two beds covered his kids but never stretched to him too.

When the family planning movement began, he was a prime target for a vasectomy. He was most unhappy about this: the Communist Party already governed heaven and earth, how come they wanted to govern the inside of his crotch as well?

But when the time came, off he trotted obediently to the commune clinic. There were various explanations as to why it was him and not his wife who went to be sterilized. He said his wife wasn't well and couldn't be sterilized. Other people said he was worried his wife would have affairs and that after being sterilized she'd cheat on him left and right. What crap, others said, everyone who got sterilized received a standard government reward of two packets of grape candy and five catties of pork; Shortie Zhao had never eaten grape candy, so he fought to go under the knife just to taste it once.

Ten or so days later, he re-emerged to come back out to work, his face clean-shaven and his complexion much rosier: grape candy, it would seem, could work miracles. The young men laughed at him and said only women went to be sterilized—when did you ever hear of a man going? Once you'd had the chop, didn't you become a eunuch? Deeply agitated, he said the government had guaranteed that wouldn't happen. Seeing the disbelieving faces massed around him, he pulled his pants down to give everyone a viewing, to clear his name of this slur.

Master Black, who still bore a grudge over the soap business, wouldn't let the matter lie: it may look the same, he said, but who knows if it still works?

"Just call your Miss Xia over, m'boy," said Zhaoqing, "then you'll know if it still works."

Miss Xia was a female Educated Youth, being courted at the time by Master Black.

Master Black reddened: "That no-good turtle-spawn hooligan!"

Shortie Zhao slowly tied his pants, "So, your heart aches at the mention of your Miss Xia? Those round buttocks of your Miss Xia, strike me down if . . ."

Before he'd finished his sentence, Master Black charged and threw him over his back with a Mongol-style wrestling move. When he raised his head, his whole face was covered with mud.

Muddy-faced, he clambered up and ran a long way away, swearing and yelling: "I've got grandsons watching the oxen, I've just had an operation, I'm a sick man just out of the hospital, even Commune Head He sent his regards and said I'd contributed to the nation, how dare you beat me, you little bastard? How dare you?"

He went back home cradling his stomach, managed to gasp out the beating had given him an internal injury and spent five or so yuan on herbal medicine. He'd walked off with a hoe belonging to Master Black, mortgaged for the time being for three yuan, a towel made up another half a yuan—Master Black had better return him the two-odd yuan he still owed him.

His vasectomy operation henceforth gave him justification for putting a premium on everything he did, became his proof of entitlement to preferential treatment wherever he went. Today he'd want to plough the fields (there were a lot of work points in ploughing) because he'd had a vasectomy; tomorrow he wouldn't want to plough (there were even more work points in pressing oil), also because he'd had a vasectomy; tomorrow he'd want the scales to be tipped (when the team head was allocating grain), because he'd had a vasectomy; today he'd want the scales to slip (when delivering manure to the team head), also because he'd had a vasectomy. He always got this to work for him, actually, and even tried his luck outside of Maqiao. When he went into the county with Fucha to buy seeds, they got on a bus at Changle. He absolutely refused to buy a ticket. He had the money all right, public family money, it wasn't earned by his own blood and sweat. But he had an instinctive, bitter, virulent aversion to parting with cash and grumbled endlessly and indignantly about any ticket price: "1.2 yuan? What d'you mean 1.2 yuan? For this hop and a skip? Should be two *jiao* at most!"

He wouldn't budge.

The ticket seller gave as good as she got: "Who asked you to get on the bus? You want a ride, this is what it costs, don't want a ride, get off right now!"

"Three *jiao*, how about three *jiao*? Four *jiao*? Four and a half?"

"This is a public bus, I can't bargain with you!"

"Funny that, business without bargaining—when we buy a bucket of manure we'll always talk terms."

"You go and buy manure, then, no one asked you to get on this bus."

"What kind of talk is this from a young girl?"

"Get a move on, one yuan two *jiao*, get your money out."

"You—you—you what're you wanting so much money for? I just don't believe it: do the tires on a bus as big as this, with all these people on, really need to turn so much?"

"Get off, get off!" His adversary impatiently pushed him down the steps.

"Help! Help!" Zhaoqing hung onto the bus door for dear life, plunking his bottom down onto the floor, "I've just had a vasectomy and the commune cadres all sent their regards to me, how dare you throw me off the bus?"

Neither the driver nor the conductor could get him to understand and the passengers crowded onto the bus were starting to yell agitatedly at the driver to hurry up and get driving. Starting to feel a bit alarmed, Fucha hastily dug out the money to buy the ticket.

Zhaoqing's face was not a pretty sight after all that: poking at the bus window, tugging at the cushions, spitting with fury, he wouldn't get off at their stop; even when, called several times by Fucha, he discovered he was the last person on the bus, he still only slouched off grudgingly. "Barbarian parts are full of crooks. For the cost of a catty of meat, you get to ride in a bus for about as long as it takes to have a piss."

Followed by a stream of filthy abuse.

On his return from the county, he said whatever happened he'd never ride on a bus again, he raged at all buses: when he spotted one on the street, a stream of "stinking whores," "fucking thieves," studded with constellations of spit, would chase at lightning speed after the bus. In the end, all buses became targets for his loathing, for his ferocious glares. That time he went to Huang City, he came upon a jeep that had run over and killed a peasant's duck and whose browbeating driver was refusing to compensate the owner of the duck—nothing to do with Zhaoqing at all. Possessed by a towering rage that came from nowhere, he pushed out of the crowd of onlookers and before anyone had time to put up any objections, with one punch toppled the driver over backwards onto the ground, face-up with a bloody nose. Although sympathetic all along with the owner of the duck, the onlookers had cowered in the face of the driver's bullying tactics and hadn't dared say anything. Now they'd seen someone else take the lead, a mass of yells and blows erupted, following which the driver and his companion paled with fright and hastily dug out some money to prevent further trouble.

The jeep screeched off in panic. The owner of the duck was brimming with gratitude toward Zhaoqing: this driver, he said, was in the county government, was a famous bully who'd often come by here in the past; he'd not only been refusing to pay compensation for the duck, he'd even accused the duck of obstructing him in his war duties. If it hadn't been for Zhaoqing's sense of justice, the driver might well have taken him off to the county government.

Zhaoqing took no notice of the gratitude and admiration of

bystanders, nor of the weighty import implied by mention of the county government: he was still muttering regretfully that the jeep had slipped away so quickly—if he'd known that was about to happen, he'd have found a carrying pole to pry off the tires.

He and Fucha went on their way: despite their attempts to get a lift with a tractor going the same way as them, driver after driver refused and they had no choice but to walk along the steaming highway. As the sweat dripped off Fucha's face while he walked, he couldn't help complaining: "Anyway, it was the team leader who gave us the bus money, why d'you insist on saving it? You're just making life difficult for yourself!"

"Cost of those tickets, the people ought to protest!" Zhaoqing was referring to the ticket price: "I'll put up with eating and wearing less, but I just can't swallow my temper."

Road sign after road sign they passed. So thirsty their throats and eyes were starting to smoke, they came across a little stand at the roadside selling tea for one cent a bowl. Fucha drank two bowls and told Zhaoqing to have a drink too. Without saying a word, Zhaoqing turned up his nose and just curled up under the shade of a tree to sleep. Braving the sun once more, they finally came across a well after another ten *li*, at which Zhaoqing borrowed a bowl from a roadside shack and drank eight bowls without pause, drank until his burps rumbled, his eyes glazed over, saliva hung down off his chin and his breath almost choked him. He gave Fucha a smug piece of advice: "You must be awakened, boy, you can't've grown hair around your dragon yet—don't you know how hard life is? People like us can't earn money for other people, we can only earn money for ourselves."

The team leader gave people traveling on business a five *jiao* meal subsidy. Zhaoqing starved himself throughout one whole day of walking, went home with the full amount *and* gained a bowl from the shack at the roadside.

☆**Purple-Teeth Soil** [朱牙土]: Purple-teeth soil is the soil you see everywhere in Maqiao, so it shouldn't take too much explaining here. It is, in a nutshell, hard, acidic, and extremely infertile. It's different from metallic loam in that metallic loam is pure white, while purple-teeth soil is deep red with white streaks, a bit like tiger skin.

The thing is, though, if you don't know about purple-teeth soil, then you can't know that much about Maqiao. For a long, long time, this has been the soil Maqiao people have had to face every day, the soil that has made countless harrows tremble, the soil that has transformed countless hands into rolls of blood blisters, into bloody pulps, soil that destroys metal faster than skin, soil that soaks your pants with sweat that runs down to the feet and congeals into salty stains, soil that leaves people dizzy and disoriented, half-alive, half-dead, soil that deletes consciousness of time, that leaves you panting so much that all desires are obliterated, soil that makes every day—the blazing heat of the summer sun, the freezing cold of serious winter—feel the same, soil that drives men to insanity, women to desperation, that leaves children prematurely aged in no time at all, soil that is eternal, inexhaustible, soil that drives people to hate, to argue, to blows, to knives, soil that multiplies hunchbacks, limps, blindness, miscarriages, imbecility, asthma, backache, and deaths, soil that drives people into exile, to suicide, soil that turns life into a daily grind, soil that, regardless of whatever form of upheaval or suffering might be occurring, remains soil upon soil upon soil upon soil upon soil upon soil.

This layer of soil rolls out from the Luo River, from the even more distant eastern mountains of Hunan, coming to an abrupt halt below Tianzi Peak, then meanders toward the villages down south. It had coagulated like a flood of molten iron, a vast, blazing sea of fire that still tortures people throughout their lives.

Zhaoqing's first son was buried alive in this soil. He'd been helping to repair the water reservoir, removing earth to build a dam, and he did what the other public laborers did to get his duties in the earthworks finished a bit faster: first he'd scoop out the soil from underneath to a certain depth, then let the upper soil cave in. This was called releasing the "fairy soil," and was a more efficient way of working. But Shortie Zhao wanted just a bit too much: having scooped out the soil to a depth of three metres, he calculated the purple-teeth soil was too solid to bring the overhanging fairy soil down right away. As he scooped up his bamboo hat, a sudden crashing noise erupted behind him and he turned to see clod upon great clod of red tumble and collapse, somersault and avalanche before his eyes, leaving not a trace, not a whisper of his son.

His son had been playing over there, just a moment ago.

He hurled himself over there, digging, digging, digging red, then more red, digging red, more red red red, digging till all his fingers bled, still without digging out even a scrap of cloth. This was his favorite son, the one who'd been able to say all sorts of things just after his first birthday, who after his second birthday had been able to recognize his own family's chickens and chase his neighbors' chickens out of the house. He'd had a large black mole on his forehead.

☆**Floating Soul** [飄魂]: Zhaoqing's death has always been a riddle to me.

The very day he disappeared, I'd gone with him to Zhangjia District to help dig a tea plantation. Hearing there'd be meat to eat at midday, he brought his kid son Kuiyuan with him, stuffing a pair of chopsticks into his hands a long time in advance; then as soon as it was time to eat, father and son strode at great speed to the front of the crowd, heading, dashing straight for the kitchen, for the sound of meat sizzling in the pot. The kid hadn't been counted in the total of mouths to feed, but his gaping jaws were very plain to everyone present. People had teamed up in groups of six, with each group entitled to a bowl of meat. No one wanted to accept an extra uncounted mouth hanging on Zhaoqing's tail, and wrangled away till Shortie Zhao flared up. "How much can one slip of a boy eat? Have you no conscience, haven't you got kids yourselves? Are you all going to be destitute old men, without descendants to look after you?"

After this, not everyone could very well continue to put up resistance, and one group was forced, rather grudgingly, to allow father and son to jostle their way in and to listen to their glugging and crunching. They also had to tolerate Zhaoqing rushing forward at the key moment to pour out meat broth for his kid first of all, into a great big ceramic bowl that was tipped bottom-up to the heavens, completely obscuring his little face.

As there was no food left in his own bowl, Shortie Zhao cadged a little green pepper from his son's.

Kuiyuan was the most important person in the world to him, and he'd never neglect to bring along this glugger and cruncher whenever there might be a meat-eating opportunity. Not long before this, I'd heard he'd dreamt at night that while messing around on the mountain Kuiyuan had had a piece of *baba* cake stolen by a figure dressed in white; even after waking from the dream he'd been still too angry to calm down, had snatched up a grass sickle and gone off to the mountain to settle scores with this figure in white. I couldn't credit it: what kind of a spirit was Old Forder that he had to recover *baba* cakes lost in a dream?

I didn't really believe this had happened. When we got into the fields, I couldn't stop myself asking him about it.

Not a word from him. Once he got onto the fields, he was totally absorbed, totally unwilling to join in with chatter that had no bearing on work efficiency.

"You've dropped some money behind you," I told him.

He turned back to look.

"There really is money, take a proper look."

"That'd be your little sister's savings, would it?" He concentrated on his digging.

It was only when he got thirsty and glanced over at my water flask that he started to get all chummy with me, giving a pretty fine imitation of the Educated Youth's barbarian accent: "I say, that flask of yours."

"If you want a drink, then drink—what are you going on about the flask for?"

"Heh-heh, what's eating you today?"

"So you'll only give me the time of day when you want something?"

"What? Have I got to kow-tow just for a gulp of your water?"

As he drank, he counted out loud without being aware of himself: one two, two two . . . Each second "two" meant two mouthfuls of water.

"If you're going to drink, just drink, why count the twos?" I said rather rudely.

"Just a habit of mine, no need for it." He laughed in embarrassment.

When he'd finished drinking, he became a little politer but remained rather vague about the business of having taken the grass sickle into the mountains: he didn't say it had happened, but neither did he say it hadn't happened. He emphasized indignantly that he'd had several dreams about this figure in white: once the figure had stolen his family's melons, once the family's chickens, another time he'd given his Kuiyuan a clip round the ears for no reason at all. What a nuisance, eh? His teeth ground as he posed the question. There was no answer I could give. From what I'd heard of what he said, those rumors about him snatching up the grass sickle and swearing to settle scores were probably all true.

It was a rum business. Why was this figure in white always barging into his dreams? How come he had so many strange dreams? I couldn't help feeling confused, as I took back the water flask.

That was the last time he borrowed my water flask. The afternoon of the following day, his wife came looking for a cadre, to report that Shortie Zhao hadn't come back home all last night and that she didn't know where he'd gone. Everyone looked everywhere, with growing looks of disquiet, as they remembered they hadn't seen him turn up for work that morning.

"Gone to Maoxing Pond, has he?" said Master Black, laughing.

"But how could he have been gone for so long?" His wife didn't understand what he was talking about.

"I was just . . . guessing . . ." Master Black dropped the subject.

"Maoxing Pond" was the name of place in a neighboring village, an isolated dwelling of no more than two households. Shortie Zhao had an old lover there, though who she actually was we had no idea. But whenever he went there to do any work, he'd gather a few branches and blades of grass from off the ground to symbolize grain and firewood, knot them into a wreath and snatch a moment to take it over to "Maoxing Pond" as a token of his affection. He'd then rush back to his work in the fields at incredible speed: nothing less than the wind itself could have moved quicker.

Fucha returned from Maoxing Pond that evening to report there was no Shortie Zhao there either, that absolutely no one had seen a trace of him. Only then did we feel things had started to get serious. Gathered round in whispering huddles, the villagers had identified one piece of news as supremely important. Someone from the lower village had just returned from Pingjiang, bearing a message from Zhihuang's former-pot wife: the dream-woman was reminding Zhaoqing to make sure he had his shoes on.

This was a common method used for warning people in Maqiao, a tip-off to those with "floating souls."

In Maqiao language, floating soul referred to an omen that occurred when people were close to death. After making some general inquiries, I found out there were mainly two sorts of situations involving floating souls:

1. Sometimes, if you saw someone walking along in front of you suddenly disappear, then reappear, you knew a hole had been made in this person's soul and they were going to scatter soon. If you were of a kindly disposition, you'd go and warn this floating soul, but you couldn't do so directly, you couldn't give it away, you'd have to ask something like, "You're running fast! Lost a pair of shoes?" and so on. Hearing this, the other person would've known the score and would rush back home to burn incense, make sacrifices, or ask a Daoist priest to come and drive out the spirits, would do his utmost to avert calamity.

2. Sometimes, while asleep or distracted, a person might dream he'd been dispatched by the King of Hell to fetch another person's soul—an acquaintance of his, perhaps. On waking, again bound by the same principle of discretion, he or she would have to find an ingenious means of giving warning to the other person. Not only were they not to give anything directly away, the two of them also had to be raised off the ground—by climbing up into a tree, for example, and whispering very quietly, to avoid Grandfather Earth hearing, then reporting to and thereby enraging the King of Hell. When the other person heard the warning, he would, of course, be full of thanks, not anger. But there could be no gift to express thanks, no clue that might risk detection by the King of Hell.

Now that the dream-woman Shuishui had mentioned shoes, the situation was of course extremely serious. But because Shuishui's family home was so far from Maqiao, by the time the bearer of the message had hurried back to Maqiao, it was too late and Zhaoqing had already disappeared before the message was delivered. While the village was sending search parties in all directions, someone remembered the business with the figure in white and sent people off to the mountain. Finally, hoarse wails from the cracked throat of Zhaoqing's wife floated in fragments on the wind down the mountain.

Zhaoqing's soul, it turned out, had already floated off. He died horrifically, facedown at the side of a stream, his severed head lying swollen about three meters away in the brook, bitten to pieces by a dense covering of ants. This violent murder sent shockwaves through the commune and the county's Public Security, and several cadres came to conduct repeated investigations. The cadres' flame was high and they didn't believe in any floating-soul business, or in fate. Their first guess was that GMD spies had been dropped from the air onto the mountain, or that oxen-rustling bad elements from near Pingjiang were responsible. In order to calm the general public and stop the strange rumors flying around, the higher-ups made strenuous efforts to solve the case, carrying out mysterious surveys, taking fingerprints, struggling a few suspicious landlords and rich peasants here and there, panicking the chickens and the dogs half to death—but still no explanation was found. The commune even arranged for the People's Militia to take turns standing guard in the evenings, to guard against tragedy repeating itself.

Standing guard was a tough job. The evenings being cold and the urge to doze off very strong, I was propped up under the armpit by a spear, my feet like two blocks of ice, and needed to jump regularly up and down to restore sensation to my toes. I heard crunching footsteps on the road leading to Tianzi Peak: every tiny hair stood up on end as I listened out again—nothing. Despite hiding in a corner out of the wind, I couldn't control my intermittent shivers. After brief hesitation, I took another few steps back and retreated to the house: even though (just as a temporary expedient) I was surveying the night from behind a window, I was still fulfilling my duties, I reasoned. In the end, my legs tortured with cold and my eyes ever returning to my quilt, I couldn't stop myself burrowing in and (half-)lying on the bed. I still reckoned I was taking frequent sidelong glances outside, not failing to keep up my revolutionary vigilance.

I was worried a figure dressed in white would suddenly skim past outside.

Dazed and confused, I woke up to discover it was already very light; in a panic, I ran outside without glimpsing a soul. Some routine yells were coming from the ox-shed—someone preparing to let the oxen out. All was quiet and peaceful.

Since I couldn't spot anyone come to investigate where the sentry had gone, I relaxed.

It was not until I was transferred to work in the county and bumped into Yanwu on a visit to the city to buy oil paint that I heard another theory concerning the strange death of Shortie Zhao. Yanwu said that at the time he'd told Public Security that Zhaoqing had definitely not been killed by a third party—it'd been suicide. Or, to be more precise, it was accidental death by suicide. Why did he die at the side of the stream? he mused. Why had there been no sign of a struggle on the scene? He must've found some fish or something else in the stream, hidden in the crack of a stone, and poked at it with the wooden handle on his grass knife. He must have poked a bit too violently, without noticing the sharp blade was pointed directly at his own neck: with one stab into the air, one pull of the knife, he lopped his own head off from behind.

This hypothesis was very daring. I've used a grass knife, sometimes called a dragon-horse knife: it's a knife with a very long wooden handle that enables you to slash cattail grass whilst standing upright, on which the blade and wooden handle are at right angles. When I thought about it, with Yanwu's deductions in mind, a chill ran right down the back of my neck.

Unfortunately, as Yanwu's class status was very poor at the time, the Public Security Bureau couldn't take any notice of what he said.

Besides, he didn't have any proof.

*Lax [懈]: And so, amidst such confused circumstances, Zhaoqing's head fell off. While on sentry duty in the middle of the night, viewing Tianzi Peak suddenly loom closer, vaster in the moonlight, I got to thinking about his life. Because he was so low, so stingy, I'd never had a good word to say about him. Only after his death did I think back to that time when (under orders from above) I'd climbed up a wall to paint Chairman Mao quotations and the ladder had suddenly started sliding unstoppably downwards; I'd only saved myself from falling by grabbing onto a horizontal beam close at hand. Quite some distance off, Zhaoqing had seen all this happen, dropped a bowl of food from his hand to the ground with a clang and ran over yelling: "help—someone help—oh my—" He jumped up and down, producing cries of extreme anguish, jumped here and there till he was dizzy, then jumped back again without having accomplished anything much, wailing and weeping as he did so.

Perhaps I wasn't in any great danger and he didn't need to wail or jump around so much—he hadn't even actually done anything to help me out. But out of all my friends and acquaintances present at that moment, not one was as terrified and panicked as he, not one shed tears involuntarily for me. I was grateful for his tears—though only for a very brief moment, though they quickly shrank back into a pair of small eyes to which I'd never be able to feel close. Later on, wherever I went, however many cities and villages I forgot, I couldn't wipe from my memory that brief glance downwards at a face below, just a face that, enlarged by perspective, had obliterated from view the scrawny body beneath, and that was showering down a noisy waterfall of yellow tears for me.

I wanted to say something to thank him, to pay him back somehow, a few yuan, a piece of soda, say, but he wouldn't have it.

I carried a bedful of cotton blankets over to his house and asked his wife to use them to cushion Zhaoqing's coffin. All his life he'd slept on carrying poles; from now on he should be allowed to sleep well. He'd been busy all his life; from now on he should be allowed to be lax.

To be "lax," in Maqiao dialect, means to "relax."

☆**Yellow-Grass Miasma** [黃茅瘴]: When I was in Maqiao, Zhaoqing told me more than once that I shouldn't go up into the mountains early in the morning, that I should wait at least until the sun had come out. He also pointed out to me something densely blue in among the scattered trees on the mountain, that floated in and out of view, hanging like threads, like bands on the branches and leaves, slowly drifting away in smoky rings: miasma, this was called. There were several different sorts of miasma: in spring there was spring-grass miasma, in summer there was yellow-plum miasma, in autumn there was yellow-grass miasma— all were highly poisonous. If people blundered into it, their skin would inevitably come out in ulcers, their faces go blue-yellow, their fingers black. It could even kill them.

He also said that you couldn't be too careful even when you went up into the mountains in daytime. The night before you went up, you couldn't eat tiny scraps of things and you definitely couldn't sleep with a woman, definitely had to give up temptations and lusts. Before going up into the mountains, you'd best drink a mouthful of rice wine to warm the body too, to strengthen the *yang*.

This was what Zhaoqing said.

It was he who told me. I remember.

☆**Pressing Names** [壓字]: I didn't recognize Kuiyuan when I bumped into him again all those years later. Both he and his Adam's apple had grown, along with a little beard; he wore a suit with rolled edges, walked around in eye-catching leather shoes, wafted fragrant breezes from his washed hair and carried a black leather bag that wouldn't zip up. He was Kuiyuan, Ma Zhaoqing's youngest, he said: Don't you recognize me, Uncle Shaogong? What a memory you have, ha-ha-ha!

I had to puzzle away for ages before I finally dredged up a child's face from long, long ago, and drew one or two points of corroborating resemblance between it and the unfamiliar face before me. I also recognized a letter he produced, written by me, true enough, to Fucha a few years ago, discussing some language-related question.

He said he'd been missing me and that he'd come to the city especially to see me. I asked him, wonderingly, how he'd managed to find me. Don't ask, he said, he'd had a devil of a time finding the way. When he'd been set down on the quay, he'd asked everywhere where I lived, but no one he'd asked had known. In the end, he'd asked where the municipal government was—still no one knew. Losing his temper, he asked where the county government was, and someone finally pointed him in some sort of a direction. I thought you were looking for me, I laughed, what did you want with the municipal and county governments? He said he had a couple of outings every year, he'd been to Wuhan, Guangzhou, Shenzhen, all sorts of places. He knew how to get about. This seemed to serve as his answer to my question.

He didn't say whether he'd actually found the government offices. But he complained about how my phone must be broken and how he hadn't been able to get through, however hard he tried. I later discovered that he hadn't in fact had my telephone number at all, so heaven only knew what number he'd been calling.

In the end, he got in a taxi and spent fifty yuan—almost all the money he'd had left on him—before finding out what university I was at. Not knowing what taxis cost here, he'd been ripped off by a crooked driver, no doubt about it.

This, of course, was no cause for worry—he'd always felt pretty detached about money matters. To sum up, he contacted the government, made a phone call, took a taxi, did everything an important visitor should, before he finally chanced across an acquaintance of mine who took him to where I lived. He'd never believed he wouldn't find me, he said, and everything had, as expected, come out in the wash: without any undue exertion, he'd miraculously pulled off a long-distance raid on my home, bringing along for good measure another young man I didn't know. Now he was home and dry, everything was fine and dandy; he took off his coat and watch, his shoes and socks, and rubbed the sweat and mud from his feet. Casting his eyes about the place, he was amazed to see I didn't have a real leather sofa, or a big, right-angled wide-screen color TV, or color-sprayed vinyl walls and mood lighting and laser-sound stereo karaoke—he knew a lot more about city life than I did. I said laser-sound stereo karaoke cost too much, forty, maybe fifty yuan for one disc. He corrected my mistake: what are you talking about, he said, a good disc would cost one, two hundred at least. Has the price gone up? I asked. It's never been less, he said. Unwilling to concede the point, I said that a friend of mine a couple of days ago had bought one at this price, a genuine, nonpirated disc. He said that wouldn't have been DDD, it wouldn't have been digital; no one serious about singing would've wanted anything to do with it.

Not understanding DDDs, I didn't dare take the matter any further and merely absorbed his instruction in silence.

After he'd washed, he put on some of my clothes and said with a smile he'd known all along he wouldn't need to bring a change of clothing: What sort of a person d'you think Uncle Shaogong is? he'd said to the folks back home. When I get to his place, there'll be clothes to wear, food to eat, work to do, no fear! When at home, rely on parents, away from home, you rely on friends. . . . He slapped me affectionately on the back as he told me this.

I removed his hand.

Things weren't that simple, I said, but let's get you settled, and then we'll see.

I took them to a hotel. When they were registering, I discovered he was no longer surnamed Ma: the surname on his I.D. card had been changed to Hu. That was how I found out that after his dad died, his mother hadn't been able to bring up all the kids and had given him away to someone else, along with an elder brother and elder sister given away elsewhere. I also found out that where they came from, adopted children had no inheritance rights before they'd "pressed names."

Pressing names was a ritual carried out to formalize entry to a clan, conducted after the funeral of the adoptive father, in which the clan elders sang the name of the adoptive father, the name of the adoptive grandfather, the name of the father of the adoptive grandfather, the name of the grandfather of the adoptive grandfather, the name of the father of the grandfather of the adoptive grandfather . . . of the person entering the clan. They sang the names of all the fathers they could possibly trace back to ensure that the person being adopted would inherit the ancestors' property and trade, and to prevent him from taking the property or land back to his original family later on. As they saw it, names were sacred and the names of the dead wielded an additionally mysterious kind of power, capable of defeating demons and punishing the unfilial. Kuiyuan said that the Hu family weren't short of property—the house was their own—but unfortunately the old man was long-lived, could still go out to work in the fields even at the age of eighty-seven. Last year he'd spend three months ill in bed, coughing up phlegm and blood, and it'd looked as if his number was pretty much up. No one had expected that, after all this time spent dying, he'd come back to life again. . . . What on earth was he meant to do? Kuiyuan's eyes widened in astonished bemusement. What he meant was that he hadn't yet been rewarded for his pains, he hadn't yet pressed names and so didn't yet have rights of ownership over the house.

And so he couldn't wait forever: he had to try and make his way in the city.

☆**Lazy (as Used by Men)** [懶(男人的用法)]: I had a friend, a big boss in the city, who employed an engineering team. I introduced him to Kuiyuan and the young man who'd come with him and they got taken on as unskilled workers—I reckoned that would just about earn them a bowl of rice.

A few days later, they were banging on my door, both faces a picture of woe: it was impossible, they said. No, it really was impossible.

"What happened?"

"Nothing, really."

"Are you streetsick?"

"I've never gotten streetsick, it was just we got . . . burned."

"D'you mean sunburned?"

"Right, mmm."

"Didn't you wear a hat?"

"Hat didn't do any good."

"Don't you get sunburned in the village?"

"I've . . . never worked in the fields."

"Well what did you do all day, then?"

"Nothing much, sometimes I'd help brother Yanwu harvest a bit of grain, collect a few debts, most of the time I'd just mess about, play cards, sit around other people's houses." Kuiyuan flashed a smile, exchanging glances with the young man who'd come with him, who just then was taking a sidelong glance at the television as he cracked sunflower seeds, but who also smiled at that moment.

"So young, the two of you, and so . . . lazy?" I pronounced a word of infinite gravity.

"Lazy, that's exactly what we are." Kuiyuan very happily joined in,

"I'm lazy around the house too, I've never cut firewood, never carried water, I still don't know how rice is washed and boiled, never done it."

The young man cracking sunflower seeds said: "Same with me: ask me where the sickle or the drill rod are in my house, ask how much our pigs eat at one meal, I won't have a clue."

"When I go out to play cards, I can be gone a couple weeks."

"I don't play cards, I go and mess around at my uncle's house in the county, ride on his motorbike, watch the TV."

I was rather nonplussed by this. I could tell from their complacent tone, from their rather exaggerated accounts of themselves, that the meaning of this word had transmogrified, that a process of linguistic renovation had begun of which I was entirely unaware. The word lazy—which was abhorrent to me—represented to them a medal for which they strove, competed, and struggled to have decorating their own chests. The indolence I had just been criticizing had to them become a synonym for ease, comfort, face, skill, to be pursued and coveted, which made their eyes shine. What else could I say to them?

Of course, the original meaning of lazy hadn't been entirely expunged: when discussing other people's wives, for example, they'd discuss whose wife was lazy and whose wasn't, and lazy women came in for repeated condemnation. What this sounded like to me was nothing less than a new, men's dictionary, compiled by them and inapplicable to women, and one in which the word "lazy" came trailing clouds of glory. If what had happened to lazy was anything to go by, then we could infer that deceiving, exploitative, violent, fiendish, treacherous, rascally, corrupt, thieving, opportunist, vulgar, rotten, low-down, obsequious, etc., could, or had already become words that connoted praise and respect in this most recent men's dictionary—at least for a sizable proportion of men. If, as they saw it, there were still men who didn't acknowledge this dictionary, this was not proof the dictionary didn't exist, it was proof only that these men were linguistic aliens, pathetic nobodies, all washed up by the tide of innovation, lagging behind the shadow of History.

Human dialogue often takes place within two, or even multiple, dictionaries. The difficulties of translating what words mean, and in particular the endless pitfalls of translating what words mean on a deep emotional level aren't easily overcome. In 1986 I visited an "artists' colony" in Virginia, U.S.A.—in other words, a creative center for artists. I couldn't rid myself of the awkward feeling the word "colony" gave me. It was only afterwards that I found out for a lot of westerners living in western sovereign states that have owned many colonies, the word colony doesn't bring with it the images of murder, burning, raping, pillaging, opium-smuggling, and the like that it does in the memories of colonial peoples; quite the contrary, it means something perfectly innocuous, it's just another name for a settlement abroad, a dwelling place; it even exudes a faintly romantic, poetic resonance of development that is tied up with all the pronouncements and professions of benevolent expansion, of maritime exploration, of the spread of civilization which are part of imperial memory. A colony is a staging house for the noble, an encampment of heroes. Westerners would never sense there was anything inappropriate in using this word to refer to the location of artistic labors.

Also in America, I met someone called Hansen, a man who understood Chinese, who'd married a Chinese woman, and who was a journalist on the Asia desk of a big news bureau. When he heard me talk about the sufferings of Chinese people, he expressed deep sympathy and anger toward the instigators of this suffering. But I suddenly noted a strange reaction behind the sympathy, behind the anger: his smiling eyes sparkled in the lenses of his glasses, his index finger drew endless lines back and forth somewhere across the dinner table, as if he was writing some word in the air, or conducting some stirring tune in his mind. Unable to control the excitement inside him, he ended up phoning some friends, inviting them to come and meet me, telling them in English how I had some stunning, amazing stories! These were, he swore, the most fantastic stories he'd ever heard! This word "fantastic" jarred on me. When my father committed suicide, when he sank to the bottom of that river, did he feel "fantastic"? When the younger brother of a friend of mine was shot following a miscarriage of justice, when, close to execution, he howled and wept, unable to find the faces of his parents in the crowd come to see him off, did he feel "fantastic"? When, after the son of a friend of mine was mistakenly killed by a gang of hooligans and the father brought his son's effects back from his university, not ever having dreamed that he would write the inscription for his son's gravestone, did he feel this was "fantastic" in any way? . . . I don't wish to cast doubts on Hansen's compassion: no, he'd always exposed injustices in his newspaper, always helped Chinese people as much as he could, which included helping me obtain the perks and financial assistance due to a visiting scholar. But his "fantastic" came from a dictionary incomprehensible to me. It was obvious that in this dictionary, suffering wasn't just suffering, it also provided material for writing or performance, it was the precondition necessary to incite revolt and revolution, and so the greater the suffering, the better, the more fantastic its radiant glow. This dictionary concealed a principle within it: in order to obliterate the instigators of suffering, more and more suffering was required as proof to convince more and more people of the urgent, lofty necessity of this struggle. In other words, in order to obliterate suffering, first there had to be suffering. The suffering of others gives rise not only to the pity, but also to the pleasure and happiness of saviors; it's an endless source of bonuses for the score-cards of their heroism.

I didn't feel like talking any more, and suddenly changed my plans: to his bemusement, I refused to let my dinner companion pay for my pizza.

I've often realized, not without a sense of disquiet, that talking isn't easy, that my words often propagate all kinds of misunderstandings once they've flown out of my mouth. I've also discovered that even a powerful propaganda machine lacks absolute controlling power over understanding and, similarly, sinks repeatedly into the mire of ambiguity. Here, I must make mention of the young man who came to my house with Kuiyuan. I later found out his surname was Zhang, that he'd been an employee of the County Film Company but had been relieved of his duties due to his exceeding the birth quota. It wasn't that he'd failed to comprehend the consequences of exceeding the birth quota: the vast truckloads of tedious state propaganda about the punishments and rewards that came with family planning regulations had bored a hole in his eardrum. Neither did he have any great love of children: the two sons he already had hardly ever caught a glimpse of him, extracted a smile from him with the greatest of difficulty, and represented to him the permanent, burdensome obstacles to divorce. He had no reason whatsoever to produce another child. After I'd spoken with him, after I'd turned it over endlessly and uncomprehendingly in my mind, there was only one conclusion I could draw: he operated on another vocabulary system, one in which a great many words transgressed ordinary people's imaginings. For example, "violating law and order" wasn't necessarily a bad or an ugly thing to do—quite the contrary, violating law and order was a proof of strength, a privilege of the strong, a crucial source of happiness and glory. If, under the category of "violating law and order," you included corruption, smuggling, official profiteering, prostitution, rushing through red lights, random spitting, eating out on public funds, and so on, then this young man would have embraced every single one of these acts with open arms. The only reason why he hadn't done these things was because at present he lacked the capability to do so.

Given that exceeding the birth quota was classified along with all those other things as a "violation of law and order," and that it lay within the range of his personal capabilities, it isn't hard to guess how he would unhesitatingly decide to act.

His exceeding the birth quota was totally illogical, sprang not from any assessment of personal benefit, but from a habit of understanding, from an impulsive pursuit of all privileged behavior. Maybe it was because in the past he'd known a director or manager who'd produced a high-and-mighty brood of three while everyone else had to toe the line, maybe he'd always secretly envied him. And so once he'd done what ordinary people didn't dare do, or couldn't do, the thing in itself made him feel like he was head and shoulders above everyone else, like he was a director or manager. His efforts to conceal the facts of his transgression from the authorities concerned were about as strenuous as someone who'd blatantly embezzled a million yuan: he quietly crowed in self-satisfaction, endlessly savoring his rash audacity.

What use was propaganda to people like him? What was the use of propaganda about legal disciplinary measures? Of course there was a use: to increase his excitement at taking desperate risks, to renew the temptation daily.

I can't find any other way of explaining it.

If the explanation given above is generally correct, then the whole affair comes down to a question of language, to an absurd coincidence of meanings interlocking and short-circuiting. In the end, the law-breaker lost his bowl of rice and paid a high price for one or two extremely ordinary words. The propaganda that the wielders of power directed at him had been entirely useless, had ended at cross-purposes: on encountering a totally alien dictionary, a totally impenetrable pair of ears, it had hastened along the birth of a furry-headed, bawling, screaming baby girl. This baby was superfluous to all parties concerned. But this mistake could never be covered up, or daubed away with correcting fluid, or deleted with an eraser.

She'd grow up, grow up into the future.

She was a mistranslated sentence made of flesh and blood.

✳**Bubbleskin (etc.)** [泡皮(以及其他)]: In Maqiao during the 1990s, a lot of new words came into fashion and passed into common usage: "television," "paint," "diet," "operate," "Ni Ping" (a well-known television host), "disco dancing," "Highway 107," "seafood," "lottery tickets," "build the Great Wall" (play mahjong), "bump-the-butt" (motorbike), "hold the basket" (act as mediator), and so on. In addition, a mass of old words which hadn't been used much between the fifties and the seventies all turned up again. Anyone who didn't know this might have mistaken them for new words. For example:

"Cut up"—originally a Red Gang (secret society) phrase, meaning
to kill someone.

"Sort out"—this also used to be a Red Gang term. Following its frequent usage in lawsuits, it later gradually grew in currency via itinerants, grew broader and broader in meaning, until it came to refer generally to any course of action that solved problems or difficulties. This word was also used in newspapers, in news headlines such as: "The Reforms Will Sort Everything Out."

"Ox-head"—this referred to a mediator or arbitrator with the authorities, a role usually taken on by the noblest, the most senior and most prestigious of the elders. The ox-head was decided neither through election nor through official appointment: whoever acted as ox-head relied during his tenure on agreement naturally reached among the people.

"Straw sandal money"—this used to refer to the tip that people who'd come from far away on public business would ask for from the person involved when the business had been completed. After this word made its reappearance at the end of the 1980s, its meaning stayed basically the same, the only difference being that straw sandal money by then was given mostly to cadres wearing leather or rubber shoes, to members of public security teams, to the well-meaning bringers of good or bad tidings and so on; and it was no longer paid in grains of rice, not like before.

"Bubbleskin"—a lazy good-for-nothing, equivalent to the Mandarin expression "roughskin," but lacking the thuggish overtones of "rough," implying something more small-fry, more cowardly and obsequious, something that resembled the insubstantial fragility of a bubble.

And so on.

It was from Kuiyuan that I heard the word "bubbleskin." In fact, Kuiyuan himself had something of the bubbleskin about him. That time in my living room, when I read him the riot act about his laziness, he immediately started nodding his head, yes-yes-yes-ing, like a chicken pecking at rice. He couldn't keep his eyes, hands or feet still, as he sought to agree with me in every possible ingratiating way. When I was his age, I said, I'd work ten hours a day; what did I mean ten hours, he said, surely fifteen hours, at the very least, I wouldn't see daylight at either end. Wasn't that right? Even in the countryside, I said, you still had a future, as long as you were willing to dig in, keep chickens, fish, pigs, you could end up with 10,000 yuan; what did I mean 10,000 yuan, he said, some became company directors, with offices abroad, surely I'd seen the stories on TV?

He overdid it a bit, turning the interrogation around on me.

In the end, stopping just short of slapping himself on the head, of shouting furiously for his own extermination, he hastily collected together the shorts and socks he'd just laid out to dry, stuffed them into the black leather bag with the broken zipper, asked me for some red plastic tape, and tightly bound the black leather bag a few times around. He took off the shirt I'd lent him and said he'd leave for home today, there was still time to catch the last boat from the quayside.

He didn't even drink his tea.

It was already late at night. I suddenly started to feel a bit bad about this abrupt departure. He didn't have to hurry back during the night, or return my shirt to me—he could at least finish his tea before he left.

"You don't need to be in such a hurry. You came, you didn't find any work, but it's all right to stay a couple of days just to mess around before you go, who knows when you'll have another chance . . ." My tone had warmed up by several degrees.

"We've messed around quite enough."

"How about going tomorrow, after breakfast?"

"When you've got to go, you've got to go—and anyway, it's cooler at night."

He and the young man with him seemed to be racing against time, unwilling to lose a moment in their haste to return to the village. They were strangers in the city, utterly clueless as to whether they'd be able to find their way, whether they'd be able to find the bus to the quay, whether they'd be able to catch the last boat, how they'd spend this long night if they didn't happen to catch the right boat. My rebuke had suddenly electrified them: you could have set mountains of knives and seas of fire before them and still they'd have leapt in without a second thought. As I was heading off to find a friend to borrow a car, planning on taking them part of the way, they called out a few times from somewhere off in the distance before they slipped into the black night and, within the blink of an eye, disappeared without a trace.

☆**Democracy Cell (as Used by Convicts)** [民主倉(囚犯的用法)]: After Kuiyuan left my house, he didn't actually return to the village. About ten or so days later, there was a knock on my door and on opening it up I found a tousle-haired, dirty-faced boy who handed me an extremely crumpled cigarette box on the top of which were written in ballpoint pen two lines of characters. The nib had obviously run out of ink and in several places had poked through the card without leaving a mark, leaving me no choice but to guess what was in the blanks.

"Uncle Shaogong, you must must come safe (save) us, quick!" It was signed: "Yor nefew (nephew) Kuiyuan." I asked what this was meant to be. My messenger had no idea either. He didn't know of any Kuiyuan. All he knew was that today, without giving any explanation, someone had stuffed ten yuan into his hands and asked him to deliver this note—that was the long and the short of it. If he'd known before he started how hard my house would be to find, he wouldn't have done it for thirty yuan. He hung around for a while, only leaving when I gave him another five yuan.

It was clear as day: Kuiyuan had committed some crime and been put in jail.

I was both furious and worried, and if old Kuiyuan had been in front of me there and then, I'm afraid we might have come to blows. But the die being cast, the damage already done, I'd have to swallow my pride, grit my teeth, and brace myself for some contact with the seamy side of life. First of all, I had to make inquiries as to where the detention center was, which involved working out the distinction between county and municipal centers, between guard centers and temporary centers and interrogation centers, and so on. All the acquaintances who answered my questions listened to my patient explanations, umming and ah-ing before simply letting the matter drop, clearly still completely mystified. Then I went to my work unit to pick up some documentation that might be useful, scooped up some money and headed for the suburbs, straight into a billowing sand storm. Because I was speeding, I was stopped and fined twice on the way by transport police, and it was already dark by the time I found the detention center. Their business hours were over, so I had no choice but to come back the next day. The next day, after producing a great many smiles, platitudes, and cigarettes, and imitating every dialect there was to ingratiate myself with every big cheese there was, I finally jostled my way into the crowd of people encircling the office and managed to talk to a female police officer who spoke with a Sichuan accent. I finally learned the details of Kuiyuan's case: gambling in a group at the quay—which, although she said it came within the parameters of the "strike hard" campaign, wasn't considered too serious, added to which the cells were impossibly overcrowded, so it was—punishable by fine. I was pleasantly surprised by these last three words and thanked her repeatedly in Sichuan dialect.

I hadn't brought enough cash, so that afternoon I took another sum of money along, handed over enough for the fine, living costs, educational materials, and so on, and took him away. One tiny twist in the story remained before I took him away: probably because there were too many convicts, the prison warden didn't know which cell he was locked up in.

Rushed off their feet, they made me sit and wait for two or three hours before they finally took pity and made an exception to the rules, allowing me to enter the cells area and look through the cells, one by one, myself. I glimpsed two long rows of grey metal doors stretching off into the distance, each door with a tiny window inset, crammed with faces; or rather, each was a square of eyes compressed in at every angle, packed denser than a block of meat fresh out of the freezer. Every eye seized hold of me, waited for me. I started with Number One: my effortful request to each square meat brick to move aside for a moment opened out a slight crack of space into which I could shout Hu Kuiyuan's name, then press my ear up close, silently listening for a movement within. I heard a miscellaneous buzz of voices, smelled a sour, rotten odor of sweat and urine, but time and time again was disappointed—no one answered.

Twenty-odd windows had gone past and my throat was beginning to crack, when a thin, weak answer floated over as if from a distant, very distant horizon, a whisper transmitted to my ear by the iron bars, drifting in and out of hearing. I was astonished: every cell was at the most twenty or thirty meters square, how could a voice sound so distant? How come it seemed to come out of a universe of infinite depth and distance, that stretched out behind the iron bars?

"Ah-ah-ah—" It sounded like someone was pinching his windpipe.

He received back from the police the black leather bag with the unzippable zipper, said many words of sincere repentance to them, then uttered nothing further, just sat on the backseat of the motorbike, getting a surreptitious measure of the expression on my face. It was only after we'd gone a few kilometers that I sensed the person behind me was wiggling his feet, dispersing their bad smell a little on the wind.

Back home, the first thing I did was tell him to stand in the doorway and not move, not sit down, not touch a single thing in my house, to take off his clothes straightaway and go into the bathroom; every single item of his clothing was collected up into a bundle by my wife and stuffed into the washing machine.

As expected, my wife, yelping with alarm from over by the washing machine, soon discovered lice, bedbugs, and traces of blood on his clothes. Slinking out of the bathroom, Kuiyuan smirked with embarrassment, asking as he combed his hair, "Where's the mirror?"

I pointed.

"I was unlucky, this time I got into a democracy cell . . ."

I didn't understand.

"I only survived by the skin of my teeth."

"What d'you mean, democracy cell?"

"Don't you know what a democracy cell is?"

"I've never committed a crime."

"It's just . . . it's just . . . everyone's democratic, right."

"What's that mean?"

"Democracy means lice, bedbugs, fights, blood, lots of them."

I still didn't understand.

He started to eat. He said in a prison cell the prison king had the best time of it, when he ate, there'd be people fanning him, singing songs, offering a towel to wipe his face. When the food came, the prison king would have first pick, nabbing all the good things, like the meat, of course. Afterwards, the "Four Daoist Immortals" and "Eight Daoist Immortals," the prison king's direct subordinates, would eat, picking out another layer of good stuff. The scraps of soup and leftover rice remaining were all the little people ate. When the prison king wanted to sleep, he took the best place. When the prison king wanted to see the female convicts, only he stood in the window opening, lifted onto the shoulders of those below, who'd sometimes support him for up to two hours at a stretch, their legs trembling with exhaustion.

A newcomer had no choice but to fall into line. If you weren't prepared to follow the fiat of the prison king, the Daoist Immortals or those convicts in waiting for promotion as Daoist Immortals would soon beat you half to death. This was called "softening you up." Or they'd stick you in the frame, show the guards in charge of discipline a nail or razor blade to prove you'd broken prison rules, and you'd end up in chains or with a yoke round your feet. He said although a prison king was pretty vicious, in a prison king's cell, people were usually quite law-abiding, generally there was a leader in everything, there were no group fights, things were kept fairly clean and hygienic, the towels hung up neatly, the quilts folded one on top of another, which kept the disciplinary cadres happy. To convicts, the democracy cell was the most terrifying thing of all, when a prison king hadn't yet emerged, or when victory and defeat between two or three prison kings remained undecided—that was no life at all. One stray comment and there'd be shouting and fighting; you'd be doing pretty well to keep your eyes, nose, hands and feet on after a few months in a democracy . . . .

Rubbing the head he'd somehow managed to keep on his shoulders, Kuiyuan said with lingering fear in his voice that the cell he'd been put in this time was neither one thing nor the other: it was a democracy, plain and simple. Three great rumbles had already been fought between the Sichuan gang, the Guangdong gang, and the Northeastern gang, without any decisive outcome. Even clapping the battle leaders in irons hadn't solved the problem for the disciplinary cadres. Terrified as he'd been every day, he hadn't had one good sleep.

I gave an icy laugh: "Got a lot of prison experience, have you?"

He anxiously leapt to his own defense: "No, no, no, nothing of the sort, I'm the most law-abiding person ever, if someone dropped their money in front of me, I wouldn't pick it up."

"How many times you been inside?"

"First time, absolutely the first time. Strike me down if I tell a lie, I swear. I've heard some things about prison from Brother Yanwu."

I couldn't remember who this was.

He couldn't believe it: "Can't you even remember Brother Yanwu? The board director, Yanzao's little brother! You know—didn't you used to play ball with him?"

When he mentioned Yanzao, it occurred to me that Yanzao, it seemed, had had a brother by this name. When I arrived in Maqiao, he was still in school, and I later heard he'd written some reactionary slogan on a stage and gone to prison—by that time, I'd already been transferred elsewhere. My memory, I realized, was getting worse and worse.

☆**Tiananmen** [天安門]: Before I revisited Maqiao, a lot of people told me that Maqiao now had a Tiananmen, that it'd become a famous scenic spot (or almost), that even senior officials out on business came, that after visiting the shrine of Qu Yuan and the County Revolution Memorial, they'd always drive out to have a look.

Strictly speaking, Tiananmen wasn't actually in Maqiao, it was on the boundary with Zhangjia District, right next to what was later National Highway 107, but its link to Maqiao lay in its belonging to Maqiao's Yanwu. It was in fact a large residence, occupying a few dozen *mu* of land, with pavilions, terraces and turrets, a lotus pond, flower gardens, bamboo woods, a winding corridor set on the water, artificial mountains and rocks. The garden was divided up within itself, each part with its own name, one called "Garden of Eden," one called "The Xiang River Lodge," an indeterminate mix of East and West. Its construction was a bit crude: few of the tiles had been laid flat or clearly aligned, they were all skewed and encrusted with dried cement that hadn't been leveled off. Not many of the windows could be opened, being permanently stuck up with something or other. This caused inevitable anxieties: if Lin Daiyu—a famously sickly Chinese literary heroine—had spent all day in the gardens pushing and pulling at windows, she'd have had her work cut out for her—how'd she still have had time to bury flowers and burn poems? The days would've gone by without her managing to croak out much more than a few lines of karaoke.

People were at work on the skeleton of a small, two-storey Western-style hotel, and it was said that after it'd been finished they'd hire ten girls from around Jiangzhe as waitresses, especially to receive journalists, writers, and other guests.

I didn't get to see the owner: people said Yanwu lived mainly up in the county, coming back only now and then to take a look around the place and check up on a couple of factories around here. I glimpsed his house from far off, a small two-storey building in the center of the lotus pond. Three or four window air conditioners were visible around its perimeters, sticking out from each wall, far more than made logical sense; when I thought about it, even the toilets must have been terrifyingly, bone-chillingly cold. The whole house looked like a cement monster overgrown with iron tumors.

Some years earlier, I'd heard that the peasants around here had gotten rich and taken to buying seven or eight electric fans at a time. When they ran out of places to put them, they set them up in the pigpens. Then the next thing you knew, it was air conditioners that were all the rage. The guide was endlessly nagging at me to count the number of air conditioners and would start counting them for me in fives and tens whenever my concentration seemed to be slipping. Every excessively enunciated figure expressed a deep envy that was tinged also with a kind of pride, and that resonated inside my eardrum, as if these iron tumors were in some way part of him, as if he felt some inner compulsion to make me admire the dazzling results of the rich peasant policy.

The guide felt this was still not enough, and at some point went looking for a manager, a young man who knew me, apparently. I'd taught a few classes in days gone by and he'd been one of my students. He produced a key, wanting to take me on a visit to the house. I could hardly refuse the offer, and not having much choice in the matter, followed him across the twists of the winding corridor, through three iron sluice gates and, with a slam and a clatter of doors, into the mansion set in the lake. Its interior, a resplendent expanse of hanging lamps and wallpaper, was really quite nicely done. Unfortunately, as the electricity wasn't powerful enough, none of the air conditioners would start, so the manager had to give everyone a rush fan to stop them from sweating. The television wouldn't play any programs either—apparently the television tower in the neighborhood hadn't yet been put up. There were two telephones, one black, one red, and from the looks of the receivers, they weren't program-controlled, so you probably wouldn't get through to that many people here—people said the switchboard operator in the local government was never on the job and spent most of her time looking after her kid.

"Have some tea, have some tea," I was being given the full courtesy treatment.

"Okay." In fact, I'd rather have found some water to wash the sweat off me.

"Watch the TV, go on."

"Okay."

After the manager had spent ages tuning it with his bottom stuck in the air, the TV finally started flickering a little less and a brightly colored picture floated up out of nowhere, some tape of a foreign music video. It played and played, then started flickering again. Maybe the tape was broken, I said, and tried to change it for one that worked. After a lengthy search, I discovered there weren't any other tapes to watch, the only other one being a Hong Kong martial-arts movie in even worse condition.

By now, my face was streaming with sweat. Steam was billowing off the lotus pond and the scarlet carpet baking underfoot was roasting everyone till they smelled of cooked meat. Panting with the heat, I had to retreat outside the door until the others had finished watching the fragmentary singing and dancing.

I only later discovered that the name "Tiananmen" referred to the main building of the compound, which was a small-scale imitation of the architecture of Tiananmen Square. To give an idea of its size: a chicken chased to extremes of panic and desperation could probably have flapped its way up onto the top of the building. The building had arches, doorways, moats, and footbridges, and was painted deep red in imitation of palace walls. In front of the main entrance stood two grimacing stone lions. Unfortunately there was no water in the moat, only scattered clumps of grass out of which a couple of toads leapt sporadically. When you stood at the head of the building, no square or memorial lay ahead, only a row of commercial alleys, a gathering of desolate noodle stalls, odds-and-ends shops and the like, an empty pool table covered with yellow dust and a crowd of young men squatting under the eaves of buildings, some crouched on stools like roosting chickens, idling away their time.

There was a house with a large shop sign hung over it, "Tianzi International Culture Club," apparently provided by the owner of Tiananmen to serve his fellow villagers for free.

As part of the club, there was also a big theater stage to the left of the building. The guide said that in the first month of this year, the county theater troupe had come to sing opera here for three whole days, again paid for solely by Yanwu for the free entertainment of his fellow villagers.

The visiting party was discussing something to do with one of the actresses in the troupe. Their argument caught the attention of the roosters perched under the eaves, finally giving their sallow gazes a focus.

I was, of course, surprised that Yanwu could build such a big mansion, and also that he'd built it in such a contentious style—if he'd built it ten or so years earlier, wouldn't it have been condemned as a counterrevolutionary conspiracy punishable by death? Only later, when I bumped into an old acquaintance, Zhihuang, did I learn the whole story that lay behind this. Zhihuang said that when Yanwu was in high school, when his family class status was very poor and he hardly counted as human, he'd once stuck a picture of Tiananmen on his bed, which had been confiscated by the class representatives. If poor and lower middle-peasants didn't own photographs like this, said the class cadre, what right did landlord scum like him have to pine for Chairman Mao? To see Tiananmen everyday? He was plotting to blow up the great leader with dynamite, now, wasn't he?

Presumably this incident had hurt him very badly, very deeply. Now that he had money, he built his very own Tiananmen before he did anything else.

In the past, he'd had no right to look at Tiananmen; now, he wanted to let everyone know that not only could he look at it, he could even build one, and build one right under all their noses. He could let his wife and two kids play with the crickets and dogs, eat sesame cakes, and sneeze in Tiananmen.

He took out large loans, was kidnapped several times by debt-collectors threatening to snap his tendons, was even taken away once in a police inspection-unit car—all for this project.

***Brutal** [狼]: In Maqiao, "brutal" means capable, skillful, a high level of technical know-how. The problem is, "brutal" at the same time implies ruthless, vicious, malicious. Uniting these two meanings in one word never made me all that comfortable. As I've said before, my handwriting was quite good, and during my time in Maqiao I'd often be ordered to paint displays of Chairman Mao's quotations everywhere in red and yellow oil paint. When the peasants saw me writing on the walls, neither using templates nor tracing out the characters, just climbing up the ladder and writing, there'd be astonished murmurs:

"This transfer kid's really brutal!"

I could never work out how much of this was admiration, how much was criticism.

Being able to write nicely was brutal, knowing a lot of characters was brutal, helping the team leader fix the grain threshing machine was brutal, being able to dive down and fill in the leaks in the pond was brutal, even factories from barbarian parts that manufactured appliances, diesel oil, chemical fertilizers, and sheet plastic (and therefore, of course, the workers) were clever, were brutal. When Maqiao people talked like this, maybe they were unaware that they were implicitly relegating knowledge and skill to the category of moral corruption, of savagery.

I suspect that, according to their past experience, people with a grasp of some particular knowledge or skill possessed a natural tendency toward violence and terror. The first time they saw a piece of rumbling machinery, it dropped Japanese bombs on them from the sky; the first time they saw a radio amplifier, it cut off their "capitalist tails" by confiscating their own private land. What was there to reassure them that clever people they later encountered wouldn't do them similar sorts of harm?

Under these circumstances, was there anything wrong in them using the word "brutal" in this way?

Maqiao language isn't unique on this point.

In a lot of places in Sichuan, people with a high level of skill are described as "fierce," a word close in meaning to "brutal." "Really fierce," that's what they say about someone with a great deal of skill.

In a lot of places in the north, people with a high level of skill are described as "wicked," again close in meaning to "brutal." "Wicked so-and-so," is what they call someone with a lot of skill.

In standard Mandarin Chinese, the term *lihai* (severe), widely used to refer to people possessing a high level of ability in some area, provides another example of the sting in the tail of praise, of the anxiety concealed within the pleasure. *Li* means fierce, severe, while *hai*, meaning evil or harm, provides a warning of even greater clarity and bluntness. In Hunanese, calling someone *lihai* refers to someone with ability who's always taking ill-intentioned advantage.

So it seems that in a lot of Chinese dialects, knowledge and skill, and evil (or brutality, fierceness, wickedness, harm, etc.) are two sides of the same coin. Two thousand years ago, Zhuangzi expressed anxiety and hatred toward all forms of knowledge and skill. "There are few good people in the world, but many bad, there are few sages that benefit the world, many that harm it" (Zhuangzi, *The Outer Chapters*, chapter 10). He believed that only by exterminating knowledge would the thieves of the nation be routed; only following the destruction of jewels would the numbers of property thieves decline; only by smashing tokens and documentation would people grow honest and contented with their lot; only by breaking the scales would people be unable to haggle and argue; only by destroying laws and religion would people be able to comprehend nature and the Way of the ultimate in human life. . . . Zhuangzi's resentment of knowledge has long since been submerged beneath the modern advance of technological progress, become a faint glimmer lying over the horizon, ignored by the majority. But in linguistic heritage, at least in the many southern dialects I mentioned above, it continues to eke out a stealthy existence.

☆**Strange Talent** [怪器]: Maqiao dialect has another term for people who demonstrate great ability: "strange talent." The *Origins of Words* (Commercial Book Center, 1988) gives three definitions for *guai*, the word for "strange" in Mandarin: the first is bizarre or unique; the second is particularly, extremely, very—presumably the gradual evolution of the first meaning into a function word; the third is censure, blame. From the looks of it, in Chinese bizarre things are forever linked with censure and blame, are perilously out of the ordinary.

Maqiao's "strangest talent" was Yanwu. When the original batch of Educated Youth had all been transferred or retired due to illness, only two remained, of whom I was one. Those who could sing revolutionary operas had all gone, and when the arts propaganda team were ordered to go out and perform, we couldn't even get the gongs going, so someone suggested Yanwu to us. He was still studying at middle school, but he responded to the call and sang very well, as it turned out; though he didn't have time to come and rehearse, and was so short he couldn't get on the stage, he concealed himself in a dark spot behind the stage, where he sang through operas from start to finish, good guys, bad guys, male roles, female roles; he just learned the words and out they came, so all the people on stage had to do was mouth. The difficult high notes he hit without batting an eye, producing an astonishing stream of rich, full sound that reverberated in the night sky over the countryside. That head of his poked in and out at everyone else's waist height: it was impossible to see his face clearly without bending at the middle. So as not to miss class, he'd run off after having finished singing, disappearing into the darkness before I'd got a proper look at him.

His singing of Peking operas and model operas was hugely renowned, and whenever there was a joint performance being given in Pingjiang County, he'd be asked to help out.

I only got a proper look at him after he graduated and returned to the village. He had a round babyface, as if he hadn't yet lost his milk teeth, that bore no particular resemblance to his elder brother Yanzao's sharp mouth and monkeylike features. After watching me play a few games of chess, he coolly took to the board himself. I dropped my guard, thinking only to give him a lesson: within a few moves he'd decimated my pieces, ravaged my defences. In another game, he plundered and pillaged to left and to right with the ruthlessness of a grand master, an implacable opponent he was, cutting me no slack, relentless in pursuit and fearsome in attack, destroying at root and branch, prepared to massacre mistakenly rather than let a single piece escape.

I suffered, in secret amazement, a devastating defeat.

"I'm so sorry, I'm no good, no good at all," he said humbly. But his forehead bore a wrinkle of undisguisable satisfaction.

Afterwards, in secret, I furiously researched through chess manuals, but when I asked him for a rematch, he was full of excuses, having to fetch a prescription or work outside the village; he hid himself far, far away, denying me an opportunity to avenge my humiliation. I could imagine, when he saw for himself my anxious impatience, my desperation, the delight on his face once he turned his back.

He didn't work much in the village or spend much time at home; he didn't even come back when his old mother was seriously ill. When the team leader allocated irrigation repair duties to everyone, his were always done for him by Yanzao. Only Yanzao ever appeared on his family's plot of land. First, he studied to be a painter, and we once met on the road, him carrying a bag of tools and covered in paint from head to foot. When I next saw him, a while on, he'd changed to studying Chinese medicine: quite the expert he looked, treating people with acupuncture and taking their pulse. Afterwards, he studied portrait painting and carving as well—it was said he sold paintings and calligraphy in Changle and in the county, as well as carved Chairman Mao's poems in plain and cursive calligraphy on customers' fountain pens, while-you-wait *and* at a fair price. In short, there was nothing much he couldn't turn his hand to, nothing that could prevent him from showing off the superlative strangeness of his talent. The fame of his strange talent spread far and wide until everyone, both old and young, knew of him. Even though he was a "traitor to the Chinese" (see the entry "Traitor to the Chinese"), Maqiao people never bore any ill feeling toward him and were always very tolerant of his frequent mysterious journeying outside the village.

Quite the contrary: he was the pride of Maqiao, the communal pride of all the villages and stockades massed around the environs of Maqiao Bow. If rumor spread that such-and-such a place had produced a university student: what of it? Maqiao people would snort. What a pity Yanwu was a traitor to the Chinese, otherwise he could have studied at three or four universities. If rumor spread that someone from such-and-such a place had been recruited as a country irrigation technician and was working for the state: What—someone like that gets to be a technician? Maqiao people would snort. What a pity Yanwu's class status was too high, otherwise this nobody wouldn't have had a chance.

Once, when Benyi's child had been ill for ages and showed no sign of recovery, Benyi made plans to send him to the county seat. Maqiao people concluded that he was sure to die: if Yanwu's prescription couldn't cure him, what use would it be to send him to the county seat? Sending good money after bad, that was. Just two weeks later, Benyi's kid was cured, in the county seat. Still, Maqiao people weren't surprised, weren't lost for words. It wasn't that Yanwu's prescription was no good, they said, nothing of the sort: the only problem was that the prescription hadn't been made up properly in the countryside. Otherwise there'd have been no need at all for Benyi's child to go to the county seat, using all that money up and suffering like he did: he even went under the knife, had his heart, liver, and lungs dug out to be washed like pickled vegetables, must've taken a good ten years off his life expectancy.

Benyi himself fully concurred with this.

Benyi, the Party Branch Secretary and an enemy of Yanwu's father, endlessly repeated how Yanwu was even more strangely talented than his old man, how he definitely had the makings of a future counterrevolutionary, of a convict. But this didn't have the slightest effect on his worship of Yanwu's strange talent, on his special regard for Yanwu: he'd ask Yanwu to come and check the pulses of his own family whenever they were ill. He wouldn't be able to rest easy before he'd done this.

Yanwu never charged for treating Maqiao's sick; and toward cadres, his manner was doubly reverent. Once, after bumming a cigarette off me, he turned and ran, disappeared in the blink of an eye. When I went to the lower village on an errand I discovered Commune Head He sitting on the grain-drying terrace, smoking away there and then on that Qiulu Mountain cigarette of mine, Yanwu standing to one side rubbing his hands, his face wreathed in simple, honest, slightly timid smiles, listening respectfully to the Commune Head's admonitions. I found out later that he didn't smoke, not because he didn't want to, but because he begrudged it. Working as a painter outside the village, as a doctor, as an artist and engraver, he carefully saved and hoarded up all the cigarettes he received as gifts, then eventually presented them with the greatest respect to cadres, and particularly to Benyi. Benyi's cigarettes were always a hodgepodge of brands for this very reason.

For a time, his relations with Commune Head He were particularly intimate: whenever Commune Head He wanted anything, he'd come as soon as he was summoned and smile as soon as he came, forever obedient, supremely gifted at demonstrating his learning whenever necessary, then returning the credit for his learning to the patronage and enlightenment of his leaders. One time, having hardly slept a wink for two days because of a painting job outside the village, he returned to Maqiao late at night, limping and staggering giddily from exhaustion. He heard from his neighbors that Commune Head He had sent a letter over, saying an alarm clock was broken and could he come and see about fixing it. Not daring to rest, he ran through the night to borrow tools from a clocksmith in Changle before hurrying on to the commune. When crossing Tianzi Peak, all it took was one lapse of concentration and you'd fall into the deep crevice. On the morning of the next day, he was eventually discovered by some passers-by, his face, hands, and exposed feet in particular plastered with stinging mountain leeches, as if his body had been overgrown with bright red fibrous roots. The passers-by all fell upon him, trying to beat the leeches off with such violence their hands were covered in blood. After they'd slapped him awake, he burst into terrified tears after one look at his blood-stained form.

If those people hadn't passed by quite so fortuitously, in another few hours Yanwu's blood would probably have been sucked completely dry by mountain leeches.

In the end, none of his displays helped him that much or got his strange talent redirected toward some higher end. Twice when universities were recruiting students from the workers, peasants, and soldiers, Commune Head He usurped Benyi's authority, pushing Yanwu forward as "Re-educable Youth," but as soon as the motion reached the higher-ups he was sent back again. What's more, on the eve of every important holiday, the peasant militia routinely ransacked his house and lectured his brothers: even if it was just a cosmetic exercise, the militia still had to do what the militia had to do.

After I'd been transferred to work in the county, I heard the county public security bureau had hauled him into jail on suspicion of writing reactionary slogans. The reactionary slogans had been discovered at the joint arts performance on National Day, apparently written along the stage just before the performance. I never found out what they actually said. All I knew was the reason the public security bureau grabbed him: at the time he'd been backstage playing the *huqin* and voice-dubbing very close to the scene of the incident, he had a reactionary family background, he had culture, he had class, he had the strangest talent, so surely he was the person most likely to get up to reactionary shenanigans under cover of darkness.

What I found surprising was that not only were all Yanwu's worshippers, the men and women, young and old of Maqiao totally unconcerned that their idol had been arrested, they even viewed his being reactionary as something that gave them face. Their response was perfectly calm, as if such an outcome was entirely natural. They'd snort with obdurate contempt whenever someone mentioned a suspect from a neighboring village: him, reactionary? Yanwu could produce handwriting as good as his with his feet, he'd never manage anything more reactionary than stealing a cow or some rice.

To them, being reactionary wasn't just petty thievery and pickpocketing, it wasn't the stuff of which ordinary men were capable. Yanwu was the most qualified to be reactionary, was the classiest reactionary: his riding off, ashen-faced, in the police car was every bit as glorious as a cavalcaded state procession to enroll at the university in the city.

There was no one else who could touch him.

People even came to blows over this business. Someone who'd come to drive pigs from Longjia Sands happened to mention in idle conversation that someone in Longjia Sands had a relative who was also a great reactionary in Xinjiang, who'd been regiment commander a few years previously, who'd had his photo taken with bigwigs like Lin Biao. Maqiao's lads weren't going to stand by and listen to this: What d'you mean regiment commander, they said, *we* heard he was only a warehouse watchman, that he had no military rank at all. If Yanwu'd been born twenty years earlier, he'd have ranked head and shoulders above *corps* commander, never mind regiment commander. He'd probably have been a high-ranking official under Chiang Kaishek and right now he'd have been in Taiwan riding in cars everyday.

The man from Longjia Sands said: "Yanwu might be a strange talent, but he's not that much of a strange talent; when he paints Chairman Mao's portrait, the head's too big and the body's too thin, he looks like Oldie Wang from the supply and marketing cooperative."

"You reckon Yanwu can't paint a likeness?" the Maqiao people said. "He's reactionary, so 'course he paints like one."

"How'd his painting make him a reactionary?"

"You haven't seen him painting dragons, he can paint one in the blink of an eye."

"There's nothing special about painting dragons, any odd-job painter can knock one out."

"He can teach, too."

"Can't Li Xiaotang teach, too?"

"Oldie Li can't hold a candle to him."

A Maqiao lad gave an example: when Yanwu explained the word "neck," the explanation took a good ten minutes. What was a "neck"? It was the cylinder of body tissue in between head and shoulders containing hundreds of blood vessels that could shrink down and turn this way and that. Pretty good, hey? How much learning could Li Xiaotang show off? A neck is a neck, Oldie Li would just give his own neck a couple of pats and leave it at that. What kind of teaching was that?

"Way I see it," said the man from Longjia Sands, "I'd rather have a couple of pats."

Long and hard they argued: over the question of whether or not Yanwu was in fact a strange talent, over the question of whether he couldn't paint a likeness of Chairman Mao or whether he deliberately didn't paint a likeness, over the question of whether or not he was actually reactionary. Then the Longjia Sands man trod accidentally on someone's foot, the victim flared up into a temper and threw tea in his face quick as a flash. If there hadn't been people nearby to restrain them, there could've been a major incident.

As I said before, the word in Mandarin for "strange" is also "censure(d)." The phrase "strange talent" always made me secretly uneasy, made me feel that no good would ever come of it. And the public security bureau and Maqiao people ended up proving this point. When presented with reactionary slogans, they suspected neither Yanwu's same-pot brother Yanzao nor other bad elements from neighboring villages, principally because neither Yanzao nor anyone else in the area could match Yanwu's strange talent. With a feeling this was perfectly justified, perfectly natural, not even worth thinking about or seeking agreement on, they defined cleverness as the enemy, brilliance as treachery—even though they secretly worshipped cleverness and brilliance. They weren't trying to eradicate reactionary slogans, as such; it was more the case that they'd long sensed that the abnormality represented by the phrase "strange talent" would sooner or later need locking up. Despite his life-long displays of cleverness, Yanwu had unfortunately never scrutinized the implications of this word, its critical undertones in Maqiao dialect; he'd been so pleased for so many years with his own strange talent, with how he'd kept in with cadres and his fellow villagers, with how he'd managed his own fate like the strange talent he was, that he'd got a little bit over-optimistic.

Whether he woke up to this in jail, I couldn't say. All I know is that he remained pretty distinctive whilst in jail, he didn't let pass any opportunities to exercise his strange talent. There, where even belts were confiscated, he actually succeeded in attempting suicide. For several nights, he rolled around wildly on the floor clutching his stomach, yelling and groaning, until he got the doctor to come and gave him an injection. He secretly hoarded the injection bottle until finally he smashed it and swallowed the pieces.

Tears streaming down his face, his mouth filled with blood and he fell into a dead faint. The guards sent him to the hospital for emergency treatment, but when the doctor heard he'd swallowed fragments of glass, he said even a fluoroscopy wouldn't be able to make out where they were and an operation was of even less use, so there was no hope of saving him. As soon as the two little convicts who'd been ordered to carry him on their backs to the hospital heard this, they burst into piercing wails. The sound of their crying brought an old man from the hospital kitchens over: luckily, he'd had a bit of experience in such matters and suggested they pour leeks down into him. Unchopped leeks, he said, lightly boiled then poured into the stomach would wrap round and tie up glass fragments before they were finally shat out. Somewhat skeptical, the doctors did as he said, but were then amazed to see the balls of leeks in his faeces unroll one after another to reveal the glass fragments inside.

☆**Reincarnation** [放轉生]: The bloody business of butchering pigs, cows, and the like is called "reincarnation" in Maqiao, a turn of phrase that makes it sound like a loftily noble undertaking. The old-timers said that domestic animals had fates, too, that they'd sinned in previous lives and were paying for it in this life, that they suffered more than any other creature, that by killing them you were letting them be reincarnated earlier, releasing them from their sea of bitterness, that it was a deed of great charity. By this reckoning, butchers could slaughter away, as if right were on their side, and diners could merrily chew and munch, their mouths running with grease, their hearts fully at ease.

Language can change the way people feel: altering a word can mitigate, even erase, the pity that scenes at a slaughterhouse evoke, until blood-letting stimulates nothing but blank, unmoved stares.

After Benyi gave up his post as Secretary, he made a living for several years as a reincarnater. Right up until his health began to fail, as long as he could still get out of bed, all it took was for him to hear the sound of a pig squealing and, quite uninvited, he'd go and stick his nose in, having a go at this person's ancestors, this person's mother—no one at the slaughterhouse would escape a tongue-lashing. He was addicted to wielding that knife of his, was pretty nifty at it too: he was the most famous butcher around here during those years, never needed anyone to catch the pig, or tie it up for him, didn't matter how big it was, or how truculent, after just one look he knew exactly what to do. Catching it unawares, he'd suddenly raise his knife, and then, as if with borrowed strength, overcome the beast with great economy of effort. One hand would grasp the pig's ear, the other would bury itself in the skin on the underside of the pig's head—meanwhile, the knife had long since plunged into its chest, turning once, deep inside, before being briskly drawn out. The pig was flat on the ground before it'd had time to squeal. Then, chuckling away to himself, he'd wipe a few bloody, smudgy marks on the quivering pile of flesh, slowly, calmly, wiping the knife clean.

This was called slaughtering on the run, or mute slaughtering—something he was a real pro at.

Sometimes, when he'd had a bit too much to drink, his hand would slip, one knife-stroke wouldn't get the job done and the floored pig would jump up and run crazily about. He'd glare furiously, all the veins in his neck throbbing with pent-up rage, chasing about the place, waving the bloody knife. At times such as these, he'd always be cursing, "Look at you run around the place, you show-off, you, think it's your lucky day, don't you, think you've got the upper hand . . ."

People didn't generally have a clue who he was cursing.

☆**Jasmine-Not-Jasmine** [栀子花，茉莉花]:

- It's going to rain, it doesn't look as if it will (concerning the weather).
- I'm full, I'm full, one more bowl and then I'll be full (concerning eating).
- I reckon the bus isn't going to come, you'd best keep waiting (concerning waiting for the bus).
- This newspaper article is well written, I can't understand a single word (concerning the newspaper).
- He's an honest man, he just doesn't talk honestly (concerning Zhongqi).

Anyone who came to Maqiao had to get used to this kind of double-talk: ambiguous, vague, slippery, vacillating, first this, then that. This rather unsettling way of talking was what Maqiao people called "jasmine-not-jasmine." I found out that Maqiao people weren't generally unsettled by this, didn't even find anything strange about it. It appeared they would quite happily produce statements that weren't really statements, that had no basis in logic. They weren't used to the principle of noncontradiction, it seemed. If sometimes they couldn't avoid speaking a little more clearly than usual, they regarded it as a hard and thankless task, a concession to the outside world which they would make while knowing it was beyond them. I could only suspect that they basically felt double-talk came more naturally to them.

It was because of this that I never really figured out how it was that Ma

Zhongqi died. Here is a summary of what people said: Zhongqi was a bit greedy, but he wasn't that greedy; he was always very above-board, it was just that he was a bit underhanded; he'd never had things that rough, it was just that he had bad luck; his wife's illness was obviously curable, it was a pity they couldn't find the right medicine; he always acted like a cadre wherever he went, it was just that he never looked like one; he built a new house, sure, but it wasn't his after he'd built it; fifth old Huang treated him best, it was just that he never helped him out; he was respected, but he didn't have speech rights; it would be unfair to say he stole things, but he walked out of the butcher's with a piece of meat he hadn't paid for; he took the yellow-vine brew himself, suicide doesn't fit the facts. . . . After all this, was anything clear to me? Or was nothing at all clear?

I know generally that for Zhongqi, who'd long nursed a sickly wife, life was very difficult and he never had enough money to buy meat. On the Double Ninth Festival, unable to help himself, he stole a piece of meat from the butcher's, was publicly arrested, and his self-criticism was stuck on a wall. He probably thought he couldn't take the shame and on the next day drank yellow-vine brew. It was that simple. But Maqiao people can't explain simple things clearly and precisely. They have to slip into an ever more ambiguous "jasmine-not-jasmine" way of talking. This can only prove that Maqiao people are unable, or unwilling, to accept a fact this simple. Perhaps they feel that outside every factual link lie yet more facts beyond explanation and clarification; thrown into confusion, crushed and scattered by all these blurred facts, their own remarks can only lapse into irrelevant nonsequitur.

Throughout his life, Zhongqi wrote innumerable "agreeds." The final one was written, through force of habit, on his own self-criticism for the theft of the meat and stuck on the wall for all to see. In the self-criticism, he cursed himself for being a thief, a shameless rogue, a reactionary element, ashamed to stand before Party and government and ancestors. Some of what he wrote was rather exaggerated in tone, indicative of the depths of his terror at the time. He'd spent his life knowing too much of other people's secrets, knowing of too much widespread deception and villainy, while he himself remained law-abiding all his life, not daring to take even a stalk of rice straw that hadn't been allocated to him. And what good did his honesty ever do him? None at all. He was cast aside by a group of people of whom he utterly disapproved, watched wide-eyed as they got rich while he fell on increasingly hard times. He couldn't even buy pork dripping, let alone afford two spare ribs to rub together. Ought he to have changed? As I imagine the scene, he walked into the butcher's, felt around in his own empty, empty pockets, breathed in the oppressive merriment of the festival atmosphere, and finally decided to make a new start with a piece of meat. Unfortunately, he didn't get any meat, only endless public humiliation and censure.

What should he have done then?

Should he have gone on being honest, or gone on being dishonest?

If he was standing before me right now and asked me such a question, I would probably hesitate a while. I would find it very difficult to give a straightforward reply. At this point, I expect I would secretly feel a haze of "jasmine-not-jasmine" creep irresistibly over me.

*Kuiyuan [虧元]: In 1968, I helped out in the making of a survey. A mass association called "Forever Eastwards" in the CCP Hunan Provincial Party Committee organ, wanted to expel two cadres from the Provincial Party Committee. Firstly, though, they had to carry out a thorough political investigation of all these cadres' relatives. So as to avoid being attacked by the opposing faction, they agreed to accept public scrutiny and invited the Red Guards to send someone along to help out with the survey. And so it was that I managed to get onto a cadre inspection team while I was still barely out of diapers, that I wangled my way onto this cushy number, onto a publicly funded pleasure trip around the whole country.

First of all we went to a number of prisons in Beijing, Jinzhou, and Shenyang to find out about a male cousin of one of the cadres. The cousin used to be a broadcaster at an important broadcasting station, but after mispronouncing the name of the important Communist Party member "An Ziwen" as that of the important GMD member "Song Ziwen" during a live broadcast in the 1950s, he was convicted and sentenced to fifteen years, and had been serving out his sentence in the above-mentioned prisons. I discovered, to my surprise, that however many appeals he wrote, all his hearers felt it was entirely right and proper that he should pay for one single written character with fifteen years of his life. By the time we spoke to him, he'd thought things through for himself, was full of apologies to the Party and to Chairman Mao, and no longer felt his own sentencing was overly harsh. "Government," he addressed me—me! all of fifteen-year-old me—"I won't appeal again, I'll concentrate on reforming my thinking."

As I walked out from under the electric wire fencing and high walls, back to the hotel where we were staying, a sudden terror rose up in me: a nameless terror toward "An," "Song," and all other such words.

Round upon round of gunfire from armed struggles resounded outside the hotel; everywhere there were street barricades, bullet holes, and gunpowder smoke; convoys of vehicles bearing yelling, screaming combatants with guns loaded and at the ready would often whistle past on the street, waking the people in the hotel up to violent starts. In Liaoning in 1968, the "Red Company" was locked in battle with the "Revolutionary Company," while the "Mao Zedong Thought" faction was encircling the "Mao Zedongism" faction. A brutal battle being fought near the station brought all the trains to a stop, trapping me and three colleagues in the hotel for a full two weeks. All this is perhaps very hard for later generations, like my daughter, for example, to understand. In the eyes of those who were born later, in terms of thinking, theory, conduct, interests, expressions, dress, or language there was nothing much to choose between those fighting on opposite sides, beyond the slight linguistic differences between, for example, "Red Company" and "Revolutionary Company"; in other circumstances, they would have done business or worked together, studied for diplomas or played the stock-market, would have done all sorts of things together. So how did these endless bouts of furious hand-to-hand fighting come about?

In just the same way, I've never been able to understand the Crusades. I've read the Catholic Bible, I've read the Islamic Koran, and apart from certain differences in wording, such as that between "God" and "Allah," I found the two religions amazingly similar in terms of ethical strictures, in admonishing people not to kill, steal, be lewd, tell lies, and so on— they're almost two editions of the same book. So why should war after far-reaching holy war erupt between the cross and the crescent? What mystical force mobilized so many people from the east to kill westwards, then from the west to kill eastwards, leaving behind a land of bare bones, and tens of thousands of weeping orphans and widows? In the great, gloomy amnesiac void that renders all memories impermanent, is history nothing but a war of words? Do the meanings of words light sparks? Do words drag themselves down into the mire? Does grammar chop off arms and heads? Does blood flow out of sentence structures, nourishing the brambles on the plains and congealing under the setting sun into smear upon gleaming smear?

Ever since language has existed in the world, it's led to endless human conflict, arguments, wars, manufactured endless death by language. But I don't for a moment believe this is owing to the magical power of language itself. No, quite the opposite: the instant that certain words take on an aura of incontrovertible sanctity, then immediately, invariably, they lose their original links to reality, and at moments of the greatest, irreconcilable tension between embattled parties, transform themselves into perfectly chiselled symbols, into the abstract simulacra of power, glory, property, and sovereign territory. If, shall we say, language has been instrumental in the advancement and accumulation of culture, then it is precisely this halo of sanctity that strips language of its sense of gravity, turning it into a force harmful to humans.

As I write this, the twentieth century will soon be at an end. As well as witnessing great strides in science and economics, this century has left behind unprecedented environmental crises, skepticism, sexual liberation, the records of two world wars and several hundred other wars, from which the numbers of war dead are in excess of numbers from the past nineteen centuries put together. Countless forms of media and language have sprung out of this century: television, newspapers, the Internet, tens of thousands of books published every day, new philosophies and slang created, renovated every week, fueling linguistic growth spurts and explosions, and forming a thick, sedimented stratum that covers the surface of the entire globe. What guarantee is there that some part of these languages won't trigger new wars?

The fetishizing of language is a civilizational disorder, the most common danger faced by language. This observation of mine won't for a minute stop me from inhaling and absorbing language every day, from ending my days rolling around in the ocean of language, from being drawn to reflection and emotion by a single word. All that my continuing recollections of that trip to Liaoning have done is increase my wariness toward language: the moment language becomes petrified, the moment language no longer serves as a tool searching for truth but comes to represent the truth itself, the moment a light of self-veneration, of self-adoration appears on the faces of language users, betraying a fetishization of language mercilessly repressive of their enemies, all I can do is think back to a story.

This story happened in Maqiao, on one July 15th, the day of an ancestral sacrifice. By this time, Yanwu's uncle Ma Wenjie had been rehabilitated and no one any longer made much mention of his father having been a traitor to the Chinese. As neither of them had been given a proper funeral before, now of course people wanted to make amends. As the richest person in Maqiao, Yanwu had hired a Western band *and* a national band to make sure it'd be a lively occasion. He also put together an eight-table banquet, and sent out red invitation cards to friends and relations from inside and outside the village.

Kuiyuan, who'd returned to the village for the ancestral sacrifice, also received a red invitation card, but when he opened it to have a look, his face immediately changed color. His full name was Hu Kuiyuan, the *kui* spelled with the character meaning "chief," or "great," but on the invitation it was written with the character meaning "lack" or "loss."

This "loss" *kui* was deeply inauspicious and dripped with animosity—even though it was probably only a result of momentary carelessness and laziness on the part of the invitation writer.

"I'll give his mother a good sticking!" (See the entry "Stick(y).")

He ripped up the red invitation in a fury.

His intolerance of this word "loss" echoed the intolerance of 1950s law courts for "Song Ziwen," the intolerance of the fighters of the Red Company faction for the two words "Revolutionary Company," the intolerance of the crusading army for the word "Allah." And so began a holy war of language.

He didn't go to the banquet. He gnawed savagely on his own raw sweet potato, as he watched people return from Yanwu's place, wiping grease from their mouths. He was going to call Yanwu's family to account, he told his family. In fact, after he went out he first of all went and sat in Zhihuang's house for a while, than went to the vegetable garden at Fucha's house to nibble on a cucumber, then ended up going to the front of Tiananmen, where he watched some young men play ping-pong, then watched some more young men play a table of mahjong—he didn't dare go looking for Yanwu. He was even afraid of Yanwu learning he'd come to make trouble. How was he ever going to dare make a fuss, if the exterior of the Tiananmen residence alone was enough to make him wet himself? Luckily, as he vacillated away, he discovered that the members of the Yanwu household, who were in the middle of decorating a shopfront, had left an electric drill on the ground; probably when the electricity had been cut off, the workers had gone off to drink tea and had forgotten to pick it up. Yanzao, who just a moment ago had been slapping some underling around, had also disappeared, presumably busy with something else. His sharp eyes darting from left to right, with nimble fingers Kuiyuan stuffed the electric drill up his shirt, scooped up two socket boards while he was at it and slipped out of the main gate; he ran to the sweet-potato patch of his third brother's house, dug a hole, and buried them before he contemplated his next move. He knew that stuff like this could later be sold anywhere.

Slowly, leisurely, he returned home, wiping his sweat and fanning himself, kicking the dog—who yelped in terror—that had followed him along, as if he'd just earned himself the right to kick it like this.

"Anyone'll need his wits about him to get the better of Kuiyuan!" he told his mother excitedly.

"What'll that Yanwu say about it?"

"What'll he say? Everything that happens now's his responsibility!"

But he didn't actually say what would happen, or how he would take responsibility. Seeing him busy removing and polishing his leather shoes, his mother forgot to press him any further on this and went off to make him something to eat. Two married women with children in their arms stood by the door for a while, half-credulous, half-doubting about what would come of the matter, forcing Kuiyuan into repeating a few blusters: "So what if Yanwu has money? When I come looking for him, he'll know about it."

After he'd finished eating, Kuiyuan was unable to sit still at home and went out in search of a television. When he reached the mouth of the road, he discovered the road was blocked by three men, of whom one, Kuiyuan discovered when he peered at them by the light of the moon, was a sidekick of Yanwu's, his manager Wang. Pretending not to have seen them, Kuiyuan tried to squeeze past.

"Where d'you think you're going?" Quick as a flash, Wang grabbed him by the chest: "You've kept us waiting long enough. You going to talk, or are we going to have to beat it out of you?"

"What're you talking about?"

"Still playing dumb?"

"You joking with me, Brother Wang?"

Smiling, Kuiyuan was about to pat the man on the shoulder when, before his hand had gone up, the other stuck his leg out, felling him with a quick rustle over the ground to half his full height, to a kneeling position. Covering his head with both arms, he yelled and screamed out: "Why'd you hit me? What d'you want to do that for?"

He took a punch from a black shadow: "Who hit you?"

"I'm telling you, I've got brothers, I have . . ."

He took another kick in the back.

"So, who hit you this time?"

"No one, no—"

"No one, eh? That's a bit more like it. Just tell us where the drill's hidden. Before we get really angry."

"I never wanted to make anyone angry in the first place. But that invitation card you sent today just went too far, I haven't told Brother Yanwu yet . . ."

"What're you talking about?"

"Ah-ah, I said I haven't told Manager Ma yet . . ." Before the words were out of his mouth, Kuiyuan felt his hair being grabbed by a hand, his head jerked roughly upwards and twisted round to face Wang's big beard. The beard within his field of vision was sharply inclined.

"Still messing around with us?"

"Talk, I'll talk, all the talk you want . . ."

"Move!"

Kuiyuan felt another sharp pain in his behind.

He led the three men to the sweet potato patch, scratched away at the topsoil with his hands, took out the electric drill and the socket board, and—quite unnecessarily—tapped the dust off the socket board and cast aspersions on its quality: "Poor quality, this is, I could tell just from looking."

"Give us some straw sandal money." The black shadows took the electric drill, snapping off Kuiyuan's watch while they were at it. "We'll let it go for now, but any more trouble from you and we'll have your ears off before we've got another word out of you."

"Righto."

Kuiyuan was completely baffled as to how they'd found him out, but he didn't dare ask. He didn't dare make any kind of a sound until the black shadows had moved off and the sound of their footsteps completely died away; only then did he get up, and weep and curse, with no thought of dignity: "Bastards, bastards, I'll get you all if it's the last thing I do—"

He rubbed his wrist, discovered it to be indeed bare, then groped around in the hole in the ground, but found that too devoid of his watch. He resolved to go and find the village head.

The village head had no time for his stories about Chief Yuan or Unlucky Yuan, about his watch (or the lack of it), for his bawls and wails, did no more than throw him a sideways glance. A fanatical opera addict, the village head went off to Tiananmen that evening to watch a show. Unfortunately there was no good opera that day. A troupe from near Shuanglong Bow took to the stage, singing some cobbled-together drum dances, their operatics, movements, costumes and make-up so scrappy they looked just like a few people who'd gotten together to thresh and dry grain on a stage. They sang utter nonsense, in fact if they ran out of words they'd produce obscenities or bits of nonsense, quite happy just to get a laugh from the audience. A lot of the audience had hurled their shoes at the stage.

Unable to lay his hands on a tattered old pair of shoes, the village head walked out of the theater and headed back home to bed. Suddenly, while on the road home, a banshee cry erupted behind him and two hands grasped his neck, toppling him over forwards. His forehead smashed on some unknown object; stars flashed before his eyes. While he was still trying to get a proper look at who was behind him, to work out what was going on, he felt a sudden chill by his right ear; when he groped at it with his hand, he discovered that side of his head was already quite seriously bereft of his . . . "Ear—" he yelled out in terror. He heard behind him the sound of clothing being ripped, heard the black shadow behind him bite speedily and squeakily on something, spit it on the ground, jump violently up and down, pick the thing on the ground up again, and hurl it violently, far away in the direction of where people were most densely assembled. All this took place in an instant.

"Hey, Wang, go fetch your fucking ear—"

This piercing, booze-soaked scream was Kuiyuan's.

"You bastard Wang, that's what happens if you don't listen to your betters, your ear ends up going to the dogs—"

It was obvious that Kuiyuan's knife had cut up the wrong person.

"Kui you bastard, you're going to get it now, you got the wrong person!" someone shouted out nearby.

More and more people gathered around. Some rushed forward, grabbing back the apparently crazed Kuiyuan by the waist. After a bout of brawling, Kuiyuan felled the new arrivals, broke past all obstacles, and headed for the dark night of the hills.

Still trembling all over, the terrified village head covered over the bleeding wound on the right side of his head and launched into an unending wail of sorrow: "Ear . . . my eyayayar . . ." He'd collapsed onto the ground on all fours, like a dog, searching. Somebody suddenly had a thought and said Kuiyuan had just thrown something toward the food-stall—could it have been the ear? At this, everyone's eyes instantly switched over in that direction, while those standing there hurriedly moved their feet out of the way to allow room for the bleeding village head, for some beams from a flashlight to sweep over the ground. Bending over, they soon found a cigarette box, a few pieces of watermelon skin, and a few piles of pig dung, but not a scrap of flesh. In the end, a sharp-eyed child found the fleshy fragment in a tattered straw sandal, but unfortunately the blood and flesh had gotten completely mangled, were embedded with grains of sand, smeared with black dirt, and were absolutely stone cold, as if they had never been part of a person. People said the only mercy in the whole unfortunate affair was that it hadn't been snapped up by a dog.

People relaxed, feeling able to tread on the ground at their ease, without worrying they might be treading on something precious. They could be confident of the ground beneath their feet once more.

By the time the village head returned from the country clinic, his head tied up with white silk, it was nearly morning. Apparently the ear had been sewn back on after a fashion, but Kuiyuan had done his dastardly work rather too well, chewing the ear till it was almost beyond recognition. The doctor said that for the time being he couldn't say for certain whether the ear would still work: they'd have to wait and see.

Lots of people thronged the door to his house, craning their necks to get a look inside.

Three months later, Kuiyuan's case was finally judged in the regional court. He'd fled to Yueyang, but was caught and brought back by the public security joint defence team dispatched by Yanwu. His crimes were grievous bodily harm and theft: one sentence of eight years covered both crimes. Having failed to get himself a lawyer, he seemed entirely insouciant about the whole process, standing in the court grinning and laughing every so often at a few mates of his behind him, giving his hair the odd carefree toss. Without the bailiff's intervention, the young men behind him would've passed a lit cigarette over to him.

"Can't I even smoke?" A look of great surprise came over his face.

When the presiding judge finally asked him if he had anything to say, another look of great surprise came over him:

"Did I do something wrong? You're kidding me—what did I do wrong? All I did was get the wrong person, my only fault was drinking too much that day. You know I don't normally drink, unless it's Remy Martin, Hennessey Cognac, dry white Great Wall Wine, Confucius wine, and a small cup at the most. My problem is I have too many friends, whenever anyone sees me they want me to drink, so what can I do? It'd be letting friends down not to drink! A gentleman should never drink alone, and all that. And anyway, it was the middle of July that day, the gateway to the spirit world was wide open, so it would've been letting the ancestors down not to drink . . ."

After he'd been cut short once by the judge, he nodded his head repeatedly, "Okay okay okay, I'll cut to the chase, get to the point. Of course, I did something a bit uncivilized, but this wasn't a crime, no crime at all; the worst you could say about it was I let my judgement cloud over just that one time, like I just lost my grip, smashed a bowl. Wouldn't you say? After today's hearing, I think this point should already be perfectly clear. The facts speak for themselves. I've already explained this to the higher-ups. Director Li from the prefectural commissioner's office will be here in a minute, that's the director of the Grain Bureau, I had a meal at his place not so long ago . . ." After the judge had once more impatiently requested him to omit his wide and varied descriptions of the weather, the surroundings, the menu of the day that meal took place, he was once more obliged to obey. "Okay, I won't say anything more about Director Li. The higher-ups have views on this matter. Chief Provincial Editor Han Shaogang also believes I've done nothing wrong.

You all know Chief Editor Han, yes? . . . What? You don't even know Chief Editor Han? He was my dad's best friend! He used to belong to our County Cultural Institute! My advice to you all is make a phone call and ask him what the provincial government actually thinks about this . . ."

His stream of consciousness lasted a good twenty minutes.

Staring at his flame-yellow teeth, the judge decided his arguments made no sense at all, refused his appeal, and told the police to take him out. The final image he left with people as he was led away was that of his overlong suit pants, their cuffs overhanging his heels, brushing back and forth over the ground in a wet, muddy mess.

*Open Eyes [開眼]: After Kuiyuan had served one year in prison, he fell ill and died. When the news reached Maqiao, his mother choked with sorrow and died. When matters had reached this pass, the enmity between the Kuiyuan and Yanwu households became even more deeply entrenched. To make a long story short, Kuiyuan's three older brothers smashed some glass in Tiananmen and injured Yanzao. Yanwu then sent his people to break in on the Kuiyuan household's funerals and hurl dogshit missiles at the soul tablet, at the offerings table, even at the two coffins. Only when the two households were threatening each other with torches and knives did the villagers ask the Ox-head to mediate between them.

The upshot of the mediation was that Yanwu made a few concessions and agreed to give the remainder of Kuiyuan's family 800 yuan in "comfort money"; in return, Kuiyuan's family would no longer harbor old grievances and old scores would be completely canceled out. In accordance with past custom, the Ox-head presided over the Open Eyes ritual: he killed a black rooster, then filled about ten bowls with its blood, which the men on both sides drank down. Representatives from both sides each produced an almost-finished bamboo arrow, each made a cut on their arrow, then put the two together and broke them with their combined strength, to show that from today onwards they would no longer fight and kill each other—each side took the broken arrow as a pledge. Finally, each side asked an old widow, someone without sons, grandsons, or any descendants, to step forward. A bowl of clear water, in which had been put a copper coin, was placed in their hands, out of which they fished the money, then slowly rubbed it over the eyes of the other widow. One said: "Ma Yanwu's family did your people wrong, you mustn't cover your eyes, you must open your eyes, from now on there will be harmony . . ." The other one said: "Hu Kuiyuan's family's samepot brothers did your people wrong, you mustn't cover your eyes, you must open your eyes, from now on there will be harmony . . ."

They started to mumble a song:

Everyone has a mouth
The ways of the right are many.
Everyone has two ears.
The ways of the right last through the years.
Open your eyes today, see clearly tomorrow,
Dear brothers, young and old, start to smile.
Today we meet, tomorrow we part,
Although separated by mountains and rivers, we are all
 under the same heaven . . .

The more wretchedly poor the woman, the more qualified she was to be the eye-opening person on an occasion like this. No one could explain why it had to be like this.

After the eyes had been opened, both sides immediately returned to calling each other brother; no one, under any circumstances, could ever bring up this phase of enmity again. In other words, all the whys and wherefores, all the enmity (or lack thereof) had been completely washed away by a bowl of water run off from the eaves.

In our present, new era, of course, the phrase "open eyes" has taken on more and more new implications. The Ox-head will discuss the here-and-nows of the national situation, the Asian Games to be held in China or family planning, for example, as a preamble to opening eyes. Both parties concerned have to give the Oxhead a red envelope (of money), not like it was in the past, when a pig's snout was enough as a thank-you gift. Both parties also have to pay "worry costs" to those who've watched the conflict unfold firsthand: heavy costs meant providing a meal, light costs meant a packet of cigarettes. Some of the young men who'd hung out with Kuiyuan had had their heads together in continual discussion over the last few days, waiting for this to happen. It was as if they were wanting to do something, but couldn't say what they wanted to do, so in the end they did nothing. They were like moths drawn to the light, always heading for where the action was, their faces masks of concern for everything, expressing a desire to put the world to rights, but when they arrived someplace, they'd have a directionless drink of tea, a direction-less smoke and assemble in directionless twos and threes, casting frequent, knowing glances or smiles at each other. Someone might suddenly get up and yell "Let's go!," which might have led an outsider to believe something was about to happen. But nothing would in fact happen: the gang of them would go and have a look at a small shop, change the tree they were sitting under, resume their waiting in groups of twos and threes, scrap among themselves over the odd cigarette—nothing more.

And that was how they worried about Maqiao for several days until finally receiving their reward: Yanwu sent someone off to buy a few cigarettes and some packs of cold drinks to keep their mouths happy; and that took care of them.

They'd originally planned to go take a look at Kuiyuan's house, but when they got there they bumped into someone called Huangbao, who blocked the road and gave them an earful. Not knowing much about him, they exchanged knowing glances and raised their eyebrows at each other until someone gave another shout of "Let's go!"—they all roared with laughter, then left.

*Standing the Body [企屍]: Kuiyuan had been adopted by the Hu family, but as he hadn't yet pressed names he didn't count as having formally entered the clan, so he was buried in Maqiao. A little big brother of his, one Fangying, who'd been married off in faraway Pingjiang County near the Luo River, hurried back when she heard the news, to weep before her little brother's coffin. She hadn't been present at the eye-opening, and would under no circumstances accept a single cent from Yanwu's family. Not only this, she even said she wouldn't let Kuiyuan go under the ground and kept guard in front of the grave, wouldn't let anyone touch it with a hoe. She asked a few people to help her put the coffin vertically upright, propping it up at the sides with a few pieces of rock.

This was called "standing the body." Standing the body was a way of voicing a grievance, a way of attracting the attention of ordinary people and of officials. The stones heaped around the coffin signified that the grievance was as vast as the mountains themselves. The upright position of the coffin, then, signified the resolution that while the grievance hadn't been fully voiced, the dead wouldn't lie still, that they were sworn not to enter the ground. Deaf to what she heard from others, Fangying had decided in her own mind that her brother had died unjustly, that he'd been persecuted to his end by Yanwu's henchmen.

She even broadcast throughout the village that she'd give 10,000 yuan as a reward to whomsoever helped her rehabilitate Kuiyuan and redress the injustice. If they didn't want the money and wanted her instead, that was fine also: she'd be a contract wife for a year, wouldn't charge anything for her labor, for doing the housework and producing children during that year. All she wanted was her body back in one piece after a year.

*Uh [嗯]: Back in the days of the Cultural Revolution, the commune ordered each stockade to dig air-raid shelters, also called war-preparation caves. The Soviet Union, apparently, was going to fight down from the north, America was going to fight up from the south, and Taiwan was going to fight over from the east, so all the war-preparation caves had to be dug before the full moon was up. It was also said a very, very large bomb indeed had already been launched from the Soviet Union and in another day or two it'd fall on us here—if our planes couldn't bring it down, that is. The team leader had no choice but to organize three revolving shifts to work on the job day and night, to keep a step ahead of the World War. Generally speaking, two men and one woman were allocated to each shift, the men to take care of digging and carrying the earth, the woman, weaker than the other two, to take care of the topsoil. And so it was that Fangying, grasping a hoe with a sawed-off handle hoe, accompanied Fucha and me into the cave.

The war-preparation cave was very small, so narrow it only permitted two people to pass by at one time. The farther in we dug, the dimmer the rays of light became, and very soon we needed the light of an oil lamp. To save oil, we lit only a tiny lamp which illuminated a small, dusky circle around where the pickaxe fell, leaving everywhere else shrouded in boundless darkness. You could only figure out your surroundings by sounds and smells: whether your partner had returned from carrying earth, whether he'd put down his bamboo hat to wait, whether he'd brought some tea or something to eat, for example. Of course, in a tiny space like this, you very easily picked up the smell of other people's bodies, distinct from the smell of lamp smoke: the smell of a woman's sweat, her hair, her saliva, for example—and some rather less specific male smells besides.

After digging for a few hours, you started to shake and sway. Several times I felt my own face bumping accidentally into another face that streamed with sweat, or brushed by a few long strands of twisted hair. As I gently moved my numbed legs while coming back out of the digging position, whenever my concentration slipped I might collide with a leg somewhere behind me in the darkness, or with a bosom—I could sense its soft fullness, and how it dodged away in panic.

Fortunately, it was very hard to get a good look at the other person's face. The flickering dusky light illuminated the mud wall your nose was rammed up against, illuminated the eternal, inescapable fate that lay before you, illuminated the dense accumulations of pickaxe marks that swarmed at you everywhere, reflecting back in places a few rays of yellow light.

It made me think of how our forefathers had described hell.

There was no difference between day and night down here, no difference between summer and winter, no recollection even of the outside world far, far away. Only accidental collisions with another sweat-streamed face startled you awake: you discovered you still existed, you were still a person, an actual person with forename and surname, for example, with a gender. For the first few days, after we'd just started, Fangying and I still managed to find a few things to talk about. But after a few startled collisions, she said no more; the most I'd get out of her was a grunted "uh." I later discovered her "uh's" covered an enormous spectrum of tones and degrees of vehemence, could express doubt, assent, even anxiety or refusal. "Uh" represented the absolute concentration of her language, an endlessly various piece of rhetoric, an inexhaustible sea of meaning.

I also noticed that she'd begun to take care to avoid collisions, that the sounds of her panting were often a long way from where I was. But every time we got off work, she'd quietly pick up clothes I'd forgotten in the cave and stuff them into my hands at an appropriate moment. When eating, she'd add two or three sweet potatoes to my bowl, while her bowl remained almost empty. And finally, as I was kneeling on the ground, sweating away, every tendon straining, I'd feel a billow of coolness on my back—a towel would mop my glistening spine.

"Leave it . . ." The sweat had got up my nose, stopped me finishing my sentence.

The towel lightly mopped my face.

"I don't need . . ."

I ducked my face away, tried to block the towel. But in the darkness, my hand wouldn't follow orders and missed the towel, ended up grabbing—after a couple of fumbles mid-air—a hand. It was only a long time after the event itself that I remembered this hand was small and soft. No, I should correct that: memories like this are imaginings, conjectures after the event. In reality, when you reach the point when physical strength is totally used up, the point when your panting is overdrawn on future panting, gender no longer exists. Chance touches are not only no longer startling: you lose all sense of touch whatsoever. Grabbing a woman's hand becomes no different from grabbing a handful of mud. Staggering, swaying, I might have brushed against her shoulder, might even have stroked her back, there might have been other might-have-beens, and others besides, but I've no memory left of this, no solid proof.

I believe that, at this moment, she too had lost her sense of touch, of shyness and reserve, that all emotional abstraction had been puffed and panted out. This is the first and only time in my life so far that I've experienced de-gendering like this.

Afterwards, as I gradually recovered my energy, she recovered her gender and retreated far, far away.

Later still, she got married. Her parents valued sons over daughters and only let her finish primary school before sending her out to earn work points in the village; once they'd found a family that could afford to eat white rice they sent her packing. The day she was sent off to be married, dressed in a new pink jacket and a pair of fairly up-to-the-minute white tennis shoes, she stood there, thronged by a crowd of twittering girls. I don't know why, but she never cast a glance at me. She would certainly have heard my voice, certainly have known I was there, but for some unknown reason, she'd talk to anybody, meet anybody's eyes—but never took a glance at me. There was nothing between her and me, nothing secret. Apart from that time digging in the cave, there'd been no other contact between us to mention. There was nothing special to be said, beyond my later imaginings and conjectures that I'd felt that hand of hers, beyond her having had the opportunity to witness my greatest sufferings. No other woman in the world would ever be so close to me in the state I'd been in then, would see me lying there like a dog, dressed in a pair of shorts and nothing else, sometimes kneeling, sometimes on my side, my whole body bathed in mud and sweat, struggling, panting underground in a darkness utterly bereft of daylight, with only the eyes in my head to prove I was human, covered with dust and smoke particles snorted around my nostrils. She'd seen a look in my eyes that would return only in death, heard groans and pants I'd make again only on the point of death, smelled my body at its most intolerable-smelling. That was all.

Of course, she'd also heard my breathless sobs. Suffering furious abuse from Benyi, we'd wanted to get the cave dug to keep a step ahead of all the bombs of the imperialists, revisionists, and counterrevolutionaries. During that time, I must've hacked five or six pickaxes to pieces. Once, when I lost my concentration, the pickaxe slipped out of my grasp and dug into my own foot—it hurt so much I burst into tears.

She cried, too. As her hands flew to help me wrap the wound, a drop of cool water fell onto the back of my foot. It wasn't a drop of sweat, I guessed: it was a tear.

We'd hit a seam of the most rock-hard purple-teeth soil. It was no fault of hers she couldn't help me much. Neither was it any fault of hers she couldn't avoid seeing my pitiful, utterly humiliated condition. And neither, moreover, was it any fault of hers that she had no way of returning this, this secret between us, to me, and was forced to carry it off with her, far away.

Since points of extremity in a human lifetime are very rare, this secret took on correspondingly vast proportions, became a jewel of priceless value embedded in her memory. Maybe Fangying had realized this early on and it had produced in her a sense of horror at the thought of an unpaid loan or of having guzzled down something belonging to someone else, and maybe that was why she didn't dare glance at me when she left.

"Looks like rain, you'd better take an umbrella with you," someone said to her.

She nodded her head and pronounced an emphatic "uh."

I'd caught it: her "uh" spread its wings, flew over the crowd, over the heads of children grabbing at candied fruits, and straight into my ears— it wasn't a reply to the comment about the umbrella, of course: it was an expression of farewell, of well-wishing.

I didn't stick around till she set off, I didn't watch her three brothers haul her trousseau onto their shoulders and a new pot onto their backs, didn't watch those few kids accompany her in rowdy pursuit as she started off on her long journey. I went to the hillside behind the mountain, sat down, listened to the whispering of the wind among the leaves, and gazed at the autumn leaves filling the mountains, watching and waiting for me. The sound of the flute playing to the departing bride suddenly rose up so loud that all the autumn grasses around started to tremble and sway, before they were drowned out of view by the tears in my eyes. I had lots of reasons to cry, of course. I was crying that my family had forgotten me (I hadn't even gotten a letter from them on my birthday), I was crying about a friend's negligence at a critical time for me (this friend, off to enjoy himself in town, had carelessly lost an urgent letter I'd nagged him about again and again, an urgent letter that concerned my future job prospects). And, of course, I was also crying about this bride, a bride who bore no relation to me whatsoever, who never could bear any relation to me, who'd been banished by the sound of the flute, her pink jacket lost to a distant and unknown family, taking those worthless "uh's" of hers away from me forever.

When I next saw her again, many years later, she was rather thinner and her face had taken on the ashen flatness of middle age. If someone standing next to me hadn't introduced us, I'd have had great difficulty making out the lines of her face as it had been all those years back. She stared momentarily, a dim flicker of recognition in her eyes, before her gaze swiftly flitted from my face. Her mind was on other things. A rural cadre who'd come to the village the same time I had was sorting out the civil dispute between her and Yanwu's family, sorting out her mother's and her younger brother's funerals, and criticizing her for running back to her parents' home to cry grievances for her brother by standing his body (see the entry for "Standing the Body"). "What more's there to say? Why won't you let the dead rest, why d'you want to make them stand! When someone's dead, doesn't matter how much fuss you make, it won't bring them back to life, doesn't matter whether you're right or wrong, no sense in making a fuss!" The cadre spoke in tones of such vexed admonition that even her brothers nodded in agreement; only she fell with a thump to her knees and, before the rural cadre had worked out what she was doing, bashed out a whole series of resonant kowtows. Two women nearby hurried forward to pull her up, tugging and yanking at her, but her face, glistening, awash with tears, kept bobbing and struggling between upright and kneeling positions as complaints continued to stream from her mouth.

Only when the women pulled her away were her hoarse sobs finally released. She had perfectly good reasons for crying, of course: for her mother and brother (who'd just passed away, who'd died in unfortunate circumstances), that there was no way she could seek redress on her own (even her little brother couldn't help her out). In my opinion, though, her sobs were perhaps even more than that, were a kind of secret reciprocation directed toward me. Twenty years, it had been, twenty years: she must have heard my sorrow on the mountainside twenty years ago, and now the tears were fighting their way unstoppably out of her eyes, trying to repay a debt of tears that could never be spoken of out loud.

The autumn grasses that filled the mountainside were a testimony to this debt of tears. They swayed in the wind, nodding in waves toward the summit. Maybe they'd silently soaked up too many human sobs, maybe that was why they'd declined into shrunken, withered reeds.

All these years later, I revisited what had formerly been the war-preparation cave. The world war had never been fought in the end. The one we'd dug had been converted into a storage cellar for potato seeds; because it was damp, the cave walls had grown green moss and the smell of moldering sweet potatoes floated from the mouth of the cave. But circular smoke stains lingered, in a few hollows where we'd placed the oil lamp.

There was another cave in the lower village, which had also been dug at about the same time by other people. The cave mouth was now blocked up by two scruffy wooden planks, with a mess of rice stalks, a few multicolored, now-discarded cigarette packets, and a pair of tattered shoes dropped behind them—as if someone was still living there.

☆**Separated-Pot Brothers** [隔鍋兄弟]: "Ah-ha, an honored guest, come sit for a while in the cave."

His face was familiar, but I couldn't quite remember who he was.

"Comrade Han, how's your health?"

"Good."

"How's work?"

"Good."

"How's study?"

"Good, quite good."

"How are your venerable elders?"

"Not bad."

"Are your honorable sons and daughters obedient?"

"I only have one daughter, but thank you for your concern."

"Eh," he inclined his head, "is industrial production in the cities good?"

"Of course . . ."

"Is the flow of commerce in the cities also . . ."

Fearing my conversation partner was about to inquire into every urban profession and trade, I hurriedly cut into this parallel sentence exchange: "I'm sorry, you are . . . ?"

"Parted so recently, and you don't recognize me?" He smiled at me. All this happened while I was visiting the air-raid shelter and a middle-aged man popped up by my side.

"I can't quite . . ."

"You are forgetful, good sir."

"It's not that surprising, I left here almost twenty years ago."

"Really? Twenty years? Now that's surprising! Can it really be that one day in the cave is a thousand years in the outside world? Tsk tsk." As he spoke, he shook his head in deepest, unfathomable puzzlement.

A distant voice, accompanied by a laugh, shouted: "That's Ma Ming!"

"Yes, my unworthy surname is Ma, informal name Ming."

"You're Ma Ming? The one from the House of Immortals . . ."

"Ashamed, bitterly ashamed."

Only now did I begin to remember, to remember how I'd gone to his house to paint quotations by Chairman Mao; I also noticed that a drip was hanging off the tip of his nose, as if on the point of falling, but—not falling. Each wrinkle on his face contained a rich seam of grime, but he didn't in fact look aged in the slightest. His face ruddy, his voice booming, he still looked exactly as he had before, dressed in a dirty, greasy, cotton jacket, with both hands resting inside his sleeves. The only change was that he seemed to have an extra badge from some county teachers' training college pinned to his chest, picked up from who knew where.

"You're still living in . . . the House of Immortals?"

"It has been my good fortune, my good fortune, to move to a new abode." He smiled, a segment of lotus root caked with mud in his hand, and gestured toward the interior of the air-raid shelter.

"You live in a place as damp as this?" I was astonished.

"You just don't understand. Men evolved from monkeys, monkeys evolved from fish, fish swim fearlessly in the sea all year long, so why on earth should they fear damp after they've turned into men?"

"You don't get ill?"

"I'm ashamed to say, in this lifetime of mine, I've eaten all sorts of delicious things but never known the taste of medicine." Just as he was saying this, a woman rushed over, saying a big pumpkin had disappeared from her family's garden and wanting to know whether Ma Ming had picked it. Ma Ming immediately began to glower: "Why don't you ask me whether I'm a murderer, too, while you're at it?" Seeing the woman's blank stare, he pressed his advantage with another growl: "Why don't you ask me whether I murdered Chairman Mao?" As a segue, he spat on the ground, forgetting all about me, his guest, and stalked off.

A few kids giggling somewhere off in the distance fled in terror after one sideways glance from him.

Off he went, spitting with anger. The last time I saw him was as I was leaving Maqiao. I spotted him standing on the mountain, as usual, leaning on a walking stick, a lone, independent figure on the hillside behind the upper village, looking far off into the vast, hazy, open fields that stretched out before him as the pink light of dawn floated over the mountain valleys. He looked to be in a complete trance. I also heard him hum a strange sort of intonation, like a moan pressed out of his gut, which turned out to be a well-known tune from television:

Where did you come from? My friend,
It's as if a butterfly has flown to my window.
I don't know how many days it'll stay,
We've been apart too long, too long . . .

I didn't dare call out to him, as it didn't feel right disrupting the aesthetic mood evoked by his butterfly.

It was only later that I found out those few words I'd got out of Ma Ming were quite the most courteous reception I could have hoped for. For a good few years lately, he'd severed all relations with the villagers and hadn't had a friendly look, let alone word, for anyone. Every day, footloose and fancy-free, he wandered through the mountains and surveyed the rivers, viewing the human world with a coldly indifferent eye. Once, a child fell into the pond unnoticed by anyone else in the village but him, as he stood on the hillside. He saved the child but refused even to contemplate the thanks of the child's mother, threw all the cured pork she sent to his door into the dung pit: "Don't pollute my mouth," he'd said. He'd rather eat ants and earthworms than eat the coarse food of coarse people, than accept favors from the villagers.

By then, he'd moved out of the House of Immortals. Maqiao's oldest residence had collapsed and Zhihuang got a few people together to rip out the foundations. A few fired bricks were still usable, so the villagers built a wayside pavilion and a small house for him. Hands in his sleeves, he went to have a look, but instead of moving into the new house uttered an uncompromising declaration of war. He chose instead to crawl into the air-raid shelter.

He didn't do that much sleeping in the cave; far more often he'd sleep in the wild, on the mountains, using the wind for a pillow, the dew for a bed. Someone once asked him if he was afraid of being eaten by something wild while asleep on the mountain. Being eaten—what was there to be afraid of in that? he asked. In his lifetime he'd eaten a good many wild things, so it was only fair that he should be eaten back by something wild in return.

In the years gone by, there were two people he hated most of all: first of all he hated Benyi, then after Benyi he hated Yanwu. "Devil's spawn," he'd always be backbiting, though no one knew the provenance of the enmity. In fact, the faces of all three shared certain points of resemblance: all had thin, pared-down faces, hooded eyes, chins slightly flattened then turned up, so that their lower lips were forced outwards. After this chance thought came to me, I was suddenly struck by a wild hypothesis. I imagined that after the deaths of Benyi and Yanwu, Ma Ming would, to the astonishment of all, weep and prostrate himself, eyes and nose running, before both their graves. I imagined that some other lazybones would in future perhaps spread a rumor to the effect that Ma Ming had said Benyi, Yanwu, and he were in fact blood relations, were all of the seed sown many years ago by Long Stick Xi (see the entry "Rough")—that they were what Maqiao people called separated-pot brothers.

Separated-pot brothers were sometimes also called borrowed-pot brothers, meaning that the brothers shared a father but, since infancy, hadn't eaten from the same pot, hadn't grown up in one family. Whether this separation was a result of legitimate adoption, or of illegitimate birth, or was forced by population drift and dispersal following bouts of pillaging, was of little import: none of this was specified. Just two factors—one, they'd been separated at the pot, and two, they were brothers—sufficed for the people of Maqiao, who seemed to stress these two crucial facts above all else. I imagine that this lazybones spreading the rumor will have asked Ma Ming, was there any proof for this allegation of his? Ma Ming would answer: when Long Stick Xi left Maqiao, he'd told him in person—at the time, he'd been just a boy and refused to believe him, he'd even spat at Long Stick Xi. Then later, as he grew up, he discovered that, in fact, in the village only Benyi, Yanwu, and he exactly reproduced Long Stick Xi's birdlike countenance; only then did he believe his real father truly had played all those dirty tricks.

I imagine that when Maqiao people hear about this, they'll all stare and gape in shock, paralyzed like a mass of poisoned cockroaches. They'll watch Ma Ming's shadow float over the drying terrace, see him cast the occasional, icy glance out of the corners of his eyes, no one having the courage to step forward and call out at him to pause and verify the facts any further.

✻**Beginning (End)** [歸元(歸完)]: In Maqiao dialect, the word for "end" (pronounced *wan* in Mandarin) is pronounced the same as the word for "beginning" (*yuan*). Two temporal extremes are thus phonetically linked. In that case, when Maqiao people say "yuan," do they mean end? Or do they mean beginning?

If things always have an end, then time always advances forward in a straight line, never repeating itself, with forward and back, this and that, right and wrong permanently in diametric opposition to each other, implying a certain standpoint for making comparisons and judgments. If, conversely, things always go back to the beginning, then time moves in a circle, always going around and starting again, with forward and back, this and that, right and wrong always confusingly overlapped and overturned.

As I see it, history's optimists insist on the division between beginning and end, viewing history as an ever-advancing straight line, in which all honor and disgrace, success and failure, praise and blame, gains and losses are always precisely recorded, ready to receive true and just final judgment. Perseverance will receive its final reward. History's pessimists, however, insist on the unity between beginning and end, viewing history as an ever-repeating loop in which their retreats endlessly advance, their losses are endlessly gained, everything is futile.

Which *yuan* would Maqiao people choose? Beginning or end?

Consider Maqiao: a little village, impossible to find, almost dropped off the map, with a few dozen households in the upper and lower village combined, a strip of land, set against a stretch of mountain. Maqiao has a great many stones and a great deal of soil, stones and earth which have endured through thousands of years. However hard you look, you won't see it changing. Every particle is a testament to eternity. The never-ending flow of its waters gurgles with the sounds of thousands of years; the pearls of dew of thousands of years still hang on the blades of grass at the roadside; the sunlight of thousands of years now shines so brightly we cannot open our eyes—a blazing white heat that buzzes on the face.

On the other hand, Maqiao is not, of course, the Maqiao of former days, or even the Maqiao of a moment ago. A wrinkle has appeared, a white hair has floated to the ground, a withered hand has turned cold, everything moves silently on. Faces appear one by one, then one by one fade away, never to return. Only on these faces can we look nervously for traces of the march of time. No power can stop this process, no power can prevent this succession of faces from sinking into Maqiao soil—just as one note plucked after another sounds and softly dies away.

☆**Vernacular/Empty Talk (*Baihua*)** [白話]: In Chinese, the word *baihua* has three meanings:

1. (Modern Chinese) vernacular (as opposed to the classical, literary language).
2. Unimportant, nonserious, unverifiable chatter, spoken only for idle amusement.
3. In Maqiao language, "bai" is also read "pa," which is a homophone of the word meaning "scary," so "empty talk" is also "scary talk," often meaning stories of ghosts or crimes told for the titillation and enjoyment of listeners.

For Maqiao people, "empty talk" was what people in other parts might call gossip. It was an activity designed for passing the time, one that took place mostly on evenings or on rainy days. This led me to suspect that the beginnings of Chinese vernacular sprang from beneath gloomy thatched eaves such as were found here, that its roots lie in sources of vulgar diversion, in the records of the fantastic and bizarre, even in tales of horror. Zhuangzi viewed fiction as trivial, superficial blather; Ban Gu proclaimed it to be "that which is spoken on the streets, in the alleys, on the roads, on the byways," both of which views generally approximate such an understanding. From the "Tales of the Supernatural" of the Wei-Jin period to the early Qing "Tales of Liaozhai"—the source from which Chinese vernacular springs—the absurd and the abnormal, in the form of demons and bizarre happenings, abound everywhere, launch repeated assaults on the nerves of listeners. Here there was no possible recourse to Confucian statesmanship, no saintly purification of mind and desire. The difference between *baihua* and the classical language was that the former has never been seen as a high, noble language, has never had the capacity to induce or depict states of spiritual extremity.

Baihua is just a daily consumer product, a language of the marketplace. Its transformation by western languages, its maturation and development in the modern era have made no difference to the prejudiced value judgments made against it by the majority view—in the dictionary used by Maqiao people, until the 1990s at the very least, *baihua* was still "empty talk," still utterly detached from any subject of serious import, still a pseudonym for "that which is spoken on the streets, in the alleys, on the roads, on the byways." Maqiao people had never sensed any urgent need to use a new name, to differentiate clearly between the three implications of *bai* mentioned above, to escape from the confusion inherent within the concept itself. Maybe they considered themselves as belonging to an inferior category of person, that of ignorant peasants. They felt they could only penetrate this base, worthless form of "emptiness," this form of linguistic degeneracy—a feeling that amounted to no less than a self-imposed confession of linguistic guilt, to exile. As they saw it, true knowledge seemed to require another kind of expressive language, one that was mysterious, unfathomable, that lay beyond their powers of expression.

Language of this kind had all but disappeared, they supposed, except in odd fragments of vocabulary handed down through their ancestors. Language of this kind lay far beyond their comprehension, was transmitted by spirits, was concealed perhaps in the spells of shamans, in the hysterics of dream-women, in rain and thunder, the sounds of nature.

These people were very thin, their skin very dark, their joints stiff, their eyes and hair yellowed. Having sold off ultimate jurisdiction over their language, sold it off to people they didn't know, they then blindly followed life's path along to its end. The unfortunate fact of the matter is, though, that my attempts at fiction and the most important linguistic memories of my youth were succored first of all by their *baihua*-filled evenings and rainy days, as we curled up in groups of threes and fours in preparation for the contented exchange of nonsense and tall stories. Bearing this immovable backdrop in mind, I'm sure they'd laugh at my fiction, sure they'd view it, in terms of moral or emotional value, as page upon page of wasted breath. In some respects, this contempt of theirs is a source of awakening for which I'm grateful. Despite my love for fiction as a genre, fiction is, in the end, fiction—nothing more. Even though humanity has produced countless beautiful novels, the wars in Bosnia and the Middle East were still fought. A Nazi who's read Dostoyevsky will continue to kill people, a cheat who's read Cao Xueqin and Lu Xun will continue to swindle. We shouldn't overstate the influence of fiction.

One could go even further and say that not only fiction, but also all language is just language, and nothing else; no more than a few symbols describing facts, just as a clock is no more than a symbol describing time. Regardless of how clocks shape our sense of time, shape our understanding of time, they can never be time itself. Even if every clock were smashed, even if all instruments for measuring time were smashed, time would still go on as before. And so we really should say that all language, strictly speaking, is "empty talk," and its importance shouldn't be exaggerated.

I've written a fair amount of fiction, as I've idled away my time as a writer over the last ten years. But essentially I've achieved no more than what anybody from Maqiao would have, my volumes of fiction amount exactly to what Fucha was doing just at that moment when he measured how deep we'd dug today, then heaved a sigh of relief. "Let's get the bad air out of us, let's have a bit of empty talk (*baihua*)." He dropped his carrying pole, stretched his arms, and grinned broadly.

It was very warm in the cave. There was no need to put any more clothes on, and we lay on our sides on the soft piles of earth, knees propped together, gazing at the lamp's hazy flickering on the cave wall.

"Go on, then."

"You go first."

"You go first. You've read all those books, you must've read a lot of empty talk."

There was something not quite right about this remark, I felt, but I couldn't quite put my finger on it.

"All right, I'll tell you something funny about Benyi, okay? This happened when we were doing People's Militia training last month, when you'd gone off for a meeting. Up he popped on the grain-drying terrace, telling me my commands weren't loud enough, so he got me to stand by and watch how he shouted. "Left turn," he shouted, "right turn," he shouted, then "back turn," finally "forward—turn." All over the place, the six guys were, didn't know what direction to turn in, but Benyi just glared, drew circles on the ground, and said this is how you turn, around and around and around and around!"

Fucha roared with laughter, his head crashing against the wall of the cave.

"Okay, my turn." By now quite excited, he moistened his throat and started to tell a ghost story. He said there once was a man from around Shuanglong who'd built a house near the mountains, very high up, projecting over the river. He lived on the top floor, and waking up one night he saw a head outside his window looking east, then west. At first he thought it was a burglar, but then realized this made no sense: if he slept on the upper floor and the window was a good twenty feet from the ground, how could a burglar have such long legs? Groping for a flashlight, he quickly turned it on, and what d'you think he saw?"

"What?" My hairs were standing on end.

"This burglar's face had no eyes, nose, or mouth—blank and flat it was, like a pancake . . ."

We heard the sound of footsteps in the cave. A quick listen told us it was Fangying back from home. She'd said a little earlier that she was going to fetch a bit of *baba* cake.

Ripping at the still-warm *baba* cake in his hand, Fucha said with a smile: "We're talking about ghosts, want to listen?"

She made a terrified "uh" noise, her footsteps fleeing into the darkness.

"Hey, aren't you afraid of the ghosts outside?"

The sound of footsteps stopped.

Fucha chuckled with delight.

"Has it snowed outside?"

No answer.

"Is the sun about to come up?"

Still nothing.

"All right, all right, we won't talk about ghosts anymore, come and sit in here for a while, in the warm."

After a moment of quiet, the rustling sound drew a little nearer. But still I couldn't see Fangying; only a metal buckle on her shoes floated up, flashed momentarily out of the darkness. This told me one of her feet wasn't too far from me.

I don't know when, but I started to hear a thumping noise above my forehead, then after a while, another dull thumping started, a quake that made the lamplight quiver; it didn't sound as if it was coming from above my head, but as if it came from in front, or from the left, from the right, from all directions. An anxious expression clouding his face, Fucha asked me what was going on. I didn't know, I said. He said there was a mountain above us and it was nighttime, there shouldn't be any noise. I agreed, there shouldn't be any noise. Could we have dug down into a tomb? he asked. Had we really found ghosts? I said I didn't believe it. He said the old guard in the production team had told him Tianzi Peak used to have a cave which could take you through to Jiangxi, could it be we'd dug through? Could it be Beijing just outside, or America?

You've been to high school, I said, d'you honestly think we've dug more than a few dozen meters? Reckon we haven't even dug as far as Benren's compost shed.

He gave a small, sheepish smile: sometimes, he said, he could think things over and over in his head without finding a solution; when somewhere was far away, why did it always have to be so far? When something was a long time ago, why did it always have to be such a long time? Couldn't there be a way, a way of digging a hole, for example, of digging and digging until you reached another world?

This had been one of my childhood fantasies—I'd burrow my head into the quilt and hope that when this head burrowed its way out again, it would find some dazzling miracle before it.

We waited and waited for new noises, but heard nothing.

Fucha yawned disappointedly: "That'll do, time's just about up, let's stop work."

"Put out the light, will you," I said

"Make sure you bundle up, it's cold outside," he said.

The lamplight was now behind me. The shadow before me suddenly, dramatically expanded and swallowed me up in one gulp.

*Officials' Road [官路]: When I look at it written down before me, the phrase "officials' road" conjures up visions of a narrow roadway paved with stone, twisting and turning as it stretched over the mountains to Maqiao—it wasn't just any old pathway that got to be called an "officials' road." I'd guess its history went something like this: way back in the past, someone from the village who'd left to take up an official post elsewhere had needed to ride back home to visit his elders; a good road being thus essential, his first act as an official was to build a road to his home village, an officials' road. Officials' roads were usually built by convicts. The official would allocate punishment through differing lengths of construction work, according to the respective gravity or levity of a crime: one hundred or two hundred feet, and so on. The construction of roads was not only a testament to wealth and honor: their growth rested on the crimes of bygone days.

Neither the officials nor criminals of Maqiao's past left their names to posterity.

As time went by, it fell into disrepair: some of the stone slabs shattered, or simply disappeared entirely. The fragments remaining sank into the surrounding topsoil, with only the part not yet grown over still poking out, trampled to a slippery gleam by passing bare feet, like a row of human spines lubricated with oil and sweat, eternally subjugated below our feet. I was once suddenly seized by an impulse to dig these spines out of the earth, to permit the skulls at the other end, slumped down into the soil, to rise up from their long darkness and look upon me—who were they?

When the soil on the officials' road began to smell of dung, that was when you'd arrived at the village. A dazzling plum-blossom tree, a rustling burst of brightness, stood there marking the place.

Panting, I turned to ask: "Aren't we in to Maqiao yet?"

Fucha was hurrying along forward, as he helped us Educated Youth haul our luggage: "Almost there, almost there, can't you see it? That's it in front, not too far now, is it?"

"Where?"

"Underneath those two maple trees."

"That's Maqiao?"

"That's Maqiao."

"Why's it called that?"

"Dunno."

My heart sank, as I took one step after another into the unknown.

Humans are linguistic animals, but speaking is actually very difficult for humans.

In 1988, I moved to the south of South China, to Hainan Island on China's southernmost tip. I couldn't speak Hainan dialect and, furthermore, I found their dialect very hard to learn. One day, going to the market with a friend to buy food, I spotted a fish I didn't know the name of, and so asked the salesman, a local. He said it was fish. I said I know it's fish, could you please tell me what fish? "Sea fish," he said, staring at me. I smiled and said, I know it's sea fish, could you please tell me what—sea—fish? He stared even more, seemingly impatient: "Big fish!"

Afterwards, my friend and I couldn't help laughing when we thought back over this dialogue.

Hainan has the largest coastal area in the country, countless fishing villages and a fishing industry with a long history. It was only later that I discovered they have the largest fish-related vocabulary of just about any people anywhere. Real fishing people have set vocabulary, have detailed, precise expressions and descriptions for all the several hundred types of fish, for every fishy part, every fishy condition, enough to compile a big, thick dictionary. But most of these can't be incorporated into standard Mandarin. Even the 40,000-odd characters in the *Kangxi Dictionary*, the largest compilation of definitions, are too remote from this island, have banished this abundant mass of deep feeling beyond its field of vision, beyond the controlling imperial brush and inkstone of scholars. When I speak standard Mandarin with the local people, when I force them to make use of a language they're not very familiar with, they can only fudge their way through with "sea fish" or "big fish."

I almost laughed at them, I almost thought they were pitifully linguistically impoverished. I was wrong, of course. To me, they weren't the people I saw, they weren't the people I've been talking about, their *chao-jiu-ou-ya-ji-li-wa-la* mocking chirping spitting babbling gabbling gibbering crying jabbering was concealed behind a linguistic screen that I couldn't penetrate, was hidden deep in a dark night that standard Mandarin had no hope of illuminating. They had embraced this dark night.

This made me think of my own hometown. For many years I've studied Mandarin. I realize this is necessary, it's necessary in order for me to be accepted by neighbors, colleagues, shop assistants, policemen, and officials, to communicate through television and newspapers, to enter into modernity. It's just that my experience in the market buying fish gave me a sudden jolt: I realized I'd been standardized. This implied that the hometown of my memories had also been standardized, that every day it was being filtered through an alien form of language—through this filtering, it was being simplified into the crude sketchiness of "big fish" and "sea fish," withering away bit by bit in the desert of translation.

This isn't to say that hometowns can't be talked about. No, you can still use standard Mandarin to talk about them, you can also use Vietnamese, Cantonese, Fujianese, Tibetan, Wei language, every foreign language there is to talk about them, but is "Beethoven's Fifth" played on a Peking Opera violin still "Beethoven's Fifth"? Does an apple that has left its native soil, an apple that's been steamed and pickled, still count as an apple?

Of course, dialect isn't the only linguistic obstacle, neither is region the only linguistic tie. Apart from regionalization, language at the very least also has epochal gradations. A few days ago, I was chatting with friends, sighing over how the development of transportation and communications was strengthening horizontal links across humanity, ever accelerating the process of cultural renewal; in the not-too-distant future, maybe regional differences in culture would be rooted out, would melt away, leading to a possible increase and intensification of epochal differences. People of the same era in the global village would eat the same kind of food, wear the same kind of clothes, live in the same kind of houses, propagate the same kind of ideas, even speak the same kind of language, but by then, for people of the 1950s to understand people of the 1930s, for people born in 2020 to understand people born in 2010, could be as difficult as it is now for Hunanese people to understand Hainanese culture, for Chinese people to understand British culture.

This process has in fact already begun. Within any one dialect, the "generation gap" shows up not only in ideas about music, literature, clothing, employment, politics, and so on, it also shows up in language—we're already used to seeing an old person having to work up a real sweat to understand his children's vocabulary. "Three-in-one," "bean coupons," "team worker," "(class) status," a whole batch of Chinese terms have rapidly become archaisms, although they haven't yet been banished to ancient manuscripts, they haven't yet been withdrawn from daily life, they remain current in a few, fixed circles of exchange, just as dialect is still current in old village circles. It's not region but era, not space but time which are producing all these new kinds of linguistic communities.

We could explore this question a bit further. Even if people can overcome the obstacles of region and era, can they still find any kind of common language? A linguistics professor once carried out a classroom experiment: he pronounced a word, such as "revolution," then got students to say the first image that flashed into their brains on hearing it. The responses were enormously varied: there was red flag, leader, storm, father, banquet, prison, politics teacher, newspapers, market, accordion. . . . The students produced totally different subconscious interpretations of the word "revolution" according to their totally different individual life experiences. Of course, having entered into the realm of public exchange, they have to submit to standards of authority such as large dictionaries. This is the compromise the individual makes to society, the compromise of lived and living feelings to cultural tradition. But who can say for sure that the ephemeral images secretly omitted in these compromises won't be stored up in some dark layer of consciousness, evolving into language that could erupt at any given moment and change the course of events? Who can say for sure, while people search for and use a broadly standard form of language, while they are overcoming all kinds of linguistic obstacles in their quest for communication with other minds, that new divergences in sound, form, meaning, regulations aren't emerging at all stages? Aren't psychological processes of nonstandardization or antistandardization constantly, simultaneously in progress?

Strictly speaking, what we might term a "common language" will forever remain a distant human objective. Providing we don't intend exchange to become a process of mutual neutralization, of mutual attrition, then we must maintain vigilance and resistance toward exchange, preserving in this compromise our own, indomitable forms of expression—this is an essential precondition for any kind of benign exchange. This implies, then, that when people speak, everyone really needs their own, unique dictionary.

Words have lives of their own. They proliferate densely, endlessly transform, gather and scatter for short bursts, drift along without mooring, shift and intermingle, sicken and live on, have personalities and emotions, flourish, decline, even die out. Depending on specific, actual circumstances, they have long or short life spans. For some time now, a number of such words have been caught and imprisoned in my notebook. Over and over, I've elaborated and guessed, probed and investigated, struggled like a detective to discover the stories hidden behind these words; this book is the result.

This, of course, is only my own individual dictionary, it possesses no standardizing significance for other people. This is just one of the many responses from the linguistics professor's class experiment; once class is over, people can forget it.

Ba: an ancient name for Sichuan, a large province in midwestern China.

Catty: five hundred grams.

CCP: the Chinese Communist Party

Double Ninth Festival: Ninth day of the ninth lunar month.

Educated Youth: high-school and university students sent down to labor in the countryside during the Cultural Revolution.

Great Leap Forward: with the Great Leap Forward (1958–1960), Mao Zedong hoped to achieve an economic breakthrough that would allow China to overtake the West. It in fact led to the worst manmade famine in human history, leaving approximately thirty million Chinese dead, most of them peasants.

Guomindang (GMD): the Nationalist Party in power in Mainland China from 1911 to 1949.

Journey to the West: one of the best-known novels of premodern China, written c. 1570, recounting the adventures of the monk Xuan Zang (Tripitaka) and the monkey Sun Wukung on a pilgrimage to India.

Li: a traditional unit of length equivalent to 0.5 km or 0.31 mile.

Lin Biao (1907–71): Communist leader and Mao Zedong's designated successor until his death in a plane crash following an unsuccessful coup d'etat.

Lin Daiyu: the tragic, sickly, poetry-writing, garden-dwelling heroine of *The Dream of Red Mansions*, probably the most famous of all Chinese novels, written by Cao Xueqin c. 1760.

Lu Xun (1881–1936): one of the most acclaimed figures in modern Chinese literature, renowned for his critical and satirical short stories and essays on modern China.

Miao: an ethnic minority of southwestern China.

Ming Dynasty: the Ming Dynasty ruled China from 1368 to 1644.

Model Operas: Eight "politically correct" revolutionary operas from the Cultural Revolution.

Mu: A Chinese unit of area equivalent to 0.067 hectares or 0.167 acres.

Poor and lower-middle peasants: The two poorest, and therefore most politically correct, classes of peasants in Maoist China.

Qing: the Qing Dynasty ruled China from 1644 to 1911.

Qingming: the Chinese grave-sweeping festival, when ancestors are commemorated.

Rice sprout dance: a traditional Chinese folk dance that Communist propaganda teams popularized from the 1940s, adding new political content. Dancers take a step forward, then a step back, in effect not moving from their original spot.

Romance of the Western Chamber: a romantic work of drama written by Wang Shifu (c. 1300).

Simplified characters: in the 1950s, the Communist government simplified the majority of Chinese written characters, reducing the number of strokes and often radically changing the appearance of the character. The original characters are now called "full-form" or "complex" characters.

Struggle: to submit (a class enemy) to class struggle was a technique of mass intimidation used particularly in Maoist China, involving mass denunciation meetings and self-criticisms.

Tujia: The Tujia nationality is found in Hunan and Hubei provinces.

Zhang Xianzhong: one of the rebels who contributed to the fall of the Ming Dynasty.

Zhan Tianyu (1861–1919): a railway engineer who invented a type of railcar coupler still in use today.

Zhuangzi (c. 370–300 b.c.): a great Daoist philosopher of ancient China.

Guide to Principal Characters

Bandit Ma: see Ma Wenjie.

Benren: Benyi's same-pot brother; fled to Jiangxi during the Great Leap Forward.

Benyi (also Ma Benyi): Party Branch Secretary in Maqiao.

Commune Head He: leader of the local commune.

Fucha: Maqiao's accountant.

Kuiyan: "lazy" son of Zhaoqing.

Long Stick Xi: a mysterious outsider who introduced "tincture of iodine" to Maqiao.

Ma Ming: leader of Maqiao's "Daoist Immortals," inhabitant of the "House of Immortals."

Ma Wenjie: Maqiao's most famous modern historical figure and former County Leader.

Master Black (also Mou Jisheng): muscular but dim Educated Youth.

Master Nine Pockets: renowned beggar king of Changle.

Shuishui: wife of Zhihuang the stonemason, later a "dream-woman."

Three Ears: unfilial son of Zhaoqing, one of the "Daoist Immortals," later lover of Tiexiang.

Tiexiang: daughter of Master Nine Pockets, later wife of Benyi and lover of Three Ears.

Uncle Luo: former village leader; Maqiao's oldest cadre.

Wanyu: Maqiao's singing star.

Xiongshi: son of Zhihuang and Shui Shui, killed in delayed blast of Japanese bomb.

Yanwu: talented younger brother of Yanzao.

Yanzao: "Traitor to the Chinese," persecuted and bullied for being a landlord's son.

Zhaoqing: notoriously stingy inhabitant of Maqiao, father of Three Ears.

Zhihuang: Maqiao's stonemason, famed for his stupidity, married to Shuishui.

Zhongqi: Maqiao's resident gossip and busybody.